THE LEGITIMACY OF INTERNATIONAL HUMAN RIGHTS REGIMES

The past sixty years have seen an expansion of international human rights conventions and supervisory organs, not least in Europe. While these international legal instruments have enlarged their mandate, they have also faced opposition and criticism from political actors at the state level, even in well-functioning democracies.

Against the backdrop of such contestations, this book brings together prominent scholars in law, political philosophy and international relations in order to address the legitimacy of international human rights regimes as a theoretically challenging and politically salient case of international authority. It provides a unique and thorough overview of the legitimacy problems involved in the global governance of human rights.

ANDREAS FØLLESDAL is Professor of Political Philosophy at the Norwegian Centre for Human Rights, University of Oslo, Norway.

JOHAN KARLSSON SCHAFFER is a senior researcher at the Norwegian Centre for Human Rights, University of Oslo, Norway.

GEIR ULFSTEIN is Professor of International Law at the Department of Public and International Law, University of Oslo, Norway.

THE LEGITIMACY OF INTERNATIONAL HUMAN RIGHTS REGIMES

Legal, Political and Philosophical Perspectives

Edited by

ANDREAS FØLLESDAL

JOHAN KARLSSON SCHAFFER

GEIR ULFSTEIN

CAMBRIDGE
UNIVERSITY PRESS

CAMBRIDGE
UNIVERSITY PRESS

University Printing House, Cambridge CB2 8BS, United Kingdom

Published in the United States of America by Cambridge University Press, New York

Cambridge University Press is part of the University of Cambridge.

It furthers the University's mission by disseminating knowledge in the pursuit of education, learning and research at the highest international levels of excellence.

www.cambridge.org
Information on this title: www.cambridge.org/9781107034600

First published 2014

Printed in the United Kingdom by CPI Group Ltd, Croydon CR0 4YY

A catalogue record for this publication is available from the British Library

Library of Congress Cataloging in Publication data
The legitimacy of international human rights regimes : legal, political and philosophical perspectives / editors, Andreas Føllesdal, Johan Karlsson Schaffer, and Geir Ulfstein.
pages cm. – (Studies on human rights conventions)
Includes bibliographical references and index.
ISBN 978-1-107-03460-0 (hardback)
1. Human rights. 2. Effectiveness and validity of law. I. Føllesdal, Andreas, editor of compilation. II. Schaffer, Johan Karlsson, 1976– editor of compilation. III. Ulfstein, Geir, 1951– editor of compilation.
K3240.L43 2013
341.4′8–dc23
2013018457

ISBN 978-1-107-03460-0 Hardback

CONTENTS

CONTRIBUTORS

RICHARD BELLAMY is Professor of Political Science and Director of the European Institute, University College London. His research focuses on democracy, citizenship and constitutionalism in modern societies. Recent publications include *Political Constitutionalism* (Cambridge University Press, 2007) and *Citizenship: A Very Short Introduction* (2008). He is currently completing a book (with Dario Castiglione) on *A Republic of European States: International Democracy and Republicanism in the EU* for Cambridge University Press.

SAMANTHA BESSON is Professor of Public International Law and European Law and Co-Director of the European Law Institute at the University of Fribourg, Switzerland. Her research focuses on international and European human rights law and theory and on the philosophy of international and European law. She co-edited the volume *The Philosophy of International Law* (2010) and is currently completing a monograph entitled *A Legal Theory of Human Rights.*

BAŞAK ÇALI is Director of the MA in Human Rights, a senior lecturer in Human Rights at University College London's Department of Political Science and a fellow of the University of Essex Human Rights Centre. Her most recent work includes *International Law for International Relations* (2010) and 'The Legitimacy of the European Court of Human Rights: A Sociological Interpretive Approach' (*Human Rights Quarterly*, 2013).

LYNN DOBSON is a senior lecturer in the Department of Politics and International Relations at the University of Edinburgh. Her recent interests and work are mainly in the areas of citizenship, representation, legitimacy and authority and political obligation, especially as they apply in non-domestic political contexts.

ANDREAS FØLLESDAL is Professor of Political Philosophy at the University of Oslo. He is Principal Investigator for the European Research Council Advanced Grant *MultiRights: The legitimacy of multi-level human rights judiciary* (2011–2016) and Director of the Centre of Excellence *PluriCourts: The legitimate roles of the judiciary in the global order.* He received his PhD in Philosophy in 1991 at Harvard University. Føllesdal publishes in the field of political philosophy, mainly on issues of international political theory, globalization/Europeanization, human rights and socially responsible investing.

KRISTEN HESSLER is an assistant professor at the University at Albany (SUNY). She received her PhD from the University of Arizona. She has published articles on international human rights law, democracy and global justice, the human rights approach to global public health and environmental justice.

IAN HURD is an associate professor of Political Science at Northwestern University. His research is on the politics of international law. Recent areas of interest include the laws of war, pre-emption, human rights and humanitarianism and international organizations. He has written widely on international organizations, international law and international relations, including the books *After Anarchy: Legitimacy and Power in the UN Security Council* (2007) and *International Organizations: Politics, Law, Practice* (Cambridge University Press, 2011). His articles and essays have appeared in *International Organization*, *International Politics*, *Foreign Affairs*, *Global Governance*, *Ethics and International Affairs*, the *Journal of International Organization Studies*, and elsewhere.

JOHAN KARLSSON SCHAFFER is a senior researcher at the Norwegian Centre for Human Rights, University of Oslo. He received his PhD in Political Science from the University of Gothenburg. His main research interests are in the areas of political and international theory. Recent publications include articles in *Review of International Studies*, *Political Studies* and *Human Rights Review.*

GEIR ULFSTEIN is Professor of International Law at the University of Oslo. In 2009–2010, he was co-director of the research project *Should states ratify human rights treaties?* at the Centre for Advanced Studies in Oslo. Ulfstein is Head of the Legal Research Team of the European Research Council Advanced Grant *MultiRights: The legitimacy of multi-level human rights judiciary* (2011–2016) and Deputy-Director of the Centre of Excellence *PluriCourts: The legitimate roles of the judiciary in the global order*. He is co-editor of the book series Studies on Human Rights Conventions, Cambridge University Press.

STEVEN WHEATLEY is Professor of International Law and Director of the Centre for International Law and Human Rights at the University of Lancaster. He has written widely on the subject of human rights and democracy in international law and is the author of *The Democratic Legitimacy of International Law* (2010).

PREFACE

The treaties, practices and institutions of international human rights seem to enjoy much support in the contemporary world, judging by ratification and vocal claims of support. Indeed, philosopher Charles Beitz has suggested that "if the public discourse of peacetime global society can be said to have a common moral language, it is that of human rights" (*The Idea of Human Rights*, Oxford University Press, 2009). Yet their legitimacy is challenged on several fronts. Not only are these international human rights commitments often breached, but states are now increasingly prepared to admit as much. Indeed, many voices now express considerable scepticism about the content, nature and justifications of such international human rights and the institutions established to uphold them. This book examines the contested grounds of legitimacy of the developing global architecture of international human rights law and the international courts and treaty bodies established by human rights conventions.

This is the third book in the Cambridge University Press series Studies on Human Rights Conventions. This series is the result of a larger research project, *Should states ratify human rights conventions?*, at the Centre for Advanced Study, Oslo, Norway. The project was led by Andreas Føllesdal and Geir Ulfstein. We are grateful for the hospitality of the Centre under Scientific Director, Gro Steinsland and Office Manager, Maria M. L. Sætre. This volume has also benefited from the European Research Council Advanced Grant #269841 *MultiRights: The legitimacy of multi-level human rights judiciary*, and the Research Council of Norway Centre of Excellence *PluriCourts: The legitimate roles of the judiciary in the global order*.

The book was developed over a period of three years, including two author meetings in Oslo. These meetings were important in shaping a common approach to this study. The chapters of the book seek to address the legitimacy challenges of the international human rights regimes. The authors have been left with considerable freedom in their choice of approach to their respective chapters.

Several people at Cambridge University Press were helpful in producing this volume. We are grateful for professional assistance and guidance, especially in contacts with Nienke van Schaverbeke, Finola O'Sullivan, Elizabeth Spicer and Richard Woodham. In Oslo, Atle Kolbeinstveit competently organized the two author meetings, and Stephanie Schmölzer provided efficient assistance in preparing the manuscript.

Last but not least, we thank all the authors who contributed to this volume for their engagement, patience and collegiality, and for a great collective learning process.

1

International human rights and the challenge of legitimacy

JOHAN KARLSSON SCHAFFER, ANDREAS FØLLESDAL AND GEIR ULFSTEIN

1. International human rights regimes: acceptance and resistance

International human rights regimes as they exist today are perplexing. On the one hand, international human rights emerged virtually out of the blue at the end of the Second World War (Mazower 2004) and had their political breakthrough in international affairs only by the mid 1970s (Moyn 2010). By now, they have become institutionalized as a set of elaborate international practices, almost universally recognized, if not always respected, by key international actors (Beitz 2009, chap.1–2). Virtually every state has ratified at least one of the United Nations' core international human rights instruments, and 80 per cent of states have ratified four or more. Regional human rights mechanisms claim a total membership of more than 150 states. In 65 countries, independent national human rights institutions monitor the state's human rights practices domestically. And not only states are implicated in this growing web of international human rights treaties: global governance institutions and multinational corporations increasingly find themselves being assessed in terms of their human rights impact in the countries with which they interact. Most notably, international human rights have inspired a vibrant international civil society. It monitors and holds to account governments, corporations and other organizations for their human rights practices, and mobilizes individuals and groups to appropriate the rights ascribed to them in international

For helpful comments on earlier versions of this introduction, we are grateful to the other contributors to the volume, as well as to Leiry Cornejo Chavez, Fredrik Dybfest Hjorthen, Pranoto Iskandar, Erik Jennische, Malcolm Langford, Juan Carlos Ochoa-Sanchez, Nino Tsereteli and Aksel Tømte.

declarations and treaties. Growing numbers of new issues of global concern – migration, trade, investment, climate change, etc. – are being framed in the vocabulary of human rights (Donnelly 2007, p.289). Thus, judging by the avowed acceptance by this multitude of actors, the practices and institutions of international human rights would seem to enjoy, on average, a broad, strong legitimacy in the contemporary world.

And yet, on the other hand, international human rights practices increasingly face potentially disabling scepticism and critique, resentment and even resistance from many of the agents involved. Across the world, governments call into question the authority of the international institutions and instruments they themselves have agreed to create or join. Critics number not only illiberal, authoritarian regimes that explicitly and wholesale reject the idea of international human rights, but also those that openly declare their sympathy for that idea. Somewhat surprisingly, governments that pride themselves as promoters of human rights and democracy both at home and abroad, increasingly complain about international human rights regimes constraining their domestic democratic affairs. Paradoxically, then, one might say that on average, the relevant international actors almost universally accept – or even endorse and support – international human rights norms (cf. Donnelly 2007), while they increasingly dispute the international institutions and practices created for the interpretation, monitoring, mediation, adjudication, enforcement and implementation of those norms.

Of course, one should not be surprised that governments increasingly resist human rights norms and the international institutions created for their protection. The doctrines of human rights stir powerful opposition because they challenge powerful groups, institutions and practices, and '[n]o authority whose power is directly challenged by human rights advocacy is likely to concede to its legitimacy' (Ignatieff 2001, pp.68, 56). International human rights doctrines disrupt not just authoritarian governments, conservative religions or traditional family structures in allegedly backwards societies, but also democratic self-rule, welfare state regimes and entrenched constitutional and legal traditions – a fact that may just have begun to dawn on some governments of liberal democracies that have traditionally considered themselves worldwide champions of human rights.

Even so, normative challenges of established authority are not necessarily justified or legitimate per se. So what are we to make of this ostensible paradox? Are governments justified in their criticism and resistance towards international human rights norms and institutions? What grounds the legitimacy of the continuously developing global architecture of international human rights law and the international courts and treaty bodies established by human rights conventions? Is there merit to the claims that international human rights courts and treaty bodies, by expanding their jurisdiction and engaging in dynamic, evolutive interpretation of their founding treaties, have outstepped the authority that states once delegated to them? When and how should a government or a domestic court defer to the judgments and decisions of international judicial institutions in the human rights area? Under which circumstances and in what ways may an international tribunal legitimately interfere in the laws, policies and decisions of a well-functioning sovereign democratic polity? What role should state consent play in a theory of legitimacy in the area of international human rights?

These are the topics that this volume addresses. It contributes to an increasingly lively research literature spanning the disciplines of law, philosophy, political science and international relations. This introductory chapter serves, first, to give some examples of the type of political controversies over international human rights regimes that motivate this volume; second, to place the volume in current academic debates about international human rights and about the legitimate authority of international institutions; and third, to outline the topics covered in the individual contributions.

1.1 International human rights regimes – universally contestable

Across the globe, we find recent examples of political contestation and controversy over international human rights norms. In this section, we first give a general account of the myriad political decisions that face governments and other actors involved in international human rights regimes, and then give a more detailed account of prominent cases of contestation over human rights mechanisms in different regions of the world. These examples demonstrate that the legitimacy of international human rights regimes is a matter of global political importance.

First, the number of international human rights treaties continues to grow, with more states becoming parties to more treaties, subjecting 'more governments, organizations and individuals than ever before to the jurisdiction of international courts. Essentially every state in the world now participates in the human rights legal regime through membership in at least one core UN treaty' (Hafner-Burton 2012). Thus, virtually all governments and their citizens are to some extent implicated in difficult moral and political dilemmas as they face choices of how to engage with international human rights regimes – choices which often involve significant yet subtle, unpredictable and long-term political consequences (cf. Cardenas 2010, p.33; Simmons 2009). Such choices include political decisions about whether the state should sign and ratify international treaties on human rights – that is, to promise to uphold the treaty's core principles or additionally to bind itself legally to comply with it. The choices also include decisions on whether and how the state should live up to its international treaty obligations, for instance in implementing human rights norms in domestic law, providing periodic reports to international human rights bodies or reacting to their decisions and criticism by altering rules and practices. A government may be required to change laws, to reform or eliminate repressive institutions or to create agencies or procedures to monitor compliance with international treaties, but also to correct persisting violations of international human rights norms, to hold past and present violators accountable and punishable for their mischief and to provide remedy or reparation to the victims.

However, international human rights regimes also structure the choices available to other types of actors: they give civil society organizations and transnational advocacy groups standards by which to evaluate the performance of state institutions. They provide additional resources for individuals and groups to seek justice before domestic courts or international supervisory organs and tribunals when they find that their rights have been violated or neglected by their governments. And when a government systematically fails to meet its human rights commitments towards its citizens, other international actors – for instance, other states, acting alone or in concert, or international organizations – may decide to take action and interfere, via diplomatic action, economic sanctions or even military intervention (Beitz 2009; Nickel 2006). Hence, all these political choices involve reflecting on the same fundamental question of legitimacy: why should the government of a sovereign state consider an international human rights regime to rightly influence or constrain its political discretion?

Thus, the legitimacy of international human rights regimes is a weighty matter confronting governments and many other agents all over the world. In recent years, we find particularly illuminating evidence of the politics of this matter in governments' increasing scepticism toward regional human rights mechanisms, which constitute important pillars in the international human rights regime. This form of politicization provides another example of the puzzles motivating this volume.

Traditionally considered an unparalleled success story and a model of regional human rights tribunals, the European Court of Human Rights (ECtHR) has recently raised intensified concern over its legitimacy and efficiency among governments, political parties and mass media commentary (see Bellamy, Føllesdal and Wheatley, respectively, in this volume). In part, this concern follows predictably after certain controversial judgments in cases brought before the court. However, that particular judgments are publicly debated is nothing new, and the potential to raise controversy lies in the very nature of a case being taken up by the ECtHR. 'Every now and then, the first reaction to a new judgment by national politicians has even been to announce that they would have a look to see if it would still be worthwhile to remain a Party to the Convention. Needless to say, such a threat has never been followed up' (Myjer 2012). Moreover, when particular judgments provoke academic and, occasionally, public debates about the legitimacy of the court, they tend to revolve around the same handful of controversial cases: *Lautsi v. Italy*, *Hirst v. UK*, *MSS v. Belgium and Greece*, etc. (Myjer 2012). Yet, those cases are hardly representative or typical of the Court's work: they provoke debate and contestation precisely because they are unusual and step on politically sensitive toes in the respondent states, but may also be essential in establishing the outer limits of the Court's competences. Michael O'Boyle (2011) argues that one reason the Court has been an easy target for populist politicians is that, like all courts, it tends not to answer back. More principally, some critics have seen dynamic or evolutive interpretation of the Convention as a way for the Court to expand its jurisdiction and authority; its supporters, by contrast, argue that this interpretive principle merely reflects an adjustment to changing social circumstances, usually anchored in a developing consensus among European states (Costa 2011; Dzehtsiarou 2011). Beyond such mediatized confrontation, support for the Court seems robust among almost all European states:

> The system has been operating for years without being called into question by the High Contracting Parties. They ratified the Convention freely, presumably because they believed in what it stood for, and it is open to them at any stage to denounce it if they so desire. Far from seeking escape from their Convention obligations, the States are keen to observe and build upon the Convention *acquis* and to reform the system so that it can perform its tasks in a more efficient manner.
>
> (O'Boyle 2011)

However, given this deeply rooted support for the European Court of Human Rights, one might argue that an equally troublesome challenge to its legitimacy is that rather than transgressing its mandate, it manages too little. The Court has positioned itself as an attractive institution for European citizens to turn to in order to have their rights defended. Its success in this regard may ironically have become an obstacle to its efficiency. Observers are worried that the European system may be overburdened by its growing backlog of cases, resulting from a complex combination of factors: the geographical expansion of the Council of Europe (it now includes 47 countries and more than 800 million people), the Court's expansive interpretation of individual liberties, endemic human rights problems in many states and distrust of domestic judiciaries in others, et cetera (Helfer 2008). The Court has 139,500 pending cases (2012), out of which only a mere 5–10 per cent will eventually be deemed admissible. More than 65 per cent of the cases are brought against only six states: Russia, Turkey, Italy, Romania, Ukraine and Serbia. The docket crisis may erode the ECtHR's reputation insofar as it offers delayed and therefore possibly ineffectual, arbitrary or incomplete protection (Dzehtsiarou & Greene 2011). A series of High Level Conferences 'have been organized in order to secure the long-term effectiveness of the supervisory mechanism of the ECHR. The resulting … declarations have proposed all kinds of measures to increase the effectiveness of the work done by the Court' (Myjer 2012). The measures considered – some of which have been implemented – include enhancing the Court's filtering capacity, attaching a cost, if only modest, for filing individual complaints, a new pilot judgment procedure to deal with repetitive complaints, but also, and perhaps most importantly, improving the national implementation and application of the Convention and reinforcing the dialogue between Strasbourg and national courts, for instance by means of an advisory opinion procedure (Helfer 2008; O'Boyle 2011).

In the Americas, the Inter-American Commission (IACHR) and Court (IACtHR) on Human Rights increasingly face criticism and resistance. The Inter-American system is the oldest and most established regional human rights mechanism outside of Europe. During the 1970s, it successfully used on-site visits and country reports to expose the human rights violations of military governments, and in the 1990s, it supported the restoration of democratic rule in Latin America (Goldman 2009). Like its European relative, it can investigate cases brought by individuals and issue judgments against states. The IACtHR has developed an innovative and creative jurisprudence, but it has also been criticized for exceeding its own mandate (Binder 2012; cf. Huneeus 2011) and neither the United States nor Canada is party to the American Convention on Human Rights.

Its authority, thus, cannot be taken for granted. For instance, the Bolivarian bloc has recently orchestrated an offensive against the Inter-American Court of Human Rights. The tribunal, based in Costa Rica, has heard a series of cases accusing Venezuela of rights abuses during Hugo Chávez's presidency (Anon 2012b; Anon 2012c). In 2012, the government of Venezuela denounced the American Convention, which means that once the withdrawal has taken effect after one year, complaints against Venezuela can no longer be brought before the IACtHR. President Chávez declared Venezuela would withdraw from the court 'out of dignity, and we accuse them before the world of being unfit to call themselves a human rights group' (Anon 2012c). The Supreme Court of Venezuela had previously recommended the government to denounce the American Convention on Human Rights, in a decision that declared a judgment of the IACtHR as non-executable (Binder 2012, p.326). The governments of Bolivia, Ecuador and Nicaragua have recently also expressed hostility toward the IACtHR, alternately calling for its elimination, linking it to the Monroe doctrine as a platform for US imperialism or condemning it as an inquisitor against member states (Picq 2012).

Brazil too, which nurtures an image as a rising power with a progressive agenda both at home and abroad, recently got into an altercation with the Inter-American system. President Dilma Rousseff previously 'strongly supported the IACHR request that Brazil create a Truth Commission to shed light on human rights violations that took place during the 1964–1985 military dictatorship' and generally 'stressed her country's engagement with the hemispheric human rights system' (Picq 2012). In 2011, however, the Inter-American Commission issued a precautionary measure requesting the Brazilian government to suspend the construction of the Belo Monte water power plant until the rights of the indigenous peoples in the area had been properly respected. Stirring controversy in Brazil for several decades, the Belo Monte hydroelectric dam on the Xingu River, a major tributary to the Amazon, is supposed to bring electricity and development to a neglected region, but the project has also raised complaints about forced evictions of impoverished, rural communities, and deterioration of water quality affecting downstream communities following the construction work. Brazil's Foreign Ministry responded by stating it was 'perplexed' by the Commission's 'unjustified' demands, adding that 'the massive construction complies with Brazilian regulations and is in accordance with an ongoing dialogue with the indigenous peoples of the Xingu River' (Anon 2011a; Anon 2011b). 'The request is absurd. It even threatens Brazilian sovereignty', said Senator Flexa Ribeiro, president of the Senate

Sub-Committee charged with oversight of the dam project (Hayman 2011). President Rousseff decided to cut all relations with the human rights body: she ordered the Brazilian ambassador before the Organization of American States (OAS) to remain in Brasilia rather than return to Costa Rica, recalled Brazil's candidate to the IACHR and suspended payment of Brazil's annual contribution.

More generally, critics have been concerned that the IACHR is expanding its jurisdiction. Traditionally focused on civil and political rights, the Commission has lately 'fueled a wave of discontent' (Picq 2012) by extending its jurisdiction to collective rights, pertaining to education, femicide and indigenous groups, and the Court has required local judicial and bureaucratic institutions to provide extensive and sometimes idiosyncratic remedies to victims (Huneeus 2011). Historically, though, the Inter-American system has coped with more severe crises of legitimacy, and it has successfully challenged regimes considerably more hostile to its authority (Goldman 2009). The system has helped many countries move from military rule and states of exception to democracy and the rule of law and supported domestic forces in holding the old regimes to account for their crimes. Democratic consolidation has brought to power political parties and movements that used to support the Inter-American system when it helped provide justice to the victims of oppression under authoritarian regimes. Now, those governments increasingly find themselves being taken to court for violations of human rights, which perhaps indicates that 'it is in the nature of power itself to resist and deny mechanisms of accountability' (Picq 2012).

In Africa, political controversy over international human rights institutions recently led to the effective dismantling of a sub-regional human rights court. In August 2012, leaders of the Southern African Development Community (SADC), a 15-member regional intergovernmental organization, resolved to renegotiate the protocol of the organization's tribunal so as to restrict its jurisdiction to advisory interpretation of the SADC Treaty only. Established in 1992, but inaugurated only in 2005, the SADC Tribunal's original mandate allowed the court to hear and decide on cases brought by individual citizens who felt their human rights had been violated by their government. However, most of the individual cases heard by the court involved allegations of human rights abuses in Zimbabwe. In 2008, in a landmark case brought by 79 farmers led by Mike Campbell, the court found the country's land reform programmes to be unconstitutional and discriminatory. The state had acquired the farms of white commercial farmers for redistribution to the landless majority; the court ordered the government to pay compensation and restore the farmers' properties (Moyo 2009). Zimbabwe's president Robert Mugabe dismissed the court's ruling as 'nonsense', and the government argued that the Tribunal could not adjudicate over the land reform programme, because it was intended to redress historical injustices. Other governments were also concerned: 'We have created a monster that will devour us all', Tanzania's president Jakaya Kikwete reportedly commented to fellow SADC leaders (Anon 2012a). Rather than jointly taking action to enforce the ruling, SADC leaders responded by suspending the Tribunal's activities. This decision prompted an international campaign to preserve the Tribunal. In the suspension period, an independent study commissioned by the SADC concluded that the Tribunal has the status of international law and is supreme to national law. The SADC 2012 summit in Maputo, Mozambique, eventually agreed to restrict the Tribunal. Human rights advocates, lawyers and political analysts, including South Africa's prominent archbishop emeritus Desmond Tutu, lambasted the decision as a major setback for the rule of law, accountable government and individual rights, which would tarnish the region's international reputation. Critics also pointed out that limiting the Tribunal's mandate to inter-state disputes would make it superfluous, because most cases heard by the Tribunal had been brought by individuals, while member states usually resolve their disputes by diplomatic means. In short, they argued, the Tribunal could no longer be seen as a legitimate and effective institution (Bell 2012; Sasman 2012).

The vast and populous Asian region has long been considered a white spot in terms of regional international human rights institutions, but that may be changing (Baik 2012). Celebrating the fortieth anniversary of the Association of Southeast Asian Nations (ASEAN) in 2007, its ten members signed the ASEAN Charter, a constitution of the intergovernmental organization which included a commitment to establish a regional human rights body. The Charter strikes a compromise between, on the one hand, promoting solemn principles of democracy, human rights, fundamental freedoms and social justice, and, on the other hand, asserting traditional ASEAN principles of non-interference in the internal affairs of member states (Ciorciari 2012, p.711). The Charter thus seems not so much to have put an end to the clash of principles of the so-called Asian values debate, but rather institutionalized the value conflict. In 2009, the human rights body took shape as the ASEAN Intergovernmental Commission on Human Rights (AICHR). Half a year later, ASEAN inaugurated a second commission focusing more specifically on the rights of women and children (Ciorciari 2012).

ASEAN has been derided as a 'club of dictators', as its membership still includes authoritarian states and some of the world's most notorious human rights violators, in particular Burma (Ginbar 2010). Democratic states therefore voiced concern over the establishment of the AICHR. The parliament of Indonesia nearly vetoed the resolution, while the Philippines raised objections. Some human rights activists and civil society organizations in the region still cautiously welcomed the establishment of a regional human rights body, and government officials of member states suggested that while the Commission would lack sharp teeth, it would be endowed with a useful tongue (Ciorciari 2012, p.713). Critics still point to the Commission's many flaws: it has a mandate limited to promoting rather than protecting human rights; it lacks independence from governments, being composed of state representatives rather than independent experts and making its decisions by consensus; it has neither investigative powers nor an ability to receive complaints from victims or their advocates and act to address the issues they raise; and its channels for participation by civil society are selective, arbitrary and opaque (Ciorciari 2012; Ramcharan 2010). 'It wouldn't be surprising to see ASEAN's misfits use the group as an excuse to whitewash their own human-rights violations', one commenter prophesied (Anon 2009).

A case in point is the AICHR's recent drafting of an ASEAN Human Rights Declaration, adopted in November 2012. Since the process lacked transparency, publicity and civil society participation, critics feared that rather than reinforcing the work to promote and protect human rights in the region, the Declaration would be used by governments to lower standards below their existing commitments to international treaties (Robertson 2012). Some human rights activists even consider the Commission a step in the wrong direction, a threat to the citizens of the member states and worse than having no regional human rights instrument at all (Ginbar 2010; Ramcharan 2010). Others have argued that much of the criticism of the AICHR misses the mark: it is a commission within the ASEAN, an organization which has always been based on non-interference – and that principle has also served the community well, by preventing powerful members from dominating weaker members (cf. Ramcharan 2010). The flaws of the AICHR may perhaps be somewhat balanced by the region's emerging network of national human rights institutions and a dynamic web of civil society groups and think tanks, which some commenters think may provide additional channels for holding governments to their commitments in the human rights area (Ciorciari 2012; Durbach et al. 2009; Ramcharan 2010; Tan 2011).

As this brief exposé – by no means exhaustive – indicates, the legitimacy of international human rights regimes is an issue on the political agenda in many corners of the world. Regional mechanisms vary in their functions and powers, and they have come to life within differently integrated regional institutional biotopes, inhabited by states that vary widely in their domestic political, social and legal institutions. Moreover, public trust in the institutions may be interlinked to support for the regional cooperative regimes with which they are associated. For instance, apart from its own veritable problems, it seems plausible that the ECtHR also experiences spill-over from the concurrent crisis of the broader project of European integration, and its much debated legitimacy deficit, just as it may have benefited in the past from periods with more resolute political and popular support for expanding and consolidating the European Union. Likewise, the contestation over the Inter-American system may be seen against the backdrop of the waning political relevance in the hemisphere of its parent regime, the Organization of American States, which reflects the weakening ties between the United States and Latin America and coincides with the recent parallel establishment of the Union of South American Nations (UNASUR), a 12-member regional intergovernmental union modelled on the European Union (Hakim 2012). As international human rights regimes do not exist in a vacuum, their legitimacy may be thought of as a relative or comparative, not absolute, property: it emerges in the interplay between international institutions, the domestic institutions of states, and individuals and groups (cf. Dobson, this volume).

Still, for all the differences among these regional mechanisms, the criticism and challenges they face seem to revolve around strikingly similar issues: with what right can an international human rights institution exercise autonomous authority over the sovereign states that once created it? The proliferation of human rights mechanisms at both global and regional levels implies additional legitimacy challenges. Some warn that this process may lead to increasingly overlapping jurisdictions between human rights instruments at various levels, to increasing fragmentation and provincialism of human rights law and to a general lapse from what many deem to be at the core of the idea of international human rights: their universal validity and global reach. On the other hand, a state may be 'more likely to give greater powers to a regional organization of restricted membership, of which the other members are its friends and neighbours, than to a world-wide organ in which it (and its allies) play a proportionally smaller part' (A. H. Robertson, cited in Durbach et al. 2009, p.224). The question, thus, is whether such accommodation of international mechanisms to regional circumstances comes at too high a cost. In reality, perhaps, the glass is neither half-full nor half-empty. Commitment to and compliance with international human rights norms is rarely uni-dimensional, but often complex, compromised, ambivalent and conditional, and therefore also often riddled with seeming paradoxes and contradictions. Under circumstances of deep disagreement, a legitimate institution, as it were, needs to strike a balance between what is desirable and what is feasible.

Partly in order to mitigate the downsides of increasing regional fragmentation of international human rights norms, partly also in response to similar problems of fragmentation, overlapping jurisdictions, weak enforcement and institutionalized politicization at the global level, academic commenters recommended a World Court of Human Rights (Goldberg 1965; Nowak 2007; Trechsel 2003). Considering the ECtHR as a model, some suggest that a world court of human rights might provide the independent, authoritative body needed to bring clarity and order to the increasingly dense patchwork of international human rights regimes, and to balance regional flaws and glitches in the protection of human rights (Ulfstein 2008). However, if it is ever created, such a global court in itself would give rise to similar issues of legitimate authority in a multi-level global human rights regime.

Furthermore, the addressees of international human rights norms are multiplying too, adding to the complexity of international human rights law and institutions. New types of corporate agents are increasingly held to account for their human rights performance, such as inter-governmental organizations, non-governmental organizations, multinational corporations, cities and other sub-state actors, and even separatist and insurgent groups. Such non-state agents might also increasingly seek to legitimate themselves as international actors by binding themselves to human rights norms. The European Union's accession to the ECHR is but one case in point (Jones 2012).

1.2 What sort of legitimacy problems does this criticism and resistance indicate?

Does the multifarious criticism, scepticism and resistance against international human rights systems signal that they face an existential crisis? The fact that various political actors discuss and dispute the legitimacy of international human rights instruments might indicate a systemic failure that needs to be addressed in order to sustain the system's efficacy. If the growing authority of international institutions does not resonate with legitimacy beliefs in the relevant communities, they will likely meet resistance (Zürn et al. 2012). As Ian Clark (2004, p.75) notes, 'we are most likely to ask questions about the legitimacy of a system only when things appear to be going wrong'. On the other hand, the fact that different actors question the authority of international human rights systems need not imply that those institutions are actually illegitimate or increasingly risk becoming so. To the contrary, their legitimacy as only indicated by the absence of resistance and criticism could be just as worrying, as such silence could indicate that subjects comply uncritically, or that the institutions are epiphenomenal to power and politically irrelevant, so that nobody cares to dispute their ostensive authority.

Indeed, one could argue that international human rights institutions should always be potentially disputable, disruptive and provoking to somebody – to some governments, for instance. Increased opposition and resistance to existing human rights regimes might even signal that they are increasingly doing their job. Why should this be appropriate? Because such conflicts are hard-wired into human rights both as a political and legal concept. If there were neat harmony of interests between national legislatures and international human rights courts, or between minority protection and majoritarian popular sovereignty, or between individual citizens and the authorities governing over them, we would hardly need international human rights treaties and tribunals in the first place.

Thus, the fact that governments criticize and challenge international human rights tribunals may say little about their legitimacy, for several reasons. First, scholars usually distinguish between subjective and objective, or descriptive and normative aspects of legitimacy, and the relationship between them is complex, both conceptually and empirically. The descriptive, subjective aspect of legitimacy refers to the attitudes and beliefs about rightful rule that members of a community hold. The normative or objective aspect of legitimacy refers to whether such beliefs are morally justified, that is, whether an institution ought to have the right to rule over its subjects. Of course, descriptive and normative accounts of legitimacy are interconnected: subjects often think they have good, justifiable reasons for regarding an authority as legitimate or illegitimate. And whether a subject is morally obligated and motivated to comply may depend on whether the agent has reason to believe that others will also endorse the norm, for instance because they regard it as legitimate, for whatever reason. The fact that some of those addressed by authority protest and critique surely does not necessarily imply that an institution is illegitimate in normative terms. On its own, general compliance is insufficient for normative legitimacy, since agents may comply with unjust rules out of self-interest, fear of sanctions, lack of alternatives or unreflective habit. Yet compliance often requires that subjects believe that an authority is normatively legitimate. Perceived normative legitimacy may also bolster the problem-solving capacity of an institution, and the reverse is also true: if a treaty or an international organization fails to secure its objective to a certain minimum extent, it risks losing normative legitimacy: individuals and other actors may no longer regard themselves as bound to comply. Second, expressions of beliefs about legitimacy are usually complex. A government may sometimes vociferously dispute an international legal norm yet comply partially or wholly with its demands (Cardenas 2010), or pledge allegiance to international law while seeking to bend it to its own advantage (cf. Hurd, this volume). The way in which a government responds to the exercise of authority by an international human rights institution is always multi-faceted, addressed to a range of domestic and international publics, and it may involve a number of state agencies and non-state actors. Hence, such responses are always open for political interpretation and continued contestation.

Expressions of legitimacy may often be more difficult to gauge and measure than expressions of illegitimacy. A recent study of the ECtHR (Çalı et al. 2011) concluded that in spite of all the political and academic debate about the Court's alleged legitimacy deficit, it actually enjoys a high level of legitimacy credit among some of its key stakeholders. Over-all, domestic politicians, judges and lawyers strongly support this supranational human rights body to actively intervene in states' internal decisions on rights protection, and while they may dispute detailed factors, their general assessments of the Court's performance are more positive. The same might be true of other international human rights treaties and bodies: states often commit to them sincerely, and seek to comply with their provisions willingly, because they believe in the values expressed in the treaties. Sometimes such beliefs may be misinformed, exaggerated self-flattery. Yet, governments, courts and other institutional actors of the state often genuinely engage in an honest dialogue about human rights with international treaty bodies, with other governments or with civil society organizations at home and abroad. But such cases may be less likely to make the headlines of international media, draw the attention of transnational civil society or provide angles for research papers.

These criticisms, challenges and contestations over international human rights systems are a key reason motivating this volume. But it would be premature to assume that such expressions of mistrust and disbelief necessarily indicate deeper crises of legitimacy, in objective or normative terms. The volume presents several contributions to debates about the legitimacy of international human rights norms, treaties and organs. The aim is not just to present solutions to the perceived problems of the legitimacy of these international institutions, but also to explicate in detail what the problem, if any, really is.

2. Academic debates about international human rights and the concept of legitimacy

As international human rights regimes increasingly seem to face challenges from the governments and other actors they seek to regulate, they have also spurred debates among scholars of law, philosophy, political science and international relations. This volume presents a selection of chapters which variously analyse the legitimacy of international human rights regimes from the perspectives of international, political and legal theory. We have selected the contributions bearing in mind that any discussion of the legitimacy of international human rights institutions must necessarily straddle disciplinary boundaries. It should address both normative concerns of what legitimate authority entails, and the empirical concerns of how to assess the legitimacy of authorities in the real world. It should be comprehensible to legal theory, political theory and international theory, since the very problem of the legitimacy of international human rights regimes may both arise and require answers across the conventional distinctions between those theoretical traditions. While much of political philosophy and democratic and constitutional theory traditionally has tended to regard its subject as an enclosed state in isolation, international human rights institutions pose a problem precisely because they seem anomalous, at face value, to such assumptions, not least because they straddle the boundary between international and national. Similarly, while theories of international relations and international legal theory traditionally regarded sovereign states as the most important, if not the only, agents in world politics, international human rights systems and their normative premises challenge such conceptions: even though sovereign states have created and consented to them, they claim authority over states, but also increasingly over individuals and non-state agents, and they grant individuals as well as certain other non-state actors a standing and independent agency in international affairs. As such, the issues this volume addresses are located at this nexus between theoretical traditions and conceptual boundaries.

Across all three disciplines, we find an increasing scholarly interest in recent years for studying *human rights* as international norms, treaties and institutions. In political science and international relations, empirical scholars equipped with increasingly sophisticated quantitative and qualitative toolboxes have recently produced a burgeoning literature seeking to understand whether and how international human rights norms impact on the behaviour of states and other actors (for overviews, see Hafner-Burton 2012; Simmons 2009, pt. I; Tsutsui et al. 2012). Research has revolved around what leads governments to participate in international legal regimes that seemingly constrain their political discretion over their citizens, the procedures by which such regimes make and craft decisions, whether they actually influence the rights behaviour of states, and the role of domestic and transnational institutions and agents in those processes. While this line of research is still in its infancy, its outcomes may provide important and sometimes provocative insights and arguments to normative analyses of international human rights regimes. Take, for instance, the finding in many studies that a state's support for particular international human rights treaties does not generally correlate with actual human rights protections in that state, and that the treaties' effects are highly conditioned on domestic politics and institutions. On the one hand, such factual findings may seem to render the political controversy surrounding international human rights norms ill-informed or misleading, exaggerating the political impact and judicial authority of international human rights treaties and treaty bodies generally. An established international court such as the European Court of Human Rights may have a significantly greater influence on its membership than global supervisory organs such as the Human Rights Committee or the Committee on the Rights of the Child. On the other hand, empirical research may also lead us to ask new, qualified questions about how to normatively evaluate the soft, subtle and conditioned influence international legal norms do have when they interact with domestic institutions of rule of law and democracy.

Political and moral philosophers have recently turned their attention to international human rights. One of the key apples of contention among philosophers concerns what a philosophical theory of human rights should do (for overviews, see Baynes 2009a, 2009b; Beitz 2009; Buchanan 2010; Ingram 2008; Valentini 2012b). The conventional approach to the philosophy of human rights has been to theorize 'a concept of human rights [as a kind of general moral rights] that can be understood without reference to the global legal-institutional phenomenon of human rights' (Buchanan 2010). In contrast to such approaches, however, philosophers have recently sought to develop a political conception of human rights. On this approach, the philosopher's task is 'to provide a critical reconstruction of human rights as they are in the international legal doctrine and practice of human rights' (Buchanan 2010). The point is not to evaluate whether this real-existing human rights practice conforms to some philosophical moral theory of what human rights are (which human rights there are, how they are justified, and so on), 'but rather to clarify the understanding (or understandings) of human rights with respect to its own practice' (Baynes 2009a). However, as Allen Buchanan points out, whether one starts in the legal-institutional phenomenon of human rights or in a moral conception of individual rights, both approaches require, sooner or later, a critical reconstruction of the institutionalized practice of international human rights. Eventually, then, the political philosophy of human rights faces questions about how best to implement and institutionalize human rights in our contemporary world, whether human rights institutions like the ones existing today are reasonable, whether the authority they exercise is legitimately binding on their subjects, and how they ought to interface with national legal and political institutions, especially procedures of democratic self-government. Hence, questions of the legitimacy of international human rights regimes should be of greatest interest to this line of scholarship in political philosophy.

The concept of legitimacy in international affairs has recently generated substantial literatures across these three disciplines. Noting how an ever growing number of multilateral organizations, global governance institutions and international courts and tribunals exercise increasingly autonomous authority over the sovereign states that have created them and delegated power to them, scholars have addressed a broad range of empirical and normative concerns relating to the legitimacy of international institutions that lack the transparency, accountability and representation we appreciate in democratic rule (Clark 2004; Dahl 1999; Keohane 2003; Keohane et al. 2009). Moreover, global governance regimes increasingly regulate not just the external relations of states, but increasingly intrude into internal affairs, blurring the traditional distinction between international and domestic spheres of policy and law (Kumm 2004; Zürn 2004).

This volume contributes to literatures on international legitimacy by focusing on international human rights systems, which present a peculiar case for a number of reasons. First, as we noted above, the institutionalization of international human rights may present certain challenges to established conceptions in all three theoretical domains. For traditional political and international theory, it seems to present a conceptual anomaly, which cannot so easily be explained or justified in terms of established concepts and principles. For instance, while democratic theory has long grappled with the issue of whether and how to constrain the majoritarian procedures of popular sovereignty in order to protect the interests of minorities and individuals, such constraints are typically revisable by democratic decisions by the people's representatives. But how could one combine international treaties and courts with normative democratic theory, given that such international entities serve this constraining function and yet are difficult, if not impossible, to revise, change, exit or supervise? Hence, international human rights norms compel theorists to reflect on standard assumptions about the state as a given unit of analysis.

Second, international human rights institutions are, arguably, qualitatively dissimilar to the sort of global governance institutions usually addressed in many studies of international institutional legitimacy, such as the World Trade Organization, the International Monetary Fund or various organs of the United Nations (e.g., see Breitmeier 2008; Coicaud 2001; Jönsson & Tallberg 2010; Koppell 2010). Empirically, the politicization of international human rights institutions apparently takes a different form than public contestation over other types of global governance institutions (cf. Zürn et al. 2012). While a broad range of civil society actors increasingly contest the growing authority of regional and global international institutions, the critics of human rights institutions are typically governments, as our previous examples indicate. Several scholars have pointed out that conventional rationalist-functionalist conceptions of international regimes, as institutionalized solutions to collective action problems that result from international anarchy, seem to be of little use for explaining why states create, delegate authority to and comply with international human rights systems (Moravcsik 2000; Simmons 2009). But if so, how should we instead think of international human rights systems and the authority they claim over states and other actors? And why does their peculiar authority trigger politicization?

Third, in academic debates about international legitimacy, respect for human rights is usually seen as an essential feature of normative legitimacy for political institutions. Indeed, on some philosophical accounts, this is a primary function of human rights: to provide a standard for inter-state toleration, to help decide when the international community should regard a state as a member entitled to sovereign non-interference (Nickel 2006). Similarly, many normative theorists suggest that respect for basic human rights provides an essential aspect of legitimacy for global governance institutions which regulate states in areas such as economy, the environment or security issues. But how should we assess international institutions which justify their existence solely in terms of promoting and protecting human rights? In the case of international human rights regimes, an account of legitimacy anchored in human rights might seem self-referential, or at any rate indeterminate.

Fourth, democracy is probably the only concept that can match human rights as a widely accepted yet essentially contested standard for evaluating the legitimacy of political institutions. Indeed, we are so used to speaking and hearing of democracy and human rights in conjunction that we often regard them as more or less synonymous. More sophisticatedly, we may think of human rights and democracy as interrelated and co-original (Habermas 2001), as defined in terms of one another (Goodhart 2005), or as expressions of a common notion of autonomy (Gould 2004) or of equal status (Buchanan 2010; cf. Hessler, this volume). Empirically, research often finds human rights and democracy not only to be compatible in practice but also to be correlated – democracy becomes difficult to realize where human rights are not safeguarded, and where democracy is lacking, the respect for human rights is usually wanting or worse. However, the issues addressed in this volume demonstrate that international human rights institutions and political practices and principles in democratic states may just as often stand in tension or outright conflict with one another. Among the central legitimacy concerns about international human rights treaties is the normative relationship between democratic rule, human rights and legitimate authority. Human rights treaties give citizens opportunities to pursue their interests vis-à-vis their own governments, while we expect democratic government to represent the interests of the citizenry. In such conflicts, which interest or principle should prevail?

Some claim that the recent worry and flurry over legitimacy in international, political and legal theory might signal a certain conservatism, or a managerialist, technocratic notion of international politics. Martti Koskenniemi warns that this academic and political 'legitimacy talk' mainly serves ideological functions, to mask power and its abuse:

> the very notion of legitimacy is ideological inasmuch as its apparent openness dissimulates a substantive void that blunts legal and political criticism and lets power redescribe itself as authority *on its own terms*. The more there is debate about 'legitimacy', the more there is pure noise, and the less we are able to hear whatever critiques 'law' or 'morality' might offer.
>
> (Koskenniemi 2003, p.367, emphasis in original)

Taking such warnings seriously, this volume nevertheless assumes that there may be more to legitimacy talk than pure noise, and that it may serve other social purposes than the ideological masking of power. At the same time, we assume that the social functions of legitimacy should be taken into account. As Ian Hurd reminds us, the sociological tradition regards legitimacy as a device to mitigate the threat that inequalities pose to social order:

> Legitimation is one source of reasons for individuals to accept the existing inequalities in society as appropriate (or natural, or defensible). It does not *eliminate* the inequalities; rather it *justifies* them and reduces their political salience. In this light legitimacy is always a conservative force that acts to defend favored values against revolution.
>
> (Hurd 2008, p.203, emphasis in original)

From a normative perspective, Buchanan and Keohane (2006) suggest that the 'circumstances of legitimacy' – that is, the circumstances under which questions of legitimate political authority arise – are situations in some sense beyond justice and self-interest: if an institution is legitimate, actors ought to comply with it, or at least not to interfere with it, even though it is neither perfectly just nor in full accordance with their self-interest. One might, arguably, even regard the circumstances of legitimacy as distinctly non-ideal. A common approach in recent political philosophy is to sketch principles of justice in ideal theory for a perfectly just society – that is, under the idealizing assumptions that everyone would act on those principles, knowing that others do the same, and that social conditions are favourable to realizing justice. Non-ideal theory, by contrast, relaxes the assumption of strict compliance and aims to formulate lower-level principles and rules to guide political decision-making 'in circumstances – our own – in which there is only partial compliance with principles' (Sangiovanni 2009, p.221; cf. Farrelly 2007; Hjorthen 2011; Valentini 2012a). Adherents of the ideal theory approach argue that it takes logical priority to non-ideal theory, as it provides the only way to identify what is ultimately desirable and to know exactly which moral demands we fail meet in our less-than-perfect world (Jubb 2012). However, the ideal theory approach has been criticized for providing insufficient practical guidance, precisely because principles of justice designed for idealized circumstances of strict compliance seem to say little about what duties and obligations apply to us under less idealized circumstances of partial compliance. Especially, a sceptic may wonder what guidance strict compliance theory can provide for theorizing legitimacy, at least in so far as we conform to the standard definition of legitimate authority as a tri-partite right to rule, to be obeyed by subjects, and to coerce those who fail to comply (Simmons 1999). Thus defined, legitimacy is a concept of non-ideal theory. In particular, the legitimacy of international human rights regimes may seem to be a topic squarely located in the domain of partial compliance theory, as the need for institutions to protect individuals and minorities from rights violations would appear to arise only if we assume that individuals, governments and other agents sometimes, or even often, do not act as they ought, whatever we take the appropriate principles to be. In the words of Kwame Anthony Appiah, 'many questions of justice only arise once people behave unjustly' (cited in Galston 2010).

3. Outline of the book

In the following chapters of this volume, a number of authors – philosophers, lawyers and political scientists – provide multi-faceted attempts to address the problems of legitimacy that international human rights regimes may entail.

In her chapter, Samantha Besson argues that before one can assess the institutional legitimacy problems involved in enforcing and specifying international human rights, one must first account for the legitimate authority of international human rights law as such. Yet this topic, she finds, has been oddly neglected in recent debates about the legitimacy of international law, perhaps because a common conventional view holds human rights as standards of legitimacy for the rest of the legal order. Setting out to cover this lacuna, Besson develops a revision of Joseph Raz's account of law's authority, where she focuses on law's ability for democratic coordination when people disagree on issues of common concern as a main justification of its authority. Applying this conception of the authority of law to human rights, Besson argues that they are both inherently moral-political and inherently legal: in a democratic polity, the law provides the best way of mutually recognizing the importance of the moral interests expressed as human rights. From this foundation, Besson analyses the legitimate authority of international human rights law through four issues, key to any autonomy-focused account of legal authority: its subjects, justification, the role of consent and sovereignty. Besson concludes that the legitimate authority of international human rights law is 'doubly piecemeal': first, following the Razian account, the justification of authority will vary depending on the circumstances and the subject's own reasons. Moreover, in the case of human rights law, such contextual variation is particularly prevalent, because given their reciprocal legal sources in domestic and international law, the legitimate authorities of international human rights and that of corresponding domestic human rights are themselves reciprocal. 'If the forum of realization of moral-political rights and as a consequence the locus of human rights legalization are situated at the domestic level', Besson concludes, 'this is also where the legitimation of international human rights ought to be sought for and promoted'.

Steven Wheatley examines the function of international human rights bodies in world society, and specifically whether their normative statements should be regarded as providing content-independent reasons for state parties to comply. To what extent should we recognize the normative authority of these international bodies to regulate domestic societies on issues where there is substantial political disagreement? Wheatley addresses the puzzle that international human rights bodies have the authority to develop the scope and content of international human rights, but in doing so, they extend the obligations of state parties beyond the original treaty text. Like Besson, Wheatley draws on the work of Raz. Applied to international human rights bodies, Wheatley argues, Raz's conception of authority implies that such institutions could only claim a right to rule where they can demonstrate that the state parties of international human rights treaties would better conform to the reasons that already apply to them by following the institution's directives than by acting independently. On Raz's interventionist account of human rights, however, the function of international human rights is to establish under what conditions external actors legitimately can take an interest in the exercise of sovereign authority in domestic societies. But this account, Wheatley argues, falls short where international human rights bodies have constitutionalized by developing a coherent jurisprudence, becoming an autonomous legal system. Such cases, where international human rights bodies adopt normative statements about the content of human rights norms and constitutional norms about norms, result in a dilemma: an international human rights body would possess legitimate authority in so far as state parties would better conform to the reasons that apply to them by following the body's directives than by acting independently, yet in most cases, domestic institutions will be better placed to determine the substance of human rights, especially so in solid democracies. Hence, in Wheatley's view, international human rights bodies need to guarantee that the procedures by which human rights norms are given content in domestic settings are consistent with democratic ideals. Therefore, such bodies may serve to provide both procedural standards for democratic political systems and to express the content of human rights treaties, consistent with a literal, logical approach to international legal norms and the 'overlapping consensus' among state parties. Democratic states may accept the authority of international human rights bodies, Wheatley concludes, as an expression of epistemic humility, as the political and legal institutions of a democratic society must admit the possibility that they have been mistaken.

Kristen Hessler explores a similar dilemma. The case she uses as a starting point for her chapter is the United Nations Human Rights Committee, which in 2006 noted concern over the United States' disenfranchisement of citizens convicted of a felony, recommending the USA to restore the right to vote to citizens who have served their sentences. If legitimate states have rights to a certain level of non-interference in their domestic affairs, Hessler asks, why should their governments consider such recommendations issued by international human rights treaty bodies as authoritative, especially as such bodies themselves do not satisfy criteria of legitimacy grounded in the values of democracy or consent? In order to resolve this puzzle, Hessler suggests, we must reconsider the conceptions of both human rights and normative legitimacy. On an institutional conception of human rights, human rights express principles of justice which apply to the structure of a society's social and political institutions (rather than ethical principles that apply directly to an agent's conduct). Hessler adopts an institutional conception according to which human rights serve, primarily if not exclusively, to secure the equal moral status of persons, and this notion of equality also, she argues, informs the most convincing accounts of political legitimacy. Now, unlike states, supranational human rights are not morally necessary to achieve justice among fellow citizens, and therefore, it is a category mistake to apply traditional conceptions of legitimacy to them. Instead, Hessler concludes, we should regard human rights treaty bodies as supranational institutions created to improve the human rights realization of states' social and political institutions – that is, as means for improving the legitimacy of states. 'To the extent that participation in international human rights regimes enables states to improve their own human rights records, such participation also improves their political legitimacy', Hessler writes and suggests that participation in international human rights regimes may improve the level of human rights protection even in states that meet standard thresholds of internal political legitimacy.

The puzzle that Başak Çalı addresses in her chapter is why domestic authorities – the judiciary, legislative or executive – should accept the interpretive authority of international human rights courts and quasi-judicial bodies. Dismissing alternative conceptions of legitimacy, Çalı suggests an instrumentalist view where questions of legitimacy – who should defer to what interpretations and who should make decisions – depend on what practices promote human rights globally in the long run. Often, the problem of legitimacy is not just to decide whether an international human rights court should prevail over a democratic state. Such a view neglects, she argues, the distinct moral value of international interpretive authorities in a world order where many political communities need to coexist with one another, and where there are many different interpretive authorities. That moral value goes beyond the domestic benefits to individuals as citizens; in exercising interpretive authority, international human rights courts help foster a global human rights culture, a debate about common standards and the common understanding that individuals have entitlements regardless of where in the world they happen to live. Noting that the long list of human rights provisions in international law might open for political manoeuvring by states, Çalı considers whether the scope of rights that international courts can legitimately interpret should be limited to a set of basic rights, while leaving the interpretation of a more extensive set of rights to domestic authorities. Rejecting this solution, Çalı instead argues that international interpretive authorities should develop standards of interpretation that take the respect for domestic democratic processes into account. When domestic authorities disagree with the interpretive authority, they should do so in a spirit of reconciliation and improvement, rather than conflict, she concludes.

In his contribution, Ian Hurd disputes common wisdom in both normative and descriptive accounts of legitimacy: that legitimacy implies compliance. Hurd studies the debates in the United States under the Bush administration about compliance with key international treaties on torture. While the international legal rules prohibiting torture are widely accepted and rarely called into question, their ostensive legitimacy coexists with state policies that permit torture – a puzzle from the conventional assumption that widespread belief in the legitimacy of an international rule will cause agents to comply with that rule. Hurd notes that even those actors who sought to open for the use of practices outlawed by conventions, such as the Convention Against Torture, accepted the legitimacy of international law, yet argued that torture practices did not constitute a violation of US obligations under international law. Hence, Hurd argues that perceiving a rule as legitimate does not preclude agents from violating it; rather, it shapes how violations are framed in order to legitimate them. International law is one tool which political actors use in the 'legitimation contest', as they fight over the meaning of compliance and, like any tool, it may be used for quite different purposes. Hence, this example demonstrates that international norms, institutions and law do not put an end to politics, but rather imply its continuation by other means.

In her chapter, Lynn Dobson seeks to offer a theory of the political legitimacy of international human rights institutions. Providing some clarifying conceptual distinctions, Dobson argues that political legitimacy must be distinguished from other types of normative justification, such as morality and justice, and pertains to the wielding of certain kinds of power by specific bodies. Specifically, legitimacy entails that a body has a right to rule over subjects who, in turn, are under a political obligation to it. On this view, it is not a capacity for coercion that makes legitimacy significant; rather, it raises a need for justification in situations where other reasons for action are insufficient to determine action. Here, Dobson makes two important claims about determining political legitimacy. First, political legitimacy is invoked comparatively, when credible candidates compete for authority in a domain that only admits one holder, and, second, attributions of legitimacy are always contextual, specifying which institution is legitimate for whom over what. Now, for international human rights institutions, this means that the question about their legitimacy boils down to the question: when should states, that believe their own institutions to be adequate to the task of applying human rights law, defer to the authority of international bodies? Here, Dobson suggests opening up the idea of pre-emptive power in legitimacy, so that both its scope and content may be variable and truncated. Consequently, an international institution's claim to legitimacy, Dobson concludes, 'would be less comprehensive and less hard-nosed than is the standard claim to legitimacy we are familiar with'. On this view of legitimacy, rather than telling states what to do, international human rights institutions hold states to account from deviations from such first-order commands.

The chapter by Johan Karlsson Schaffer explores whether international human rights institutions can be assessed by certain complex, hybrid standards of legitimacy that cosmopolitan theorists have suggested for global governance regimes. While such regulatory regimes may perhaps enjoy a prima facie justification in terms of the benefits they help states obtain, such a rationalist-functionalist view of institutions has difficulties making sense of international human rights institutions, which do not serve to solve collective action problems among states, but to regulate the internal relation between governments and their citizens. If we conceive of international human rights institutions in this way, they are justified to the extent that they provide to individuals and groups certain benefits, such as the opportunity to assert their interests vis-à-vis their governments. If so, state consent may offer a standard of legitimacy more plausible and feasible than recognized by certain cosmopolitan authors, he concludes.

Richard Bellamy starts from a number of recent controversial decisions by the European Court of Human Rights, which, similarly to Hessler's empirical example, relate to the disenfranchisement of prisoners serving custodial sentences. Drawing on the debate about the case of *Hirst v. the United Kingdom* as an illustration, Bellamy examines from a normative perspective whether international courts may legitimately interfere with the legal and political decisions and processes of well-established democracies, given that such states may seem to possess greater democratic legitimacy than most international arrangements. Bellamy explores the issue from the theoretical vantage point of political constitutionalism, which emphasizes the constitutional qualities of actual processes of democratic self-government and thereby offers an alternative to the dominant legal constitutionalist understanding of the role of international human rights conventions. Just as political constitutionalism only rules out strong forms of judicial review, weak review by international human rights organs may also be considered legitimate from this theoretical perspective. An international human rights convention can be regarded as an extension of the domestic political constitutions of democratic states to the extent that it results from, and is regulated by, a voluntary and fair association among democratic states, where its competences remain under their equal control and are limited to weak, contestatory review, respecting a principle of subsidiarity in its judgments. Bellamy finds that while the European system falls short of some of these criteria, it could easily be adjusted to fulfil the political constitutionalist model's demands.

Similarly engaging with the authority of international human rights courts over well-functioning democracies, Andreas Føllesdal presents a partial democratic defence of the judicial review by the European Court of Human Rights. The chapter addresses some of the tensions between sovereignty, international human rights review and legitimacy, and brings these findings to bear on the proposals for reform of the ECtHR that would reduce its authority over national legislatures and judiciaries. The objectives of such review are not obvious, the causes of non-compliance are contested, as is the legality of dynamic treaty interpretation; all of which hamper efforts to assess proposed improvements. Føllesdal first presents some relevant aspects of the ECtHR and reviews some of the recent criticism against the ECtHR practice of judicial review to protect human rights in 'well-functioning' democracies, in terms of various forms of legitimacy deficits. The chapter also presents some of the recent proposals for reform of the ECtHR. Subsequently, he lays out some reasons why such judicial review of majoritarian democratic decision-making may be defensible, also for well-functioning democracies, and responds to some of the criticisms, presenting a partial defence. Some standard objections are not well targeted against the practices of the ECtHR, Føllesdal argues, partly due to the division of responsibility between the Court and national public bodies, and the different roles of legislators and of judiciaries. His chapter concludes by considering some of the important remaining normative challenges, this partial defence notwithstanding.

Bibliography

Anon, 2009. Asean's toothless council. *The Wall Street Journal*. Available at: http://online.wsj.com/article/SB10001424052970203517304574303592053848748.html [Accessed 31 August 2012].

2011a. Brazil furious with Human Rights Commission decision cuts all relations. *MercoPress*. Available at: http://en.mercopress.com/2011/04/30/brazil-furious-with-human-rights-commission-decision-cuts-all-relations [Accessed 11 September 2012].

2011b. Brazil rejects request for suspending Amazon dam construction. *RTTNews*. Available at: www.rttnews.com/1592840/brazil-rejects-request-for-suspending-amazon-dam-construction.aspx [Accessed 11 September 2012].

2012a. SADC summit: Beheading the monster. *The Economist*.

2012b. Venezuela denounces American Convention on Human Rights as IACHR faces reform. *International Justice Resource Center*. Available at: http://ihrlaw.org/2012/09/19/venezuela-denounces-american-convention-on-human-rights-as-iachr-faces-reform/ [Accessed 12 October 2012].

2012c. Venezuela withdrawing from regional human rights court. *bdnews24.com*. Available at: http://bdnews24.com/details.php?id=228878 [Accessed 6 September 2012].

Baik, T.-U., 2012. *Emerging regional human rights systems in Asia*, Cambridge University Press.

Baynes, K., 2009a. Discourse ethics and the political conception of human rights. *Ethics & Global Politics*, 2(1). Available at: www.ethicsandglobalpolitics.net/index.php/egp/article/view/1938 [Accessed 16 November 2010].

2009b. Toward a political conception of human rights. *Philosophy & Social Criticism*, 35(4), 371–390.

Beitz, C., 2009. *The idea of human rights*, Oxford; New York: Oxford University Press.

Bell, A., 2012. Southern Africa: SADC lawyers vow not to support changes to regional court. *SW Radio Africa*.

Binder, C., 2012. The prohibition of amnesties by the Inter-American Court of Human Rights. In A. von Bogdandy & I. Venzke, eds. *International judicial lawmaking*. Beiträge zum ausländischen öffentlichen Recht und Völkerrecht. Springer Berlin, Heidelberg, pp. 295–328. Available at: www.springerlink.com/content/g47117768p52g1r4/abstract/ [Accessed 1 October 2012].

Breitmeier, H., 2008. *The legitimacy of international regimes*, Farnham, England; Burlington, VT: Ashgate.

Buchanan, A., 2010. The egalitarianism of human rights. *Ethics*, 120(4), 679–710.

Buchanan, A. & Keohane, R. O., 2006. The legitimacy of global governance institutions. *Ethics & International Affairs*, 20(4), 405–437.

Çalı, B., Koch, A. & Bruch, N., 2011. *The legitimacy of the European Court of Human Rights: The view from the ground*, Strasbourg.

Cardenas, S., 2010. *Conflict and compliance: State responses to international human rights pressure*, Philadelphia: University of Pennsylvania Press.

Ciorciari, J. D., 2012. Institutionalizing human rights in Southeast Asia. *Human Rights Quarterly*, 34(3), 695–725.

Clark, I., 2004. Legitimacy in a global order. *Review of International Studies*, 29(S1), 75–95.

Coicaud, J.-M., 2001. *The legitimacy of international organizations*, Tokyo; New York: United Nations University Press.

Costa, J.-P., 2011. On the legitimacy of the European Court of Human Rights' judgments. *European Constitutional Law Review*, 7(02), 173–182.

Dahl, R. A., 1999. Can international organizations be democratic? A skeptic's view. In I. Shapiro & C. Hacker-Cordón, eds. *Democracy's edges*. Cambridge University Press, pp. 19–37.

Donnelly, J., 2007. The relative universality of human rights. *Human Rights Quarterly*, 29(2), 281–306.

Durbach, A., Renshaw, C. & Byrnes, A., 2009. 'A tongue but no teeth'? The emergence of a regional human rights mechanism in the Asia-Pacific. *University of New South Wales Faculty of Law Research Series 2009*. Available at: http://law.bepress.com/unswwps-flrps09/art30 [Accessed 5 September 2012].

Dzehtsiarou, K., 2011. European consensus and the evolutive interpretation of the European Convention on Human Rights. *German Law Journal*, 12(10), 1730–1745.

Dzehtsiarou, K. & Greene, A., 2011. Legitimacy and the future of the European Court of Human Rights: Critical perspectives from academia and practitioners. *German Law Journal*, 12(10), 1706–1715.

Farrelly, C., 2007. Justice in ideal theory: A refutation. *Political Studies*, 55(4), 844–864.

Galston, W. A., 2010. Realism in political theory. *European Journal of Political Theory*, 9(4), 385–411.

Ginbar, Y., 2010. Human rights in ASEAN – setting sail or treading water? *Human Rights Law Review*, 10(3), 504–518.

Goldberg, A. J., 1965. The need for a World Court of Human Rights. *Howard Law Journal*, 11, 621.

Goldman, R. K., 2009. History and action: The Inter-American human rights system and the role of the Inter-American Commission on Human Rights. *Human Rights Quarterly*, 31(4), 856–887.

Goodhart, M., 2005. *Democracy as human rights: Freedom and equality in the age of globalization*, Routledge: New York.

Gould, C. C., 2004. *Globalizing democracy and human rights*, Cambridge University Press.

Habermas, J., 2001. Constitutional democracy – A paradoxical union of contradictory principles? *Political Theory*, 29(6), 766–781.

Hafner-Burton, E. M., 2012. International regimes for human rights. *Annual Review of Political Science*, 15(1), 265–286.

Hakim, P., 2012. The incredibly shrinking vision: US policy in Latin America. *Politica Exterior*. Available at: www.thedialogue.org/page.cfm?pageID=32&pubID=3011 [Accessed 4 October 2012].

Hayman, M., 2011. Brazil breaks relations with Human Rights Commission over Belo Monte dam. *Latin America News Dispatch*. Available at: http://latindispatch.com/2011/05/03/brazil-breaks-relations-with-human-rights-commission-over-belo-monte-dam/ [Accessed 11 September 2012].

Helfer, L. R., 2008. Redesigning the European Court of Human Rights: Embeddedness as a deep structural principle of the European human rights regime. *European Journal of International Law*, 19(1), 125–159.

Hjorthen, F. D., 2011. *Rescue beyond ideals: Guiding action in political theory*. Master's thesis. University of Oslo. Available at: http://urn.nb.no/URN:NBN:no-30279 [Accessed 18 October 2012].

Huneeus, A., 2011. Courts resisting courts: Lessons from the Inter-American Court's struggle to enforce human rights. *Cornell International Law Journal*, 44, 493.

Hurd, I., 2008. Myths of membership: The politics of legitimation in UN Security Council reform. *Global Governance*, 14(2), 199–219.

Ignatieff, M., 2001. *Human rights as politics and idolatry*, Princeton University Press.

Ingram, J. D., 2008. What is a 'right to have rights'? Three images of the politics of human rights. *American Political Science Review*, 102(04), 401.

Jones, C., 2012. The EU's accession to the European Convention on Human Rights: A cause for celebration or concern? *Statewatch Journal*, 21(4). Available at: www.statewatch.org/analyses/no-187-echr.pdf [Accessed 28 September 2012].

Jönsson, C. & Tallberg, J., eds., 2010. *Transnational actors in global governance: Patterns, explanations, and implications*, Basingstoke: Palgrave Macmillan.

Jubb, R., 2012. Tragedies of non-ideal theory. *European Journal of Political Theory*, 11(3), 229–246.

Keohane, R. O., 2003. Global governance and democratic accountability. In D. Held & M. Koenig-Archibugi, eds. *Taming globalization: Frontiers of governance*. Cambridge: Polity, pp. 130–159.

Keohane, R. O., Macedo, S. & Moravcsik, A., 2009. Democracy-enhancing multilateralism. *International Organization*, 63(01), 1.

Koppell, J., 2010. *World rule: Accountability, legitimacy, and the design of global governance*, University of Chicago Press.

Koskenniemi, M., 2003. Legitimacy, rights and ideology: Notes towards a critique of the new moral internationalism. *Associations*, 7(2), 349–373.

Kumm, M., 2004. The legitimacy of international law: A constitutionalist framework of analysis. *European Journal of International Law*, 15(5), 907–931.

Mazower, M., 2004. The strange triumph of human rights, 1933–1950. *Historical Journal*, 47(2), 379–398.

Moravcsik, A., 2000. The origins of human rights regimes: Democratic delegation in postwar Europe. *International Organization*, 54(2), 217–252.

Moyn, S., 2010. *The last utopia: Human rights in history*, Harvard University Press.

Moyo, A., 2009. Defending human rights and the rule of law by the SADC Tribunal: Campbell and beyond. *African Human Rights Law Journal*, 9, 590.

Myjer, E., 2012. The success story of the European Court: The times they are a-changin'? *Netherlands Quarterly of Human Rights*, 30(3), 264–271.

Nickel, J. W., 2006. Are human rights mainly implemented by intervention? In R. Martin & D. A. Reidy, eds. *Rawls's law of peoples: A realistic utopia?* Oxford: Blackwell, pp. 263–277.

Nowak, M., 2007. The need for a World Court of Human Rights. *Human Rights Law Review*, 7(1), 251–259.

O'Boyle, M., 2011. The future of the European Court of Human Rights. *German Law Journal*, 12(10), 1862–1877.

Picq, M., 2012. Is the Inter-American Commission of Human Rights too progressive? *Al Jazeera*. Available at: www.aljazeera.com/indepth/opinion/2012/06/2012658344220937.html [Accessed 5 September 2012].

Ramcharan, R., 2010. ASEAN's Human Rights Commission: Policy considerations for enhancing its capacity to protect human rights. *UCL Human Rights Law Review*, 3, 199–235.

Robertson, P., 2012. ASEAN's road to nowhere? Subverting standards within the ASEAN Human Rights Declaration. *Strategic Review*. Available at: www.sr-indonesia.com/2011-08-09-22-09-10/commentaries/187-aseans-road-to-nowhere-subverting-standards-within-the-asean-human-rights-declaration [Accessed 11 September 2012].

Sangiovanni, A., 2009. Normative political theory: A flight from reality? In D. Bell, ed. *Political thought and international relations: Variations on a realist theme*. Oxford University Press, pp. 219–239.

Sasman, C., 2012. Southern Africa: SADC leaders neuter tribunal. *The Namibian*.

Simmons, A. J., 1999. Justification and legitimacy. *Ethics*, 109(4), 739–771.

Simmons, B., 2009. *Mobilizing for human rights: International law in domestic politics*, Cambridge University Press.

Tan, H.-L., 2011. *The ASEAN Intergovernmental Commission on Human Rights: Institutionalising human rights in Southeast Asia*, Cambridge University Press.

Trechsel, S., 2003. A World Court for Human Rights? *Northwestern University Journal of International Human Rights*, 1(1).

Tsutsui, K., Whitlinger, C. & Lim, A., 2012. International human rights law and social movements: States' resistance and civil society's insistence. *Annual Review of Law and Social Science*, 8(1), 367–396.

Ulfstein, G., 2008. Do we need a World Court of Human Rights? In O. Engdahl & P. Wrange, eds. *Law at war: The law as it was and the law as it should be: Liber Amicorum Ove Bring*. International humanitarian law series. Leiden. Available at: http://papers.ssrn.com/sol3/papers.cfm?abstract_id=1937580 [Accessed 28 September 2012].

Valentini, L., 2012a. Ideal vs. non-ideal theory: A conceptual map. *Philosophy Compass*, 7(9), 654–664.

2012b. In what sense are human rights political? A preliminary exploration. *Political Studies*, 60(1), 180–194.

Zürn, M., 2004. Global governance and legitimacy problems. *Government and Opposition*, 39(2), 260–287.

Zürn, M., Binder, M. & Ecker-Ehrhardt, M., 2012. International authority and its politicization. *International Theory*, 4(01), 69–106.

2

The legitimate authority of international human rights

On the reciprocal legitimation of domestic and international human rights

SAMANTHA BESSON

1. Introduction

International human rights have been part of international law since the 1950s. Today, they bind more than 80 per cent of the world's states qua treaty law[1] and, although this is more controversial, all or most of them qua customary international law and general principles of international law.[2] Having been an important part of international law for the past fifty years, human rights have become an object of interest for political and legal theorists alike. Not only have they become the lingua franca of most recent accounts of international relations (Raz 2010; Tasioulas 2002), but they are often put forward as the ground for the legitimate authority of international law and institutions (Buchanan 2004, 2008; Goodin 2007) and, as a result,

Early drafts of this chapter were presented at the Osgoode Hall Law School's Nathanson Centre Seminar Series on Legal Philosophy between State and Transnationalism in Toronto on 16 October 2009, at the workshop on democratic authority of the APA Annual Conference in New York on 29 December 2009, at the Cardozo-NYU ICON Seminar on 14 April 2010 and at the Authority, Coercion and Paternalism Conference in Graz on 27 and 28 May 2011. I would like to thank Allen Buchanan, Jean Cohen, Ken Ehrenberg, David Enoch, Michael Giudice, Leslie Green, Johan Karlsson Schaffer, Mattias Kumm, David Lefkowitz, Lukas Meyer, Gianluigi Palombella, Gerry Postema, Sophia Reibetanz-Moreau, Michel Rosenfeld, Joseph Raz, Stefan Sciaraffa, François Tanguay-Renaud, Detlef von Daniels, Timothy Waligore, Wil Waluchow and Joseph Weiler for their comments and questions. Special thanks are owed to my research assistant, Tancrède Scherf, for his help with the editing and formal layout of the chapter, and to Andreas Føllesdal for his feedback and editing.

[1] For an overview of international human rights treaties, see: www2.ohchr.org/english/law/index.htm.

[2] On the sources of international human rights law, see the two seminal pieces by J. F. Flauss (1998) and Simma & Alston (1989).

for that of individual states' legal orders (from an international perspective (Beitz 2009; Buchanan 2004; Raz 2010), but also arguably from a domestic one (Føllesdal 2007; Forst 2010)) and even of regional organizations' legal orders (e.g. the European Union's[3]). Surprisingly, however, very little attention has been given so far to the legitimacy of international human rights law itself (Benhabib 2008, 2009; Besson 2011a, 2011e; Buchanan 2010a; Cohen 2008; Donoho 2003; Hessler 2005).

At a basic level, the question of the legitimacy of international human rights, and more precisely its legitimate or justified authority as I will understand it here,[4] can be elucidated along the lines of the legitimacy of international law. The legitimacy of international law amounts to the imposition of moral duties of obedience on its subjects, i.e. categorical and exclusionary moral reasons for action (Raz 1986: 23). Those moral duties are duties to obey international law not because it is just, morally correct and justified, but qua law. They are moral duties, however, and are distinct therefore from the legal duties to obey the law because it is law (Raz 1995: 342–343). Furthermore, the existence of international law's legitimacy is the result of an objective evaluation: international law may have legitimate authority whether or not its subjects think it does and whether or not they have consented to its authority. In other words, it is not the perceived or sociological legitimacy of international human rights law this chapter is concerned about, but its normative legitimacy (Raz 2006: 1006–1007).[5] While the former can be established from the striving international human rights discourse (Çalı, Koch & Bruch 2011), the latter needs to be argued for in other ways.

Of course, in recent years, the various prudential or non-prudential, and self-regarding or cosmopolitan reasons states may have to ratify and then to comply with international human rights instruments have been at the centre of many sociological and political empirical studies (Hafner-Burton & Tsutsui 2005; Moravcsik 2000; Risse, Ropp & Sikkink 1999; Simmons 2009). Some of those reasons have also been assessed and discussed from a philosophical or jurisprudential perspective (Buchanan & Powell 2008:

3 See e.g. European Court of Justice, *Yassin Abdullah Kadi and Al Barakaat International Foundation v. Council of the European Union and Commission of the European Communities*, judgment of the Court (Grand Chamber) of 3 September 2008, European Court Reports 2008 Page I-06351; German Bundesverfassungsgericht, Beschluss vom 30. Juni 2009, Lissabonsvertrag, 2 BvE 2/08.

4 In what follows, I will use 'authority' to mean legitimate authority (see also Besson 2009a). For the same use of the term, see Raz (1986, 1995, 2006).

5 See also Buchanan (2004). See, however, Franck (1988); Franck (2006: 88, 91 and 93) who conflates the sociological and normative approaches to legitimacy.

330 ff.; Gardbaum 2008). The various reasons there may be to ratify and/or to comply with international human rights norms ought not, however, to be confused with content-independent moral reasons to obey those norms qua legal norms.[6] There may be moral reasons to create and support international human rights guarantees and institutions because they are morally valuable[7] or just (Rawls 1971: 114–117 and 333–337; Waldron 1993: 3) independently from human rights law's legitimacy. They ought not be confused, as a result, with moral reasons to obey the legal human rights applied or generated by those states and international institutions.[8]

Recently, some authors have started looking more closely at the question of the legitimacy of international human rights institutions and their decisions.[9] The question of those institutions' legitimacy, however fascinating, is distinct from that of international human rights law itself.[10] True, international law's authority is the authority of international legal norms, but also accordingly of their law-making and legal interpretation processes and hence in part a product of the legitimacy of the domestic or international institutions involved in those processes.[11] One cannot indeed distinguish a legal norm from its interpretation. In the context of international human rights law, there are reasons, however, to address the two issues separately, or at least to address the legitimacy of human rights norms generated by states before that of international human rights institutions, on the one hand, and of their decisions and interpretations in the context of international human rights, on the other.

On the one hand, it is true that international human rights institutions can make or contribute to making international human rights law by interpreting and hence specifying international human rights further and issuing application decisions. They are not usually involved in making those norms in the first place, however, or at least not independently from states themselves. Furthermore, some international human rights instruments

[6] See, for example Raz (1986: 66 ff.; 1995; 2006), on the distinction.

[7] See on those different justifications, e.g. Buchanan (2008) and Buchanan & Powell (2008).

[8] See, for example Raz (1986: 66 ff.; 1995; 2006), on the distinction. See also Buchanan (2008).

[9] This has been the case especially for international judicial human rights institutions and decisions: see e.g. Besson (2011b); Føllesdal (2007, 2008); Hessler (2005); Letsas (2008).

[10] The article focuses on legal authority in contrast to private authority, but also to political authority in general. On the distinction, see Raz (1979; 1986: 23, 38 and 70; 1995: 210, 341 and 355; 2003; 2006:1004–1005).

[11] See Besson (2009a); Buchanan (2008). Of course, the correlation is not perfect: illegitimate institutions may produce legitimate laws, and legitimate institutions may produce illegitimate laws.

do not have international bodies connected to them or, on the contrary, have many of them without clear division of labour: some specialized and some general; of many different kinds: some judicial, some quasi-judicial and others political; and implying different subjects: states, but also individuals. As to those institutions' decisions, on the other hand, they are quite rarely binding and almost never self-executing. Even when they are, their alleged contribution to the interpretation of international human rights norms (their so-called jurisprudential authority or *erga omnes* effect) is deeply contested and rarely recognized by states. This is because international human rights norms are to be interpreted and applied in priority (or, in some cases, only) by states in their domestic legal orders and with the help of all their national institutions, and only in a subsidiary fashion (and never completely anyway) by international human rights bodies (Besson 2012a; contra: Letsas 2010). Thus, while the legitimacy of international human rights institutions and their decisions in their vast diversity raises intriguing and important questions, those questions cannot be addressed without first considering the legitimacy of international human rights law itself. The purpose of this chapter therefore is to address this first question only, leaving the question of international human rights institutions' legitimacy per se and in relation to domestic institutions for another time.

So far, very few studies have focused on the justified authority of international human rights law qua law. Presumably, however, the contribution of international human rights norms to the legitimation of other national and international legal norms will depend in part or entirely on their legitimacy. Taken on their own, furthermore, ascertaining the existence and the scope of their justified authority over states is important. The existence of an entirely illegitimate, albeit valuable for different reasons (Tasioulas 2010a), set of human rights norms would not be sustainable in the long run. The law's distinctive contribution to the advancement of valuable goals lies precisely in successfully laying down authoritative directives to reach those goals (Tasioulas 2010a). Furthermore, the fact that valid human rights law necessarily claims to be legitimate implies that it should be capable of being legitimate and hence be produced so that it can be. In those conditions, ensuring the legitimacy of international human rights law has a key influence on the organization of international human rights law-making and decision-making processes. This will prove particularly important when addressing potential conflicts between international human rights norms and/or their interpretations by international human rights bodies with national human rights law (Hessler 2005). Finally, due to the increasingly direct impact of international human rights norms on individuals and public authorities in areas previously exclusively covered by domestic human rights law (Gardbaum 2008; Stone Sweet & Keller 2008), a legitimacy gap is gradually widening and the legitimacy of international law in those areas has become more pressing (Kumm 2004). This is particularly obvious when international human rights constitute direct limitations on democratically legitimate decisions and legislation at domestic level.

The neglect of those issues is even more surprising as discussions of the legitimacy of international law in general have become more common in recent years (Besson 2009a; Bodansky 2008; Charlesworth & Coicaud 2010; Franck 1988, 2006; Goldsmith & Posner 2005; Kumm 2004; Tasioulas 2010a; Teson 2005; Wolfrum 2007). Curiously, however, the legitimacy of international human rights is barely ever mentioned in that context or only to stress that it is precisely not in contention.[12] Indeed, the more robust and the more intrusive supranational human rights law becomes in the domestic sphere, the more effective (Helfer & Slaughter 1997), but also, interestingly, the more legitimate it is perceived to be (Bayefsky 2001). Their subjective or sociological legitimacy would therefore seem to be in greater tension with their objective or normative legitimacy than is the case for other international legal norms. Furthermore, the more other international institutions and legal norms are in need of legitimacy, the more those justifications are sought after, by analogy with what applies domestically, within international human rights law whose legitimacy itself cannot as a result be in contention (Buchanan 2004: 189; Buchanan 2008; Goodin 2007).

A first kind of explanation for this neglect or at least for this presumption of legitimacy resides precisely in the prima facie counterintuitive nature of the question in the domestic context. Among domestic legal norms, human rights norms are those whose legitimate authority is usually the least likely to be doubted. This is, primarily, because the direct bearers of the duty to obey human rights are public authorities and not individuals, and, second, because human rights norms create rights to the benefit of all individuals and corresponding rights-based duties for all public authorities. Finally, the special authority of domestic human rights usually stems from their constitutional nature, and hence from the highly inclusive and democratic adoption procedures of constitutional

[12] See e.g. Gardbaum (2008: 768). On the unquestionability of human rights, see O'Neill (2005: 439).

norms due to their constraining role on ordinary democratic procedures. Democracy and human rights are indeed often regarded as being grounded by reference to the same value: political equality, and work as necessary mutual constraints when protecting that value.[13] Human rights are deemed as necessary for the democratic process and as having to be protected from it, albeit in a way that is democratic. As a result, human rights and democracy are commonly regarded as mutually reinforcing at domestic level and their interdependence turns human rights into an inherent part of the democratic legitimation from which they have to benefit. It follows that their democratic credentials and accordingly their legitimacy are bound to be different from that of other domestic law norms.

While the two former characteristics may be true of international human rights as well, the legitimacy of international law pertains mainly to states' duties to abide by international law. Thus, the fact that the duty-bearer in both cases is a state cannot explain the lack of concern for the legitimacy of human rights at the international level. As to the third explanation, it cannot simply be transposed onto international human rights without further argument. Of course, some authors may argue that international human rights actually contribute not only to the democratic legitimation of international law, but also to the democratic legitimation of states and that as a result trying to assess their democratic legitimacy, even from an international perspective, is not feasible (Buchanan 2004: 189). It remains, however, that international human rights have not been deliberated and adopted by highly inclusive international democratic procedures the way constitutional rights have; they are deliberated and adopted by both democratic and non-democratic states, and through procedures that are not necessarily inclusive, egalitarian and transparent (Donoho 2003: 27 ff.; Gould 2004). Not to mention the lack of correspondence between those adopting international human rights and those actually bound by them and whose political equality is protected. Even if they are approved democratically at domestic level before being ratified at an intergovernmental level, they have not been deliberated over through democratic channels. As a result, international human rights are not usually regarded as source-based superior constraints on such procedures whether domestic or

[13] See Christiano (2008: 130 and 260–264) on the mutual grounding of democracy and liberal rights in the principle of public equality. See also Brettschneider (2007: 23–26) on equality as one of the core values of democracy and substantive rights.

international.[14] This explains why international human rights do not per se take priority over domestic constitutional law. Nor do they necessarily take priority, either due to their source or to their content, over other norms or regimes of international law. If they cannot be associated in a straightforward fashion with the legitimation of international law the way they are in domestic law, their legitimating role in the process cannot be held against trying to account for their own legitimacy through that process. While it would be wrong to reduce human rights to democracy and prioritize the latter over the former, the contrary would be equally wrong and oblivious of their mutually supportive albeit complex relationship.[15]

A second explanation for this differentiated take on international human rights may be that they stem from international agreements between democratic states. And indirect democratic consent through the consent of democratic states is usually put forward as a major justification for international law's authority. This explanation fails to persuade, however. Consent is neither a sufficient nor a necessary condition of legitimacy per se (Besson 2009a; Buchanan 2004). This applies both at the domestic and the international levels. Of course, as we will see, state consent still has an important role to play in the ascertaining and strengthening of international legal authority, but it is not in and of itself a justification for obligations to obey the law. Nor is it correct to identify democratic consent with democratic legitimacy (Besson 2005a, 2009a; Hershovitz 2003). Again, in the absence of international democracy, consent may play an identification role in the generation of state duties in a fair association model (Christiano 2012), but this should not be mistaken for democracy itself.

A third explanation may actually be that the adoption of international human rights instruments historically found part of their justification in the reinforcement of national democracies when democracy did not fare that well as a binding international principle and was replaced by human rights (Letsas 2008; Moravcsik 2000). On this view, if human rights are there to consolidate national democracy, their democratic legitimacy itself cannot be questioned. In a similar vein, if international human rights instruments were initially adopted to curb democratic violations of human rights, accounting for their legitimacy in democratic terms would be counterproductive. These arguments come close to the democratic precommitment

[14] This explains why some authors try to conceive international human rights as a form of international or domestic (thick) constitutional law (see Gardbaum 2008 for the various arguments). For a democratic critique of this argument, see Besson (2009b: 381–407).

[15] See for the same balanced approach to the legitimacy of international human rights: Benhabib (2008, 2009); Cohen (2008).

argument that is often used in the context of discussions of the democratic credentials of constitutional rights. Even if this historical explanation pertains, times and circumstances have changed, however; national democracies have developed and consolidated, including through domestic human rights catalogues and judicial institutions of their own. Furthermore, neither democracy nor human rights alone suffice to provide full legitimacy to any law; as they are mutually supportive, privileging one over the other would amount to providing an impoverished account of legitimacy. Finally, precommitment types of argument based on the protection of human rights (including the right to self-government) against themselves raises well-known difficulties in the domestic context, that are magnified when brought to the international level (Besson 2005b; Waldron 1999).

A fourth explanation may be found in the moral nature of human rights and the widespread belief in their universal moral justification. The alleged straightforward relationship between universal moral rights and legal human rights is sometimes regarded as dispensing the latter's authority from having to be justified the way the authority of other legal norms would in a content-independent fashion: their uncontested moral justification and the corresponding moral duties suffice (e.g. Gardbaum 2008: 768). Or else, if the possibility of reasonable moral disagreement is contemplated, the difficulty is said to lie exclusively in the lack of universal scope of legitimate authority in the context of the cultural parochialism or exceptionalism debates, but not in the possibility of moral justification per se. While parochialism raises important questions that will be broached at the end of this chapter, the moral nature of international human rights is not exclusive of their legal nature and is not left untouched by their legalization, hence the need to account for their legitimacy qua legal norms. Legal specifications of moral human rights may be controversial and trigger important reasonable disagreements of their own. Moreover, the institutional recognition and the legalization of human rights do affect their moral counterparts (Besson 2011a) and, as I will argue, it is precisely there that the key to their legitimacy may be found.

Finally, yet another explanation for the absence of discussion of the legitimacy of international human rights may lie in the specific nature of human rights qua rights and the kind of legitimate authority rights may claim to have. Rights are interests which are regarded as sufficiently important to give rise to duties. Qua entitlements and source of a normative relationship, rights correspond to correlative duties albeit with a justificatory priority over those duties. Legal rights are legally recognized, specified or created moral rights and trigger as a result both legal and moral duties. When moral agents are bound by a legal right, they are bound by the primary moral duties corresponding to the right and by the secondary moral duties to obey this right qua legal norm and to abide by its corresponding moral duties. Those duties are usually reduced to each other and go unnoticed at the domestic level. The same may be said about the right-holders of both kinds of duties in a democracy where the group of those affected in their fundamental interests and the citizens overlap: they are all the citizens in a given polity. And this in turn may explain why the justification of the second-order duties to abide by a legal right and its duties is not usually regarded as an additional requirement. That does not necessarily apply to the international level, however. International human rights can bind states as international legal norms but generate corresponding human rights duties for other subjects as well whether on the international or the domestic plane: state authorities in their domestic setting, IOs, etc. The same may be said about the right-holders of both kinds of duties: states and arguably the international community as a whole for the second-order duty to abide by international human rights law and individuals for the first-order duty to respect human rights. As a result, the question of the legitimacy of those second-order duties can be regarded as an important one and its justification as logically distinct from the justification of first-order human rights duties, albeit intrinsically related to it.

All five explanations provide interesting insights into the specificity of international human rights norms and about the ways one may justify their authority. It reveals, if need be, how complex the enquiry into those different justifications is bound to be: it requires a good understanding of difficult issues such as the nature and justification of moral and legal human rights, and the relationship between their moral justification and their legitimate authority, a good grasp of law's and human rights' authority and a view of the relationship between human rights and democracy at the domestic level, on the one hand. It also requires, however, explaining how one can make all three questions travel to the international level and back to the domestic level and how to adapt our accounts of the relationship between democratic legitimacy and domestic human rights when the human rights and/or the democratic processes at stake are international, on the other. A separation between domestic and international law in the field of human rights would make no political and legal sense in the light of existing human rights practice that straddles the different sources of human rights[16] and hence no sense in terms of legitimacy either.

[16] On the domestic constitutionalization of international human rights in Europe, see Gardbaum (2008); and on the ECHR in domestic human rights reasoning in the United Kingdom and Ireland, see Besson (2008).

In order to know whether international human rights norms have a justified claim to legitimate authority over states, the chapter focuses on their normative or 'supply' side and in particular on their corresponding duties (O'Neill 2005: 430). It starts by assessing what kind of duties and hence what kind of reasons states have by virtue of recognizing human rights. This implies determining whether those norms can be described as legal human rights in the first place with the respective legal and moral duties they imply and what is the relationship between domestic and international human rights law in that context. Then it turns to the different conditions of their legitimate authority and to the issue of how the reasons given by international human rights law can not only match corresponding states' reasons, but also contribute to improving conformity to those reasons. It is the interdependence between human rights and political equality and the role of human rights for democratic authority at domestic level that is at the core of the argument about the mutual legalization and legitimation of international and domestic human rights.

To that effect, the argument in this chapter is three-pronged: in the first section, I start by general considerations about the model of legitimate authority of international legal norms, before discussing the moral-legal nature of international human rights and the relationship between domestic and international legal guarantees of human rights in the second section (Besson 2009a, 2011c). The third step of the argument enables us to bring those two groups of considerations together and address the question of the legitimate authority of international human rights law, by looking at four basic issues: how states may bind themselves to create human rights duties for themselves, what the justification for the duty to obey those rights could be, whether they can consent to more than they have to and, finally, whether sovereignty can be invoked against the legitimate authority of international human rights.

2. The legitimate authority of international law

The model of legitimate authority of international law that is used in this chapter is best captured by explaining, first, the concept of legitimate authority of international law that is chosen and, second, the conception that is applied to international human rights law.[17]

[17] This section is borrowed and summarized from Besson (2009a).

2.1 *The concept of legitimate authority of international law*

The first difficulty facing any explanation of the legitimacy of international law lies in the identification of a concept of legitimacy that can account for the legitimacy of (at least some part of) international law. The differences between international and national law in that respect are well known (Buchanan 2008): international law is mostly the product of horizontal interstate law-making practice and, to be more precise, of different interstate practices. Some international legal norms are more akin to making contractual promises and others to general legal rule-making for all subjects of international law. As a result, international law is said to lack a centralized and hierarchical ensemble of law-making institutions and processes that may be equated with domestic law-making authorities and legislating procedures, on the one hand, and is mostly exempt from sanctions backing up its norms, on the other.

To make things more complex, new forms of international law have arisen in recent times that question the exclusivity of the horizontal interstate law paradigm. Subjects no longer only include states making law for other states, but also international organizations (IOs) and individuals as subjects of rights and obligations. With respect to its object, international law no longer pertains only to interstate relations, but also, for instance in the case of international human rights, to intrastate relations and therefore directly regulates the life of individuals alongside domestic law. Finally, and maybe as a result, the sources of international law and its law-making processes have become more diverse and have developed to include, besides the 'famous three' (treaties, customary law and general principles), general multilateral interstate law-making processes that often associate individual actors, and unilateral legislation by IOs. Interestingly, those very sources which include subjects of international law other than states regulate matters previously covered by domestic law only and often through majority rule (Besson 2009a; Kumm 2004; Wolfrum 2007). In terms of normativity as well, international law no longer offers a unified face. International legal norms can bind subjects universally or not (e.g. *erga omnes* and *omnium* duties) and to varying degrees (e.g. *jus cogens norms* and, more controversially, soft law) (Tasioulas 1996; Weil 1983).

Thus, either the concept of legitimacy that is chosen accounts for the legitimate authority of both national and international law, but in a way that can capture not only their differences but also the sheer diversity of international law-making itself, or two (or more) separate concepts of legitimacy are used in each case. Given the increasing intermingling of international and domestic legal orders and, arguably, their reciprocal legitimation (Buchanan 2011), but especially given the common individual subjects of those legal orders, authors writing about the legitimacy of international law ought to choose and use one of the concepts of legitimate authority developed for the domestic context and apply it in a transitive manner (Besson 2009a; Tasioulas 2010a). Of course, this does not imply that the specific justifications for the authority of international law or its consequences will be the same as those applicable to domestic law given the differences identified before between those two legal orders. The remainder of this chapter is actually devoted to exploring the specificities of the legitimacy in international law, and in international human rights law in particular. Rather, what matters for our purpose is that the concept that is used when assessing the legitimacy of legal norms stemming from both orders is the same.

Besides the virtues of conceptual unity in a pluralist legal order, it is important, when choosing a concept of legitimate authority of international law, that it can also be applied to individual legal subjects and not only to states.[18] When states are bound by obligations of international law, their institutions and subjects are bound indirectly and have to comply with them through the actions of their state, when they are not bound directly. As a result, assessing the legitimacy of international law and national law with the same concept, but on an interstate basis in the case of international law and on a state-individual basis in the case of national law is unhelpful. The legitimacy of international law can only be understood if the reasons for action it provides to all subjects of that authority are assessed at the same time and by reference to individual subjects as ultimate subjects of authority. Of course, this is not to deny that international law may provide different subjects with different reasons: states with some reasons and individuals with others. However, because the relationship between those subjects is one of constituency, separating the justifications for those reasons or, worse, eluding some of them blinds to an essential connection between them. When a state is bound by an international legal norm, its institutions and subjects are bound at the same time, whether directly or indirectly, and this must necessarily affect in return the way in which the state itself can be bound (Kumm 2004: 910; Murphy 2010).

Those two points are particularly important in the case of international human rights law whose content overlaps with that of domestic human

[18] See Besson (2009a). For a similar argument but in relation to the application of the international rule of law to states, see Besson (2011d); Waldron (2011).

rights law and whose subjects overlap with those of domestic human rights law. This correspondence of content and scope is actually part of what international human rights are about: providing a subsidiary and minimal set of human rights guarantees that prevent a levelling-down in domestic human rights protection. Moreover, when states bind themselves through international human rights law, they bind the domestic polity and in turn contribute to mutually securing the equal status of each of its individual members within the polity itself. In that respect, it is very important to assess the legitimate authority of international human rights law for the state but with individual members of the domestic polity in mind.

2.2 The conception of legitimate authority of international law

2.2.1 Razian authority

Joseph Raz's seminal and refined account of authority, and of legitimate legal authority in particular (Raz 1986, 1995, 2006), constitutes a useful starting point for any discussion of international law's authority (Tasioulas 2010a). It is also the conception that constitutes the basis of the model of democratic authority that I propose, albeit complemented with a democratic procedural requirement.[19]

In a nutshell, the Razian conception of legal authority comprises two elements: A has legitimate authority over C when A's directives are (i) content-independent and (ii) exclusionary reasons for action for C. In other words, the directives are authoritative reasons for action, first, by virtue of the fact that A issued them and not because of the content of any particular directive (Raz 1986: 35 ff.; 2006: 1012–1020), and, second, because these reasons are not simply to be weighed along with other reasons that apply to C but, instead, have the normative effect of excluding some countervailing reasons for action (Raz 1986: 57 ff.; 2006). The authority of those reasons for action is justified, according to Raz, if two conditions are fulfilled: (i) the dependence condition (DC); and (ii) the normal justification condition (NJC). Both conditions are intrinsically related. First, A's directives have to match (objective) reasons that apply to C independently of A's directives (Raz 1986: 42 ff.; 2006). Second, A has legitimate authority over C if the latter would better conform with those reasons that apply to him or her if he or she intends to be guided by A's directives than if he or she does not (Raz 1986: 53; 2006: 1014). So, an authority is legitimate

[19] I have argued elsewhere for this complement to the Razian basic account of legal authority: Besson (2005a, 2005b).

when its subjects would likely better conform with the reasons that apply to them by treating the authority's directives as content-independent and exclusionary reasons for action than if they did not. This is what is meant by the so-called 'service conception' of legitimate authority: it facilitates its subjects' conformity with the (objective) reasons that already apply to them and hence respects their autonomy (Raz 2006: 1012 ff.). By autonomy, I mean having and exercising the capacity to choose from a range of options (Griffin 2008: 33).

Among the content-independent reasons that may trigger the application of the NJC, one usually mentions the authority's epistemic expertise, its cognitive, decisional or volitional ability, its executive capacity or its coordinative ability (Raz 1986: 75 ff.). The specific justification will vary depending on the circumstances and the concrete ability of each legal norm or set of legal norms, on the one hand, and the subject's own objective reasons, on the other. This explains the piecemeal nature of law's legitimate authority in Raz's account, i.e. the fact that the law cannot have general legitimate authority over all subjects at one given time, and this realization is quite illuminating when the piecemeal nature of legal authority is contrasted with the law's general claim to authority.

2.2.2 Revised Razian authority

One of the major content-independent sets of reasons for action that can be provided by a public authority in the legal context is a salient set of coordinative reasons.[20] When there is an independent reason to choose one single interpretation or course of action in circumstances of reasonable disagreement and hence to coordinate, legal authority can help identify some of the conflicting reasons for action or orderings of reasons as salient and hence can help legal subjects coordinate over them.

In fact, as I have argued elsewhere, coordination on issues of common concern is a much more common requirement in the pluralist circumstances of contemporary politics than legal theorists are usually ready to concede. In conditions of pervasive and persistent reasonable disagreement about justice, the creation of a legal order as a means of general coordination over matters of justice is actually in itself a requirement of justice (Besson 2005b; Finnis 1984: 115–138; Waldron 1993; 1999: 101–113). And the law constitutes the best coordination mechanism one may think of: it provides a framework through which one may identify in a

[20] See, for coordination-based accounts of legal authority founded on Razian authority, Besson (2005b); Waldron (2003).

determinate and public manner a salient solution from a range of morally eligible solutions. This has to do with its decisional and expressive abilities, but also, although not only, with the sanctions it can provide in case of non-conformity (Besson 2005b: 459, 503; Waldron 1999: 101–113). As a result, the reason to coordinate over certain issues is not restricted to certain contexts and legal areas where so-called 'coordination problems' arise, such as environmental law, migration law or disarmament law, but it is a more general reason to constitute a legal system and then to abide by the rules of that legal system as a whole, whether or not those rules effectively solve coordination problems in practice.

The kind of coordination I have in mind here is (partial-conflict) coordination over moral concerns when people disagree reasonably over them and therefore have an independent reason to coordinate over a common take on those issues if they know others will do so as well and can identify what all of them will coordinate over – even if this means not doing things the way they separately think would be the right way to go about doing them.[21]

Scope precludes expanding here on the question of law and coordination, but any form of coordination over matters of common concern cannot be judged in the same way. Democratic coordination provides the most legitimate mode of coordination in circumstances of reasonable disagreement over matters of justice.[22] It respects equality by including all those affected in the decision-making process over issues of disagreement. Democratic legitimacy is another dimension that escapes most recent accounts of law's authority that are still, and questionably so, focused on a hierarchical divide between rulers and governed.[23] In any case, since democracy is incremental and rarely fully realized, the proposed account of coordination-based authority does not exclude less or non-democratic forms of legitimate coordination (Raz 2006: 1031 fn. 20, 1037–1040). In a nutshell, democratic decision-making is intrinsically valuable because it respects basic political equality in circumstances of pervasive and persistent reasonable disagreement about morality. More precisely, majority rule provides all participants with an equal chance of giving salience to their

[21] On the difference between consent and coordination, see Besson (2005b: 473–475); Waldron (1993: 25–27). Consent can enhance coordination, but is not necessary for coordination to take place.

[22] See Besson (2005b: 459 ff.); Waldron (1999: 101–113) on democratic coordinative authority. See for a non-coordination-based account of democratic authority that is very similar, Christiano (2008: 231–259).

[23] See, for example Hershovitz's (2003: 209–210) critique of Raz's account of legal authority.

own views over what ought to be done over matters of common concern and thus by taking turns in the decision-making process.[24]

If all this pertains, (democratic) coordination provides one of the main justifications for the law's authority. It is a justification that may actually overlap with some of the others mentioned above, including epistemic expertise and executive or volitive ability in certain cases (Raz 2006: 1031), but it also applies much more broadly than most. This has consequences for the piecemeal approach to legal authority presented before – although law's legitimate authority is not necessarily as general as the law claims it is, its scope can be much broader than conceded by proponents of the Razian account. This does not mean, however, that other justifications of authority cannot apply on an individual basis and complement the democratic coordination-based legitimacy of the law.[25] Nor does it prevent the coordination-based account from coexisting with other reasons for respect and recognition of law's authority that usually fill the gap between the law's general claim to legitimate authority and the piecemeal scope of its objective legitimacy.

Importantly, the coordination-based approach to authority just presented ought not be understood as an alternative to the Razian account described before, but, on the contrary, as a re-interpretation of that account in circumstances of ordinary law-making and public authority (Besson 2005a: 89; 2005b: 490–498).[26] This re-interpretation requires specifying the concept of justified authority and its conditions, in order to accommodate the way the law provides a whole class of subjects, and not each of them separately, and a class of subjects who are also authors of the law they are subjected to, rather than dominated by the law and its authors, with reasons for coordinated action over matters of justice and common concern.

Thanks to its minimal and flexible features, the revised democratic coordination-based account of Raz's service conception of authority provides the perfect account of the legitimacy of international law and of international human rights law in particular. It is piecemeal and does not

[24] In contrast to what is often said (see, for example, Tasioulas 2010a) and presumably derived from a skewed idea of participatory practices in a democracy, individual consent ought not therefore be conflated with democracy as a justification of authority. See Hershovitz (2003: 215).

[25] See Waldron (2003: 66) on the contrast between purely individual and coordination-based individual reasons to obey the directives of a public authority.

[26] See Besson (2005a: 89; 2005b: 490–498); Waldron (2003). See also the replies by Raz (2003; 2006: 1040–1044).

understand the legitimate authority of law to be general and applicable to all subjects in a similar fashion, on the one hand, and it encompasses many different justifications that can fit different social and cultural contexts, on the other. Those two features fit the many authors, subjects and sources of international human rights law. The proposed conception of legitimacy corresponds, in other words, to the fragmented and non-monolithical nature of international human rights law.

3. The nature of human rights

The notion of human rights that is used in this chapter is best captured by explaining, first, the moral nature of human rights and, second, what lies in their legalization and how legal human rights relate to the universal moral rights they recognize, modulate or create.[27]

3.1 Moral human rights

In a nutshell, human rights may be considered a subset of universal moral rights (i) that protect fundamental and general human interests (ii) against the intervention, or in some cases non-intervention of (national, regional or international) political institutions (iii). Those three elements will be presented in turn.

To start with, a human right exists qua moral right when an interest is a sufficient ground or reason to hold someone else (the duty-bearer) under a (categorical and exclusionary) duty to respect that interest vis-à-vis the right-holder (Raz 1984b: 195). For a right to be recognized, a sufficient interest must be established in a particular social context (Raz 1984b: 200, 209). Rights are, on this conception, intermediaries between interests and duties (Raz 1984b: 208). It follows, first of all, that a right may be recognized and protected before specifying which duties correspond to it (MacCormick 1977: 201). Once a duty is specified, it will be correlative to the (specific) right, but the right may pre-exist abstractly without its specific duties being identified. The relationship between rights and particular duties is justificatory therefore, and not logical (MacCormick 1977: 199–202; Raz 1984b: 196, 200). As a result, the determination of the duty-bearer(s) of a right and its claimability are not conditions of the existence of a moral right (Tasioulas 2007). A right is, second, a sufficient ground for holding other individuals under all the duties necessary to protect the

[27] This section is borrowed and summarized from Besson (2011c).

interest rather than in terms of the details of these duties (Waldron 1984: 10–11). It follows that a right might provide for the imposition of many duties and not only one. Rights actually have a dynamic nature and, as such, successive specific duties can be grounded on a given right depending on the circumstances (Raz 1984b: 197–199). This application indeterminacy of rights also implies that rights need to be localized to be fully effective; it is only in local circumstances that the allocation and specification of duties can take place (Buchanan 2004: 180–186).

Turning to the second element in the definition, human rights are moral rights of a special intensity and universal moral rights, in that the interests protected are regarded as fundamental and general interests that all human beings have by virtue of their existence and not of a given status or circumstance. They include individual interests when these constitute part of a person's well-being in an objective sense. That person need not believe that it is the case for her interest to require protection as a human right.

What makes it the case that a given individual interest is regarded as sufficiently fundamental or important to generate a duty and that, in other words, the threshold of importance and point of passage from a general and fundamental interest to a human right is reached, may be found in the normative status of each individual qua equal member of the moral-political community, i.e. their political equality or equal political status.[28] A person's interests are owed equal respect in virtue of her status as member of the community and of her relations to other members in the community; those interests are recognized as socio-comparatively important by members of the community and only then can they be recognized as human rights (Besson 2012b, 2013a; Buchanan 2005, 2010b). The recognition of human rights is done mutually and not simply vertically, and as a result human rights are not externally promulgated as such but mutually granted by members of a given political community (Cohen 2004: 197–198; Forst 2010). Of course, human rights are not merely a consequence of individuals' equal status, but also a way of actually earning that equal status and consolidating it. Without human rights, political equality would remain an abstract guarantee; through human rights, individuals become actors of their own equality and members of their political community (Cohen 2004; 2008: 585–596). Human rights are power-mediators, in other words:[29] they enable political equality. Borrowing Hannah Arendt's

[28] See Forst (1999: 48; 2010). On the relationship between political equality and human rights more generally, see e.g. Christiano (2008: 138, 156).

[29] For the original idea of mediating duties, see Shue (1988: 703). See also Reus-Smit (2009). On liberal rights and the exercise of power in general, see Christiano (2008: 134).

words: 'we are not born equal; we become equal as members of a group on the strength of our decision to guarantee ourselves mutually equal rights' (Arendt 1951).

In short, the proposed account of the nature of human rights follows a modified interest-based theory: it is modified or complemented by reference to considerations of equal moral-political status in a given community.[30] Thus, this relationship between human rights and political equality bridges the sterile opposition between the individual and the group.[31] Under a purely status-based or a purely interest-based model, the Manichean opposition between the individual and the group, and between his private and public autonomy would lead to unjustifiable conclusions that are tempered in the proposed account (Tasioulas 2010b).

It is important to pause at this stage and clarify what is meant by political equality or inclusion into an organized political society.[32] Political equality is a normative idea according to which a person's interests are to be treated equally and taken into consideration in a given political group's decision. Human rights protect those interests tied to equal political membership and whose disrespect would be tantamount to treating them as outsiders. Of course, some human rights, such as civic and political rights, are more closely tied to actual political membership, while others such as the right to life, for instance, are closer to basic demands of humanity and hence to access to political membership. Even the latter rights, however, constrain what equal membership can mean if it is to be legitimate and the kind of interests it must protect. By submitting individuals to genocide, torture and other extreme forms of cruel treatment, a community excludes them and no longer treats them as equal members, thus violating the threshold of recognition of human rights: political equality. This is in line with the republican idea of the political community qua locus of rights (Cohen 2008: 604 fn. 47).

This idea of equal political status or membership may also be referred to as democratic membership, as will be the case in the remainder of the present article. Democracy is indeed morally required by the commitment to the equal political status of persons. And one may even add that, just

30 Scope precludes discussing the notion of political equality to a full extent here. It suffices to say I am using it to refer to equal political status as opposed to distributive equality, and as a minimalist requirement of transnational justice. On the importance of equal status, see e.g. Anderson (1999); Waldron (2002). See also Besson (2013a).

31 The proposed account comes very close to, but is distinct from Forst (1999: 48–50; 2007; 2010).

32 The following argument is a specific development of Cohen (2004: 197–198)'s argument.

as human rights, democracy enlivens and enables political equality. Their common grounding by reference to political equality actually confirms the mutual relationship between human rights and democracy. Of course, just as human rights, democracy implies more than political equality. Scope precludes discussing it extensively, but democracy qua political regime also implies egalitarian deliberation and decision-making procedures.

This brings me to the third element in the definition of human rights: human rights are entitlements we all have equally against each other, and hence against our public institutions (national, regional or international). They generate duties on the part of public authorities not only to protect equal individual interests, but also individuals' political status qua equal political actors. Public institutions are necessary for collective endeavour and political self-determination, but may also endanger them. Human rights enable the functioning of those institutions in exchange for political equality and protection from abuse of political power. This is why one can say that human rights both are protected by public institutions and provide protection against them; they exist because of collective endeavour in order both to favour and constrain it. Of course, other individuals may individually violate the interests protected by human rights and ought to be prevented from doing so by public institutions and in particular through legal means. This ought to be the case whether those individuals' actions and omissions may be attributed to public authorities or not qua *de jure* or de facto organs. However, public institutions remain the primary addressees of human rights claims and hence their primary duty-bearers.

3.2 Legal human rights

It follows from the moral-political nature of human rights that the law is an important dimension of their recognition and existence. It is time to understand exactly how this is the case and to unpack the inherently legal dimension of human rights.

Just as moral rights are moral propositions and sources of moral duties, legal rights are legal propositions and sources of legal duties. They are moral interests recognized by the law as sufficiently important to generate moral duties (Raz 1984a: 12; 2010). The same may be said of legal human rights: legal human rights are fundamental and general moral interests recognized by the law as sufficiently important to generate moral duties.

Generally speaking, moral rights can exist independently from legal rights, but legal rights recognize, modify or create moral rights by recognizing moral interests as sufficiently important to generate moral duties.

Of course, there may be ways of protecting moral interests or even independent moral rights legally without recognizing them as legal 'rights'. Conversely, some legal rights may not actually protect pre-existing moral rights or create moral rights, thus only bearing the name of 'rights' and generating legal duties at the most. The same cannot be said of human rights more specifically, however.

First of all, it is true that not all universal moral rights have been or are legally recognized as legal human rights. Some are even expressly recognized as universal moral rights by the law even though they are not made into legal rights or modulated by the law. A distinct question is whether they ought to be legalized and hence protected by law. Again, respect for universal moral rights ought to be voluntary in priority, and this independently from any institutional involvement. However, the universal moral rights that will become human rights create moral duties for institutions, and hence for the law as well, to recognize and protect human rights (Raz 2010). Based on the moral-political account of human rights presented previously, the law provides the best and maybe the only way of mutually recognizing the socio-comparative importance of those interests in a political community of equals.[33] It enables the weighing of those interests against each other and the drawing of the political equality threshold or comparative line.

In short, the law makes them human rights. As a result, in the moral-political account of human rights propounded here, the legal recognition of a fundamental human interest, in conditions of political equality, is part of the creation of a moral-political human right. In other words, while being independently justified morally and having a universal and general scope, human rights qua subset of universal moral rights are also of an inherently legal nature. To quote Jürgen Habermas, 'they are conceptually oriented towards positive enactment by legislative bodies' (Habermas 1998a: 183; 1998b: 310–312). Thus, while legal rights stricto sensu are necessarily moral in nature (qua rights), human rights (qua rights) are also necessarily legal and they are as a result both moral and legal rights.

Second, legal human rights necessarily also pre-exist as independent universal moral rights. However, the law can specify and weigh moral human interests further when recognizing them as legal human rights.

[33] Cohen (2008: 599–600); Forst (1999, 2010); see even Pogge (2005: 3 fn. 26) who concedes this point in the case of civil and political rights. It seems, however, that the egalitarian dimension of human rights and hence their inherently legal nature would apply even more to the case of social and economic rights.

One may imagine certain political interests whose moral-political significance may stem from the very moral-political circumstances of life in a polity. As a result, the law does not create universal moral rights, but it can modulate them when recognizing them. The inherently legal nature of human rights and the role the law plays in recognizing given interests as sufficiently important in a group as to generate duties and hence human rights make it the case that the law turns pre-existing universal moral rights into human rights and hence actually makes them human rights. As a result, human rights cannot pre-exist their legalization as independent moral human rights, but only as independent universal moral rights.

The next question pertains to the locus of legalization of human rights, i.e. the legal recognition and modulation of universal moral rights qua human rights. It could per se take place at the domestic or at the international level: through national or international law. The locus of legalization of human rights ought to be domestic in priority, however. International human rights provide an external and minimal entrenchment for human rights legalized and hence recognized domestically.

Given what was said about the interdependence between human rights and political equality, indeed, the political process through which their legalization takes place ought to be democratic and include all those whose rights are affected. As a result, using international law to recognize fundamental and general human interests as sufficiently important to generate state duties at the domestic level is delicate. Not only does international law-making include many other states and subjects than those affected, but the democratic quality of its processes is not secured, at least not yet (Christiano 2010; Cohen 2008: 599–600). Unless international legal human rights refer to and correspond to existing domestic (moral-political and legal) human rights, therefore, they cannot be regarded as human rights for lack of a moral-political community. What this means is that so-called international human rights can at least be regarded as legally protected universal moral rights and most of the time as legal rights as well. One of those universal moral rights is the universal moral right to have rights, i.e. the right to equal membership in a moral-political community. According to Arendt, the 'right to have rights' is a right to political membership and includes the right to have all other human rights that make individuals equal members of the moral-political community (Arendt 1951; Cohen 2008: 604 fn. 47; Forst 2010). That right would prohibit submitting individuals to genocide, torture and other extreme forms of cruel treatment, through which a community would exclude individuals and not treat them as equal members (Cohen 2008: 587).

Qua legal rights, international human rights norms guarantee rights to individuals under a given state's jurisdiction, on the one hand, and to other states (or arguably IOs) (international human rights are usually guaranteed *erga omnes*), on the other, to have those rights guaranteed as 'human rights' within a given domestic community. They correspond to states' (and/or arguably IOs') duties to secure and ensure respect for those rights as 'human rights' within their own jurisdiction. In that sense, international human rights law's duties are international legal second-order duties for states (and/or arguably IOs) to generate first-order human rights duties for themselves under domestic law, i.e. international duties to have domestic duties.

Interestingly, the normative considerations presented before about the locus of legitimation and hence of legalization of human rights are reflected in contemporary processes of legalization of human rights under domestic and international law. They fit and justify, in other words, our current international human rights practice. To start with, one observes that human rights guarantees in international law are usually minimal. They rely on national guarantees and their common denominator (often referred to as 'consensus') to formulate a minimal threshold which they reflect and entrench internationally (Besson 2012a). More importantly, they are usually abstract and meant to be fleshed out at domestic level, not only in terms of the specific duties attached to a given right but also in terms of the right itself. Although they share the same content and scope, both levels of protection are usually regarded as complementary and as serving different functions, therefore, rather than as providing competing guarantees. This complementarity between international and domestic guarantees explains why the national reception of international human rights within domestic law is favoured or even required by international human rights instruments. Domestic human rights law does more than merely implement international human rights therefore: it contextualizes and specifies them. One actually often talks of 'reception' within the domestic legal order in that respect (Stone Sweet & Keller 2008). Through domestic legal reception, national authorities determine democratically what the actual threshold of importance of various human interests is to be and what duties that human right will give rise to in practice. Gradually, as domestic human rights are fleshed out in similar fashions across the board, the minimal human rights consensus among states is becoming thicker and can feed back into international human rights law that will constrain domestic authorities in return.

Besides its explanatory force faced with current human rights practice, this approach to international human rights has the further benefit of fitting the structure of the international legal order more generally. It puts international human rights law back into its political context. State sovereignty and political self-determination constitute indeed one of the pillars of the international order, a pillar which is complemented and not replaced or, strictly speaking, even restricted by the second pillar of international human rights law.[34] Through those two pillars and its dualistic structure, the international legal order protects the very interdependence between democracy and human rights alluded to before and hence keeps the tension between the individual and the group at the core of international law-making. International law guarantees the basic conditions for political equality and self-determination by protecting peoples through state sovereignty, on the one hand, and by protecting individuals through human rights, on the other.

4. The legitimate authority of international human rights

Among the various key questions usually addressed in any autonomy-based account of legal authority, there are four main features that deserve particular attention in the international context. Those four questions pertain to: whose autonomy it is we are concerned about; how that autonomy can be said to be enhanced by authority; how consent relates to the best exercise of one's autonomy; and, finally, whether autonomy can sometimes be said to be best protected on its own. In international terms, the questions pertain to: the identity of the subjects of authority in international law and in particular the relationship between states and individuals; the justification of the authority vested in international horizontal law-making processes and in particular the democratic coordination justification; the role of additional reasons for respect for the law one encounters in international law and in particular the role of state consent; and, finally, the compatibility between the service conception of authority and state sovereignty.

4.1 The subjects: double-binding

One of the first difficulties facing an account of the authority of international human rights lies in the identification of its subjects, i.e. the

[34] See for a similar argument, Cohen (2008: 595–597); Macklem (2007: 577).

determination of those subjects in authority and of those submitted to their authority.

In the domestic context, the subjects of authority are usually taken to be the law and, more exactly, a centralized set of state institutions, on one side, and individuals or groups of individuals, on the other. Given the prevalence of the vertical model of political authority, the (state) institutions v. individuals model of authority is usually transposed without further thought in the legal context. While it matches the reality of legislative politics, the model has been criticized, however, for personifying law-making authority (Raz 1986: 70). It also obfuscates the identity between law-makers and legal subjects in a democratic legal order,[35] on the one hand, and eludes the coordinative relationship between law-making institutions,[36] on the other. The former inability to explain democratic authority is particularly problematic when accounting for the legitimate authority of human rights given the identity between right-holders and duty-bearers in a democracy.

In the international context, the vertical model has become an even more important source of confusion. To start with, there is no centralized and hierarchical law-making process, but many processes and without a hierarchical order between them, ranging from treaty-making and customary law-making to unilateral law-making by IOs (Boyle & Chinkin 2007; Lowe 2000).

Second, the law-makers are manifold and are implicated to different extents in those different processes; they range from states and IOs to individuals (Alvarez 2006; McCorquodale 2004). The same applies to the subjects of those laws, which are diverse; they range from natural persons to collective entities like states and IOs. Third, contrary to what applies at the domestic level, not all subjects of international law are direct subjects of authority, i.e. subjects to (legitimate) duties to obey international law; some are merely subjects of rights, while others may be subjects to duties to obey, but without the means to claim their rights and duties at the international level. This is the case, according to traditional approaches, of individuals in international law. Finally, at least in traditional international law-making processes such as treaties or customary law, given the overlap between states qua law-makers and states qua legal subjects, there is prima facie no clear separation between law-makers and legal subjects.

[35] See e.g. Hershovitz (2003). See, however, Raz (2006: 1031–1032).

[36] See e.g. Waldron (2003). See, however, Raz (2006).

As a result, the relationship seems horizontal as opposed to the vertical domestic relation of authoritative law-making.

This is why I have argued elsewhere that it is essential we lift the state veil to understand the scope of the authority of international law.[37] A state may or may not be conceived as an entity 'over and above' the people who constitute it, but if states can act, and be held in duty, this is only because there are people involved. This is true even if legal doctrine, in treating corporate entities such as states as legal persons, neglects the relationship those entities have to people. The potential moral effect of the law on people is in need of justification. This does not mean that all legitimate authority of international law is, in the end, authority over individuals. It means that practices of ascribing duties to collectives of people like states must make moral sense and this means that the moral position of individuals cannot be ignored.[38]

In what follows, the relationship between international law-makers and international legal subjects is addressed in more detail. Of course, the coordination-based justification of authority defended here relies on a democratic model of law-making where legal subjects participate in a collective law-making exercise or, at least, where institutions (states or IOs) are both officials and proxies for legal subjects in that exercise. This is particularly important in the human rights context where states are bound towards other states in the international community to respect their human rights duties towards individuals: in short, they acquire an interstate duty to generate and then conform to a state-individual duty and are double-binding themselves as it were. More precisely, states' primary or first-order human rights duties are duties they owe to individual right-bearers within their jurisdiction, whereas states' secondary or second-order duties to abide by those primary duties are duties they owe to all other states as well (qua (subset of or entire) international community).[39] A second caveat is in order: the coexistence of different subjects of authority implies different authoritative reasons and this is in line with the piecemeal account of legitimate authority presented before. Although all subjects of authority are discussed here, scope precludes discussing the specific justifications of authority for each of them later on in the chapter, and I shall focus mostly on states and individuals hereafter.

[37] Besson (2009a). I owe this expression to Murphy (2010).

[38] See Murphy (2010). See also, albeit in the domestic context, Raz (1986: 72).

[39] See O'Neill (2005: 433) on international human rights and duties qua second-order duties.

4.1.1 Authority by whom

States are the original law-makers in international law. This is at least the case for the main sources of international law such as treaty law, customary law and general principles of international law. Traditionally, states are understood as being both the primary law-makers and the primary legal subjects in international law, and hence as making laws for themselves on a horizontal basis. This horizontal conception of international law-making fits the consensualist view of international law whose authority is allegedly based on state consent: states make laws like individuals enter into contracts and they are only bound by what they have acquiesced to. However, unlike individuals directly or indirectly involved in the domestic law-making context who act qua officials either as representatives or as citizens and not in their private capacity, this approach sees the involvement of states in international law-making qua individuals rather than qua officials.

Such an approach is deeply misleading on more than one count. First, and as Waldron rightly argues, states are not just makers of the international legal order as private individuals would be the makers of a web of contractual promises; they are also its officials (Waldron 2006: 23–25; 2011). Except in the cases where IOs' institutions are involved in international law-making, international law has few institutional resources of its own. It depends on states for the making, but also for the enforcement of its provisions. Governments are the officials or officers of the international legal system. Second, although states are free, rational agents, they are not themselves human individuals and cannot therefore act as those would. In the last resort, states are not the bearers of ultimate value. They exist for the sake of human individuals. In the international context, states are recognized by international law as trustees for the people committed to their care. Ultimately, international law is oriented to the well-being of human individuals, rather than to the freedom of states (Waldron 2011: 23 ff.). This, of course, becomes clear from international human rights law, but it is also the point of most norms of international law. Finally, states cannot be viewed as independent law-makers separately from the individuals they ought to care for as officials and whom they bind indirectly when binding themselves. The fact that states no longer make laws only for themselves but also directly for other international subjects, such as IOs or individuals, is further evidence of their role as officials. Unless states are conceived of as officials and as trustees in international law-making processes, this lack of congruence between international law-makers and legal subjects cannot be bridged.

This is particularly important in the human rights context where states are binding themselves in order to bind their own authorities in domestic law in order to protect individual interests. In a democracy where there is an identity between the right-holders and the duty-bearers of human rights, this amounts to binding all individuals in favour of all individuals in any given state. It contributes to enhancing political equality, but it also implies tinkering with the relationship of interdependence between human rights and democracy as this reinforcement of political equality is done from outside the national polity and from outside domestic democracy.

These considerations about the role of states as international law-makers have important normative consequences. First, states do not make international law just for themselves as free, rational agents, but as officials or representatives for their respective populations. Their role as officials constrains their competence not only in terms of internal accountability, but at the international level itself (Chayes 1965: 1410). States are bound by the rule of international law, i.e. the set of values and principles associated with the idea of international legality (Rawls 1971: 236–269; Raz 1979: 212–219; Waldron 2006: 15). Second, when acting as officials, whether in the law-making or law-enforcement process, states have to coordinate among themselves, the way officials in a democratic state would (Waldron 2003). However, this kind of coordination among officials differs from what applies in the domestic context. States act as law-making officials, but also, as will be shown, as proxy-subjects. As a result, both the coordination among officials and that between subjects are often merged and cannot easily be dissociated.

A ready objection is the lack of legal security this would imply in international relations. If states can only act as official authorities in international law-making when they are democratic and represent their citizens, this drastically reduces the number of states which can produce binding international laws.[40] Another objection in the human rights context would be that non-democratic states would have no means of contributing to the development of international human rights law from the outside and bind themselves internally on the basis of international human rights norms. Here again it is important to remember the interdependent relationship between human rights and political equality, and the counterproductive idea of committing to one without the other.

[40] See Christiano (2010) for a discussion of the representativity objection and potential remedies.

4.1.2 Authority over whom

States are the primary subjects of binding international norms. Most duties stemming from international legal norms directly constrain the action of states. Following the analogy between states and individuals entering private contracts discussed before, states are generally held as being able to bind themselves as free, rational agents.

This approach is misleading in this context as well, however. The service conception of authority adopted in this chapter contends that authority can only be justified if it facilitates its subjects' conformity with the (objective) reasons that already apply to them and hence respects their autonomy. Its application therefore has a prerequisite: the subject bound by a legal norm needs to be an autonomous subject, as it is only so that its freedom to choose from a range of options can be furthered by an authoritative directive.

The analogy between authority for states and individuals presupposes therefore that the value of autonomy extends to the choices and actions of states. At first sight, it seems plausible that it does, given the value of shared membership in a national political community and, as a result, of the collective self-determination of such communities (Christiano 2010). The problem is that the value of state autonomy can only be explained in terms of the autonomy of the individuals constituting it. States are quite unlike individuals when it comes to the value of their autonomy. Their autonomy cannot simply be equated with that of any of their domestic legal subjects, but is the product of those subjects' autonomy as a political entity (Waldron 2006: 21). As a result, states can only be bound by international legal norms when they represent those subjects as officials and hence can bind them as proxy subjects to international law. When a state is morally bound by a norm of international law, the duties imposed on it will require action that burdens individuals either indirectly, through international state action that is costly to national resources, or directly through the duty to enact domestic laws in order to transpose international law into domestic law (or implement the latter directly in the domestic sphere). This affects individuals' balance of reasons as a result and explains why the autonomy of states and its ability to be bound depends on its constituency's autonomy and hence on its ability to represent the latter.[41]

This is particularly important in the human rights context where by binding themselves, states bind all their authorities and hence all their legal subjects mutually, and hence bind them to an even greater extent

[41] See also the discussion in Crawford & Watkins (2010: 283–298); and in Murphy (2010).

than in other fields of international law. The fact that it is done with other states, and from outside the democratic polity, makes it even more important that all individuals are adequately represented.

Of course, states remain free, rational (albeit artificial) agents and as such they can enter into binding agreements the way an individual would enter into a contract. This can be the case for many contract-like treaties and other international agreements, although consent does not necessarily bind in all cases (Raz 1986: 87–88). The opposite view would simply strip states of their right to bind themselves and hence from any of the meaningful implications of their quality as primary international legal subjects.[42] Further, states' international legal obligations to obey would remain in place even if they are illegitimate, as they are often backed up by legal sanctions. And so would states' moral obligations to abide by morally correct directives which bind individuals (and states for them collectively) in any case. But populations unrepresented by those states would not be morally bound by those legal directives qua law. Nor could those states be bound in that way as a result.

Of course, this constitutes a risk and it could eventually weaken some states' credentials at the international level and hence the possibility for them to bind themselves even only as subjects. At the same time, however, it could also provide an important incentive to democratize states from within, thus eventually leading to an increase in the overall legitimacy of international law itself. This is particularly important in the case of human rights where benefiting from human rights without being able to take part in national and hence international decision-making is not only highly unlikely, but profoundly counterproductive. Human rights can only be truly respected in practice qua legal human rights if those they protect are self-governing and contributing to the identification of their equal rights.

One way around this difficulty may be to consider international human rights treaties as contract-like treaties generating second-order inter-state duties that only bind states the way promises would and to condition the possibility for those second-order duties to give rise to first-order state duties towards their individual members within domestic law in respect of the democratic requirements of representativity mentioned before. This distinction between second-order and first-order human rights duties would actually explain the greater authority in practice of international human rights agreements in democratic states than in non-democratic ones.

[42] See Buchanan (2008: 53) on the 'Vanishing Subject Matter Problem'.

4.2 *The justifications: piecemeal authority*

4.2.1 Coordinating authority

The next question one ought to address in any account of legal authority pertains to the justification of authority, and more precisely to how individual autonomy can be said to be enhanced by a given authority. The virtue of the service conception of authority used in this chapter is that it does not rely on the existence of a general duty to obey international human rights law; their legitimate authority can be piecemeal depending on the states and their reasons, on the one hand, and the international human rights norms at stake, their sources and their qualities, on the other.

First of all, and by virtue of the dependence condition, the reasons given by international law need to match the state's pre-existing reasons. If the state's duty to comply with an international legal norm implies a duty to abide by a duty, and e.g. a duty to abide by a human rights duty, then that state must have a matching pre-existing reason for action.

In the case of human rights, the justification of authority implies increasing the state's conformity with its own reasons to protect fundamental and universal human interests. In view of the diversity of those reasons between states, the legitimate authority of international human rights can be regarded as piecemeal. Given what was said before about the moral-political nature of human rights and their relationship to political equality, the legitimate authority of international human rights only makes sense if the state has human rights-based moral duties and therefore if it is democratically organized and guarantees human rights domestically (politically or legally). The justified authority of human rights corresponds to the justification of the correlative duties. As a result, human rights and their corresponding duties can only arise in a given political context where interests can be compared and balanced against each other and recognized as equally important and vulnerable. The legitimate authority of international human rights is therefore a function of that of the corresponding domestic human rights. The mutual legalization of international and domestic human rights law described in the previous section is reflected in their mutual legitimation and vice versa.

In a non-democratic state, by contrast, there would be at the most reasons to protect fundamental moral interests qua human rights and those reasons would be the only ones that could be matched by the reasons given by international human rights law. In those circumstances, international human rights would provide second-order reasons to adopt domestic human rights law rather than first-order reasons to comply with human rights directly. In other words, the universal right to have rights would be the only international legal human right and corresponding duty that would meet a state's pre-existing moral duty, i.e. the duty to bear human rights duties. Importantly, that minimal content of international human rights and their inclusive and consensual development bottom-up helps placate an important critique, i.e. that of parochialism that targets the DC and the correspondence between the second-order reasons to generate first-order human rights duties and the states' existing reasons.

Second, and by virtue of the normal justification condition, the content-independent reasons that are given by international law ought to help the state better conform to its own reasons, and individuals within states to theirs. There are many different justifications that may be given in this context. Not only is democratic coordination the best justification in the proposed revised service conception of authority, but it is actually one of the best justifications of the authority of international law. And this also pertains in the context of international human rights law.

First of all, the horizontal nature of most relationships between subjects of international law makes justifications of authority based on a vertical ruling relationship between an authority and governed subjects less probable. The legitimacy of major international law-making processes, such as customary law-making, multilateral treaty-making or international institutional law-making, is therefore well accounted for by a coordinative justification of the authority of international law. Second, the lack of centralized and hierarchical law-making processes in international law confirms the need for various levels of coordination within the same regime, but also across regimes. Coordination can ensure coherence between sets of norms and across regimes, without hierarchy (Besson 2005b: 192–195; Waldron 1999). It can also account for the existence of a public authority and multilateral and multi-level law-making community despite the absence of a centralized law-making process and institution.[43] This distinction is made difficult in the international context given the dispersed nature of public authority. Coordination provides that very distinctive feature and justification. Furthermore, states are a small group in number and are as a result easy to coordinate over issues of common concern such as human rights.

Third, the coordination-based justification of authority fits the need for international regulation on difficult matters of common concern among subjects whose diversity of views creates pervasive and persistent

[43] See Waldron's (2003) critique of Raz's account of legal authority at the domestic level.

reasonable disagreements. This applies in cases of classic coordination problems such as: problems related to epidemic diseases, economic instability, environmental degradation, the proliferation of weapons of mass destruction, migration movements that cannot be addressed by individual states acting alone but only through coordination. It also applies, however, to conflict and partial conflict coordination cases where there is disagreement about issues of justice and common concern. On such issues, it is better that all coordinate over the same set of international norms rather than acting individually (even correctly) according to their own reasons. In a legal system characterized by deep divergence in ethical, religious and political beliefs and practices, democratic coordination provides one of the best justifications of authority to escape irreducible substantive controversies.

This third argument applies particularly well to international human rights. In circumstances of moral and social pluralism, where values are diverse and conflict with each other, and where their ranking can vary from one culture to the other, the fundamental interests protected by human rights are bound to conflict or at least vary and states to disagree reasonably over them. Based on their universal moral duty to protect human rights and the corresponding universal moral right to have human rights, states ought to coordinate on minimal interstate second-order duties to generate and protect full-blown first-order human rights duties in domestic law. External and minimal human rights protection can help them to avoid a levelling-down in domestic protection. This can only be done, however, if those minimal human rights guarantees are identified bottom-up on the basis of states' human rights practices. The coordinated minimal content of international second-order duties to adopt domestic first-order human rights duties can then evolve with the further development of domestic first-order human rights duties. Of course, for that to happen, further coordination ought to take place at the domestic level when identifying and specifying the state's first-order human rights duties in domestic law. The need to coordinate on one set of minimal external human rights duties that protect a right to have human rights in the domestic context explains how the NJC can be saved from the exceptionalist critique that claims that some states may have reasons corresponding to the ones given by international human rights law (DC) but can respect them better on their own.

Besides coordination, other justifications for the authority of international legal norms may also be mentioned. This is the case of the volitional, decisive and cognitive abilities of certain norms of international law.[44] In most cases, however, as in the domestic context, the coordination justification of authority encompasses a lot of those other justifying grounds and it constitutes the most important justification of international law's authority. As a matter of fact, coordination captures precisely those other grounds that compensate for the predominant circumstances of epistemic limitations. This is likely to be even more pertinent in international law given the diversity of the objects of international law, of its subjects and of their relationships.

4.2.2 Democratic authority

As in the domestic context, the coordination-based justification of international law's authority is enhanced in circumstances of disagreement about justice if the coordination procedure and functioning is democratic (Buchanan 2008). This is particularly the case with coordination over international human rights given the interdependent relationship between human rights and political equality, and the legitimizing role of human rights in domestic democracy. Due to the interdependence between human rights and political equality, the democratic requirements on international law-making process are actually higher when the legitimacy of human rights norms is at stake than for other international law norms.

What democracy means in the international law-making context is a difficult issue and scope precludes fully addressing it here.[45] In a nutshell, and as I have explained elsewhere, global democracy does not equate either with indirect state democracy nor with a state-like global democracy at the international level (Besson 2009c: 213 ff.). On the contrary, it groups all democratic processes that occur within and beyond the state and whose outcomes affect individuals within that state, but in ways that link national democracies among themselves and to other transnational, international or supranational democratic processes (Besson 2006, 2009d).

Importantly, global democracy on that model can only strive if states are democratized from within at the same time; this is actually a key feature of the legitimate authority of international law for states, as discussed before. Indirect state democracy does not replace direct individual participation or representation in international processes, however, at least from the perspective of the authority of international law over individuals.

[44] See Waldron (2003) for a detailed discussion of those justifications in the context of international law.

[45] See, for an excellent discussion, Christiano (2010).

There are many reasons for this. To start with, their interests might diverge from those of their national polity, because they are members of a minority at the national level (Besson 2009c: 216; McCorquodale 2006). In fact, even in a democratic state, the international or external interests of that state might actually differ from those of the sum or the majority of that state's citizens, given the primary and increasing role of the executive in foreign policy and international negotiations. Furthermore, even when individual interests match their government's, the rule of international democracy, and in particular majoritarian rule in multilateral law-making (but also veto rights in the case of unanimous voting), cannot always guarantee international results that are in line with individual national will, or at least respect the principle of political equality in terms of the proportionality of votes to the size of the populations represented. Thus, indirect international democracy models face the famous dilemma between states defending their citizens' interests at the expense of other states and their citizens on the one hand, and following the rules of international democracy at the expense of their own citizens' interests, on the other (Archibugi 1993). Moreover, not all individuals subjected to international law are citizens of democratic states, and hence have a say in national democratic processes pertaining to international issues, or are represented by democratically elected representatives in international fora. This creates an inequality in legitimacy (Christiano 2010).

It is clear, however, that in current conditions of international law-making, the equal inclusion of all those subjected and the means to get an equal say even in an iteratively democratic process are simply not guaranteed yet.[46] One of the main shortcomings of international law-making processes at this time is the lack of respect for political equality and as a result for human rights themselves. It would be even more paradoxical, indeed, than at the domestic level to be enacting guarantees of international human rights and not to enable the beneficiaries of those rights to exercise them when deciding about those very rights and about their membership in the community of right-holders. At the same time, however, democratic coordination between states requires minimal guarantees of human rights to function properly and these should therefore be respected within international law-making processes themselves (Besson 2005b: 319–323).

Of course, this difficulty raises the same issues of apparent circularity one meets when contemplating the democratic legitimacy of human rights

[46] See Christiano (2010) on the democratic shortcomings of both his fair association of states model and his global democracy model.

at the domestic level and the role of human rights in that very legitimation. In those circumstances, it would certainly be vain to look for an alternative foundation for the legitimacy of international law in international human rights law, as some authors have suggested (Goodin 2007; Teson 1998, 2005). Rather, international law-making should be organized so as to both provide the enacting of human rights with deliberative and inclusive legitimacy and bolster that deliberative process by protecting minimal human rights.[47] This is a consequence of the mutual relationship between democracy and human rights that lies in their respective grounding by reference to political equality.

As a matter of fact, this legitimacy bootstrapping between human rights and democracy does not only occur at the international level itself and is actually less likely to occur at the international level than domestically. This is mainly due to the underdeveloped democratic features of international law-making presented before. The legitimation of international human rights actually mostly involves the domestic level where international human rights and domestic democracy can be understood as standing in a mutually reinforcing relationship. International human rights become vernacularized or contextualized through domestic democratic law-making processes and that outcome can in return become a source of international human rights law. As I have argued elsewhere, this mutual legitimation between domestic and international human rights or, more exactly, between citizens' rights and human rights, is particularly important in the case of international human rights and their corresponding domestic human rights: the recoupling between human rights and democracy that were decoupled in 1945 through the internationalization of the legal protection of human rights cannot operate horizontally (yet), but works vertically across legal orders and levels of governance (Besson 2011c).

As indicated in the previous section by reference to their legal sources, international human rights' guarantees are often abstracted bottom-up from domestic guarantees as general principles and then constrain those domestic practices in return. As a result, the legalization of human rights is a two-way street that is not limited to a top-down reception or a bottom-up crystallization, but is a retroactive process. And this corresponds to the way in which international human rights law is legitimized. Only those polities that respect international human rights are legitimate in

[47] See Besson (2010); Buchanan (2008, 2010a). See also Cohen (2008) on the human right to have rights.

specifying the content of those rights qua citizens' rights and hence in contributing to the recognition and existence of those rights qua international human rights that constrain polities in return and so on. This corresponds to what Allen Buchanan has referred to recently as 'reciprocal legitimacy'; it implies that international law may contribute to the legitimacy of corresponding domestic legal norms and vice versa (Buchanan 2004: 187–189; Buchanan 2011; Besson 2013b, 2013c).

4.3 Other reasons to comply: consent

Like in the domestic context, it may of course happen that some international legal norms are not legitimate on any of the grounds just mentioned or, at least, not for all states at once. This even more so with democracy: even defined as it is in this chapter, it is still limited and largely incremental in the international context. This is particularly problematic when the international norms to legitimize are human rights norms given the interdependence between human rights and political equality; the democratic requirements on international law-making process are higher when the democratic legitimacy of human rights norms is at stake than otherwise.

Of course, and although democracy is particularly relevant, other justifications for their authority may still be available (Besson 2009a). Moreover, it is important to emphasize that this conclusion does not affect the legal validity and as a result the legal authority of human rights norms under current international law. Nor does it impact the moral reasons there may be for states to adopt or recognize international legal guarantees of a given human right in the first place, whether those reasons are self-regarding or cosmopolitan (Buchanan & Powell 2008: 330 ff.). There may be other reasons than ones of legitimacy for states to actually respect and comply with international human rights, some instrumental (e.g. democratic peace) and other justice- or fairness-related. While those reasons are no justifications for the authority of a legal human right, they are reasons for compliance that coexist and are important in international law.

So, the hiatus between the general scope of the claim to legitimacy laid by international human rights law and the effective scope of its legitimacy in practice is likely to be more significant than in the domestic context, in the absence of a single centralized set of law-making institutions and processes. This need not be a source of concern, however, in view of the widespread de facto authority of international human rights law and of the coexistence of other reasons to respect international law (and not to obey it) (Raz 1986: 88 ff.; 1995: 80–94; 2006: 1028–1029). These reasons might, as a matter of fact, explain how international law's claim to general legitimacy may seem entirely granted in practice, although international law does not and cannot have general legitimate authority over all its subjects at any given time.

One of the complementary reasons for respect of international law is consent. Interestingly, consent theory is the dominant account of legitimacy among international lawyers and this is traditionally captured by the general principle of international law *pacta sunt servanda*. The popularity of consent in accounts of the legitimacy of international law may partly be explained by the widespread failure to distinguish between the normative and sociological senses of legitimacy: at least on the basis of an individual analogy, there seems to be some empirical connection between believing a norm is binding and having previously consented to it (Raz 1995: 360 ff.; 2006: 1037 ff.; Tasioulas 2010a). In normative terms, however, consent fails to provide independent authoritative reasons to obey the law (Hart 1994: 224 ff.; Raz 1995: 355–369). Scope precludes rehearsing the many shortcomings of the consent-based justification of political authority,[48] whether consent is thought of as express or tacit, and as actual or hypothetical.

Following Raz, therefore, one may argue that consent to a legal authority is effective as a source of obligations only if the authority respects autonomy and hence satisfies an independent test of legitimacy.[49] Of course, consent can still have some impact on legitimacy; it can strengthen obligations to obey and can express a citizen's trust in their public authorities (Raz 1986: 90; 1995: 368–369). However, consent cannot generate legitimacy.

In international law, there are further specific reasons why (democratic)[50] state consent is neither a sufficient nor a necessary condition of legitimacy (Buchanan 2004: 301–304; Buchanan 2008). Despite similar or even greater limitations of consent qua source of legitimate authority to those applying in the domestic context, consent is paradoxically even more important as a source of recognition and respect of the authority of international law than in the domestic context.[51] This has to do with the fragmentation of international law and institutions and the absence of a centralized legal order and of central political institutions. In the current

[48] For a general discussion of the shortcomings of the consent-based justification of political authority, see Simmons (1979).

[49] See Raz (1986: 89; 1995: 355–369). See the discussion in Hershovitz (2003: 201, 215).

[50] On the limitations of democratic state consent, see Besson (2009c: 214–217); Buchanan (2004).

[51] See Lefkowitz (2005) for a similar argument; Christiano (2012).

and non-ideal circumstances of international law-making, the equality of states qua referential political entities through which self-determination can be exercised is particularly important and that equality expresses itself through state consent. Moreover, since individual political equality is not yet fully secured in current international law-making processes and in view of their inherent democratic limitations, the equality of states and the state consent of democratic states are the best approximation that may often be secured (Christiano 2010, 2012).

To start with, due to the plurality of subjects involved in international law-making and their manifold roles, as is particularly clear from the role of states qua subjects and officials, consent can clarify the existence of justifications for the authority of international law for specific subjects. Furthermore, consent can often be used as a normative strengthener when states consent to abide by duties of justice[52] or to authoritative international legal norms. This is particularly important in international law, as consent can ease coordination by clarifying participants' intentions to coordinate and their trust in public authority, and hence can further legitimize authority. Finally, the pre-eminence in traditional international law, but also in certain areas of international law today, of contract-like promises between states, and the difficulty in distinguishing obligations stemming from those promises from obligations to obey the law qua law, explains how consent could usually account for widespread cases of de facto authority of international law. For instance, qua rational collective agents, states can bind themselves legally through consent and promises under certain conditions (Raz 1986: 87–88), even when they cannot be deemed authoritatively and morally bound by those obligations because they do not act as officials for their constituency. And even if they do act as officials for their constituency, it is difficult in practice to distinguish cases of legitimate authority from cases where they are bound through mutual promises.

Of course, there are conditions to be respected before consent can be deemed to strengthen or even extend independent authoritative reasons – conditions which may themselves overlap with justifications of authority itself (Lefkowitz 2005). First, consent cannot be used to bind oneself to immoral acts. Second, state consent ought to be free and unconstrained, on the one hand, and duly informed, on the other.[53]

[52] Estlund (2008: 127) on normative consent.

[53] See Christiano (2012) on the conditions of fair state consent.

In the human rights context, states may consent to international human rights norms that do not bind them legitimately. Their consent cannot make up for the lack of legitimate authority of those norms, but it can reinforce those rights' sociological legitimacy or confirm other reasons a state may have to comply with those rights, and in particular self-regarding or even other-regarding justice-based reasons (Simmons 2009). Moreover, in cases described before where the existence of second-order interstate human rights duties of non-democratic states cannot be justified except by reference to contract-like promises, consent does play an important role.

5. The exceptions: sovereignty

One of the main challenges to the legitimacy of international law is that it allegedly fails to respect the autonomy of states, intruding upon domains in which they should be free to make their own decisions. State sovereignty is often understood in international law as a competence, immunity or power, and in particular as the power to make autonomous choices (so-called sovereign autonomy). The legitimate authority of international law is as a result often opposed to state sovereignty.

Based on the service conception of authority discussed before, authority can only be justified if it facilitates its subjects' conformity with the (objective) reasons that already apply to them and hence if it respects their autonomy. There is per se no conflict between justified authority and autonomy. Regarding some matters, however, it is more important that a person reaches and acts on his or her own decision, rather than take a putative authority's directives as binding, even if doing the latter would result in decisions that, in other respects, better conform to reason (Raz 1995: 365–366; 2006: 1014). This is what Raz has referred to as the independence condition (Raz 2006). It is difficult, however, to distinguish those cases from cases where legitimate authority can apply, the incompatibility being at the most contingent and relative to certain circumstances (Tasioulas 2010a).[54]

The contingency of the independence condition is even more clearly the case in international law. If states are deemed as officials both qua law-makers and qua proxy-subjects of authority in the international legal order, their autonomy cannot simply be equated with that of any of their domestic legal subjects. It is the product of those subjects' autonomy as a political entity and the value of that autonomy itself depends on that of the

[54] Tasioulas (2010a). See, however, the discussion in Raz (2006: 1015 ff.).

individuals of which it is constituted. Considered in both its internal and external dimensions, a state's sovereign autonomy is a purely legal construct, as a result, and not something whose value is to be assumed as a first principle of normative analysis. In its internal dimension, the state works as a legal organization – it is the outcome of organizing certain rules of public life in a particular way (Waldron 2006: 21–22). Its sovereignty is artificial and it is legally constructed for the benefit of those whose internal interests it protects. In its external dimension, the sovereignty and the sovereign autonomy of the individual state are equally artefacts of international law (Murphy 2010). There can be no international legal order without sovereign states, but equally there can be no sovereign states without international law (Endicott 2010; Hart 1994: 223). What a state's sovereignty is and what it amounts to is not given as a matter of the intrinsic value of its individuality, but determined by the rules of the international legal order. Those rules define state sovereignty so as to protect the internal and external interests of the political community qua sovereign equal to others, but also to protect the interests of other subjects of international law.

If this is correct, the potential cases of incompatibility between the service authority and state freedom are likely to be even more contingent in the international legal order than in the domestic context. The only possible incompatibility under the independence condition therefore would be that between service authority, on the one hand, and the individual autonomy of a state's subjects and their collective autonomy qua democratic polity as they are represented by those states at the international level, on the other. As a result, provided states act qua officials and proxy-subjects when making international law and the other conditions of the democratic authority of international law discussed before to protect individual subjects' autonomy are fulfilled, state sovereignty seems to be necessarily compatible with justified international legal authority.

True, sovereign states are collective entities and as such their relationships are likely to be even more riddled with disagreement than individuals'. Moreover, one of the values of sovereignty being self-determination, it is clear that decisional independence is of value in the case of sovereign states as well. Finally, given the circumstances of social and cultural pluralism that prevail globally, it is likely that state autonomy can be exercised valuably in very different manners. All this makes self-determination over certain matters just as important to sovereign states as it is to individuals, albeit for different reasons. This is clearly the case when deciding over constitutive standards in a democracy such as human rights and democracy itself.

In sum, state sovereignty is not necessarily compatible with the authority of international law. It is only the case when the latter has legitimate authority, i.e. furthers state autonomy and the reasons that underlie state autonomy. Those can be understood by reference to the values that make a good state or more generally a good political entity such as self-determination, democracy and human rights, but also the values that make a good international community of equal sovereign entities. However, this should not be taken to mean that state sovereignty is only incompatible with international law's authority when the latter is illegitimate. There may be cases where autonomy requires legitimate authority, but others where self-direction is valuable despite the prima facie justification of international law's authority. Too much international regulation would empty sovereign autonomy from its purpose (Endicott 2010). In short, it would be wrong to explain sovereignty only by reference to the legitimacy of international law, but also, conversely, to account for the legitimacy of international law only by reference to sovereignty. It is with respect to the values they both serve that the authority of international law can be justified in some cases, together with the prima facie restrictions to state autonomy this implies.

Of course, the absence of independent state autonomy distinct from that of the sum of its legal constituents does not mean that states cannot be deemed as collective agents and hence relate as free, rational agents. In that context, however, as discussed earlier, states do not act to promote their constituency's autonomy and cannot therefore be deemed as authoritatively bound by their actions in moral terms. But this does not preclude legal obligations, as well as moral reasons to abide by morally correct directives. Furthermore, as discussed before, complementary sources of non-authoritative reasons for action such as consent or trust usefully complement those legal duties. To that extent, their sovereignty may have to be protected, but not against the legitimate authority of international law.

What the relationship between international legal authority and state sovereignty means in the human rights context is primarily that the traditional prima facie opposition between state sovereignty and human rights is a false one (Besson 2012c). State sovereignty cannot be dissociated from the protection of the political equality and human rights of the individuals constituting that state, and cannot be invoked against them as a result.

Of course, this is not to say that state sovereignty cannot be in tension with international human rights law. Importantly, international sovereignty protects a collective entity of individuals – a people – and not individual human beings per se. True, their fates are connected, the way democracy and human rights are correlated. But sovereignty, and sovereign equality in particular, protects democratic autonomy in a state's external affairs and remains justified for this separately from international human rights. Thus, the tensions between international human rights and state sovereignty are reminiscent of those between popular sovereignty and human rights in the domestic context. The difference is that one of them is international while the other remains domestic.

In short, state sovereignty cannot be dissociated from the protection of the political equality and human rights of the individuals constituting that state, and cannot per se be regarded as incompatible with the values it is meant to help pursue. However, given the value of both individual and collective autonomy in the human rights context and their potential contradictions, two different consequences follow depending on the kind of international human rights norms at stake.

First of all, sovereignty cannot be invoked to escape the legitimate authority of the universal moral right to have rights at domestic level. Sovereignty can only protect political autonomy when it exists in a normative sense; it cannot therefore be opposed to the legitimate authority of the right to have rights. In such a case, self-determination is undermined and sovereignty forfeited. Second, this also means, however, that, with respect to international human rights more generally, states may not commit to and abide by more than their constituency could and what that right to have rights or self-government authorizes. When the legal norms at stake pertain to the basic rules of political legitimacy at domestic level and the details of human rights protection, both state sovereignty and international human rights law have met their intrinsic limitations. Deciding on what makes us members of a political community and how to protect our equal rights as such is the least likely issue to leave the scope of collective self-government and hence of sovereignty.

This in turn explains why international human rights norms are usually minimal, abstract and indeterminate so as to grant states a lot of autonomy in their specification and implementation. Even when minimal international human rights duties are fleshed out on the basis of states' practice, a given state may still invoke its margin of appreciation or the principle of the maximization of protection in controversial cases despite the prima facie legitimate authority of those human rights duties. This confirms that (the limits of) domestic legitimate authority ought not necessarily be conflated with (the limits of) national sovereignty.

6. Conclusion

International human rights may be facing grave enforcement problems and even specification problems, but their most important problem, I have argued, is legitimacy. Focusing on the former before addressing the latter is putting the cart before the horse and risks looking for solutions to failing enforcement and deep indeterminacy where they cannot be found. Nor is the problem of the legitimacy of international human rights simply a matter of settling the conflict between their claim to legitimacy and that of domestic human rights law. Settling that question is important, but it requires understanding of how international human rights' authority is justified in the first place and this implies understanding their complementarity to domestic human rights.

International human rights cannot be fully grasped without referring to their corresponding duties and this requires taking the normative side of human rights more seriously. This is even more important if what is at stake is their legitimacy. To know whether international human rights norms have a justified claim to authority over states, one needs to start by assessing what kind of duties and hence what kind of reasons for action states have by virtue of recognizing human rights. This implies determining whether those norms can be described as legal human rights in the first place with the respective moral duties they imply. Then only can one turn to the different conditions of their legitimate authority and of how the reasons given by international law not only match corresponding states' reasons but also contribute to improving conformity to those reasons. By virtue of their correlative duties, human rights are such that their legal validity and legitimacy are more closely related than they are in the case of other legal norms.

More specifically and given their close relationship to political equality, I have argued that human rights are moral and legal in nature. Their legalization ought to take place at domestic level in priority and international human rights norms can only be regarded as human rights if they match an existing set of domestic human rights. International human rights are best understood, therefore, as international law second-order duties to adopt and abide by first-order human rights duties in domestic law. Those second-order duties correspond to the universal moral right to have rights, i.e. the right to political membership with all the human rights that right requires for its realization. In turn, the moral and legal reality of human rights affects their legitimacy: not all states can be bound to respect all human rights duties for lack of pre-existing reasons in the absence of first-order domestic human rights duties or democratic representation; while democratic coordination is the best justification one may give for the legitimacy of international human rights in circumstances of pervasive social and moral pluralism, it is not necessarily sufficiently democratic to justify the authority of rights that are central to democratic legitimation at the domestic level; finally, even though the value of state sovereignty and autonomy is defined by reference to human rights, sovereignty can constitute an exception to the legitimate authority of human rights when the boundaries of self-government are met.

Unsurprisingly, as a result, international human rights' legitimate authority, like that of other international law norms, is piecemeal: it varies from one state to the other, and from one human right source or norm to the other. In fact, the legitimate authority of international human rights is doubly piecemeal by virtue of the indeterminate nature of human rights and the dynamic and specifiable nature of their corresponding duties: states' duties to create human rights duties will also vary as a result by reference to the latter. Those state to state and right to right variations are even higher in the case of human rights than for other international legal norms which have no functional domestic equivalent or corresponding norms: given their reciprocal legal sources in domestic and international law, the legitimacy of international human rights and that of corresponding domestic human rights are closely related and somehow reciprocal.

If the forum of realization of moral-political rights and as a consequence the locus of human rights legalization are situated at the domestic level, this is also where the legitimation of international human rights ought to be sought for and promoted. Recurrent and seemingly banal human rights practices such as the domestic reception and specification of international human rights, the exhaustion of domestic remedies as a condition of admission before international human rights bodies, the margin of appreciation in the interpretation of international human rights or the domestic determination of the best means of enforcement of international human rights decisions seem therefore to have found their moral justification. There is nothing vacuous or, worse, politically worrying as a result in international human rights minimalism and their piecemeal authority. Quite the contrary: it corresponds not only to the legality of international human rights, but also to their moral reality.

Importantly, those conclusions about the legitimacy of international human rights should not be mistaken with a denial of the existence of other self-regarding or cosmopolitan reasons for states to ratify and respect international human rights law. Those reasons are actually very important and may help enhance the sociological legitimacy of international human rights law and compliance with those rights. So should democratic states' consent that constitutes an important reason for them to respect international human rights law even if it cannot palliate the absence of legitimate authority of those norms. After all, those international human rights norms are valid legal duties, whose validity and legal authority remain, at least in the short run, unaffected by the absence of generalized legitimate authority. Nor should one underestimate states' and individuals' imperfect duties of global justice; human rights do not exhaust the field of moral duties in international relations as one too often tends to forget.

Bibliography

Alvarez, J., 2006. *International Organizations as Law-makers*, Oxford University Press.

Anderson, E., 1999. What is the Point of Equality? *Ethics*, 109, 287–337.

Archibugi, D., 1993. The Reform of the UN and Cosmopolitan Democracy: A Critical Review. *Journal of Peace Research*, 30 (3), 301–315.

Arendt, H., 1951. *The Decline of the Nation-State and the End of the Rights of Man. The Origins of Totalitarianism*, London: Penguin.

Bayefsky, A., 2001. *The UN Human Rights Treaty System in the Twenty-First Century*, Ardsley: Transnational Publishers.

Beitz, C. R., 2009. *The Idea of Human Rights*, Oxford University Press.

Benhabib, S., 2008. The Legitimacy of Human Rights. *Deadalus*, 137 (3), 94–104.

2009. Claiming Rights across Borders: International Human Rights and Democratic Sovereignty. *American Political Science Review*, 103 (4), 691–704.

Besson, S., 2005a. Review Article: Democracy, Law and Authority. *Journal of Moral Philosophy*, 2 (1), 89–99.

2005b. *The Morality of Conflict*, Oxford: Hart Publishing.

2006. Deliberative Demoi-cracy in the European Union: Towards the Deterritorialization of Democracy. In S. Besson & J. L. Martí eds, *Deliberative Democracy and its Discontents*, Aldershot: Ashgate Limited Publishing, pp. 181–214.

2008. The Reception of the ECHR in the United Kingdom and Ireland. In H. Keller & A. Stone Sweet eds, *A Europe of Rights. The Reception of the European Convention on Human Rights*, Oxford University Press, pp. 31–106.

2009a. The Authority of International Law – Lifting the State Veil. *Sydney Law Review*, 31 (3), 343–380.

2009b. Whose Constitution(s)? International Law, Constitutionalism and Democracy. In J. Dunoff & J. Trachtman eds, *Ruling the World? Constitutionalism, International Law and Global Governance*, Cambridge University Press, pp. 381–407.

2009c. Ubi Ius, Ibi Civitas. A Republican Account of the International Community. In S. Besson & J. L. Martí eds, *Legal Republicanism and Republican Law – National and Post-National Perspectives*, Oxford University Press, pp. 204–237.

2009d. Institutionalizing Global Demoi-cracy. In L. Meyer ed., *Justice, Legitimacy and Public International Law*, Cambridge University Press, pp. 58–91.

2011a. Human Rights – Ethical, Political ... or Legal? First Steps in a Legal Theory of Human Rights. In D. Childress ed., *The Role of Ethics in International Law*, Cambridge University Press.

2011b. European Human Rights, Supranational Judicial Review and Democracy – Thinking Outside the Judicial Box. In P. Popelier, C. Van den Heyning & P. Van Nuffel eds, *Human Rights Protection in the European Legal Order: Interaction between European Courts and National Courts*, Cambridge: Intersentia, pp. 97–145.

2011c. Human Rights and Democracy in a Global Context – Decoupling and Recoupling. *Ethics & Global Politics*, 4 (1), 19–50.

2011d. International Law, Sovereignty and Democracy: A Reply to Waldron. *European Journal of International Law*, 22 (2), 373–387.

2011e. The Human Right to Democracy – A Moral Defence, with a Legal Nuance. In *Souveraineté populaire et droits de l'homme: Definition and Development of Human Rights and Popular Sovereignty in Europe*, Collection Science et Technique de la Société, 49. Strasbourg: Editions du Conseil de l'Europe, pp. 36–62.

2012a. The Erga Omnes Effect of ECtHR's Judgements – What's in a Name? In S. Besson ed., *The European Court of Human Rights after Protocol 14 – First Assessment and Perspectives*, Zurich: Schulthess.

2012b. The Egalitarian Dimension of Human Rights. *Archiv für Sozial- und Rechtsphilosophie Beiheft*, pp. 19–52.

2012c. Sovereignty. In R. Wolfrum et al. eds, *Max Planck Encyclopedia of International Law*, Oxford University Press.

2013a. International Human Rights and Political Equality – Implications for Global Democracy. In E. Erman & S. Näsström eds, *Equality in Transnational and Global Democracy*, Palgrave, forthcoming.

2013b. International Human Rights and Constitutional Law – Patterns of Mutual Validation and Legitimation. In R. Cruft, M. Liao & M. Renzo eds, *Oxford Handbook on Human Rights*, Oxford University Press, forthcoming.

2013c. Human Rights Pluralism in Europe. In K. Tuori & M. Maduro eds, *Transnational Law – Rethinking Legal Thinking*, Cambridge University Press, forthcoming.

Bodansky, D., 2008. The Concept of Legitimacy in International Law. In R. Wolfrum & V. Röben eds, *Legitimacy in International Law*, Berlin: Springer, pp. 308–318.

Boyle, A. & Chinkin, C., 2007. *The Making of International Law*, Oxford University Press.

Brettschneider, C., 2007. *Democratic Rights – The Substance of Self-government*, Princeton University Press.

Buchanan, A., 2004. *Justice, Legitimacy, and Self-Determination: Moral Foundations for International Law*, Oxford University Press.

2005. Equality and Human Rights. *Politics, Philosophy & Economics*, 4 (1), 69–90.

2008. Human Rights and the Legitimacy of the International Order. *Legal Theory*, 14, 39–70.

2010a. The Legitimacy of International Law. In S. Besson and J. Tasioulas eds, *The Philosophy of International Law*, Oxford University Press, pp. 79–96.

2010b. The Egalitarianism of Human Rights. *Ethics*, 120 (4), 679–710.

2011. Reciprocal Legitimation: Reframing the Problem of International Legitimacy. *Politics, Philosophy & Economics*, 10 (1), 5–19.

Buchanan, A. & Powell, R., 2008. Constitutional Democracy and the Rule of International Law: Are they Compatible? *Journal of Political Philosophy*, 16 (3), 326–349.

Çalı, B., Koch, A. & Bruch, N., 2011. The Legitimacy of the European Court of Human Rights: The View from the Ground. UCL Working Chapter. Available at: http://ecthrproject.files.wordpress.com/2011/04/ecthrlegitimacyreport.pdf [Accessed 27 May 2013].

Cassese, A. & Weiler, J. eds, 1988. *Change and Stability in International Law-Making*, Berlin, New York: Walter de Gruyter & Co.

Charlesworth, H. & Coicaud, J.-M. eds, 2010. *Fault Lines of International Legitimacy*, Cambridge University Press.

Chayes, A., 1965. *A Common Lawyer Looks at International Law*. Harvard Law Review, 78 (7), 1396–1413.

Christiano, T., 2008. *The Constitution of Equality*, Oxford University Press.

2010. Democratic Legitimacy and International Institutions. In S. Besson & J. Tasioulas eds, *The Philosophy of International Law*, Oxford University Press, pp. 119–137.

2012. The Legitimacy of International Institutions. In A. Marmor ed., *Routledge Companion to the Philosophy of Law*, London: Routledge.

Cohen, J. L., 2004. Minimalism about Human Rights: The Most We Can Hope for? *Journal of Political Philosophy*, 12 (2), 190–213.

2008. Rethinking Human Rights, Democracy and Sovereignty in the Age of Globalization. *Political Theory*, 36 (4), 578–606.

Crawford, J. & Watkins, J., 2010. International Responsibility. In S. Besson & J. Tasioulas eds, *The Philosophy of International Law*, Oxford University Press, pp. 283–298.

Donoho, D. L., 2003. Democratic Legitimacy in Human Rights – The Future of International Law-Making. *Wisconsin Law Journal*, 21 (1), 1–60.

Endicott, T., 2010. The Logic of Freedom and Power. In S. Besson & J. Tasioulas eds, *The Philosophy of International Law*, Oxford University Press, pp. 245–260.

Estlund, D., 2008. *Democratic Authority, A Philosophical Framework*, Princeton University Press.

Finnis, J., 1984. The Authority of Law in the Predicament of Contemporary Social Theory. *Notre Dame Journal of Law, Ethics and Public Policy*, 1, 115–138.

Flauss, J. F., 1998. La protection des droits de l'homme et les sources du droit international. In Société Française pour le Droit International, *La protection des droits de l'homme et l'évolution du droit international*, Colloque de Strasbourg, Paris: Pédone, pp. 11–79.

Føllesdal, A., 2007. Why International Human Rights Judicial Review Might Be Democratically Legitimate. *Scandinavian Studies in Law*, 52, 103–122.

2008. International Judicial Human Rights Review – Effective, Legitimate or Both? In J. Sihvola, P. Korkman & V. Mäkinen eds, *Universalism in International Law and Political Philosophy, Helsinki: COLLeGIUM*. Available at: www.helsinki.fi/collegium/e-series/volumes/volume_4/10_follesdal_2008_4.pdf [Accessed 27 May 2013].

Forst, R., 1999. The Basic Right to Justification: Toward a Constructivist Conception of Human Rights. *Constellations*, 6 (1), 35–60.

2007. *Das Recht auf Rechtfertigung. Elemente einer konstruktivistischen Theorie der Gerechtigkeit*, Frankfurt: Suhrkamp.

2010. The Justification of Human Rights and the Basic Right to Justification. A Reflexive Approach. *Ethics*, 120 (4), 711–740.

Franck, T., 1988. Legitimacy in the International System. *American Journal of International Law*, 82 (4), 705–759.

2006. The Power of Legitimacy and the Legitimacy of Power: International Law in an Age of Power Disequilibrium. *American Journal of International Law*, 100 (1), 88–106.

Gardbaum, S., 2008. Human Rights as International Constitutional Rights. *European Journal of International Law*, 19 (4), 749–768.

Goldsmith, J. L. & Posner, E. A., 2005. *The Limits of International Law*, Oxford University Press.

Goodin, R., 2007. Enfranchising All Affected Interests, and its Alternatives. *Philosophy & Public Affairs*, 35 (1), 40–68.

Gould, C., 2004. *Globalizing Democracy and Human Rights*, Cambridge University Press.

Griffin, J., 2008. *On Human Rights*, Oxford University Press.

Habermas, J., 1998a. *Die Legitimation durch Menschenrechte. Die postnationale Konstellation. Politische Essays*, Frankfurt: Suhrkamp, pp. 170–192.

1998b. *Faktizität und Geltung. Beiträge zur Diskurstheorie des Rechts und des demokratischen Rechtsstaats*, Frankfurt: Suhrkamp.

Hafner-Burton, E. M. & Tsutsui, K., 2005. Human Rights in a Globalizing World: The Paradox of Empty Promises. *American Journal of Sociology*, 110 (5), 1373–1411.

Hart, H. L. A., 1994. *The Concept of Law*, 2nd edn, Oxford: Clarendon Press.

Helfer, L. R. & Slaughter, A.-M., 1997. Toward a Theory of Effective Supranational Adjudication. *The Yale Law Journal*, 107 (2), 273–391.

Hershovitz, S., 2003. Legitimacy, Democracy, and Razian Authority. *Legal Theory*, 9, 201–220.

Hessler, K., 2005. Resolving Interpretive Conflicts in International Human Rights Law. *Journal of Political Philosophy*, 13 (1), 29–52.

Kumm, M., 2004. The Legitimacy of International Law: A Constitutionalist Framework of Analysis. *The European Journal of International Law*, 15 (5), 907–931.

Lefkowitz, D., 2005. Customary Law and the Case for Incorporationism. *Legal Theory*, 11 (4), 405–420.

Letsas, G., 2008. *A Theory of Interpretation of the European Convention of Human Rights*, Oxford University Press.

2010. Strasbourg's Interpretive Ethic: Lessons for the International Lawyer. *European Journal of International Law*, 21 (3), 509–541.

Lowe, M., 2000. The Politics of Law-Making: Are the Method and Character of Norm Creation Changing? In M. Byers ed., *The Role of Law in International Politics*, Oxford University Press, pp. 207–226.

MacCormick, N., 1977. Rights in Legislation. In P. Hacker & J. Raz eds, *Law, Morality and Society: Essays in Honour of H. L. A. Hart*, Oxford University Press, pp. 189–209.

Macklem, P., 2007. What is International Human Rights Law? Three Applications of a Distributive Account. *McGill Law Journal*, 52 (3), 575–604.

McCorquodale, R., 2004. An Inclusive International Legal System. *Leiden Journal of International Law*, 17 (3), 477–504.

2006. International Community and State Sovereignty: An Uneasy Symbiotic Relationship. In C. Warbrick & S. Tierney eds, *Towards an International Legal Community*, London: British Institute of International and Comparative Law, pp. 241–265.

Moravcsik, A., 2000. The Origins of Human Rights Regimes: Democratic Delegation in Postwar Europe. *International Organization*, 54 (2), 217–252.

Murphy, L., 2010. International Responsibility. In S. Besson & J. Tasioulas eds, *The Philosophy of International Law*, Oxford University Press, pp. 299–319.

O'Neill, O., 2005. The Dark Side of Human Rights. *International Affairs*, 81 (2), 427–439.

Pogge, T., 2005. Human Rights and Human Responsibilities. In A. Kuper ed., *Global Responsibilities: Securing Rights by Defining Obligations*, London: Routledge, pp. 3–35.

Rawls, J., 1971. *A Theory of Justice*, Cambridge, MA: Harvard University Press.

Raz, J., 1979. *The Authority of Law: Essays on Law and Morality*, Oxford: Clarendon Press.

1984a. *Legal Rights. Oxford Journal of Legal Studies*, 4 (1), 1–21.

1984b. On the Nature of Rights. *Mind*, 93 (370), 194–214.
1986. *The Morality of Freedom*, Oxford: Clarendon Press.
1995. *Ethics in the Public Domain*, Oxford: Clarendon Press.
2003. Comments and Responses. In L. Meyer, S. Paulson & T. Pogge eds, *Rights, Culture and the Law: Themes from the Legal and Political Philosophy of Joseph Raz*, Oxford University Press, pp. 253–278.
2006. The Problem of Authority: Revisiting the Service Conception. *Minnesota Law Review*, 90, 1003–1044.
2010. Human Rights in the New World Order. *Transnational Legal Theory*, 1 (1), 31–47.
Reus-Smit, C., 2009. On Rights and Institutions. In C. R. Beitz & R. Goodin eds, *Global Basic Rights*, Oxford University Press, pp. 25–48.
Risse, T., Ropp, S. C. & Sikkink, K. eds, 1999. The Power of Human Rights. *International Norms and Domestic Change*, Cambridge University Press.
Shue, H., 1988. Mediating Duties. *Ethics*, 98, 687–704.
Simma, B. & Alston, P., 1989. The Sources of Human Rights Law: Custom, Jus Cogens and General Principles. *Australian Yearbook of International Law* 12, 82–108.
Simmons, A. J., 1979. *Moral Principles and Political Obligations*, Princeton University Press.
Simmons, B. A., 2009. *Mobilizing for Human Rights: International Law in Domestic Politics*, Cambridge University Press.
Stone Sweet, A. & Keller, H., 2008. *A Europe of Rights*, Oxford University Press.
Tasioulas, J., 1996. In Defence of Relative Normativity: Communitarian Values and the Nicaragua Case. *Oxford Journal of Legal Studies*, 16 (1), 85–128.
2002. Human Rights, Universality and the Values of Personhood: Retracing Griffin's Steps. *European Journal of Philosophy*, 10 (1), 79–100.
2007. The Moral Reality of Human Rights. In T. Pogge ed., *Freedom from Poverty as a Human Right: Who Owes What to the Very Poor*, Oxford University Press, pp. 75–101.
2010a. The Legitimacy of International Law. In S. Besson & J. Tasioulas eds, *The Philosophy of International Law*, Oxford University Press, pp. 97–116.
2010b. Taking Rights out of Human Rights. *Ethics*, 120 (4), 647–678.
Teson, F., 1998. *A Philosophy of International Law*, Boulder, CO: Westview Press.
2005. *Humanitarian Intervention: An Inquiry into Law and Morality*, 3rd edn, Ardsley: Transnational Publishers.
Waldron, J., 1984. Introduction. *Theories of Rights*, Oxford University Press.
1993. Special Ties and Natural Duties. *Philosophy and Public Affairs*, 22 (1), 3–30.
1999. *Law and Disagreement*, Oxford University Press.
2002. *God, Locke and Equality*, Cambridge University Press.

2003. Authority for Officials. In L. Meyer, S. Paulson & T. Pogge eds, *Rights, Culture and the Law: Themes from the Legal and Political Philosophy of Joseph Raz*, Oxford University Press, pp. 45–71.

2006. The Rule of International Law. *Harvard Journal of Law and Public Policy*, 30, 15–30.

2011. Are Sovereigns Entitled to the Benefit of the International Rule of Law?. *European Journal of International Law*, 22 (2), 315–343.

Weil, P., 1983. Towards Relative Normativity in International Law? *American Journal of International Law*, 77 (3), 413–442.

Wolfrum, R., 2007. Legitimacy in International Law. In A. Reinisch & U. Kriebaum eds, *The Law of International Relations – Liber Amicorum Hanspeter Neuhold*, The Hague: Eleven International Publishing, pp. 471–482.

3

On the legitimate authority of international human rights bodies

STEVEN WHEATLEY

1. Introduction

The idea of 'human rights' has established itself as the dominant discourse in world society without a coherent understanding of its proper function or meaning. There is no agreement among legal and other scholars on the relationship between international human rights and domestic systems; the identity of the subjects of international human rights law, or the holders of the correlative duties; on the importance of enforceability; or indeed the object and purpose of international human rights law, and consequently the function of international human rights bodies (IHRBs) established under human rights treaties.[1] The role of IHRBs is understood by scholars in a number of ways, including, for example, ensuring that States parties comply with their international obligations; delimiting the circumstances in which it is appropriate for external actors to take an interest in the treatment of human persons within the State; and/or elaborating an idealized conception of the 'just' society. The focus of this essay concerns the extent to which we should recognize the claims of IHRBs to normative authority, i.e. to be able to regulate domestic societies on issues of social, economic and political controversy.

International human rights bodies do not possess the capacity to 'legislate' human rights; their normative power is exercised through an elaboration of the scope and content of abstract international law norms adopted

Professor of International Law, University of Lancaster. The author would like to thank the editors for their helpful and constructive comments on an earlier draft and the other contributors for the stimulating discussions and comments at the various meetings.

[1] The definition excludes bodies such the United Nations Security Council, whose primary concern is international peace and security, and the Human Rights Council, which is not established by a constitutive human rights treaty.

in the form of Concluding Observations, Views, Recommendations and General Comments. The requirement for interpretation results from the fact that human rights norms are (radically) indeterminate, and it is not possible to cover all possible scenarios within the text of an international law instrument. The claim by IHRBs to a 'right to rule' rests on providing an authoritative interpretation of human rights norms and making a determinative evaluation as to whether a State party has complied with its obligations under the treaty. Any analysis of the role of international human rights bodies is made complex by three factors: first, IHRBs have not constrained themselves to a literal interpretation of the text of human rights treaties; second, given that the treaties construct the States parties as democratic societies, IHRBs are required to engage with a political conception of rights in the absence of a meaningful political community; and third, the 'constitutionalization' of human rights regimes means that we can no longer understand certain (if not all) human rights regimes in terms of an expression of the wills of the States parties.

The objective of this chapter is to make sense of the proper function of international human rights bodies in light of these complexities. It first outlines the traditional understanding of the right to rule in world society, i.e. the de facto exercise of sovereign power, before observing the emergence of human rights in the period of the United Nations. The extant literature on 'human rights' (beyond the doctrinal treatment of the subject in international law) can be divided into two: first, arguments that certain moral rights that we possess simply by virtue of 'being human' should be recognized by the international community in international law, with correlative obligations imposed on States and non-State actors, including international organizations and institutions; second, arguments that ground the idea of 'human rights' in the practice that has emerged since the adoption of the Universal Declaration in 1948, and which can be seen as reflecting a political settlement; or an overlapping consensus of ethical perspectives; or an overlapping consensus of the practice of sovereign States. The objective of both the moral analysis and the practice-based analysis is to understand the idea of human rights and its regulatory function in world society. By contrast, the argument here is that we should examine the idea and function of international human rights law from the perspective of legitimate political authority, i.e. examine the regulatory claims of human rights law and international human rights bodies from the perspective of the normal justification thesis for the recognition of authority developed by Joseph Raz. The normal justification criterion establishes that IHRBs can only claim a right to rule where they can demonstrate that the States parties of international human rights law regimes would better conform to the reasons that already apply to them by following the normative directives of the IHRB than by acting independently. The argument here is that, given the development of a political conception of international human rights, there is a requirement for IHRBs to engage meaningfully with the political and democratic conception of rights if they are to be recognized as possessing the right to rule by democratic States parties. The analysis concludes that the work of John Rawls on the role of constitutional courts in a deliberative democracy provides the basis for conceptualizing the function of IHRBs, and considers the consequences of this understanding for any evaluation of the work of IHRBs.

2. International human rights law

There has been something of a backlash against the idea of 'human rights', with concerns being expressed by politicians, scholars, the media and citizens about the involvement of international human rights bodies on issues of social, economic and political controversy in democratic States. The most prominent of these debates in the United Kingdom relates to the judgment of the regional European Court of Human Rights on the right of prisoners to vote in elections – a right not expressly contained in the European Convention on Human Rights (ECHR).[2] British Prime Minister David Cameron has stated that the thought of implementing the judgment makes him feel 'physically ill' and, according to one opinion poll, nearly two out of three voters in the UK believe that the British Parliament and Supreme Court should have the final say on issues of human rights and not 'a foreign court' (Helfer 2012).

The critique of the European Court of Human Rights is representative of the concerns around the function that IHRBs have abrogated to themselves in world society. A senior judge in the United Kingdom (now retired), Lord Hoffmann, outlines the argument in the following way: 'I have no difficulty about the text of the [ECHR] … The problem is the Court; and the right of individual petition, which enables the Court to intervene in the details and nuances of the domestic laws of Member States' (Hoffmann 2009). Hoffmann's critique is not only concerned with the functioning of the Court and the quality, or otherwise, of its justices and/or judicial reasoning; it is informed by an understanding that 'human rights are universal

[2] Cf. Article 3, Protocol to the Convention for the Protection of Human Rights and Fundamental Freedoms, Paris, 20 March 1952, into force 18 May 1954, CETS No. 9.

in abstraction but national in application' (Hoffmann 2009: para. 23). He continues: even if the Strasbourg judges were 'omniscient, knowing the true interests of the people of the United Kingdom better than we do ourselves, it would still be constitutionally inappropriate for [certain] decisions … to be made by a foreign court' (Hoffmann 2009: para. 43). It is not surprising, Hoffmann argues, that, 'to the people of the United Kingdom', the European Court of Human Rights does not enjoy the constitutional legitimacy of a Supreme Court, and that 'detailed decisions about how [the legal system] could be improved should be made in London, either by our democratic institutions or by judicial bodies which … are integral with our own society and respected as such' (Hoffmann 2009: para. 39). Hoffmann's argument is that the content of abstract human rights norms should become determinate through the decisions of domestic political and legal institutions, which, in a democratic system, are accountable to the people and sensitive to the social, economic and political values of the community. The problem is that the very idea of international human rights implies that policy decisions on human rights should be settled at the global level and not by political and legal institutions of the State.

The idea of 'human rights' emerged following World War II as one part of a settlement that rejected the absolute claims of sovereign authority which had underpinned the allocation of political power following the Peace of Westphalia (1648). During the Westphalian epoch, the dominant positivist narrative understood the right to rule in terms of the exercise of sovereign authority, excluding the claims of natural or divine law, and positive morality. The de facto ability to exercise political power was sufficient to establish a *de jure* right: positive law is, according to the best known account, the command of a sovereign backed up by sanctions (Austin 1885: 88). The justification for the recognition of sovereign authority is the requirement to establish coercive government to protect subjects from external threats and internal instability. Individuals in the state of nature recognize that their rational self-interest requires the establishment of a political community and the transfer of regulatory power to the sovereign in order to establish the conditions of justice. Following the establishment of sovereign authority through a social contract between free individuals, political power can only be legitimately exercised in the interests of subjects (Grotius 1901: Bk. I, Ch. I, § 14; de Vattel 1916: Bk. I, Ch. IV, § 39). For Thomas Hobbes, Leviathan is the sole judge of the interests of the people, with that judgment held to be infallible (Hobbes 1968: 87); for John Locke, lawful power is understood in terms of constitutional government and majority rule (Locke 1960: Bk. II, § 96), with the function of government held to be the protection of the lives and properties of the members of the community (Locke 1960: Bk. II, § 135).

According to the positivist analysis, normative power is legitimate (legitimacy as legality) following an expression of sovereign will framed in terms of domestic or international law. Internally, following Jean Bodin, sovereignty was understood as the exclusive right to determine the normative situation of subjects without reference to any other temporal body or person (Bodin 1992: 8); externally, following Hugo Grotius, a law of nations was identified, which derived its authority 'from the consent of all, or at least of many [sovereign] nations' (Grotius 1901: Bk. I, Ch. I, § 15). In the absence of an agreement by the State to accept limitations on the exercise of political power internally, the treatment of the citizens remained an issue of domestic concern, with the principle of sovereignty precluding external interference in the internal affairs of a sovereign political community. Human rights provisions might be adopted as one part of the domestic constitutional order, as in the United States, but with the exception of ad hoc instances of humanitarian intervention, the imposition of obligations concerning minorities on States by the Great Powers, and attempts to regulate slavery, specifically the slave trade, the international community was not concerned with the treatment of human persons within States, allowing Hermann Goering to proclaim on the subject of the Holocaust: 'But that was our right! We were a sovereign State and that was strictly our business.'[3]

The dystopian Nazi regime demonstrated the fatuity of understanding the right to rule in terms of the de facto exercise of sovereign will, with the international community coming to the conclusion that a government that mistreats part of its own population cannot be trusted as a reliable partner in inter-State relations – at least this is the narrative that we international lawyers tell ourselves.[4] The de facto ability to legislate and enforce political law norms within State borders could no longer be accepted as sufficient to establish *de jure* political authority. The revised world order, reflected in the Charter of the United Nations, recognized the importance of sovereignty and human rights,[5] and one of the earliest acts of the United Nations was to adopt a Universal Declaration on Human Rights.

[3] Quoted in Lauren (2003: 202–204).

[4] See Kennedy (2007: 650). Compare, however, Moyn (2010); also Moravcsik (2000); Mazower (2004).

[5] Cf. Article 2(7) (domestic jurisdiction) and Articles 1(3) and 55 (human rights), Charter of the United Nations, San Francisco, 26 June 1945, into force 24 October 1945.

The preamble to the Declaration links the protection of human rights to the establishment and maintenance of international and domestic peace and security, asserting that '[the] recognition of the inherent dignity and of the equal and inalienable rights of all members of the human family is the foundation of freedom, justice and peace in the world' and that 'it is essential, if man is not to be compelled to have recourse, as a last resort, to rebellion against tyranny and oppression, that human rights should be protected by the rule of law'.[6]

The language of the Universal Declaration reflects in parts that of natural or moral law, whereby certain rights are assumed to be possessed by all persons, at all times, in all places – the Declaration is described in the preamble as 'a common standard of achievement for all peoples and all nations'. Article 1 provides that '[a]ll human beings are born free and equal in dignity and rights'. The substantive provisions do not support a natural law reading, however, with the Declaration recognizing human rights to physical integrity;[7] to equality and non-discrimination;[8] to personhood[9] and personal autonomy, which is developed in the context of the community;[10] to political participation through democratic procedures;[11] to property;[12] to education[13] and welfare;[14] to the judicial protection of rights;[15] and to the right to be free from arbitrary interferences in the enjoyment

[6] GA Res. 217(III)A, adopted 10 December 1948, 'Universal Declaration of Human Rights'.

[7] Article 3 (life, liberty and security of person); Article 5 (prohibition on torture); Article 9 (freedom from arbitrary arrest, detention or exile); and Article 14 (to seek and to enjoy asylum).

[8] Article 2 (non-discrimination in the enjoyment of rights); and Article 7 (equality before the law).

[9] Article 4 (prohibition on slavery); Article 6 (right to recognition everywhere as a person before the law); Article 15 (to a nationality); and Article 16 (to marry and to found a family).

[10] Article 29 (duties to the community and limitations on rights); Article 12 (privacy, family, home and correspondence); Article 13 (freedom of movement and residence); Article 18 (freedom of thought, conscience and religion); Article 19 (opinion and expression); Article 20 (peaceful assembly and association); Article 26 (education directed to the full development of the human personality); and Article 27 (right to participate in the cultural life of the community).

[11] Article 21.

[12] Article 17, including intellectual property (Article 27).

[13] Article 26.

[14] Article 22 (social security); Article 23 (work, and fair conditions of work); Article 24 (to rest and leisure, including reasonable limitation of working hours and periodic holidays with pay); and Article 25 (welfare support for a standard of living adequate for health and well-being).

[15] Article 8 (effective judicial remedy for the violation of rights); Article 10 (hearing by an independent and impartial tribunal); and Article 11 (fair trial).

of rights.[16] A general limitation clause allows for restrictions on the enjoyment of rights solely for the purpose of securing the rights and freedoms of others, and 'of meeting the just requirements of morality, public order and the general welfare in a democratic society'.[17] The content of the Universal Declaration on Human Rights conceptualizes 'human rights' in terms of the relationship between an autonomous human agent and a democratic State government, which is required to establish judicial and educational systems, and provide welfare support.

Following the adoption of the Universal Declaration, the United Nations moved to delegitimize certain policies, notable discrimination against women and groups identified on the basis of race and religion, and in 1966 the General Assembly adopted its International Bill of Rights in the form of the International Covenant on Economic, Social and Cultural Rights, and International Covenant on Civil and Political Rights (ICCPR).[18] A body of United Nations human rights law has been developed,[19] with the core human rights instruments establishing supervisory mechanisms in the form of supranational international human rights bodies: the Human Rights Committee (established under the International Covenant on Civil and Political Rights); Committee on Economic, Social and Cultural Rights; Committee on the Elimination of All Forms of Discrimination Against Women; Committee Against Torture; Committee on the Elimination of Racial Discrimination; Committee on Migrant Workers; Committee on

[16] Cf. Article 9 (freedom from arbitrary arrest, detention or exile); Article 12 (arbitrary interference with privacy, family, home or correspondence); Article 15 (arbitrary depravation of nationality); and Article 17 (depravation of property).

[17] Article 29.

[18] International Covenant on Economic, Social and Cultural Rights, New York, 16 December 1966, into force 3 January 1976, 993 UNTS 3; International Covenant on Civil and Political Rights, New York, 16 December 1966, into force 23 March 1976, 999 UNTS 171.

[19] The core international human rights instruments – in addition to the International Covenant on Economic, Social and Cultural Rights, and International Covenant on Civil and Political Rights – are as follows: International Convention on the Elimination of All Forms of Racial Discrimination, New York, 7 March 1966, into force 4 January 1969, 660 UNTS 195; Convention on the Elimination of all Forms of Discrimination against Women, New York, 18 December 1979, into force 3 September 1981, 1249 UNTS 13; Convention Against Torture and Other Cruel, Inhuman or Degrading Treatment or Punishment, New York, 10 December 1984, into force 26 June 1987, 1465 UNTS 85; International Convention on the Protection of the Rights of All Migrant Workers and Members of Their Families, New York, 18 December 1990, into force 1 July 2003, 2220 UNTS 3; Convention on the Rights of the Child, New York, 20 November 1989, into force 2 September 1990, 1577 UNTS 3; Convention on the Rights of Persons with Disabilities, New York, 13 December 2006, into force 3 May 2008, 2515 UNTS 3.

the Rights of the Child; and Committee on the Rights of Persons with Disabilities.[20]

These international human rights bodies employ a number of mechanisms to promote the compliance by States parties with their international law obligations. First, States parties are required to submit a report to the relevant IHRB, which allows for the possibility of a dialogue between States parties and the IHRB at meetings to discuss the report, prior to the IHRB adopting Concluding Observations on the compliance of the State party with its obligations under the treaty. Second, a number of instruments allow for the possibility of inter-State complaint, which is rarely invoked, and, more importantly, for individuals to bring a complaint to the IHRB that they have been a victim of a human rights violation. In arriving at a view on an individual application, the IHRB is required to interpret the scope and content of a convention right and evaluate its application in the particular case. The importance of allowing for individual complaints lies in the ability of the IHRB to develop a detailed jurisprudence on the substantive content of human rights through an application of the legal principles of treating like cases alike; the requirement to give reasons for decisions; and the practice of following, or not following, previous decisions on similar or the same facts. Third, a number of IHRBs issue General Comments on the content of primary human rights norms and the secondary rules about rules, concerning, for example, reservations to treaty norms, continuity of obligations, the nature of the general legal obligations imposed on States parties, and the ways in which States parties should respond to the directives and judgments of IHRBs.

One could argue that while the normative statements of IHRBs contribute to a global discourse on 'human rights', allowing for dialogue around the idea and emergence of new methodologies for problem-solving, they do not form part of the discipline of international law and are not binding as a matter of law (cf. Luhmann 1985: 256, 262), i.e. that they do not provide a content-independent reason for compliance, but can be seen as mere 'advice' to States parties (cf. Raz 1979: 14, 24). Nobody doubts that IHRBs are important discursive agents, influencing international and domestic elites and publics in the formulation of policy on human rights. IHRBs do not, however, expect States parties to take their normative statements as another reason in the balance of reasons which influence the

[20] See, also, developments at the regional level, in relation, for example, to the African Commission on Human and Peoples' Rights, Inter-American Court of Human Rights and European Court of Human Rights.

actions of domestic governments. IHRBs expect States parties to act on their directives, because they are the directives of the relevant supervisory body, often framing Concluding Observations, Views, Recommendations and General Comments in terms of the binary divide 'lawful' or 'unlawful', in contrast, for example, to suggestions that the actions of States parties are not in accordance with best practice, etc. As Niklas Luhmann observes, from the perspective of a law, impugned conduct is either 'legal' or 'illegal', with an autonomous legal system constructing its own boundaries through the operation of the binary distinctions between norms and facts and legal/illegal (Luhmann 2004: 58).

Consider, for example, the position of the Human Rights Committee, established under the International Covenant on Civil and Political Rights, which provides that the Committee 'shall study the reports submitted by the States Parties [and] shall transmit its reports, and such general comments as it may consider appropriate, to the States Parties'.[21] The Committee has interpreted the provision as providing a right to issue Concluding Observations on the compliance of a State party with its obligations under the ICCPR and to adopt General Comments that provide a 'general statement of law that expresses the Committee's conceptual understanding of the content of a particular provision, and as such is a very useful guide to the normative substance of international human rights obligations' (OHCHR 2004). The Human Rights Committee has further developed a quasi-judicial mechanism under the Optional Protocol to the ICCPR, which allows the Committee to receive individual petitions. The relevant provision provides that '[t]he Committee shall forward its views to the State Party concerned and to the individual'.[22] From the commencement of the work of the Committee, as Dominic McGoldrick observes, its views have followed 'a judicial pattern and are effectively decisions on the merits'.[23] While a number of academics conclude that the views of the Human Rights Committee 'lack any binding legal force' (Helfer & Miller 1996; Tomuschat 2008), a number observe the quasi-judicial nature of the individual petition mechanism (Crawford 1997: 257; Buergenthal

[21] Article 40(4), International Covenant on Civil and Political Rights.

[22] Article 5(4) of the Optional Protocol to the International Covenant on Civil and Political Rights, New York, 16 December 1966, into force 23 March 1976, 999 UNTS 171.

[23] McGoldrick (1994: 151). McGoldrick observes that, in the drafting the International Covenant on Civil and Political Rights, the term 'view' was preferred to the 'stronger terms "suggestions" and "recommendations" ' (1994: 150) and that it is clear from the drafting work that the views of the Human Rights Committee 'do not constitute a legally binding decision as regards the State party concerned' (1994: 151).

2001: 368), and it is noteworthy that a factsheet produced by the United Nations describes the views adopted under the Optional Protocol as consisting of 'either a finding of violation, or a finding of non-violation' of the Convention (OHCHR 2004: 26).

In relation to the procedure for receiving individual applications, the Human Rights Committee has stated that, while its function 'is not, as such, that of a judicial body, the views issued by the Committee under the Optional Protocol exhibit some important characteristics of a judicial decision', specifically 'the considered interpretation of the language of the Covenant, and the determinative character of the decisions'.[24] The Committee has concluded that its views represent an 'authoritative determination' of the legal position of States parties,[25] and that it expects them to 'use whatever means lie within their power in order to give effect to the views issued by the Committee'.[26] The Human Rights Committee's self-understanding of its function is supported by the International Court of Justice, which has concluded that it will ascribe 'great weight' to the case law of the Committee, which was 'established specifically to supervise the application of [the] treaty'. The International Court of Justice observed that the Committee 'has built up a considerable body of interpretative case law, in particular through its findings in response to the individual communications … and in the form of its "General Comments" '. The reliance on the 'jurisprudence' of the Human Rights Committee is justified by reference to the need to achieve 'the necessary clarity and the essential consistency of international law, as well as legal security, to which both the individuals with guaranteed rights and the States obliged to comply with treaty obligations are entitled'.[27]

The Human Rights Committee provides just one example of an IHRB that has developed a more extensive function for itself than that envisaged in the text of the relevant international instrument, specifically in providing an authoritative interpretation of the content of human rights norms and correlative obligations of States parties. Where IHRBs interpret the obligations of States parties in accordance with a literal understanding of convention rights, the function can be understood as a delegation of

[24] Human Rights Committee, General Comment No. 33, 'The Obligations of States Parties under the Optional Protocol to the International Covenant on Civil and Political Rights', adopted ninety-fourth session, UN Doc. CCPR/C/GC/33, para. 11.

[25] Ibid., para. 13.

[26] Ibid., para. 20.

[27] *Case Concerning Ahmadou Sadio Diallo* (*Republic of Guinea v Democratic Republic of Congo*), Merits, Judgment, ICJ Rep. 2010, p. 639, para. 66.

sovereign authority, i.e. the external expression of sovereign will in accepting the obligations that follow accession to the treaty is understood to limit the possibilities of internal political self-determination, with IHRBs performing a further 'check and balance' on the exercise of domestic political power (this might be particularly important where political law norms reflect the taken-for-granted cultural norms of the majority of the population, or domestic political conflicts are conceived of in terms of a zero-sum-game). Where, however, IHRBs develop an interpretation that goes beyond the literal expression of the text of the treaty, they can appear to be imposing restrictions on the internal freedom of action without clear evidence that States parties have consented to the limitation, and without the possibility of 'constitutional over ride' as the positions adopted by IHRBs are not subject to reversal and revision by domestic or international judicial or political institutions, and there is limited possibility of reform of the substantive provisions through treaty amendment, which requires the consent of all States parties. There is, then, a difficulty in accepting an extensive function for international human rights bodies.

Before going on to consider the arguments for recognizing the normative authority of IHRBs, the chapter first develops a conceptual framework for understanding the idea of legitimate political authority, i.e. the basis for accepting that an actor or institution has the right to determine the normative situation of the subjects of a regulatory regime.

3. Authority: the right to rule

The most influential account of authority is provided by Joseph Raz, who follows John Lucas: 'A man, or body of men, *has authority* if it follows from his saying "Let *X* happen, that *X* ought to happen' (Lucas 1966: 16 quoted in Raz 1979: 11, original emphasis). Authority is relational and dyadic; it is the ability to change the normative situation of others, involving the issuing of directives – framed in terms of norms, standards, principles, doctrines, etc. – to a subject. Where an individual recognizes an actor or institution as an 'authority', she should subject herself to the directives of the authority and not seek to reflect on, or deliberate about, the relevant issues, or come to an independent judgment. An authority directive must express a view about what ought to be done and it should be possible for the subject to comply with the authority directive without recourse to the reasons or considerations on which the directive purports to adjudicate. Raz' concept of legitimate political authority establishes that the directives of legitimate authorities are reasons for action, or inaction, on the part of the subjects, who are expected to follow the authority directive regardless of their view on the underlying merits and indeed without attempting to form a judgment on the merits of the relevant issue (Raz 1994: 212).

Raz argues that the normal way to establish that a person has authority over another (the 'normal justification thesis') '*involves showing that the alleged subject is likely better to comply with reasons which apply to him (other than the alleged authoritative directives) if he accepts the directives of the alleged authority as authoritatively binding and tries to follow them, rather than by trying to follow the reasons which apply to him directly*' (Raz 1986: 53).[28] The normal justification criterion establishes that A has (legitimate) authority over B, if B would better conform to the reasons that already apply to B by following the directives of A (i.e. by treating the directives of A as content-independent and exclusionary) than by acting independently.

The normal justification thesis is an ideal-type theory, establishing how authorities are supposed to function; it can be contrasted with sociological concepts of legitimacy, concerned with the identification of those actors and institutions which are, in fact, recognized as having the right to rule, for whatever reason.[29] The normal justification thesis contains both normative and sociological elements: legitimate authority depends on the actor or institution regulating in accordance with the interests and preferences of subjects, with the evaluation as to whether, or not, this is the case made by 'subjects'.[30] Consequently, the ways in which authority is recognized by subjects may differ from time to time and place to place, i.e. it is context-dependent, and it is not possible to identify universal criteria for the exercise of legitimate authority. This conclusion conflicts with the general understanding in world society that the right to rule at the level of the State is dependent on a minimum level of compliance with human rights. Perhaps we might accept that the idea of 'human rights' is implied by the normal justification criterion, which provides that the exercise of normative power is only legitimate where exercised in accordance with the interests of subjects of the regime? Raz accepts that fundamental human rights

[28] Emphasis in original.

[29] Raz does not understand the right to rule in terms of the de facto ability to ensure compliance through coercive government institutions, although it is the case that most *de jure* authorities will also be de facto authorities.

[30] See Raz (2006: 1018). The argument applies equally to the scope of authority accepted by subjects. Actors might accept the authority of an actor or institution on certain issues, but not others – consider for example the competing directives of the State and organized religion. Consequently, while an institution might be an authority in relation to subject matter 'X', it might not be in relation to subject matter 'Y'.

are a basis for the challenge of authority directives, even when the directive is clear as to what is required and that the grounds for challenging the directives of an authority 'determine the conditions of legitimacy of the authority and the limits of its rightful power' (Raz 1986: 46). The idea of fundamental rights is not though defined, with Raz concluding that fundamental liberal rights 'are valid moral rights deserving legal-institutional protection over and above the normal legal protection, because they express values which should form a part of morally worthy political cultures' (Raz 1986: 46). The argument appears, however, to be focused exclusively on the domestic political cultures of liberal and democratic States (and not an understanding more generally of the idea of legitimate political authority), with Raz outlining a different function for international human rights in subsequent writings.

3.1 *Raz' interventionist account of human rights*

In contrast with his understanding of human rights in liberal States, Raz understands 'human rights' in world society as moral rights recognized in international law 'because they are thought to combine exceptional importance and universality' (Raz 2010a: 39). Once a human right is identified 'there is a duty to establish and support impartial, efficient and reliable institutions to oversee its implementation and protect it from violations.' There is no difficulty with IHRBs or other outsiders judging the actions of domestic governments against international human rights law norms because human rights are 'those rights that all people living today have in virtue of the common conditions of life today'. For that reason, 'no special knowledge of the circumstances of this country or that [is] required to know that its citizens have those rights' (Raz 2010a: 43).

According to Raz' interventionist account, 'human rights' delimit the circumstances in which it is appropriate for those outside of the State (including other States, international organizations and institutions and international non-governmental organizations) to take an interest in the internal affairs of the State, disabling any claim that sovereignty should cloak those with political power from external interest and intervention (Raz 2010b: 331).[31] The approach is underpinned by the idea that many

[31] Human rights might consequently be understood as a correlative to sovereignty, with the idea only making sense in the context of the State and a world society comprised of States. Raz rejects this conclusion, however, arguing that human rights are not only held against States, but also international organizations and against political institutions in domestic settings: 'The claim is only that being rights whose violation is a reason for action against

of the moral principles that govern social relations depend on contingent practices at the level of the State. The justification for excluding external intervention lies in the moral value of the independence and autonomy of the State, with Raz concluding that we should be prepared to accept '[some] variability in the precise content and scope of rights which apply in different political societies' (Raz 2010b: 331).[32] Human rights are, according to the interventionist account, sovereignty-limiting measures, and we should not confuse the idea of legitimate political authority with State sovereignty, which limits the permissibility of outsiders interfering in the affairs of a State, 'even when the State is in the wrong' (Raz 2010b: 328). It follows that not every action of a State government that exceeds its legitimate authority can provide a justification for intervention by other States (Raz 2010b: 330).

Raz does not address in detail the role of international bodies in ensuring the protection of human rights, although the account implies that their function should be to delimit the circumstances in which intervention in the internal affairs of the State is justified by the seriousness of the human rights violations, with the consequence that the interpretive function of IHRBs is limited to establishing the minimum content of human rights. A 'minimalist' account is not reflective of human rights, according to human rights practice, and international human rights bodies have elaborated in some detail the scope and content of the various convention rights, with the consequences that the normative position of States parties is established by the treaty, as interpreted by the international human rights body. There is then a requirement to establish the authority of IHRBs, which in the practice of human rights can appear to be determining the normative situation of States.

The de facto ability of IHRBs to regulate States parties does not, of course, according to the normal justification thesis, establish a *de jure* right to rule. One function of IHRBs might be to determine the circumstances in which external actors may take a legitimate interest in the internal affairs of States parties to human rights treaties, but there remains the question as to whether IHRBs can establish a right to rule, i.e. whether States parties should accept the normative directives of IHRBs – adopted in the form of Concluding Observations, Views, Recommendations and General

States in the international arena is distinctive of human rights, according to human rights practice' (Raz 2010b: 329).

32 Raz draws a direct analogy with the moral value of the independence and autonomy of the individual.

Comments – as providing a content-independent reason for action, or inaction.

3.2 *The authority of international human rights bodies*

According to Raz' normal justification criterion, legitimate political authority is established where the subjects of the regulatory regime would better conform to the reasons that already apply to them by following the directives of the authority than by acting independently. The normal justification thesis can be applied to the exercise of legitimate political authority by actors and institutions over non-human legal actors, including States.[33] The authority of international human rights bodies can be located in one of two sources: the authority of the human rights treaty established under international law or the authority of the human rights law regime following the 'constitutionalization' of the regime (where this occurs). Once the authority of an international human rights body is accepted by States parties, compliance is assumed, except where a State party does not accept the scope of authority claimed by the IHRB, or the IHRB goes beyond its authority, understood in terms of its legitimate regulatory role. Raz concludes that – at the level of the State – there might be a political obligation to support just institutions even when the government exceeds its legitimate authority; that individuals may have prudential reasons for obeying the rules of an actor or institution even when it goes beyond the scope of its authority; or they may comply where not obeying will do more harm than good. Further, he does not regard it as problematic for the State to enforce moral duties that should be recognized and enforced through the law and legal institutions, giving the example of certain human rights (Raz 1986: 102–103). Consequently, even where a State party regards the IHRB as going beyond its legitimate authority (or even does not regard an IHRB as an independent authority, distinct from the human rights treaty), it has a political obligation to consider the importance of supporting the work of the IHRB as a 'just institution' and the prudential consideration of supporting the function of IHRBs in world society. Further, Raz' argument about the exercise of political power by the State in recognizing and enforcing moral duties may have a particular resonance in relation to the acceptance

[33] The argument constructs the exercise of authority in relation to subjects capable of autonomous reasoning, i.e. capable of deciding whether it would be better to follow the directives of the authority or to act independently, and of evaluating the justification advanced by the authority, i.e. the claim of the right to rule: Raz (2009: 140).

by democratic States parties of the regulatory role of international human rights bodies.

Many scholars locate the argument for accepting the regulatory function of IHRBs in the sovereign consent of States parties to the establishment of the human rights treaty regime. The normal justification criterion establishes that the international law system is an authority in relation to States where States recognize that they would better conform to the reasons that already apply to them by following the rules of international law than by acting independently. In this context, States recognize the importance of maintaining inter-State contractual bargains (*pacta sunt servanda*); the value of developing norms through the collective experience of legal actors in the absence of a centralized authority (customary international law); and the importance of a coherent system of general international law, reflected in the acceptance of the authority of 'international law' and the norms and principles of general international law.[34] Sovereign consent – and an acceptance of the authority of the international law system – could provide the basis for establishing a regulatory role of IHRBs if the following criteria were met. First, the importance of *pacta sunt servanda* was established, either as an independent moral value around the keeping of promises, or as part of an argument for accepting the authority of international law. Second, the treaty accorded interpretive autonomy to the international human rights body, although this is not the case in relation to the majority of IHRBs. Third, IHRBs interpreted the obligations of States parties in a way that was consistent with the principles established by States under international law, specifically in accordance with the principles for interpretation recognized in the Vienna Convention on the Law of Treaties, which provides that a treaty 'shall be interpreted in good faith

[34] John Tasioulas observes the following justifications for States accepting the authority of international law: international law and its institutions might enjoy cognitive advantages over its subjects – customary international law, for example, is founded on the experiences of States; international law might cure volitional defects where the self-interest of States mitigates against action, for example in relation to humanitarian intervention; international law might enjoy decision-procedural benefits in terms of requiring multilateral as opposed to unilateral decision-making procedures; and international law might enjoy certain executive advantages in terms of coordination and cooperation, in relation for example to air transport: Tasioulas (2010: 101–102). Tasioulas concludes that not all of the fragmented systems of international law enjoy the same authority, observing that the 'hopelessly vague and endless proliferating' norms around the idea of 'human rights' cannot make the same claim to legitimate authority as the Charter of the United Nations regime on the use of force (2010: 102–103).

in accordance with the ordinary meaning to be given to the terms of the treaty in their context and in the light of its object and purpose'.[35]

International human rights bodies have not though interpreted the terms of human rights treaties in line with the ordinary meaning, nor have they adopted a restricted approach to the interpretation of human rights treaties that seeks to avoid the imposition of international law obligations on sovereign States in the absence of the clearly expressed consent of States parties.[36] The European Court of Human Rights has, for example, concluded that the European Convention on Human Rights[37] is not an international treaty of the 'classic kind', involving 'mere reciprocal engagements between contracting States'.[38] The object and purpose of the ECHR is the collective enforcement of human rights and fundamental freedoms,[39] and the Convention cannot be interpreted 'solely in accordance with the intentions of their authors as expressed more than forty years ago'.[40] A dynamic and teleological approach to the interpretation of human rights treaties is not only adopted by the European Court of Human Rights. A report by the International Law Commission observes the development of self-contained regimes in the field of human rights and emergence of principles of international human rights law, which are assumed '[to] differ from what the general law provides for analogous situations' (International Law Association 2006: para. 129). The Report refers to the development of 'the principle of "dynamic" or teleological interpretation[,] [which] is much more deeply embedded in human rights law than in general international law' (International Law Association 2006: para. 130).

The dynamic or teleological approach to interpretation has led IHRBs to construe human rights norms in a way that is not consistent with the sovereign political wills of States parties reflected in the adoption of the international law instrument and their accession to the regime. Consider, for example, the conclusion of the Human Rights Committee that a prohibition against private homosexual behaviour in the Australian state of Tasmania constituted an arbitrary interference with the right to privacy and that discrimination on the grounds of 'sex' included sexual

35 Article 31(1), Vienna Convention on the Law of Treaties, Vienna, 23 May 1969, into force 27 January 1980, 1155 UNTS 331.

36 Cf. *Golder v United Kingdom*, A18, Separate Opinion of Judge Sir Gerald Fitzmaurice, paras 37 and 39.

37 Convention for the Protection of Human Rights and Fundamental Freedoms, Rome 4 November 1950, into force 3 September 1953, CETS 005 (as amended).

38 *Ireland v United Kingdom*, Ser A25, para. 239.

39 *Soering v United Kingdom*, Ser A161, para. 87.

40 *Loizidou v Turkey* (Preliminary Objections), Ser A310, para. 71.

orientation.[41] Whatever the moral and intellectual arguments in support of this view, it is difficult to conclude that it is in line with the position of a majority of States at the moment of the adoption of the International Covenant on Civil and Political Rights, or at the present time.[42]

Through the adoption of Concluding Observations, Views, Recommendations and General Comments, international human rights bodies are able to develop a coherent normative understanding of the convention rights and the correlative obligations of States parties. The following process of constitutionalization – understood as the development of a legal system organized in accordance with a basic norm, with accepted constitutional laws about law-making – can be observed in the practice of certain international human rights bodies, transforming certain international human rights regimes from regimes of inter-State contract to regimes of global governance.[43] Following the establishment of the human rights treaty and the functioning of the IHRB for a period of time, a relatively coherent human rights regime is identified (by academic writers and legal practitioners) in the Concluding Observations, Views, Recommendations and General Comments of the IHRB. The human rights regime becomes operationally closed through self-reference to its own normative statements (Luhmann 2004), for example where an IHRB refers to its own previous views in a conclusion on an individual application, or its own General Comments. The IHRB becomes constitutionally 'self-aware' through the development of rules about rules and the location of the regime within a wider political and legal institutional framework, with reference in the 'jurisprudence' to non-binding resolutions adopted by representative assemblies such as the General Assembly of the United Nations. The defining moment occurs where the IHRB asserts the authority of the human rights regime over other legal regimes, if only implicitly,

[41] *Toonen v Australia*, HRC Communication No. 488/1992, UN Doc CCPR/C/50/D/488/1992 (1994).

[42] The Human Dignity Trust reports that over 80 States have laws criminalizing homosexuality. See generally Hamzic (2011).

[43] This work does not argue that all international human rights law regimes have undergone a process of 'constitutionalization', although the argument can be made in relation to certain International Human Rights Bodies. The most compelling case is made in relation to the European Convention on Human Rights, with the European Court of Human Rights describing the ECHR as a 'constitutional instrument of European public order' in the field of human rights: *Bosphorus Hava Yollari Turizm Ve Ticaret Anonim Sirketi v Ireland*, Reports of Judgments and Decisions 2005-VI [GC], para. 156. In relation to the academic literature, see Greer (2003: 407); Gardbaum (2009: 233, 247); and Klabbers, Peters & Ulfstein (2009: 218).

i.e. where the IHRB asserts that *its* understanding of the convention rights will prevail over other interpretations, including those of the States parties, and that it will have the final say on the terms of engagement between the international human rights regime and other legal orders (domestic and international), i.e. that the human rights law system is not subject to the authority of any other legal system. At this point, an autonomous human rights system can be identified, where autonomy is understood in terms of a legal system organized in accordance with its own basic norm or rule of recognition. Following this development, while the international human rights body remains ultimately subject to the political influence of States parties, who could, for example, withdraw funding for the IHRB, it cannot rely on the original consent of States parties to justify its regulatory role: the international human rights body must demonstrate a right to rule in its own terms.

The normal justification criterion provides that an IHRB has legitimate political authority over States parties where it is established that States parties would better conform to the reasons that already apply to them by following the directives of the IHRB than by acting independently in relation to 'human rights'. The authority of IHRBs is not dependent on the ability to ensure compliance, but the ability to ensure acceptance by States parties: IHRBs must persuade States parties to recognize their authority in the area of human rights by demonstrating that they are in a better position to establish the content of abstract human rights norms than the States parties.

While the normal justification thesis does not establish a democratic conception of legitimate political authority (Raz 2006: fn. 20), it can be read as requiring the introduction of democratic procedures and mechanisms for the exercise of legitimate political authority *in relation to democratic societies* (Sadurski 2006). The normal justification criterion establishes that an actor or institution has legitimate authority over a subject if the subject would better conform to the reasons that already apply to her by following the directives of the putative authority than by acting independently. The understanding of subjects as to whether the authority is better placed will be determined, at least in part, by the political culture of the community. In the case of democratic societies, it is likely that subjects will conclude that the only way in which the government can establish the reasons that already apply to them is by engaging with subjects through democratic procedural mechanisms. The political culture of democratic States, i.e. the way in which political debate is conducted within democratic societies, is not sympathetic to any claim to 'know better' by an actor or institution on issues of social, economic and political controversy, i.e. where there is disagreement, including on the elaboration of the content of abstract human rights norms or the necessary balance between the rights of the individual and the interests of the wider political community. A democratic conception of epistemic authority provides that an actor or institution is in a privileged position concerning the 'just', 'correct' or 'right' course of action only where public policy positions have been established through democratic procedural mechanisms.

The normal justification thesis establishes that the exercise of authority is legitimate where subjects accept that the authority is better placed to regulate the conditions of social, economic and political life than the subjects themselves. In a democratic political system – with a democratic political culture – the subjects of the State law regime will conclude that the only way in which governmental authority can ascertain the reasons that apply to them is by engaging with subjects through decision-making procedures which are responsive to interests and preferences of subjects. The argument here is that it is implausible to conclude that political elites and the citizens of democratic States (who influence – directly and indirectly – domestic political elites) will apply a democratic conception of legitimate political authority within the State and at the same time recognize the claims of international organizations and institutions to 'know better' on issues of collective concern in the international community.[44] Democratic States are only likely to accept the regulatory function of supranational institutions on 'political' issues on which there is reasonable disagreement where the normative directives of global institutions can make a claim to democratic procedural legitimacy.[45] The conclusion has a particular significance in relation to the regulatory function of international human rights bodies. The Universal Declaration on Human Rights conceptualizes States in the international community as democratic societies, providing a human right to participate in free and fair elections,[46] and only permitting restrictions on the enjoyment of rights for the purpose of meeting the

[44] This is the basis for concerns over the democratic deficit in global governance. See, generally, Wheatley (2011).

[45] This is not to conclude that democratic States will only recognize and accept the right to rule of international organizations and institutions that regulate in accordance with the democratic ideal. Democratic states might, for example, accept other bases of legitimate political authority by global actors which are not defined by reference to the idea of democratic legitimacy – the authority of the Security Council of the United Nations might, for example, rest on its ability to deal effectively with problems around international peace and security.

[46] Article 21(3), Universal Declaration of Human Rights.

general welfare in a 'democratic society'.[47] Further, with the exception of the Convention Against Torture, which is focused on an absolute and non-derogable human right that applies to all States irrespective of their political system, the core United Nations human rights instruments provide a right to vote and participate in the democratic process[48] and/or establish that restrictions on individual rights can only be justified in the interests of a 'democratic society'.[49] Given that the States parties to human rights treaties are constructed as democratic States, the exercise of regulatory authority by IHRBs must be justified either by the original delegation of sovereign authority or in accordance with the democratic conception of legitimate political authority.

3.3 *IHRBs and the political conception of human rights*

A political conception understands human rights to be the product of an act of political will formation. While arguments from moral philosophy might inform debates around the nature, meaning, content and identity of rights, the concept of human rights only becomes meaningful at the point at which moral norms are codified in positive law. International human rights norms are the result of deliberation, debate and compromise and a positive act of political will formation by global institutions, notably the General Assembly of the United Nations, which adopted the core human rights instruments – and which express an under-theorized and inchoate account of certain of the necessary conditions of global political justice. In these circumstances, it seems implausible to conclude that democratic States will accept the claims of international human rights bodies to 'know better' on the subject of human rights. A further complexity emerges in the construction of the States parties to human rights treaties as democratic States, given that, in a democratic political system, all constitutional and political law norms, including human rights law norms, may be subject to contestation and challenge by reasonable citizens. Policies in a democratic

[47] Article 29, ibid.

[48] Article 25(2), International Covenant on Civil and Political Rights; Article 5(c), International Convention on the Elimination of All Forms of Racial Discrimination; and Article 7, Convention on the Elimination of All Forms of Discrimination against Women.

[49] Articles 14, 21, 22(2), International Covenant on Civil and Political Rights; Articles 4 and Article 8, International Covenant on Economic, Social and Cultural Rights; Article 15(2), Convention on the Rights of the Child. See also General Recommendation No. 32, The meaning and scope of special measures in the International Convention on the Elimination of Racial Discrimination, Committee on the Elimination of Racial Discrimination (Seventy-fifth session, August 2009), para. 16.

system are 'just', 'correct' or 'right' to the extent that they are consistent with the requirements of right process and substantive democratic principles, concerning for example political equality and public reason.

The importance of a self-government conception of democracy is confirmed by the facts of reasonable disagreement and imperfect knowledge in political discussions; the importance of private autonomy and public participation for the individual citizen; the requirement for (at least hypothetical) consent for the exercise of political authority; and the need for members of a political community to commit themselves to a process of collective decision-making that takes into account the interests of others within the community. A self-government conception does not understand human rights to be in an antagonistic relationship with political will-formation,[50] as it requires each democratic society to work out its own conception of 'human rights' through political deliberation and legal argument.[51] The approach can be seen in Jürgen Habermas' deliberative ideal of democracy, in which certain rights are viewed as essential for the functioning of the democratic system: the general right to equal liberties; membership rights; guaranteed legal remedies; and the right to the provision of basic living conditions required for citizens to have equal opportunities to exercise the other legal and democratic rights. Beyond these basic rights, the framework of rights and liberties that structures the social context of human existence is established through a process of political dialogue in accordance with the principle of public reason, with valid laws – including human rights provisions – receiving the assent of all affected citizens (Habermas 1996). Habermas also accepts a role for a world organization, such as the United Nations, in relation to human rights (Habermas 2007), with the domestic 'deliberative' conception of human rights developing in a way that is consistent with international human rights norms. Habermas concludes that all deliberative democracies will share similar visions of the just society, reflected in the standards recognized in universal human rights instruments, which give expression to the collective experiences of democratic peoples (Habermas 1998: 190).

John Rawls also refers to the ideal of a 'deliberative [or well-ordered constitutional] democracy', although in a different sense to Habermas.[52] Rawls

[50] This is in contrast to liberal theories that hold rights to be both prior and superior to democratic laws, typically 'rights as trumps' over collective positions. See Dworkin (1977).

[51] The requirement for legal argument is provided by the fact that human rights are, by their very nature, juridical rights.

[52] In Habermas' counterfactual ideal, the legal system emerges through a consensus arrived at through dialogue in which positions are accepted as legitimate only where agreed through

argues that the definitive idea of democracy is deliberation: the exchange of views and perspectives on political questions, with arguments supported by reasons. The concept of public reason applies in public political fora, i.e. to the discourses of judges in their decisions, in particular the discourses of judges on a constitutional court; the discourses of officials exercising governmental authority; and those of candidates for public office. The subject of public reason is the good of the public and the issue of political justice. The requirement of public reason does not apply to political law norms (although this is desirable), only to the constitutional essentials and questions of basic justice, including the nature, scope and content of human rights norms. The political community must reach a narrow constitutional consensus on the necessary political procedures of democratic government and a broader and deeper overlapping consensus on the constitutional essentials and elements of political justice, including certain substantive rights, such as freedom of conscience and thought; equality of opportunity; and the basic requirements of the human person (Rawls 2005: 163–164). Rawls argues that the overlapping consensus on human rights emerges through political debate and judicial review by the courts. Deliberation on the idea, nature, identity, scope and content of human rights is conducted by elected and appointed government officials and candidates for public office in accordance with the principle of public reason. Abstract and concrete human rights norms are then adopted, or not, as one part of the constitutional settlement. The function of judicial review is to develop the best interpretation of constitution norms, including human rights norms, that can be justified in terms of the public concept of justice and public reason, based on the relevant body of constitutional materials and precedents (Rawls 2005: 236). The constitution is not, however, the product of judicial decision-making and judicial reasoning: 'it is what the people acting constitutionally through the other branches eventually allow the Court to say it is' (Rawls 2005: 237). One of the functions of the constitutional court is to ensure that political discussions that address the content of human rights norms are undertaken 'in line with the political values of justice and public reason' (Rawls 2005: 239).

un-coerced rational discourses by those affected by the outcomes. In the practice of deliberative democracy, given that it is not possible for all persons to engage directly on all issues, citizens must be represented by others in parliamentary institutions responsible for the adoption of law norms; the function of the judiciary is limited to ensuring the procedural legitimacy of established law norms and interpreting the scope and content of laws established through political procedures. Cf. Habermas (1996).

Rawls' understanding of the role of constitutional courts, i.e. judicial bodies allocated the function of uncovering the meaning of a constitutional text, provides the basis for beginning to think about the role of international human rights bodies.[53] According to Rawls, the establishment of human rights norms within a deliberative community represents an overlapping constitutional consensus, which is reflected in the Constitution, Bill of Rights and other relevant instruments. The establishment of an agreed interpretation of the content of abstract human rights norms proceeds through parallel political and legal discourses. Government officials, candidates for public office and civil society actors engage in public political deliberations around the meaning of abstract human rights norms and their application in a particular context. The function of judicial review is to provide the best interpretation of the human rights provisions in the constitution, based on the constitutional materials and judicial precedents – in line with the political values of justice and public reason expressed in those public discourses.[54] The human rights recognized in the international law instruments reflect an 'overlapping consensus' on the idea of 'international human rights'. A human rights treaty can be understood as a constitutional text, with the function of the international human rights body established under the treaty, in line with Rawls' argument, being to interpret the primary human rights norms and the secondary norms about norms in accordance with the best interpretation of the text that can be justified in light of the terms of the text of the treaty and other relevant materials, including the *travaux préparatoires*, and the prior normative statements adopted by the IHRB in its Concluding Observations, Views, Recommendations and General Comments – in line with the overlapping consensus that emerges among the States parties to the regime.[55]

[53] The argument applies to international human rights law regimes that have undergone a process of 'constitutionalization'. In relation to other human rights regimes, the authority of IHRBs is established by the authority of international law and the requirement for the interpretation of international law instruments in accordance with the original will and intent of the States parties, taking into account the object and purpose of the treaty as a 'human rights' instrument.

[54] The process is also constrained by the disciplinary understandings of the interpretive community of lawyers: legal terms have specific meanings in the context of 'law' and must be understood in that context.

[55] In relation to the qualified autonomy rights in the European Convention on Human Rights (Articles 8–11), the European Court of Human Rights accepts that national authorities have direct democratic legitimation, and that States parties enjoy a certain 'margin of appreciation' in the application of convention rights, which will vary according to a number of criteria, including the existence (or otherwise) of a 'European consensus', reflected in national

There is no difficulty in identifying the judicial function of international human rights bodies in the development of a deeper understanding of the scope and content of international human rights law norms. The problem lies in the seeming absence of any parallel political discourses, in contrast to the position within the State, as international human rights law regimes do not provide a formal public space for political deliberation: actors can only influence the regime directly as participants in legal processes, as applicants, lawyers, etc. This is problematic, given Rawls' conclusion that human rights are the subject of public reason, i.e. deliberative reasoning, and that judicial decision-making and judicial reasoning on the content of human rights norms is subject to popular self-government through legislative and constitutional control. It would, though, be a mistake to conclude that IHRBs are completely insulated from deliberative reasoning within States parties and the deliberative reasoning of States parties in international organizations and institutions. First, and most obviously, IHRBs are informed about domestic political debates through an examination of the reports submitted by States parties on compliance with their human rights obligations; further, the submission of 'shadow reports' by non-governmental organizations can enhance the understanding of IHRBs through the highlighting of issues not raised by the government, or by asserting that the report of the State party does not reflect the true situation. Second, where an IHRB is empowered to receive individual complaints, it is able to consider both claims and counter-claims – and associated reasoning – as to whether a recognized human right has been violated (the prohibition against torture, for example) and arguments around the scope and content of abstract human rights norms (whether, for example, the right to privacy includes a right to a sexual identity). Third, the public reasoning of States parties, or, at least the reasoning of the government, is manifested through the adoption of treaties, resolutions and declarations on human rights by international organizations and institutions following deliberation and debate, which often occurs in representative fora, such as the General Assembly of the United Nations.

It is then possible to apply a revised conception of the Rawls' understanding of the function of constitutional courts to recognize a legitimate role for international human rights bodies in developing an understanding of the content of abstract human rights norms. The function of IHRBs

laws and the adoption of international instruments: cf. *Marckx v Belgium*, A31, para. 41; and *Goodwin v United Kingdom*, Reports of Judgments and Decisions 2002-VI, para. 85.

is not to give expression to moral rights, i.e. inherent rights we possess simply by virtue of 'being human', but to give expression to the overlapping consensus of the subjects of the regime on the issue of human rights: IHRBs are required to develop the best interpretation of the human rights norms recognized in the treaty, based on the text, and other relevant materials, and the legal reasoning developed in Concluding Observations, Views, Recommendations and General Comments, in line with the political values of justice and public reason expressed by States parties in domestic and global public discourses.

4. Conclusion

Drawing on the normal justification thesis developed by Joseph Raz, the objective of this chapter was to evaluate the extent to which States parties to international human rights law treaties should regard the Concluding Observations, Views, Recommendations and General Comments adopted by international human rights bodies as providing a conclusive, content-independent and exclusionary reason for action, or inaction. A democratic reading of the normal justification criterion establishes that States will accept the exercise of authority by IHRBs on two related grounds: first the delegation of authority by States parties in the establishment of the human rights regime, often following domestic democratic debates and procedures for the approval of accession to treaty regimes;[56] and, second, *either*, that the IHRB undertakes its function in accordance with the established principles for the interpretation of international law treaties, *or*, following the constitutionalization of the regime, that the international human rights body can demonstrate that it is better placed than the States parties to determine the content of abstract human rights norms through the development of an overlapping consensus based on the text of the treaty and the political debates occurring within the political systems of States parties and in international organizations and institutions.

The first step – the adoption of the international human rights treaty by sovereign States – is a necessary requirement, as there are no examples of human rights regimes emerging in the absence of a prior commitment by sovereign States to establish a human rights instrument. Whatever the motivations for adopting the treaty, once the Convention is in force, States

[56] In the majority of states, the mechanisms for adopting treaties are the same as for adopting national legislation: Hathaway (2008: 1362 ff.).

parties are expected to comply with their international law obligations – a position consistent with the normal justification thesis. States accept the authority of international law; the binding nature of international law agreements; and the international law principles for the interpretation of treaties, although there is general agreement that these principles are modified to some extent in the case of human rights treaties. The text of the treaty represents an agreement to recognize abstract moral norms in positive international law, but no commitment to develop a determinate understanding of 'human rights' or the introduction of measures to ensure their implementation within domestic legal systems.[57] The approach of the drafters of human rights law treaties appears in line with that of Lord Hoffmann, regarding 'human rights [as] universal in abstraction but national in application'.[58]

The complexity in the understanding of the regulatory function of IHRBs follows the second step – the constitutionalization of the human rights regime, following the adoption, by the international human rights body, of normative statements concerning substantive human rights provisions and the 'constitutional' norms about norms. The normal justification criterion establishes that IHRBs have legitimate authority in their own right where States parties would better conform to the reasons that apply to them by following the directives of the IHRBs than by acting independently. This is problematic given that the determination of the substantive content of 'human rights' will, in most cases, be better achieved at the domestic level – this is certainly the case in relation to functioning democracies, and it is to be remembered that human rights treaties construct the States parties as democratic States. Much of the detailed content of human rights must, then, be decided by domestic political and judicial processes, for the reason that there is no 'overlapping consensus', reflected in the text of the human rights instrument or the public political discourses that take place within States parties and international organizations and institutions. There is consequently a requirement for

[57] Consider, for example, the function of the Human Rights Committee, which – according to the International Covenant on Civil and Political Rights – is to provide 'reports' and 'general comments', and adopt 'views' on individual complaints. See above note 21 ff. (and accompanying text).

[58] Hoffmann (2009). In relation to the European Court of Human Rights, the States parties have committed themselves to a more extensive role in the text of the human rights instruments, with the European Convention on Human Rights providing that '[t]he jurisdiction of the Court shall extend to all matters concerning the interpretation and application of the Convention': Article 32(1), European Convention on Human Rights.

IHRBs to ensure that the content of abstract human rights norms in domestic settings is established (as far as possible) in accordance with a democratic procedural ideal. It follows that a primary function of IHRBs is to outline the necessary procedural requirements for domestic political systems, including, for example, requiring the involvement of representative institutions in decisions on important human rights issues; that the conduct of political debate proceeds in accordance with the principle of public reason; that all those affected by domestic regulations are able to participate effectively in democratic procedures; and that any interferences in the enjoyment of rights can be justified by reference to relevant legal principles, such as non-discrimination in the enjoyment of rights, and proportionality in the balance between individual rights and community interests.

A second primary function of international human rights bodies is to provide an interpretation of the content of human rights treaties consistent with a literal and logical approach to interpretation of international law norms and the overlapping consensus among the States parties on the convention rights, based on the treaty and other relevant materials, including the *travaux préparatoires*, and the legal reasoning developed in Concluding Observations, Views, Recommendations and General Comments. A complex picture emerges in which the understanding of human rights norms is developed through a constitutionalist reading of the treaty, in line with the 'precedents' established in the previous normative statements of the international human rights body (which may be the subject of critical commentary within the interpretive community of international human rights lawyers), with the juridical conception of human rights developing in parallel with the various political discourses around the idea in the domestic political systems of States parties and the debates in international organizations and institutions in which the States parties are engaged.

One final question: why would the democratic States parties of international human rights regimes accept the normative authority of international human rights bodies, i.e. why would a functioning democracy accept that a supranational court or tribunal were better placed to determine the content of abstract human rights norms? The answer lies in the idea of epistemic humility which is inherent in the practice of democracy, and which explains, for example, the function of judicial review in a democratic system. The claim of the democratic procedural system is that it is better placed to regulate the subjects of a State law regime than the subjects themselves, or any other political system, for the reason that a democratic procedural system is in a privileged position concerning knowledge of the 'just', 'correct' or 'right' course of action, expressed in terms of public policy positions and the adoption of political law norms, established through democratic procedural mechanisms, reflecting, in the counterfactual (deliberative) ideal, the consent of all those citizens affected by the policy. This is the claim that democracy makes to epistemic authority. Epistemic humility concerns the uncertainty that actors or institutions feel in the claim to 'know better', given that, in the practice of democracy, the political system will inevitably rely on 'majoritarianism', and one function of 'human rights' is to give expression to the idea that public policy positions and political law norms should not result in an injustice being applied to democratic minorities through an application of policy positions with majority support, but which cannot be justified in terms of the non-discrimination norm, the requirement of public reason or prohibition on the imposition of a disproportionate burden on democratic minorities, etc. In the practice of democracy, political and legal institutions must remain open to the possibility that they have failed to regulate in accordance with the interests and perspective of subjects, and that the coercive enforcement of law norms by government institutions constitutes an injustice for those unjustifiably subject to law norms.

The normal justification thesis establishes that the exercise of authority is legitimate where subjects accept that, in conditions of uncertainty and complexity, the authority is better placed to regulate the conditions of social, economic and political life than the subjects themselves. In a democratic system, the subjects will conclude that the only way in which governmental authority can ascertain the reasons that apply to them is by engaging with subjects through decision-making procedures which are responsive to interests and preferences of subjects. It seems, however, reasonable to conclude that existing and prospective democracies will share some minimum conception of legitimate democratic political authority, which can be expressed in terms of a morally worthy political culture (in Raz' terms) – as understood by democratic societies. The adoption of a human rights law treaty reflects a commitment by the State government to exercise political power in accordance with the values of a morally worthy political culture, and an acceptance of the difficulties of establishing such a culture in isolation from other political communities sharing a similar commitment. If this were not the case, democratic States would seek to develop an autonomous version of 'human rights'. The text of the human rights treaty represents an expression of the idea of a morally worthy political culture at a particular moment in time; it does not represent an understanding that the idea, scope and content of human rights has been settled, and there is an expectation that public political discourse on the idea of human rights will continue within States parties and between the States parties in global public discourses. The importance of international human rights bodies lies in their capacity to give expression to the logical and literal understanding of human rights norms and the overlapping consensus on 'human rights' (where the human rights treaty constructs States parties as democratic societies), reflecting a commitment by the democratic States parties to uncover together a collective understanding of the morally worthy political culture, and the inherent limits of legitimate political authority in democratic States. The role of IHRBs is not to provide an idealized expression of a moral reading of international human rights law, but to determine the normative obligation of States parties – and correlative convention rights of individuals – and this is only possible (following the normal justification thesis) where the States parties accept the authority of IHRBs. The understanding of the determinate content of abstract human rights norms will not reflect a moral conception of legitimate political power, or 'human rights', or a reading that results only from an autonomous reading of the international law instrument. The function of IHRBs in world society is to articulate the minimum content of the political conception of the morally worthy political culture as understood by the States parties, and reflected in the text and other relevant materials, the precedents and judicial reasoning developed by the IHRB and the overlapping consensus on human rights, as presently constructed in domestic and global political debates.

Bibliography

Austin, J., 1885. *Lectures on jurisprudence, or, The philosophy of positive law*, fifth edn, revised and edited by R. Campbell, London: John Murray.

Bodin, J., 1992. *On sovereignty: four chapters from The Six Books of the Commonwealth*, edited and translated by J. Franklin, Cambridge University Press.

Buergenthal, T., 2001. The UN Human Rights Committee. In J. A. Frowein & R. Wolfrum eds, *Max Planck yearbook of United Nations law*, 5, 341.

Crawford, J., 1997. An international criminal court? *Connecticut Journal of International Law*, 12, 255.

Dworkin, R., 1977. *Taking rights seriously*, London: Duckworths.

Gardbaum, S., 2009. Human rights and international constitutionalism. In J. L. Dunoff & J. P. Trachtman eds, *Ruling the world: constitutionalism, international law, and global governance*, Cambridge University Press, p. 233.

Greer, S., 2003. Constitutionalizing adjudication under the European Convention on Human Rights. *Oxford Journal of Legal Studies*, 23, 405.

Grotius, H., 1901. *The rights of war and peace, including the Law of Nature and of Nations*, translated from the Original Latin of Grotius, with Notes and Illustrations from Political and Legal Writers, by A. C. Campbell with an Introduction by D. J. Hill, New York: M. Walter Dunne.

Habermas, J., 1996. *Between facts and norms: contributions to a discourse theory of law and democracy*, transl. by W. Rehg, Oxford: Polity.

1998. *The inclusion of the other: studies in political theory*, Cambridge, MA: MIT Press.

2007. A political constitution for the pluralist world society? *Journal of Chinese Philosophy*, 34, 331.

Hamzic, V., 2011. The case of 'queer Muslims': sexual orientation and gender identity in international human rights law and Muslim legal and social ethos. *Human Rights Law Review*, 11, 237.

Hathaway, O., 2008. Treaties' end: the past, present, and future of international law-making in the United States. *Yale Law Journal*, 117, 1236.

Helfer, L. R. 2012. The burdens and benefits of Brighton. *ESIL Reflections*, 1(1). Available at: http://esil-sedi.eu/node/138. Last accessed 6 July 2012.

Helfer, L. R. & Miller, A. M., 1996. Sexual orientation and human rights: toward a United States and transnational jurisprudence. *Harvard Human Rights Journal*, 9, 61.

Hobbes, T., 1968. *Leviathan*, edited with an introduction by C. B. Macpherson, London: Penguin.

Hoffmann, Lord, 2009. The universality of human rights. Judicial Studies Board Annual Lecture, 19 March 2009. Available at: www.judiciary.gov.uk/media/speeches/2009/speech-lord-hoffman-19032009. Last accessed 10 May 2012.

Human Dignity Trust, www.humandignitytrust.org/. Last accessed 19 July 2012.

International Law Commission, 2006. Fragmentation of International Law: Difficulties Arising from the Diversification and Expansion of International Law. Report of the Study Group of the International Law Commission, Finalized by Martti Koskenniemi, UN Doc. A/CN.4/L.682, 13 April 2006.

Kennedy, D., 2007. One, two, three, many legal orders: legal pluralism and the cosmopolitan dream. *New York University Review of Law and Social Change*, 31, 641.

Klabbers, J., Peters, A. & Ulfstein, G., 2009. *The constitutionalization of international law*, Oxford University Press.

Lauren, P., 2003. *The evolution of international human rights*, second edn, Philadelphia: University of Pennsylvania Press.

Locke, J., 1960. *Two treatises of government*, edited with an introduction by P. Laslett, Cambridge University Press.

Lucas, J., 1966. *The principles of politics*, Oxford: Clarendon Press.

Luhmann, N., 1985. *A sociological theory of law*, transl. by E. King & M. Albrow, London: Routledge & Kegan Paul.

2004. *Law as a social system*, transl. by K. Ziegert, Oxford University Press.

Mazower, M., 2004. The strange triumph of human rights, 1933–1950. *The Historical Journal*, 47, 379.

McGoldrick, D., 1994. *The Human Rights Committee: its role in the development of the International Covenant on Civil and Political Rights*, Oxford: Clarendon.

Moravcsik, A., 2000. The origins of human rights regimes: democratic delegation in postwar Europe. *International Organization*, 54, 217.

Moyn, S., 2010. *The last utopia: human rights in history*, Cambridge, MA.; London: Belknap.

OHCHR 2004. UN Office of the High Commissioner for Human Rights, Factsheet No. 15 (Rev.). Civil and Political Rights: The Human Rights Committee. Available at: www.ohchr.org/Documents/Publications/FactSheet15rev.1en.pdf. Last accessed 24 July 2012.

Rawls, J., 2005. *Political liberalism*, New York; Chichester: Columbia University Press.

Raz, J., 1979. *The authority of law*, Oxford: Clarendon Press.

1986. *The morality of freedom*, Oxford University Press.

1994. *Ethics in the public domain: essays in the morality of law and politics*, Oxford: Clarendon.

2006. The problem of authority: revisiting the service concept. *Minnesota Law Review*, 90, 1003.

2009. *Between authority and interpretation: on the theory of law and practical reason*, Oxford University Press.

2010a. Human rights in the emerging world order. *Transnational Legal Theory*, 1, 31.

2010b. Human rights without foundations. In S. Besson & J. Tasioulas eds, *The philosophy of international law*, Oxford University Press, p. 321.

Sadurski, W., 2006. Law's legitimacy and 'democracy-plus'. *Oxford Journal of Legal Studies*, 26, 377.

Tasioulas, J., 2010. The legitimacy of international law. In S. Besson & J. Tasioulas eds, *The philosophy of international law*, Oxford University Press, p. 97.

Tomuschat, C., 2008. International Covenant on Civil and Political Rights. United Nations Audiovisual Library of International Law. Accessible at: http://untreaty.un.org/cod/avl/ha/iccpr/iccpr.html. Last accessed 24 July 2012.

de Vattel, E., 1916. *Le droit des gens, ou, Principes de la loi naturelle: appliqués à la conduite et aux affaires des nations et des souverains*, with an

introduction by A. de Lapradelle, Washington, DC: Carnegie Institution of Washington.
Wheatley, S., 2010. *The democratic legitimacy of international law*, Oxford, Hart.
2011. A democratic rule of international law. *European Journal of International Law*, 22, 525.

4

Equality, human rights, and political legitimacy

KRISTEN HESSLER

1. Introduction

States that ratify international human rights treaties also sign on to the process of interpretation via the treaty body system, which oversees the implementation of the major international human rights treaties within states that have ratified them. While such oversight might be obviously justifiable regarding illegitimate states that egregiously violate human rights, the UN treaty bodies oversee implementation in legitimate states as well. For example, in 2006, the Human Rights Committee (HRC), which monitors implementation of the International Covenant on Civil and Political Rights (ICCPR), issued its "concluding observations" in response to the United States' reports. In these comments, the HRC noted with concern that in the United States "about five million citizens cannot vote due to a felony conviction, and that this practice has racial implications." The HRC continued:

> The State party should adopt appropriate measures to ensure that states restore voting rights to citizens who have fully served their sentences and those who have been released on parole … The State party should also assess the extent to which such regulations disproportionately impact on the rights of minority groups and provide the Committee with detailed information in this regard.
>
> (United Nations Human Rights Committee 2006, p. 11)

I thank the editors for inviting me to be a part of this project, and the other contributors for helpful feedback on very early drafts. I am indebted to Jonathan Mandle for valuable discussions on the broader issues in this paper, and to Joseph Boskovski for many illuminating discussions about felon disenfranchisement laws. And for constructive comments on an earlier draft, I thank Joseph Boskovski, Allen Buchanan, Andreas Føllesdal, Johan Karlsson Schaffer, Christopher Wellman, and the attendees at Binghamton University's Conference on Philosophy and International Law in April 2012.

Notice that these recommendations include both a procedural one regarding the HRC (that the USA provides information to the HRC), and a substantive one (that the USA changes its laws and policies regarding felon disenfranchisement). My question in this paper is whether recommendations of either kind by UN treaty bodies are authoritative for legitimate states. At the limit, regarding the HRC's substantive policy recommendations as authoritative interpretations of the treaty provisions would seem to require the USA to change state-level policies *because* the HRC recommended doing so. However, legitimate states traditionally have been thought to have rights to nonintervention in their domestic affairs that are incompatible with granting such interpretive authority to treaty bodies. Compounding this problem is the fact that UN human rights treaty bodies do not themselves seem to satisfy traditional standards of domestic political legitimacy grounded in the values of democracy or consent. In this vein, for example, Kenneth Anderson asks: "We count democratic legitimacy to be the sine qua non of legitimacy of the sovereign national state, but why, I wonder, do we suddenly jettison it when it comes to the international system … ?" (Anderson 2000, p. 103). This question suggests that international human rights institutions may turn out to be illegitimate themselves, if we judge them by the same standards of legitimacy that we use for states.

I argue that an adequate analysis of this problem requires careful consideration of our particular conceptions of both human rights and normative political legitimacy. Underlying the most promising accounts of political legitimacy and human rights is the value of the equal moral standing of citizens. Only a sufficiently institutional conception of human rights – one that, in Thomas Pogge's terms, understands human rights "primarily as claims on coercive social institutions and secondarily as claims against those who uphold such institutions" (Pogge 2002, pp. 44–45) – can adequately diagnose whether the organization of a state's social and political institutions is consistent with the equal standing of its citizens. Moreover, the equal standing of citizens is an important foundation for Rawls's liberal principle of political legitimacy, which grounds the right of legitimate states to noninterference in the collective right to self-determination of the members of a political community of equals. I argue that this sense of legitimacy is essential for connecting human rights and the self-determination of legitimate states. According to this account, legitimacy is not a clearly demarcated threshold concept, but rather a scalar predicate that can be more or less realized along multiple dimensions of both political procedures and their policy outcomes.[1] Moreover, given that equality of citizens is a foundational value for both legitimacy and human rights, a state's improved human rights record also improves its internal political legitimacy. Thus, UN treaty bodies should be seen as supranational institutions designed to improve the legitimacy of states by improving the realization of human rights in state-level social and political institutions. For these reasons, states have strong reasons, connected to both their obligations to realize human rights and their own internal legitimacy, to regard the procedural recommendations of treaty bodies for their participation in these regimes as authoritative. Moreover, while treaty bodies are not constituted with the political power to effect policy changes within states, my argument nonetheless suggests that agents with political power within states have strong reasons to advocate for changes along the lines of treaty body recommendations. Finally, it follows from this argument that treaty bodies need not meet traditional standards of legitimacy for states, given that they do not govern in the same sense as states, but rather are a means of improving the legitimacy and human rights records of states.

2. The concept of normative legitimacy

A theory of normative political legitimacy is intended to specify conditions under which the exercise of political power is morally justified. This contrasts with a sociological or descriptive concept of legitimacy, according to which an institution is legitimate if its directives are, as a matter of fact, widely accepted as binding by those it claims the authority to direct. The sociological and normative concepts of legitimacy are importantly connected. Institutions are often said to be legitimate in the descriptive or sociological sense if their subjects and other salient agents generally believe that they are legitimate in the normative sense. Thus, the sociological concept of legitimacy typically assumes some conception of normative legitimacy, attributed to the subjects of the relevant institution.[2] Conversely, conceptions of normative legitimacy typically assume (sometimes tacitly) that legitimate institutions should be capable of being recognized and supported as such by those whom they purport to command.

[1] In this way, liberal political legitimacy is analogous to Thomas Pogge's description of democracy as "a scalar predicate, as political systems can be more or less democratic in multiple dimensions" (Pogge 2002, p. 147).

[2] Though Thomas Christiano argues that Thomas Hobbes and John Austin held that "[s]ubjects need not think of the authority as a legitimate authority" (Christiano 2013).

As John Rawls has argued, the circumstances of political decision-making include the pervasiveness of deep and persistent reasonable disagreement, not only about the content of political decisions but also about how such decisions should be made, and by whom. It is in the context of such disagreement that questions of political legitimacy arise. According to Thomas Christiano, for example:

> The role of considerations of inherent political legitimacy is to define a fair system of collective decision-making when there is disagreement on the substance of the decisions and fundamental interests are at stake. It answers the question: by what right has this decision been made and imposed on all? It determines who has the right to make certain decisions. If a system of decision-making is legitimate then the decisions become legitimate as well (within some clearly defined limits). Members then have content-independent reasons to go along with decisions even if they think them unjust. These reasons are grounded in the right of the legitimate decision-maker.
>
> (Christiano 2010, p. 120)

To the extent that subjects have "content-independent reasons" to comply with the exercise of political power by legitimate institutions, assessments of legitimacy must go beyond justifying the substance of the rules or commands issued by a legitimate authority. In other words, legitimacy necessarily concerns the structures or procedures of the relevant political institutions, and not just the content of their commands. One important implication of this is that considerations of legitimacy are at least to some extent divorced from substantive standards of justice – that is, it is perfectly consistent to argue that an institution is justified in exercising political power even if that institution is not completely just (or if the question whether it is completely just is itself a matter of reasonable disagreement). Indeed, some scholars emphasize the distance between justice and legitimacy as an element of the concept of normative legitimacy itself. As Allen Buchanan and Robert Keohane argue, for example:

> actors must not assume that an institution is worthy of support only if it is fully just. We thus need a standard of legitimacy that is both accessible from a diversity of moral standpoints and less demanding than a standard of justice. Such a standard must appeal to various actors' capacities to be moved by moral reasons, but without presupposing more moral agreement than exists.
>
> (Buchanan & Keohane 2006, p. 409)

A further implication of the fact that subjects of legitimate institutions have content-independent reasons to comply with their directives is that even unjust directives do not, by themselves, undermine the right of legitimate institutions to exercise political power. There is a limit to how unjust the directives of legitimate institutions can be before their legitimacy is undermined by their injustice; as Rawls writes, "[l]egitimacy allows an undermined range of injustice that justice might not permit" (Rawls 1993, p. 428). Thus, legitimacy confers a moral justification in the exercise of political power, which in turn confers at least some right against interference and correlative duties on both subjects and outsiders not to undermine legitimate institutions.

Taking these analyses of the concept of normative political legitimacy together, three important features emerge: first, questions of legitimacy arise in the context of reasonable disagreement, including disagreement about justice; second, subjects of a legitimate political institution have content-independent reasons to comply with that institution's directives (at least within certain limits); and third, legitimate institutions are entitled to a certain level of noninterference.

3. Legitimacy, sovereignty, and human rights

Given this analysis of the concept of normative legitimacy, a foundational challenge to the normative legitimacy of international human rights bodies is constituted by the fact that legitimate (even if not fully just) state governments already exist, and are entitled to at least a certain level of noninterference. If legitimate states with substantive laws, policies, or practices that do not comply with international human rights law are nonetheless entitled to noninterference regarding their domestic policies, including those relevant to implementing human rights within their borders, then the best we can do is to strike some kind of balance between interfering in legitimate states to support human rights, or respecting state sovereignty at the expense of human rights.

Working within this general framework, Christopher Wellman recently argued that "if we take human rights as seriously as we should, then even a legitimate state has no principled objection to outsiders' intervening in its internal affairs if this interference will prevent just a single human rights violation" (Wellman 2012, p. 119). I argue in this section that Wellman's argument is flawed but instructive, insofar as it relies on a traditional but problematic conception of human rights, and insofar as it fails to account for the full moral significance of political legitimacy. When we approach the question with better accounts of both concepts, we shall see that legitimate states have a much stronger claim against intervention (even interventions on behalf of human rights) than Wellman concedes.

Wellman's argument takes aim at what he takes to be roughly the consensus view among philosophers: "that all and only legitimate states are entitled to self-determination, where a state is legitimate just in case it satisfactorily protects the human rights of its constituents and respects the rights of all others" (Wellman 2012, p. 121). On Wellman's reconstruction, the received view incorporates a fairly stringent view of sovereignty, understood as "moral dominion over its self-regarding affairs – a right of self-determination which includes a claim against external intervention" (Wellman 2012, p. 119). Human rights, on Wellman's view, "are the protections generally needed against the standard and direct threats to leading a minimally decent human life in modern society" (Wellman 2012, p. 119). As Wellman notes, when legitimate states fail to protect the rights of their citizens (while still remaining legitimate), this would seem to create a moral conflict for external agents, because they cannot respect both the state's right to nonintervention and the human rights of the state's subjects.

Wellman's main argument centers around the following example:

> Imagine that I live in a state which performs the requisite political functions flawlessly. That is to say, it assigns itself all and only the tasks a state may permissibly undertake, and it performs each of them perfectly ... This all changed yesterday, however, when I was wrongly convicted of kidnapping, torturing, and then killing two young boys. Suppose however, that, while I am entirely innocent and therefore was wrongly convicted, the state was in no way culpable in arriving at this judgment. That is, all of my procedural rights were fully respected, and the police, prosecutors, judge, and jury all acted as they should have in arresting me, prosecuting me, and finding me guilty. (To make this somewhat believable, suppose that I was cleverly framed and/or that, because of some freak biological coincidence, my DNA matched that of the actual perpetrator.)
>
> (Wellman 2012, pp. 124–125)

Wellman's argument that intervention would be permissible in such a case starts with his plausible assertion that he is under no moral obligation to remain in jail, if he had the opportunity to escape (if, for example, he was in possession of a Ring of Gyges which could turn him invisible so he could sneak out of jail). He then argues that his mother, knowing his innocence, could permissibly help him escape:

> What if she had two Rings of Gyges, and she could turn herself invisible, sneak into the jail, give me the second ring, and then help me escape? Is there any reason that she may not do so? I do not see why. After all, if I do indeed act permissibly in escaping, it is hard to see why she should not aid my efforts.
>
> (Wellman 2012, p. 125)

Wellman modifies the example in three more steps. If his mother is permitted to help him escape, he argues, it should not make a difference that his mother is actually a Swedish citizen (rather than a fellow-citizen of his fictional perfectly legitimate state). Nor should it affect the substance of the argument if his mother is actually the Prime Minister of Sweden, he argues. And finally, assuming that the Prime Minister of Sweden is not his mother, she should still be permitted to help him escape. Wellman concludes that, in this example,

> we have step by step arrived at a situation in which a political leader may permissibly intervene in the execution of a foreign country's criminal sentence of a person who was duly convicted of a crime which was committed on that country's territory against that country's constituents. In other words, we have an (admittedly idiosyncratic) humanitarian intervention into a legitimate state which is justified by its promise to prevent a single rights violation.
>
> (Wellman 2012, p. 125–126)

3.1 *What are human rights?*

Wellman's argument crucially depends on his understanding of human rights as "the protections generally needed against the standard and direct threats to leading a minimally decent human life in modern society" (Wellman 2012, p. 119). This brief account is obviously not supposed to be a complete theory of human rights, but rather a marker indicating that Wellman is working within a family of theories according to which human rights are indexed to human needs. Theories of this general type explain the urgency of human rights by reference to the urgency of the needs they represent. They tend to generate sparse rather than lengthy lists of human rights (in Wellman's formulation, this is due to the idea of a "minimally decent human life"). Needs-based accounts of human rights also rely on some account of the good human life, which generates the list of needs that grounds human rights. Each of these features has theoretical advantages and disadvantages. For example, the urgency connected with a minimal list of human rights allows theorists to explain why human rights generate overriding moral obligations to protect them, and also provides a bulwark against the proliferation of rights claims; however, the same minimalism may lead to contentiously short lists of human rights. Moreover, basing an account of human rights on a conception of what is needed for a minimally decent human life raises concerns about parochialism regarding how a minimally decent human life is defined.

For our purposes, however, a different and more general feature of Wellman's conception of human rights in this argument is more salient. This is that Wellman's argument neglects what Thomas Pogge calls the institutional dimension of any adequate conception of human rights. On Pogge's institutional understanding of human rights, human rights are understood "primarily as claims on coercive social institutions and secondarily as claims against those who uphold such institutions" (Pogge 2002, pp. 44–45). By contrast, an "interactionist" conception of human rights "presents human rights as placing the treatment of human beings under certain constraints that do not presuppose the existence of social institutions" (Pogge 2002, pp. 44–45). As an example of this contrast, Pogge argues that having one's car stolen by a thief is not obviously, by itself, a human rights violation, even if "the car may be its owner's most important asset," while "[a]n arbitrary confiscation of her car by the government, on the other hand, does strike us as a human-rights violation, even if she has several other cars left. This suggests that human-rights violations, to count as such, must be in some sense official, and that human rights thus protect persons only against violations from certain sources" (Pogge 2002, p. 57).[3]

While Wellman's example does implicate official conduct, since the state is the agent of the wrongful imprisonment in the example, by itself the identity of the actor does not capture the force of the institutional account. Beyond "implicating official conduct in some way," an institutional account of human rights holds that asserting a human right to X implies "that any society or other social system, insofar as this is reasonably possible, ought to be so (re)organized that all its members have secure access to X, with 'security' always understood as especially sensitive to persons' risk of being denied X or deprived of X officially: by the government or its agents or officials" (Pogge 2002, p. 64). Assessing whether this standard is met requires an examination of the structure of social and political institutions in a particular society, not just the presence or absence of discrete human rights violations. Consider the following contrasting cases:

> A person may fully enjoy X even while her access to X is insecure (as when persons relevantly like her, say blacks or vocal government opponents, are beaten or threatened). Conversely, a person may be temporarily deprived of X, through a crime by a rogue government official perhaps, in a society that is very effective in preventing crimes of the relevant type. Opposite to

[3] Note also that this example strains the connection between human rights and needs.

> the interactional understanding, my institutional one regards only the first case as a human-rights problem.
>
> (Pogge 2008, p. 71)

Notice that Pogge uses the term "human rights problem" in his comparative analysis of these two cases. This is because shifting to an institutional conception of human rights requires paying attention to whether human rights are fulfilled in the institutional order as a whole; information about the existence of discrete human rights violations will not suffice, on the institutional model, to establish the existence of a "human rights problem." As Pogge interprets the institutional account of human rights, therefore, it links "human rights fulfillment with insecurity rather than violation":

> On the interactional understanding of human rights, governments and individuals have a responsibility not to violate human rights. On my institutional understanding, by contrast, their responsibility is to work for an institutional order and public culture that ensure that all members of society have secure access to the objects of their human rights.
>
> (Pogge 2008, p. 71)

Recall that in Wellman's example of his wrongful imprisonment as a human rights violation, all the protections that a state can provide against such a miscarriage of justice were, *ex hypothesi*, in place. Given that the state in the example performed all "requisite political functions flawlessly," there is literally nothing within the realm of possibility the state could have done, much less should have done, to have avoided the unfortunate miscarriage of justice. Thus, while the wrongful imprisonment in Wellman's example may turn out to be a human rights violation, an appropriately institutional account of human rights would also note that human rights against wrongful imprisonment are as fulfilled as it is possible for any institutional order to ensure in this fictional state. Thus, all the institutional considerations available in this case suggest that the state in question had no human rights problem at all, despite the existence of this particular human rights violation.

The question then shifts to whether the existence of a single human rights violation provides an appropriate standard to use in arguments about political legitimacy and justified intervention, or whether it is better instead to index such arguments to the degree of human rights fulfillment in the institutional order. While I offer a more detailed argument against basing arguments about legitimacy and nonintervention on single human rights violations in the next section, for now I point out that two features of Wellman's argument suggest caution regarding such an approach. The first is that, in Wellman's example, the Prime Minister of Sweden, in rescuing the wrongfully imprisoned man, does not act in her official capacity qua head of state; indeed, she does not act publicly at all, but rather secretly, using a Ring of Gyges. Given this, we should be skeptical that any principle that follows from this case can convincingly carry over to the question of how official cross-border interventions might be morally justified. Second, each of the specific interventions that Wellman argues would be justified in his example are all cases in which individual agents have the power to successfully intervene to prevent a grave harm to a specific individual, "without any collateral damage or otherwise deleterious diplomatic side-effects" (Wellman 2012, p. 130). Given this, it seems likely that what is doing the intuitive work in Wellman's example is not so much a theory of human rights, but rather intuitions about the moral duty of rescue. In other words, while the case for rescuing the wrongly imprisoned man in the example is strong, it's not at all clear that this implies that "even a legitimate state has no principled objection to outsiders' intervening in its internal affairs if this interference will prevent just a single human rights violation" (Wellman 2012, p. 119). Legitimate states may have strong principled objections grounded in considerations of political legitimacy (or so I will argue); these principled objections may turn out to be overridden by the moral duty of rescue in this exceptional case, but that does not establish that they don't exist in the first place.

3.2 *How are institutions relevant?*

Recall that Pogge describes an interactional conception of human rights as one that "presents human rights as placing the treatment of human beings under certain constraints that do not presuppose the existence of social institutions" (Pogge 2002, pp. 44–45). But, importantly, Wellman's argument does not literally proceed as if institutions do not exist – after all, he specifies the exceptional virtues of the political institutions of his fictional state, and the conclusion of his argument is that a sitting Prime Minister may permissibly intervene in a legitimate state to rectify a human rights violation. So, institutions do appear in Wellman's argument. However, the moral duties at work in Wellman's example do not themselves adequately track the moral significance of these institutions; instead, all the moral duties and constraints in Wellman's argument themselves exist independently of the workings of any social or political institutions. The institutions in Wellman's example function merely as stage-setting; morally, they are inert.

When we describe the point this way, it becomes clear that Wellman is not alone in discussing human rights in insufficiently institutional terms. For example, Onora O'Neill has persistently cautioned against reliance on human rights in theorizing about international justice, on grounds that human rights obscure what she takes to be the central question of justice; namely, who ought to do what for whom. In contrast to liberty rights, which assign to others only negative obligations, O'Neill argues that

> [r]ights to goods and services can be thought of only in the hazy way which the rhetoric of rights favours and allows until they are at least partly institutionalized. It may be possible to state what ought to be provided or delivered, but it will be impossible to state who ought to do the providing or delivering, and who can be called to account when deliveries are botched, or nothing is delivered, unless there are established institutions and well-defined special relationships. Rights to goods and services are easy to proclaim, but until there are effective institutions their proclamation may seem bitter mockery to those who most need them.
>
> (O'Neill 2000, p. 105)

Here O'Neill ascribes an essential role to institutions in specifying the obligations correlative with human rights and assigning them to particular agents. However, and importantly for my purposes, O'Neill does not regard political institutions as sources of moral obligations in their own right, nor do they transform the moral obligations correlative to human rights in any substantive way. This leaves out a significant aspect of an institutional perspective on human rights, which is captured best in one of Pogge's descriptions of the distinction between the institutional and interactional accounts of human rights:

> An *institutional* conception postulates certain fundamental principles of social *justice*. They apply to institutional schemes and are thus second-order principles: standards for assessing the ground rules and practices that regulate human interactions. An *interactional* conception, by contrast, postulates certain fundamental principles of *ethics*. These principles, like institutional ground rules, are first-order in that they apply directly to the conduct of persons and groups.
>
> (Pogge 2002, p. 170, original emphasis)

Rather than providing standards for assessing shared practices that are mediated by political institutions, O'Neill's analysis relegates institutions merely to the instrumental role of specifying and allocating the obligations determined by ethical theory to correlate with human rights. In Pogge's terms, institutions for O'Neill serve only to make first-order obligations determinate and actionable.

While theorizing about human rights understood primarily in interactional terms is important for some philosophical questions, the institutional conception of human rights is clearly more relevant to questions about the relationship between political legitimacy, human rights, and justified cross-border interventions.

3.3 *Equality as a foundational value for human rights*

Thus far, I have argued that an institutional conception of human rights is essential for capturing the relevance of human rights for political legitimacy. In this and the following subsections, I pursue a positive argument to the effect that an institutional account of human rights is required in order to accommodate the value that equal moral standing of citizens plays in both human rights and in the most convincing account of political legitimacy.

There is currently no real consensus among philosophers on the moral values that ground human rights.[4] For our purposes, however, it is salient that several theorists recently have argued that any adequate understanding of human rights must recognize their concern for the equal moral standing of citizens in social and political institutions. In a recent paper, for example, Allen Buchanan argues that international human rights practice embodies an idea of equal status for all human beings. Buchanan notes that "philosophers have failed to appreciate that, in the historical process by which IHR [international human rights] emerged, equality of status has been a central concern" (Buchanan 2010, p. 688). In particular, according to Buchanan, the history of the practice as it emerged out of the global movement to end the slave trade, anti-colonialism, and in the aftermath of the Holocaust, reveals a consistent concern with equal status as an animating drive of the international human rights movement itself. Rainer Forst also argues that the earlier history of the concept of human rights reveals a foundational concern with equality, arguing that "the original meaning of human rights was a republican rather than a classic liberal one," in which the Levellers claimed rights to "property, liberty, and freedom" as "the means that would make them

[4] See, for example, the very different views in James Griffin (2008) and Charles Beitz (2009).

independent social and political agents, free from feudal domination or tyrannical rule" (Forst 2010, p. 717).

In addition to an historical concern for equality, both Buchanan and Forst find (different) substantive ways in which human rights practice embodies a commitment to institutional recognition of the moral equality of persons. For example, Buchanan notes that human rights practice ascribes human rights and equality before the law to all citizens (not, for example, just to whites, or to men, or to those wealthy enough to secure their rights for themselves). Moreover, international human rights practice articulates strong claims on behalf of all individuals to rights of political participation, social and economic rights sufficient for a decent life (and to enable one to participate in political life), and explicit rights against discrimination on the basis of race or gender. Finally, both the right to work and rights to an adequate standard of living are understood in human rights practice in what Buchanan calls a "social-comparative way": that is, as both recognizing the equal moral status of all individuals and protecting this status against the risks of being regarded as a noncontributor (if one does not work) or of being humiliated by one's poor standard of living. Most philosophical theories of human rights accept a requirement of reasonable fidelity between the list of rights endorsed by philosophical theory and the lists of rights found in international human rights practice. It is this requirement that Buchanan has in mind when he writes: "My point is not that the protection of equal status is the sole value that grounds modern human rights, only that it is sufficiently prominent that a critical reconstruction of IHR [international human rights] ought to take it into account" (Buchanan 2010, p. 690).

Forst, taking the same line of argument further, argues that moral equality of persons is, in fact, the sole grounding value of human rights:

> The moral basis for human rights, as I reconstruct it, is the respect for the human person as an autonomous agent who possesses a right to justification, that is, a right to be recognized as an agent who can demand acceptable reasons for any action that claims to be morally justified and for any social or political structure of law that claims to be binding upon him or her. Human rights secure the equal standing of persons in the political and social world, based on a fundamental moral demand of respect.
>
> (Forst 2010, p. 719)

Notice that Forst's view of human rights is necessarily what Pogge would call an institutional account – one in which human rights claims are understood primarily as claims on the organization of political institutions.[5] Even on Buchanan's more limited view of the role of status equality in human rights, this element of human rights is primarily a set of requirements on the structure of a state's social and political institutions. Insofar as a solely interactionist theory of human rights focuses on discrete human rights violations, rather than on the structure of the institutional order in which those violations take place, it cannot adequately account for a commitment to the equal moral status of citizens; that is, we cannot adequately diagnose violations of the status egalitarian element of human rights without careful inquiry into the structures of the relevant political institutions.

An example may help to make this clearer. As the Human Rights Committee noted in its comments on the report by the United States on the implementation of the ICCPR, the practice of felon disenfranchisement in the USA is extensive, and, importantly for our purposes, has strongly disproportionate negative impacts on nonwhite racial groups. Currently, only 2 states do not disenfranchise even those who are currently in prison; the remaining 48 states "vary widely over whether those on probation or parole are disenfranchised, and whether fines and assessments must be paid in full, even if that means an ex-convict who typically will have limited employment prospects, may be effectively disenfranchised for life" (Chin 2007, p. 330). As one study notes, "Among postindustrial democracies, the United States is virtually the only nation to permanently disenfranchise ex-felons as a class in many jurisdictions, and the only country to limit the rights of individuals convicted of offenses other than very rare treason or election-related crimes" (Uggen & Manza 2002, p. 778). When this is combined with the fact that "the United States is also exceptional for the rate at which it issues felony convictions" (Uggen & Manza 2002, p. 778), the impacts of felon disenfranchisement on voting rights across the population are severe.

The disproportionate impact of felony disenfranchisement along racial lines is striking: approximately 13 percent of black men in the United States cannot vote due to a current or past felony conviction (The Sentencing Project 2012). In addition to the disproportionate numbers of black men who are currently prohibited from voting as a result of these laws, research

[5] Similarly, Jamie Mayerfeld argues that an account of human rights must incorporate the principle that "people deserve to be recognized and treated as equals," which in turn "upholds a claim to be accorded equal standing in the communities, especially the political communities, to which we belong" (Mayerfeld 2009, p. 59).

has shown that adoption of felon disenfranchisement laws in the first place was historically more likely in jurisdictions with a reasonable expectation of disproportionate racial impacts; for example, one study showed that "[s]tates with greater nonwhite prison populations have been more likely to ban convicted felons from voting than states with proportionally fewer nonwhites in the criminal justice system" (Behrens, Uggen, & Manza 2003, p. 596).

Given that "felon disenfranchisement laws are 'race neutral' on their face" (Behrens, Uggen, & Manza 2003, p. 560), their disproportionate impact along racial lines can only be seen at the aggregate population level. This example helps to demonstrate an important practical difference between interactional and institutional approaches to human rights: it is difficult to see how the interactional conception of human rights could capture the extent to which existing felon disenfranchisement laws might amount to a violation of the civil and political rights of racial minorities as a group in the United States. However, evidence that felon disenfranchisement laws, passed in some states with explicitly racist agendas,[6] and with disproportionate impacts on the political voice of racial minorities, strongly supports the conclusion that racial minorities do not enjoy civil and political rights as securely as whites in the United States. While it is beyond the scope of this paper to determine whether felony disenfranchisement laws in the United States constitute a human rights violation,[7] it should be clear that arguments on this topic must contend with the disproportionate impacts of actual felon disenfranchisement laws on the political and social status of nonwhite citizens. For this purpose, we need an institutional account of human rights – one that primarily assesses whether the "institutional order and public culture" combine to "ensure that all members

[6] For example, the unanimous Mississippi Supreme Court decision *Ratliff v. Beale* (1896) explicitly describes this agenda as a way of working around the prohibitions on direct discrimination against "the negro race," which the Court described as "a recently enfranchised race, unfitted by educational experience for the responsibility thrust upon it." Therefore, the opinion declares, the state of Mississippi instead "discriminated against its characteristics and the offenses to which its weaker members were prone ... Burglary, theft, arson, and obtaining money under false pretenses were declared to be disqualifications, while robbery and murder and other crimes ... were not" (20 So. 868, cited in Chin 2007, p. 331).

[7] For example, Andrew Altman argues that "a democratic citizenry has a collective right to make its own decision to disenfranchise for the duration of their imprisonment felons who commit serious crimes" (Altman 2005, p. 271). This principled conclusion is detached in Altman's argument from an analysis of American felony disenfranchisements in their particular historical context, but Altman argues that his conclusion counters some of the most salient arguments against felon disenfranchisement even when this context is taken into account.

of society have secure access to the objects of their human rights" (Pogge 2008, p. 71).

3.4 Legitimacy and collective self-determination

Considerations of status equality in the institutional order are essential for evaluating not only the level of human rights fulfillment within a state, but also, I argue in this section, a state's internal political legitimacy. To make this argument, I need to distinguish between two senses of "legitimacy." In Wellman's argument, legitimacy functions as a lower standard than full justice, though sufficient to qualify for rights of sovereignty:

> [R]ather than insist that a state can be legitimate only if it performs the requisite political functions perfectly, it seems more appropriate to demand merely that it do an adequate job. If the requisite political function is thought to be protecting human rights, for instance, it seems unreasonable to insist that a state cannot be legitimate unless it ensures that none of its constituents ever has her human rights violated. Such a high standard is not realistically achievable in this world, so it seems more natural to specify that a state can qualify as legitimate just in case it does a satisfactory job of protecting the rights of everyone within its jurisdiction.
>
> (Wellman 2012, p. 121)

In understanding legitimacy in this way, Wellman builds on an aspect of legitimacy as it functions in Rawls's work. Rawls articulates this element of legitimacy in *Political Liberalism*: "A significant aspect of the idea of legitimacy is that it allows a certain leeway in how well sovereigns may rule and how far they may be tolerated" (Rawls 1993, p. 427). Moreover, in *The Law of Peoples*, Rawls distinguishes "decent" peoples, which respect Rawls's truncated list of human rights and maintain a nonaggressive foreign policy, from outlaw states, which do not. For Rawls, this distinction marks the boundary of toleration on the international stage: outlaw states have no right to be tolerated as members in good standing of the international community (though Rawls himself does not use the term "legitimacy" in this context).

However, the description of legitimacy as merely a lower standard than justice leaves out an important component of the concept of legitimacy – namely, the argument for why legitimacy entails toleration. This is easiest to see if we look first at Rawls's more demanding conception of legitimacy, as he develops it in his later work on domestic political philosophy. As Rawls states it, the "liberal principle of legitimacy" maintains that "our exercise of political power is fully proper only when it is exercised in accordance with a constitution the essentials of which all citizens as free and equal may reasonably be expected to endorse in the light of principles and ideals acceptable to their common human reason" (Rawls 1993, p. 137). This conception of liberal legitimacy, Rawls argues, plays "a special role in democratic institutions," which is "to authorize an appropriate procedure for making decisions when the conflicts and disagreements in political life make unanimity impossible or rarely to be expected" (Rawls 1993, p. 427). In this sense, "[a] legitimate procedure is one that all may reasonably accept as free and equal when collective decisions must be made and agreement is normally lacking" (Rawls 1993, p. 427). This sense of legitimacy emphasizes the existence of persistent reasonable disagreement about matters of justice, and insists that political procedures must therefore respect the equal moral standing of all citizens, for only such procedures will generate laws and policies that citizens can accept as free and equal in spite of their reasonable disagreements. This fairly demanding understanding of legitimacy is, still, a "lower" standard than full justice – after all, the liberal principle of legitimacy may be satisfied even though the ideally just law or policy is not chosen by the political process. However, this conception of legitimacy incorporates demanding procedural requirements for what it takes to ensure the moral freedom and equality of persons in their role as citizens.

On this strong conception of liberal legitimacy, legitimate political procedures embody certain important values, which in turn ground the respect owed to these institutions by both subjects and outsiders. On several strands of liberal political theory, the value served by legitimate political institutions is nothing short of making justice possible – that is, political institutions create justice. According to Kant's political philosophy, for example, only in what he calls "a civil condition" can we establish just relations with one another.[8] This is because in a state of nature not only is there no impartial judge, but more fundamentally, there are no settled, determinate laws. In order to avoid subordination in the choice among equally permissible sets of rules (for example, equally permissible but different sets of rules regarding property acquisition and transfer), a political

[8] I am indebted here to Jon Mandle's account of Kant in Mandle (2009). Mandle cites Arthur Ripstein's *Force and Freedom* as his source for this understanding of Kant. Moreover, if Mandle's interpretation is correct, then Rawls's political philosophy mirrors Kant's in important respects, most saliently in the understanding of the moral freedom and equality of persons and the importance of nondomination as the foundational political value. See Mandle (n.d.).

mechanism is required in which all are situated as equals. For Kant, then, only under political institutions can we reliably maintain our equal moral freedom; the state of nature, by contrast, is "a state devoid of justice" (Kant 1996). However, one need not be a Kantian to accept this point. For example, Thomas Christiano, in a move that parallels this aspect of Kant's political theory, argues that democratic political procedures are required by justice because "[t]he main purpose of the state is to establish justice among persons within a limited jurisdiction … What the state does, if it is reasonably just, is settle what justice consists in by promulgating public rules for the guidance of individual behavior" (Christiano 2004, p. 281). Christiano argues that it is precisely the requirement of justice that all be respected as equals that makes a public system of rules morally necessary, which in turn makes the state morally necessary.

On this view of political legitimacy, then, the duty of outsiders not to interfere with the outcomes of a legitimate state's political procedures is grounded in the political community's right to self-determination. Political legitimacy, therefore, should not be understood as merely a compromise on justice, as if we were obligated to refrain from interfering in legitimate states only because interference is likely to do more harm than good. Rather, subjects of legitimate political institutions have a moral claim, proportional to the legitimacy of their institutions, that the outcomes of their political procedures not be undermined, given the distinctive moral values those institutions serve.

Notice that institutions can be more or less legitimate in this sense, as Rawls notes:

> At some point, the injustice of the outcomes of a legitimate democratic procedure corrupts its legitimacy, and so will the injustice of the political constitution itself. But before this point is reached, the outcomes of a legitimate procedure are legitimate whatever they are. This gives us purely procedural democratic legitimacy and distinguishes it from justice, even granting that justice is not specified procedurally. Legitimacy allows an undetermined range of injustice that justice might not permit.
>
> (Rawls 1993, p. 428)

Even the lower standard of legitimacy as mere toleration on the international stage can be understood as grounded in the values served by (minimally) legitimate institutions. For example, in *The Law of Peoples*, "decent" states must meet what Jon Mandle calls "a certain minimal threshold of legitimacy" necessary for toleration on the international stage, which Mandle argues obtains when "the constitution has widespread support, effectively protects basic human rights, and generates law according to a procedure that affords all citizens input in determining the common good" (Mandle 2006 pp. 81, 85). Such institutions, while falling short of realizing the robust equality required for full democratic legitimacy, serve important political values for their subjects, establishing basically just, if not fully just, relations among them.

4. The normative legitimacy of international human rights bodies

On my view, the measurements of legitimacy and of human rights are to some extent complementary. By itself, however, this observation doesn't differentiate my view from Wellman's. What my view does is explain why this should be so: at root, because both human rights and political legitimacy are largely informed by the equal moral status of persons.

My argument so far has been, first, that an institutional account of human rights is required to account for the value of status equality in human rights, and second, that a legitimate state's political institutions serve distinctive values connected to the moral equality of the members of the political community, which in turn ground that state's claims to self-determination. Together, these points have the further result that Wellman is wrong to say that legitimate states have no principled objection to intervention if the intervention prevents even a single human rights violation. While certain interventions to prevent human rights violations in legitimate states may turn out to be justified, this cannot be because legitimate states have no general, principled claim to nonintervention.

We have now returned to the problem with which we began: should states regard the procedural and substantive recommendations of UN treaty bodies as authoritative? It might seem that my argument has made it more difficult to answer this question in the affirmative. I have defended a much stronger account (than Wellman's, for example) of the moral claim legitimate states may make against intervention; to the extent that international human rights bodies function by intervening to change state-level laws and policies, it seems we might be forced to conclude that supranational human rights bodies are themselves illegitimate. However, the fact that supranational institutions are not morally necessary in the way that legitimate states are creates space in which to construct an alternative account of legitimacy for the particular functions they serve. Because legitimate states create (some level of) justice among fellow citizens, international human rights bodies do not need to serve this function; therefore, traditional conceptions of political legitimacy for states need not apply to them. Thus, requiring international human rights bodies to prove their democratic credentials, or otherwise conform to standards of legitimacy developed for states, is making a category mistake. Questions (such as Kenneth Anderson's) about why we do not require supranational institutions to meet the same standards of legitimacy as states, can be answered in terms of the very different functions served, and values realized, at different levels of governance.

I suggest that we should understand international human rights bodies as supranational political institutions designed to improve the legitimacy of states by better structuring state-level political institutions to realize human rights.[9] Legitimate states that better realize human rights, especially the status egalitarian elements of human rights, also thereby improve their own legitimacy. To the extent that participation in international human rights regimes enables states to improve their own human rights records, such participation also improves their political legitimacy. We can see this by returning to the issue of felon disenfranchisement in the United States. It is important that the effects of such laws in the US context include the disproportionate diminishment of the political rights of racial minorities, so that the human rights problem in turn reduces the political legitimacy of the United States. Moreover, this example is not so different from other kinds of human rights problems in the United States, including others that the HRC commented upon in its response to the United States' report, such as the disproportionate number of blacks who are homeless, "reports of *de facto* racial segregation in public schools," "allegations of widespread incidence of violent crime perpetrated against persons of minority sexual orientation," and concerns about employment discrimination against women (United Nations Human Rights Committee 2006). Such concerns raise the possibility not just of the existence of specific policies that lead to discrete human rights violations (in an interactionist sense), but, more worrisomely, to the existence of networks of policies and laws that systematically entrench the unequal status of certain groups of citizens in both social and political life, which in turn impugns the legitimacy of the political system itself. Importantly, on my analysis in this chapter, the erosion of political legitimacy in turn weakens a state's claim to political self-determination.

Given this background, states' participation in UN human rights regimes is instrumentally essential to realize the human rights of their citizens, even for even states (like the USA) that meet most standard thresholds

[9] Allen Buchanan has advocated a similar position; see Buchanan (2011).

of internal political legitimacy. There are a number of ways in which the level of human rights protection even in legitimate states (which by definition fulfill human rights requirements above some threshold level) can be improved by participation in international human rights regimes. First, human rights are universal ideals. Ratifying international treaties regarding the content of human rights doctrine helps to ensure that the standards of human rights within particular states are largely consonant with the existing international consensus on human rights, and participation in the oversight process directed by the treaty bodies facilitates further deliberation with the international human rights community and with other states regarding the substantive content of human rights. Both of these effects in turn serve to ensure that the human rights standards within participating states are not inappropriately narrow or parochial. Second, while the UN treaty bodies have no direct coercive power, the treaty body regime does constitute, for states parties, at least some formal external accountability regarding how human rights are realized within the state, which in turn provides states with an opportunity for self-reflection in the creation of reports and responses to comments from the treaty bodies or other states. Finally, participation in the treaty body regime provides credibility for agents within states working for human rights, most notably when a treaty body raises the same human rights concerns that domestic activists are working on. For these reasons, states risk reducing their own internal legitimacy by shunning international human rights regimes.[10]

This argument might seem to justify some interference in legitimate states for the sake of improving their internal human rights records, along with their legitimacy. However, given my argument so far, casting the issue as one of external interference is misleading. Rather, what is at stake is that states have strong reasons, connected to concern for their own internal legitimacy, to participate in good faith in international human rights treaty regimes. Moreover, while such participation requires regarding the procedural recommendations of treaty bodies as authoritative, this loss of self-determination (if it can be called that) must be balanced against the fact that such participation strengthens the state's case for self-determination grounded in the legitimacy of its internal political institutions.

[10] Nonparticipation also risks their external legitimacy, to the extent this is measured by respecting the human rights of outsiders. Indeed, many of the concerns and recommendations of the HRC in response to the US reports focused on the treatment of non-US citizens in the context of the wars in Afghanistan and Iraq, as well as detention in US facilities at Guantanamo Bay, Cuba.

Recall that the directives issued by the HRC to the United States regarding felon disenfranchisement were of two kinds: procedural (the HRC directed the United States to furnish it with data regarding the disproportionate racial impact of felon disenfranchisement laws) and substantive (the HRC noted that the United States "should adopt appropriate measures to ensure that states restore voting rights to citizens who have fully served their sentences and those who have been released on parole"). According to my analysis, a strong argument can be made for the authority of the HRC's procedural recommendations to legitimate states; that is, there are strong moral reasons for legitimate states to engage in the HRC procedures in good faith, and doing so (on my argument) increases its legitimacy.

The case of the substantive recommendations is more complicated. The political legitimacy of states is clearly a scalar predicate, and many considerations of both substantive policy as well as political procedures influence the internal legitimacy of states. Moreover, many of these are imbricated within each other; for example, felon disenfranchisement in the United States affects assessments of both whether the US policies are justifiable from a human rights perspective as well as whether political processes within the USA are sufficiently egalitarian to be considered legitimate. It is therefore not the case that legitimate states, in the world as it is, warrant no further international scrutiny. For this reason, treaty bodies have an important role to play both in improving the legitimacy and the human rights records of legitimate states. Despite this substantial room for improvement, however, there is good reason to regard the outcomes of the political processes within broadly legitimate states as themselves legitimate.

Advocates of human rights might argue (with Wellman) that this conclusion fails to take human rights seriously, insofar as it entrusts change in the direction of greater human rights fulfillment to legitimate, though admittedly defective, political institutions within states. A full defense of my view would have to consider relevant alternative proposals for changing state-level laws and policies that fall short of full realization of human rights, which I do not have space for here.[11] As a gesture towards a reply, however, I conclude by noting reason for cautious optimism regarding felon disenfranchisement laws in the United States. As I have argued, given the disproportionate racial impacts of

[11] For a comparative analysis of whether states or treaty bodies would more reliably interpret international human rights law, which reaches a similar conclusion using a different normative framework, see Hessler (2005).

felon disenfranchisement in the United States, the effect of such laws is to compromise the political legitimacy of the United States by undermining the equal status of racial minorities in the political process. While it might not seem a promising strategy on behalf of human rights to trust to the functioning of compromised political institutions, change is in fact occurring in the United States regarding these policies. In a recent report, The Sentencing Project notes that between 1997 and 2010, "23 states have amended felony disenfranchisement policies in an effort to reduce their restrictiveness and expand voter eligibility" (Porter 2010, p. 1). As the report notes: "As the public has become increasingly aware of these restrictive policies, there has been a groundswell of support for change. Public opinion surveys report that 8 in 10 Americans support voting rights for persons who have completed their sentence and nearly two-thirds support voting rights for persons on probation or parole" (Porter 2010, p. 3).

One possible explanation for this phenomenon is that the value of equal moral standing that underpins the liberal conception of political legitimacy provides a powerful argument within the political culture for internal reform of institutions that fail to respect this value. Part of the point of respecting the outcomes of legitimate institutions is precisely to respect the equal freedom of citizens, by respecting their collective self-determination. This respect may entail a compromise on full justice, but the evidence on felon disenfranchisement laws suggests that this compromise is not a hopeless one.

Bibliography

Altman, A., 2005. Democratic self-determination and the disenfranchisement of felons. *Journal of Applied Philosophy*, 22, 263–273.

Anderson, K., 2000. The Ottawa convention banning landmines, the role of international non-governmental organizations and the idea of international civil society. *European Journal of International Law*, 11, 91–120.

Behrens, A., Uggen, C., & Manza, J., 2003. Ballot manipulation and the "menace of negro domination": racial threat and felon disenfranchisement in the United States, 1850–2002. *American Journal of Sociology*, 109, 559–605.

Beitz, C., 2009, *The Idea of Human Rights*, Oxford University Press.

Buchanan, A., 2010. The egalitarianism of human rights. *Ethics*, 120, 679–710.

2011. Reciprocal legitimation: Reframing the problem of international legitimacy. *Politics, Philosophy and Economics*, 120, 5–19.

Buchanan, A. & Keohane, R., 2006. The legitimacy of global governance institutions. *Ethics and International Affairs*, 20, 405–437.

2011. Precommitment regimes for intervention: Supplementing the security council. *Ethics and International Affairs*, 25, 41–63.
Chin, G., 2007. Felon disenfranchisement and democracy in the Jim Crow era. *Ohio State Journal of Criminal Law*, 5, 329–340.
Christiano, T., 2004. The authority of democracy. *The Journal of Political Philosophy*, 12, 266–290.
2010. Democratic legitimacy and international institutions. In S. Besson & J. Tasioulas, eds. *The Philosophy of International Law*, pp. 119–137. Oxford University Press.
2013. Authority. In E. Zalta, ed. *The Stanford Encyclopedia of Philosophy*. http://plato.stanford.edu/archives/spr2013/entries/authority/, accessed June 11, 2013.
Forst, R., 2010. The justification of human rights and the basic right to justification: A reflexive approach. *Ethics*, 120, 711–740.
Griffin, J., 2008. *On Human Rights*, Oxford University Press.
Hessler, K., 2005. Resolving interpretive conflicts in international human rights law. *Journal of Political Philosophy*, 13, 29–52.
Kant, I., 1996. *The Metaphysics of Morals* (ed. M. Gregor), Cambridge University Press.
Mandle, J., 2006. *Global Justice*, Cambridge: Polity Press.
2009. Distributive justice at home and abroad. In T. Christiano & J. Christman, eds. *Contemporary Debates in Political Philosophy*, pp. 408–422. West Sussex, UK: Wiley-Blackwell.
n.d. Reconciling freedom and equality. Unpublished manuscript.
Mayerfeld, J., 2009. The democratic legitimacy of international human rights law. *Indiana International and Comparative Law Review*, 19, 49–88.
O'Neill, O., 2000. Women's rights: Whose obligations? In *Bounds of Justice*, pp. 97–111. Cambridge University Press.
Pogge, T., 2002. *World Poverty and Human Rights*. Cambridge: Polity Press.
2008. *World Poverty and Human Rights*. 2nd edition, Cambridge: Polity Press
Porter, N., 2010. *Expanding the Vote: State Felony Disenfranchisement Reform, 1997–2010*. The Sentencing Project.
Rawls, J., 1993. *Political Liberalism*. New York: Columbia University Press.
The Sentencing Project: Research and Advocacy for Reform, 2012. www.sentencingproject.org/template/page.cfm?id=133, accessed April 15, 2012.
Uggen, C. & Manza, J., 2002. Democratic contraction? Political consequences of felon disenfranchisement in the United States. *American Sociological Review* 67, 777–803.
United Nations Human Rights Committee 2006. Concluding Observations of the Human Rights Committee. CCPR/C/USA/CO/3/Rev.1.
Wellman, C., 2012. Taking human rights seriously. *Journal of Political Philosophy*, 20, 119–130.

5

The legitimacy of international interpretive authorities for human rights treaties: an indirect-instrumentalist defence

BAŞAK ÇALI

1. Introduction

In its 2006 report to the monitoring body (the Human Rights Committee) of the United Nations Covenant on Civil and Political Rights (ICCPR), the USA challenged the Committee's interpretation of what the term 'within the jurisdiction' of a state meant in Article 2 of the ICCPR.[1] While the Human Rights Committee stated that the term jurisdiction should be understood as a function of a state's control over persons wherever such control may be, the US authorities said that jurisdiction was a function of a state's control over its own territory and not a function of its control over persons outside that territory. Consequently, the USA refused to answer questions on issues that fell outside its own interpretation of jurisdiction.[2] This meant the Human Rights Committee was unable to monitor actions by the USA in military bases and detention camps outside the USA, such as those in Afghanistan or Iraq. The Human Rights Committee, like any other international interpretive or judicial authority, has no authority to enforce its interpretations. Therefore it simply announced its concern about the USA's lack of respect for its interpretive authority and argued

I would like to thank Richard Bellamy, Mat Coakley, Lynn Dobson, Andreas Føllesdal, Kristin Hessler, Johan Schaffer, Geir Ulfstein and Rachael McGill for comments on earlier drafts, and Alice Wyss for research assistance.

[1] US report to the HRC, UN Doc. CCPR/C/USA/Q/3, 26 April 2006, Annex 1.

[2] Ibid. See also Consideration of Reports Submitted by States Parties under Article 40 of the Covenant, UN Doc. CCPR/C/USA/CO/3/Rev.1 (2006), para. 10.

that it deserves such respect as the monitoring organ of the ICCPR, a global human rights treaty with 167 state parties.[3]

This is just one example of a current puzzle in international human rights law – namely, what is the basis of the authority of international interpretive institutions? Do these bodies possess the legitimacy to interpret human rights treaties and demand respect from domestic institutions? Are there good reasons for domestic authorities to refuse to follow the interpretations of these international institutions? The puzzle is normative as well as practical. There are currently nine quasi-judicial interpretive human rights bodies at the level of the United Nations, two regional human rights commissions and three human rights courts.[4] Every country in the world has signed up to at least one international human rights treaty (Hafner-Burton 2012). Each treaty has a monitoring body to interpret its provisions. These institutions deliver an impressive amount of interpretations of international human rights law. It is of paramount importance to assess whether there are good reasons to follow such interpretations, even if one disagrees with them, and what those reasons might be. Conversely, it is of equal importance to assess whether a decision not to follow such interpretations can be defended and on what grounds.

In this chapter I aim to defend one view in favour of the legitimacy of international interpretive authority for human rights treaties. This view holds that there are good indirect instrumentalist reasons for starting

[3] United Nations Treaty Collection Database, http://treaties.un.org/Pages/ViewDetails.aspx?src=TREATY&mtdsg_no=IV-4&chapter=4&lang=en accessed on 11 July 2011. In its Fourth Periodic Report to the same Committee, the USA recognised that human rights law can apply extra-territorially, but that the international law of armed conflict displaces international human rights law as *lex specialis*. Report of 30 December 2011 www.state.gov/j/drl/rls/179781.htm accessed on 29 November 2012.

[4] At the United Nations level, these are the Human Rights Committee, Committee on Economic, Social and Cultural Rights, Committee on the Elimination of All Forms of Racial Discrimination, Committee on the Rights of the Child, Committee on the Elimination of All Forms of Discrimination Against Women, Committee Against Torture, Committee Against Enforced Disappearances, Committee on Migrant Workers and Committee on the Rights of Persons with Disabilities. There are also two regional commissions that decide on individual cases, the Inter-American Commission on Human Rights and the African Commission on Human and Peoples' Rights, both of which have interpretive powers. There are also three regional human rights courts: the Inter-American Court of Human Rights, the European Court of Human Rights and the African Court of Human and Peoples' Rights, which can deliver legally binding judgments.

with a presumption of deference towards international human rights interpretive authorities at the expense of domestic interpretive authorities, namely the domestic judiciary, legislature and executive, when interpreting the scope and application of international human rights law. In particular, I propose that we should treat questions of who should defer to which interpretations and who should make decisions as ultimately hinging on which institutional practices will, in the long term, promote an instrumental non-legitimacy-based goal: the promotion of a human rights respecting culture globally. I shall further argue that international interpretive authorities are best placed to further this goal because of the background conditions that define the state of human rights protections in the world today: significantly weak human rights protections, underdeveloped human rights jurisprudence in domestic contexts and persistent risks of parochial interpretation by domestic courts, legislatures and executives. While formal commitment to international human rights treaties for the most part imply that domestic authorities are committed to the ideal of respect for human rights in the abstract, interpretation of human rights treaties is necessary for the development of a human rights respecting culture. I hold this argument to apply both to human rights treaty-interpreting bodies solely with powers of recommendation (such as those of the United Nations) and to human rights courts which deliver legally binding judgments (regional human rights courts). This is because, as far as emitting interpretation goes, both types of institutions engage in similar types of activity. Alongside interpretive authority, human rights courts also have adjudicative authority, as well as the authority to declare remedies for human rights violations. In this chapter, I focus solely on the interpretive authority of international human rights bodies, understanding this type of authority as the authority to specify, clarify and infer specific standards of policy and action from the general international human rights law clauses enshrined in international human rights law treaties. Whether states should respect international human rights law outside of their own territory and what procedures they have to put in place to do so is one such interpretive question.

International interpretive authorities face the risk of 'getting it wrong' as much as any other interpretive authority. I therefore offer an argument that includes a framework for assessing under which conditions domestic interpretive authorities, be they domestic courts, parliaments or governments, might have good reasons to refuse to defer to the interpretations of international authorities.

2. The value of legitimacy in the international context

The value of employing a legitimacy discourse in the international context is a matter of dispute. Asserting that an institution is legitimate implies that the institution has the right to impose duties on others and that those duty holders must be compelled to fulfil those duties regardless of the content of the duty (Raz 2006). Legitimate institutions, therefore, generate content-independent reasons to act for the subjects of legitimacy. Some conceive those reasons as trumping other reasons to act or not to act (Raz 2006). Others hold that legitimacy-based reasons coexist with other reasons and in some circumstances can be trumped by them (Buchanan 2004). The central point of the dispute on legitimacy's value in the international context lies in larger disagreements about the types of relationship that exist in the international sphere. Some argue that there is not much point in even talking about whether international institutions are legitimate or not as international institutions cannot impose duties on states. States accept duties by voluntarily agreeing to them and may withdraw their agreement if and when they see fit (Goldsmith & Posner 2005). Others argue that international institutions do impose duties on states, but they can never attain standards of domestic legitimacy because they are not democratically legitimate (Von Bogdandy & Venzke 2012). A key difficulty in employing the notion of legitimacy to international institutions is, therefore, not only about which standards of legitimacy apply, but also whether legitimacy is at all relevant to discussions of international institutions.

In the field of international human rights law, the dispute about the legitimacy of international interpretive bodies also suffers from this difficulty. International human rights bodies do not dispense orders or commands; they dispense interpretations of international human rights law and expect that state institutions conduct their present and future affairs in ways that are compatible with those interpretations. In some instances, a human rights treaty interpretation may not require domestic institutions to act in a specific way. It may simply point out the permissive range of interpretations, blocking some interpretations but not others. In other cases – as in the case of the interpretation of the term 'jurisdiction' – there may be competition between two alternative interpretations demanding actors to choose the interpretation of the international institution or the one advanced by the domestic institution.

There are then two distinct questions we can ask about the legitimacy of human rights bodies. The first is whether legitimacy – as defined above – is at all relevant in the characterisation of the relationship between states and treaty-monitoring bodies. Do state institutions have content-independent reasons to follow the interpretations of these bodies? The second is whether and to what extent these reasons are exclusionary reasons and how they fare against other reasons that may point to the legitimacy of state institutions rather than of international bodies.

To return to the US example given at the start of this chapter, one can map three possible ways of reading the reasoning that may have informed the position of the US domestic interpretive authorities in 2006 when rejecting the HRC's interpretation of the term 'jurisdiction'. They point to different conclusions regarding the relevance of legitimacy as well as the relevant standards of legitimacy:

1. The US authorities opted for an evaluation of the interpretation of the Committee only on 'its merits', disagreed with it and decided to discard it.
2. The US authorities considered the legitimacy relationship to be non-applicable in the case of an international institution and a state. They therefore decided to disregard the interpretation without assessing its merits.
3. The US authorities judged the Human Rights Committee to have legitimate authority to issue this interpretation, but they thought that this particular interpretation failed some sort of 'reasonable interpretation' test and decided to disregard it.

All three readings above imply an overall normative conclusion about the value and relevance of legitimacy in the international context.

In reading 1, it is implied that the reasons for following the interpretation of a human rights treaty body are content-dependent, and that legitimacy-based arguments are of no relevance. This is a view about the nature of international institutions. The USA does not replace its own interpretation of human rights treaties with that of the treaty body because it regards this international institution as having persuasive authority rather than binding authority. This suggests that the USA could follow another interpretation of the Human Rights Committee on the basis that it agreed with the content of that interpretation. There is, however, no legitimacy-based authoritative relationship between the Human Rights Committee and the USA that would generate any reasons for the USA to follow its interpretations. This is akin to an anarchist view about how people interact with institutions: the reasons the institution provides are only relevant if we agree with those reasons ourselves (Wolff 1970). The view is echoed in the will-based theories of international law, where the will of individual states is at the centre of international law making and interpretation (Goldsmith and Posner 2005).

In reading 2, the outcome is the same as in reading 1. Part of the reason for not following the human rights treaty body, however, is a view about the superiority of the legitimacy of state authorities *over that of* international institutions. This view holds that state authorities have *more* legitimacy in comparison to international institutions. Both a democratic legitimacy standard that holds that states have more democratic legitimacy than international institutions (Hessler 2005) and a sovereignty legitimacy standard that holds that states have more sovereignty than the international legal system can support this conclusion. Under this reading, the USA refuses the interpretation of the Committee not because it disagrees with its content, but because it believes that the Committee lacks the legitimate authority to emit any interpretation.

In reading 3, there is, again, a theory of legitimate authority. This holds that interpretive authority for the treaty body exists within limits. A human rights treaty body cannot demand respect for treaty interpretations that do not meet a test of reasonable interpretation. The USA could argue that the interpretation of the 'scope of jurisdiction' does not pass this test.

A shared outcome of readings 1 and 2 is that the interpretive authority of the domestic authorities remains intact, albeit for different reasons. In reading 3, a more nuanced notion of legitimate authority operates, in which neither the USA nor the human rights treaty body has exclusive interpretive authority.

How do we evaluate and make moral sense of these readings? What attitude should we adopt towards legitimacy-based views in the context of the relationship between domestic authorities and international institutions? Reading 1 suggests that the interpretations of human rights bodies should be followed based on a 'merits only' analysis. Reading 2 suggests that we adopt a standard that tells us what makes an interpretive authority legitimate and support the institution, which fares better based on that standard. The structure of reading 3 deviates from reading 2 in that it accepts that institutions can share common goals, but be regarded as legitimate based on different types of standards. This demands an attitude of deference for an international institution, but also admits that there can be a case for rebuttal of that deference. This notion of legitimacy suggests that the more an institution gets the interpretation 'wrong', the weaker the presumption of deference becomes. A domestic authority that rightfully challenges one bad decision is still under a duty to defer to the next decision of the international interpretive body, but an international institution that continually delivers bad decisions may gradually lose its claim to legitimacy. This understanding of legitimacy is not too far removed from domestic accounts of legitimacy in one sense: in the domestic arena, the case for civil disobedience against illegitimate rule is recognised (Singer 1973; Rawls 1996). In the international human rights context, the risk is not the emergence of tyrannical rule over time, but the possibility of manifestly bad interpretations of human rights treaties, which would ultimately harm the emergence and entrenchment of a global human rights culture.

In what follows I aim to provide reasons in support of the structure in reading 3 (though not necessarily in support of the outcome in the US example), arguing that international institutions should enjoy deference, but that such deference should be subject to an assessment of the body's interpretive performance.

3. The case for presumption of deference to international interpretive authorities

Reading 3 defends a presumption of deference to international interpretive bodies rather than domestic interpretive bodies in the field of human rights treaty interpretation. It is often argued that there is nothing controversial in this if the state authorities we have in mind are human rights states with bad human rights records and weak rule of law (Buchanan 2004; Hessler 2005). What reasons do states with good human rights records with strong interpretive authorities of their own have to defer to international human rights bodies? I offer support for this hierarchy of deference by arguing that the institution of international interpretive authorities in the field of human rights passes an important indirect instrumentalist test: international interpretive authorities make *a distinct moral contribution* to an area of global concern that is more than the contributions of individual interpretations (Rawls 1955). In other words, there is an added institutional value to international interpretive authorities that individual domestic interpretive authorities, individually or collectively, cannot secure. Domestically, high courts, the legislature or the executive can prove to have very high standards of human rights interpretation. Furthermore, states can look to each other's interpretations and learn from them. The literature on citing foreign judgments also focuses on the value of this (Waldron 2005). The possibility of learning from other domestic interpretive authorities, however, is predicated on the motivation to do so. Only those domestic authorities that are willing to improve their human rights standards would seek alternative views and interpretations elsewhere. The added institutional value of an international human rights interpretive authority is that it removes the optional character of learning about outside perspectives and obliges all domestic interpretative actors to become part of the international human rights law interpretive process. This means that the motivated, the ambivalent and the non-motivated, are all included on an equal footing in the common interpretative process. It is the ability to situate *all* domestic interpreters in a position to take account of international human rights law that makes the international institution distinct from any domestic authority with similar expertise.

This positioning is key to the realisation of the central purpose of international human rights treaties: to increase awareness about human rights law and principles, to contribute to their recognition and effective entrenchment across all state parties and to foster a good faith discussion about the most appropriate interpretative strategies of human rights law. The recognition of and engagement with international human rights law by domestic judiciaries, parliaments and the executive, through engaging with the interpretive authorities, is precisely what entrenches the global human rights culture.

This duty to attitude of deference makes the international interpretive authorities of human rights treaties different from political forms of international human rights dialogue or adjudicatory human rights practices. A political forum, such as that of the United Nations' *Universal Periodic Review*, for example, is not an interpretive authority. This institution allows for inter-state peer review of the human rights performance of states every four years. States make recommendations to each other in order to improve their human rights practice. The reviewed state is free to accept or reject such recommendations.[5] The case for interpretive authority is also weaker than that of adjudicatory authorities. Once a human rights court adjudicates on a human rights case, the domestic authorities do not have the option of disagreeing with the individual judgment. This is because the authority to adjudicate is by its nature a final authority: to challenge the specific outcome of adjudication would contradict the acceptance of its powers. Interpretive authority, on the other hand, obliges domestic authorities to join in the conversation on how to best interpret international human

[5] On how the *Universal Periodic Review* works, www.ohchr.org/en/hrbodies/upr/pages/BasicFacts.aspx accessed on 9 May 2011.

rights law, but also recognises the competent authority of domestic actors. Creating independent international interpretive authorities also ensures that no state imposes its own interpretations on others.

Domestic authorities across the world have different levels of human rights protections due to different political and constitutional arrangements, cultures and/or religions. Ratification of an international human rights treaty represents a commitment to the ideal of convergence of interpretive standards. It is, however, an ideal that is open to good faith debate, and this debate, by its very nature, should be carried out on a level above the domestic.

The case for international interpretive authority is neither a top-down recipe for a World Constitution nor an attempt to standardise or micro-manage all domestic legal and political systems in the name of convergence of human rights standards. That the interpretations of the international authorities must be subject to challenge by the careful arguments of domestic interpreters is an important safeguard against the imposition of one-size-fits-all rules. For example, the right to fair trial in Article 14 of the ICCPR is a right to a fair process. This process is respected through different means in common law and civil law countries. The international interpreters would face a challenge if they insisted that fair trial could only be protected through civil law. Rather, the interpretation of the right to a fair trial is about the list of standards one must consider regardless of the domestic institutions in place. The convergence of interpretive standards also does not mean identical outcomes must obtain when standards are applied. Article 14 of the ICCPR requires fair trial without undue delay, but concrete determinations of undue delay would vary based on the complexity of the case, the conduct of the parties and the necessary procedures that a judge needs to follow to decide on a case.

The deferential relationship between international interpretive authorities and domestic ones is ultimately justified by the aspiration of equal respect and concern for each individual globally.[6] For example, my right to freedom from torture should not alter in content if I move from Oslo to Islamabad and, from there, to a US overseas detention facility, because

[6] The Preambles of the International Covenant on Civil and Political Rights and the International Covenant on Economic, Social and Cultural Rights state this as 'recognition of the inherent dignity and of the equal and inalienable rights of all members of the human family'. www2.ohchr.org/english/law/cescr.htm and www2.ohchr.org/english/law/ccpr.htm accessed on 14 July 2011.

domestic interpreters have applied different standards of interpretation based on a nationalist interpretation of what torture entails. The authoritative interpretations offered by the Human Rights Committee and the Committee against Torture, which cover all three of these countries, is an important assurance against such domestic variations of interpretation based on a right to auto-interpretation argument. To emphasise, this does not mean that there could be no variations of interpretation based on arguments of a reasonable kind in interpretations of various rights provisions in human rights treaties. For example, the scope of some rights depends on how they fare when balanced against public interest or other rights in specific contexts; some domestic authorities may argue that they provide a higher standard of protection to human rights than international human rights treaties. These distinctions, however, form part of the interpretation process of international human rights law.

This discussion of legitimacy takes place in the context of real world conditions. Very different standards of human rights protections are present in different parts of the world, and there are principled disagreements about the best interpretations of human rights standards. In my view, justifying the prima facie deference to international interpretive bodies is also the most prudent option to enable the maturing of the debate about human rights standards and to work towards greater consistency in the range of human rights considerations and the level of protection in all parts of the world. This is an indirect instrumentalist account of legitimacy, in that I treat questions of legitimacy as ultimately hinging on what practices will in the long term promote the non-legitimacy-based goal of the promotion of human rights. I justify this indirect form of instrumentalism with reference to current historical conditions. In a world with a different level of human rights protection, for example in a supranational state, other arguments might be more fitting.

This account of the interpretive authority of human rights bodies and courts is tied strongly to the *circumstances* of legitimacy at the international level: the existence of international institutions and the reasons for deferring to them only make sense in terms of their contribution to shared moral aims and in the light of the international institutional background (Çalı 2009). The circumstances of legitimacy have two dimensions. First, we must consider questions of the legitimacy of international institutions against the backdrop of a larger web of moral concerns of which the legitimacy of human rights treaties forms part. Broadly speaking, the core of these concerns is the promotion of human rights and the need to ensure that such promotion does not come at the expense of other moral goals. For example, the promotion of human rights should not undermine democracy or justice. The legitimacy of an international institution makes sense in reference to or in competition with other moral values (Dworkin 2008). Second, consideration of the circumstances of legitimacy requires attention to the relevant institutional landscape and relationships encountered.[7] Multi-level governance structures in the international context and the existence of competing and complementary domestic interpretive authorities define the field of human rights.[8]

4. Legality

Why not use a simple test of transfer of authority from states to treaty-monitoring bodies to settle questions on the order of deference? This has obvious practical advantages. It prevents ambiguity in cases of disagreement between states and treaty bodies. If there were a legal obligation to follow the interpretations of treaty bodies, then the conduct of the USA in the above example, or of other states making similar arguments, would be wrong. If there were no legal obligations, they would not be making the arguments. Legality solves problems about legitimacy by pointing to legal recognition or pedigree (Føllesdal 2006). However, to understand legitimacy exclusively as legality raises problems: legitimacy as legality is only able to tell us whether a particular interpretation issued by an institution is justified within that legal structure (Buchanan 2010). It does not address the question of whether the ongoing legal structure is *itself* justified or legitimate, or whether there are circumstances in which, despite its legality, the treaty-interpreting body might lack legitimacy.

Collapsing legality together with legitimacy raises further questions. How do we establish that there is a legal obligation to respect the interpretive authority of international institutions? What type of consent is needed to establish this? What type of an obligation is it? Should states follow all

[7] The approach to circumstances of legitimacy in this respect shares common features with Rawls' method of 'initial situations' developed for setting out social contract doctrines (Rawls 2007: 16–17).

[8] This need not always be the case. For example, in the field of peace and security, there is a strong case for conceiving international authorities as morally primary rather than competing. Alternatively, in the field of global justice, international institutions might be conceived as subsidiary.

international interpretations – even the most far-fetched ones – where there is clear legal recognition, and ignore all other interpretations – even the most sound ones – because there is no clear legal obligation? The rule of recognition is silent on these issues. Legality solves the problem of whether international interpreters can override domestic interpreters, but does not address what makes the authority of the interpreting institution legitimate, or what basic principles we should rely on when deciding whether to respect the interpretations of human rights handed down by international treaty bodies and courts. It is, therefore, incomplete in offering a moral account for legitimacy as a framework of deference between states and interpreting bodies.

Finally, legality as a standard of legitimacy is not sensitive to the existence of potentially potent competing interpretive authorities at the domestic level, who may also have a legal mandate to interpret human rights under their constitutions (Sloss 2009; Çalı 2012). To demand that each and every interpretation of an international body should be followed is an extreme conclusion to reach in the context of these multiple interpretive structures. It is also one that interpretive authorities, be they international courts or other bodies, cannot subsequently enforce. Even the decisions of supranational human rights courts can ultimately be rejected or overturned by domestic referenda or domestic legislative change, due to the differentiation between interpretive authority and enforcement authority at the international level (Drzemczewski 1998). International interpretive authorities make a rightful demand that domestic authorities respect their decisions, but they have no control over the enforcement authority, which ultimately rests with the domestic authorities. Legality, therefore, is a very high standard to employ in this context. It is a better fit with concepts of legitimacy in the context of a single state: i.e. the justification of coercion or the duty to obey from the perspective of individual moral agents (Coakley 2011).

5. Primary deference to domestic interpreters: isolationism and democracy

If legality is insensitive to the existence of multiple interpretive authorities, accounts which focus on democratic standards of legitimacy from the perspective of a single state are insensitive to the distinct moral value of international interpretive authorities. The legitimacy account developed here for international institutions parts ways, too, with accounts that seek to transfer a view of legitimacy developed in the domestic context to the international context. Accounts that do not make room for the interpretive authority of international bodies often share a common notion of seeing a single political community in isolation, ignoring the coexistence of that political community with others at the international level. They conceive the benefits of human rights treaty interpretation primarily as benefits for individuals *qua* citizens. The context of the relationship between multiple states and human rights interpreting institutions is missing in such accounts. The normative justifications for interpretive authority are developed from the perspective of an isolated single state rather than from the circumstances of an association of states as representatives of individuals on the international plane.

One feature of isolationism is the comparison of states with international interpretive authorities in order to ask which of these institutions can carry out the task better. In one account of this kind, Hessler turns to qualities that make a state human rights respecting domestically in order to justify that state's claim to legitimate authority in interpreting international human rights treaties (Hessler 2005: 29–52). She argues that a strong prima facie case exists for one type of domestic interpretive authority: 'appropriately deliberative and participatory state governments should have final interpretative authority' (2005: 30). This is because such domestic mechanisms increase the likelihood that a diverse range of views will be reflected in the final decisions of domestic actors and contribute to a 'better shared understanding of the abstract moral principles relevant to a political decision' (2005: 35). Liberal, democratic states have stronger mechanisms for participation and deliberation and are, therefore, more likely to issue better and more reliable interpretations of human rights provisions, providing us with a moral reason to accept their interpretations as authoritative (2005).

There are appealing aspects to this account. In the case of liberal democratic states, with functioning parliaments, courts and deliberative democratic mechanisms, the interpretation of human rights treaties may ensure respect for the autonomy of each citizen, as they are able to participate in the interpretative process through direct mechanisms of accountability. In the case of international human rights bodies, citizens are involved indirectly, through the deliberations of experts elected by states and by way of governmental and non-governmental access to interpretative debates. Hessler's account places emphasis on the more direct participation of citizens in the interpretive processes within their own state.

It is, however, unclear whether this account succeeds in ensuring better protection of human rights law globally. First, there is the question of whether the account is workable – i.e. whether it can offer a criterion for selection. The second question is whether citizen participation in decision-making processes is the most appropriate yardstick to use to assign interpretive authority. As to workability, there is an issue of possible conflation of the question of whether democratic liberal states are better than non-democratic ones with the question of whether they are better than international independent judicial non-state bodies. The former does not necessarily mean the latter is correct, and in this context the latter is the key concern. No international interpretive authority in a world of sovereign states can meet the legitimacy standards developed for liberal democratic states. This is a test that all international institutions are bound to fail. This, therefore, begs the question of whether the test is a fair one and whether we should compare domestic interpretive authorities and international ones based on theories of democracy.

Nor does the account solve the disagreement between the state and international interpretive institutions. It merely translates this into another disagreement, i.e. whether the state is a liberal democratic state that satisfies criteria of participation or deliberation to such an extent that it can be immune from the interpretive authority of international institutions. The implicit argument here is that an international interpretive body fares better than a non-democratic state. This is not necessarily the case. Even a non-democratic state needs protection from the bad decisions and interpretations of a benevolent international interpreter. Hessler's criterion of 'participatory local institutions' which have access to local knowledge and 'directly involve people' in the process of decision-making as being key features of liberal democracies is a moving target (Hessler 2005). It does not solve the interpretive conflict, but makes it subject to an empirical assessment of levels of participatory democracy in each and every state (Hessler 2005). So, if one can show that the USA falls below the liberal democratic standard, then there is a case for legitimately demanding the US to follow the interpretations of the Human Rights Committee. The interpretive conflict is not, therefore, resolved. States could potentially reject interpretations from human rights bodies based on their assessments of the health of their domestic regimes.

Although Hessler's legitimacy standard of democracy is undesirable for the global protection of human rights for the reasons given above, it does address an important sensitivity that needs attention in any account in support of international interpretive authorities. Namely that international interpretive authorities can undermine domestic democratic institutions and the principle of political equality underpinning them through bad interpretations (Bellamy 2007).

Liberal contractarians have responded to this critique with the idea that international interpretive authorities cut both ways: these authorities are not in and of themselves a threat to political equality, and they can also improve it. The risk of international authorities undermining political equality can be offset by the weak judicial review powers of international interpretive institutions (Føllesdal 2007, Bellamy in this volume). Føllesdal's argument, in particular, focuses on the inability of direct participation to deliver equal concern for each and every citizen. Minorities in liberal democracies are often vulnerable to the hostile preferences of majorities and are unable to make their voices heard. This situation calls for a duty to provide assurances to minorities within liberal democracies. Føllesdal holds that this duty is a good domestic reason to constrain democratic authority through submission to international human rights review (Føllesdal 2007). In particular, provided that the review of international interpretive authorities is not designed to take decisions on behalf of democratic states, such a review has an important value in alleviating the doubts of citizens that domestic institutions are not doing their share of human rights protection.

In the instrumentalist account developed here, I argue that the distinct value of these authorities goes beyond their domestic benefits. This emphasises the role human rights treaties play internationally in encouraging orientation and structured debate about common standards, and in fostering the understanding that all individuals have entitlements to human rights, regardless of which sovereign state they live in. It is a more stable basis of interpretive authority than assurances to domestic minorities. The latter invites challenges from those who hold that some states simply do not need such assurances and that domestic assurances can also be designed domestically. The core content of international assurance is different. It does not derive from a desire for equal respect for citizens who associate with each other, but from concern for the moral integrity of individuals and their vulnerability in their interactions with political institutions. Citizenship is the only form of protection for individuals, and it has been sociologically proven to be weak in the face of the global movement of peoples (Benhabib 2004). International human rights treaties provide indirect, but global protection for human rights through their contribution to the development of a reasonable range of interpretations of human rights anywhere in the world. A domestic interpretive authority cannot fulfil this purpose. It lacks the standing to facilitate debate and discussion among a large number of states at the same time.

In practice, the interpretations of international human rights treaty bodies might lead to more meaningful improvements in human rights protections in states with bad human rights records than they do in liberal democratic states. But this is the potential outcome of international interpretive authority, not its value. Individuals have a prima facie reason to demand that any government defer to international human rights treaty bodies because such bodies concern themselves with the treatment of individuals qua individuals. They are concerned with that treatment regardless of the state in which an individual may happen to find him or herself.

6. The problem of bad interpretations

One scenario must be addressed in order for my account of deference to these institutions to gain widespread acceptance, namely that of bad interpretations delivered by international interpretive authorities. The problem of bad interpretations has two distinct dimensions. The first is the definitional threshold of a 'bad interpretation'. What kinds of arguments are relevant to show that an interpretation is a bad interpretation and that the domestic interpretive authorities are therefore justified in deciding to withdraw their presumption of deference? The second is that of the design of international interpretive bodies: what normative safeguards would prevent bad interpretations?

6.1 Bad interpretations

The distinct institutional contribution of international interpretive authorities on which this account of deference rests requires that states strive to find 'true' human rights law interpretations globally by submitting themselves to the interpretive authority of an international interpretive body. Most domestic authorities are perfectly capable of interpreting human rights law themselves. That is why they are also under a duty to provide reasons why an interpretation offered by the interpretive authority is bad and therefore should not be followed to its word, but needs to be reworked or reconsidered. This assumes both an initial acceptance of the potential integrity of international human rights law as a body of principles (Higgins 1989) and the possibility of reasonable disagreement on the concrete application of human rights law between domestic and international interpretive authorities.

This account does not operate by imposing a definition of a 'bad human rights interpretation'. This would require the adoption and defence of a substantive theory of international human rights law that is prior to the interpretive process itself. Rather the account operates by imposing a framework that filters the kinds of reasons that would be fit for making assessments of bad interpretations. In this framework, the burden of proof of a bad interpretation rests with the domestic authority. That is, the domestic authority must show through reasoned argument why an interpretation is unreasonable for *any* domestic authority. Challenging an interpretation, therefore, is still an act of active engagement with building a common human rights culture globally, and not a diversion from it. Domestic interpreters with advanced human rights protections play an important role in providing checks and balances. The fact that an international interpretive authority is under constant surveillance by domestic interpreters, and the fact that individual interpretations are subject to rebuttal, are both safeguards to ensure the normative performance of international interpretive authorities.

There are clear-cut cases of bad interpretation even under this procedural scheme. An interpretation that comes with no justificatory framework, i.e. an arbitrary interpretation, is a bad interpretation. The same would be true for interpretations that are internally incoherent. An important aspect of the duty to detect bad interpretations, however, has to do with the kinds of reasons that domestic interpreters can put forward to challenge international authorities. As the domestic interpreters and the international interpreters do not have conflicting reasons for action, but merely different sources of authority, domestic interpreters should be barred from using 'comprehensive doctrines', to borrow a term from Rawls (Rawls 1996), as the sole ground for declaring interpretations to be 'bad'. State authorities should not, for example, use their own history, culture or laws as the sole basis for rejecting the interpretations of human rights bodies. They should appeal to reasons that can be understood and recognised by anyone engaged in human rights interpretation. This is because an important part of the ideal of human rights law is that it does not fully depend on any comprehensive doctrine (Nickel 2006). International human rights law claims are those that seek to rise above such doctrines.[9]

The fact that domestic interpreters cannot rely solely on comprehensive doctrines plays an important filtering role in deciding which

[9] It is a matter of dispute how this is justified. For a review of various normative strategies, see Beitz 2001.

reasons are selected and how they are formulated. In particular, arguments based on the 'original intent' of the domestic drafters of human rights law treaties would be suspect (Pellet 2001). In the example introduced at the beginning of this chapter, for example, the US authorities put such an original intent argument forward. The USA argued before the Human Rights Committee that, at the time it participated in the drafting of the treaty, it did not intend the term 'jurisdiction' to mean anything more than accepting US responsibility for human rights within its own territory.[10] If one were to accept the original intent doctrine, the Human Rights Committee would have to accept that 167 separate interpretations of the treaty exist, based on the original intent of every single state party. This is at odds with the fact that international human rights treaties are more than international contracts that seek to legalise a particular transaction of goods or services between two states: they aim to set standards for the protection of human rights globally (Craven 2000). This means that a purposive reading of international human rights treaties is required by the very nature of these treaties by all interpreters, domestic and international alike.

The requirement of reason-giving I develop here approaches situations of disagreement in two different ways. First, it demands that a continuous attitude of deference is adopted on the part of the domestic authorities. This attitude is necessary for there to be continuing global debate about what human rights law requires in practice. Second, state authorities have the burden of proof in explaining to the treaty-monitoring body (and to the global audience that the treaty serves) why a particular interpretation is unworkable given the purposes of international human rights law. This can be described as the 'duty to take into account' an interpretation by a treaty-interpreting body. It brings with it the responsibility to provide normative reasons that advise against a particular interpretation and to offer solutions to interpretive deadlock. As Sen puts it, 'the admissibility of a domain of continued dispute is no embarrassment to a theory of human rights' (Sen 2004). The duty to take into account, therefore, requires a constructive process, so that interpretive disagreements do not undermine the legitimate authority of these bodies to continue to foster an international debate about human rights protections.

The duty to take into account rests on a commitment to constructive dialogue on human rights interpretation. It does not regard states and

[10] Supra Note 2. US report to the HRC, UN Doc. CCPR/C/USA/Q/3, 26 April 2006, Annex 1.

international bodies in a hierarchical relationship, but in a relationship of cooperation towards the same goal, the fostering of a human rights culture internationally. The duty to take into account still points to a special type of influence that one agent has over another, in that the directions of the international body constitute a distinctive reason for the action for the domestic authorities (Freeman 1990). It does not, however, imply that the States should exercise no judgment in deciding the scope of their engagement with human rights treaty bodies.

My account of the process of establishing relevant reasons in order to contest bad interpretations could be criticised for being too optimistic, given the diversity and multiplicity of human rights provisions in international law, as well as the strong possibility of more granular disagreements. Human rights provisions include economic, civil, political, social and cultural rights as well as special rights regimes for the disabled, the migrant worker, the child and women. It could be argued that if domestic authorities are in a position to challenge too many interpretations made by international authorities there is little point in insisting that a presumption of deference exists that favours the international authority in principle. One solution to this problem would be to limit the scope of rights that international interpretive authorities can legitimately interpret.[11] For example, such authorities could be mandated to focus on a limited range of 'basic rights' and be required to defer to domestic authorities for rights or rights-related issues that are beyond the scope of basic rights. This proposal aims to minimise the constant challenging of international interpreters by proposing a distinction between human rights that require international interpretation and those rights that are best interpreted by domestic, democratic authorities. I do not support this proposal because this pre-imposed framework lacks the international validation and global ownership process through which human rights interpretation moves. Ultimately, an international interpreter, carefully checked by domestic interpreters of democracies, ought to achieve standards of interpretation that incorporate deference to judicial (and to some extent political) processes in democracies for some rights. However, it is still worth noting that a global and collective discovery process of the relationship between human rights and democracy has value in and of itself.

[11] I am grateful to Richard Bellamy for bringing this point to my attention.

6.2 *The design of international interpretive authorities*

The design of international interpretive authorities should reflect the values such authorities serve, and should offer adequate opportunities for the individual interpretations of these authorities to be rebutted. These general principles have consequences for the make-up of interpretive bodies, their proceedings and powers. The discussion below aims only to sketch out some of the relevant design issues in the light of the purposes of interpretive authorities, and is not intended to be a full list of design features.

A key principle in the design of these institutions should be the widest possible representation of the world's traditions of rights interpretations, to ensure global debate. This requires adequate and high-quality representation of those traditions. The European Court of Human Rights, for example, has a 'one country, one judge' principle. At the United Nations a structure of regional representation, informed by Cold War divisions, is used. Treaty-interpreting bodies have between 10 and 23 members. The bodies with the largest interpretive mandates and adjudicative powers, the Human Rights Committee and the Committee on Economic Social and Cultural Rights, each have 18 members. This is a relatively small number to satisfy global coverage in the case of those treaties that make up the International Bill of Rights. The quality and knowledge of the interpreters also needs to be subject to control and scrutiny through a verification and vetting procedure.

The proceedings of interpretive authorities should provide for ample opportunity for international interpretive bodies to consider alternative interpretations offered by domestic authorities. This requires a transparent process of exchange before an interpretation is issued. Interpretive authorities should be able to collect any relevant information that impinges on the interpretive process. This has design implications for the expertise and support such authorities receive.

The account I provide here does not distinguish between international human rights courts and quasi-judicial bodies in terms of what entitles them to a presumption of deference. This is because of the distinction I make between the standard of justification for interpretive and adjudicatory authority (and the authority to deliver remedies). The justification of interpretive authority is grounded in similar principles for both types of institutions: neither courts nor quasi-legal bodies have a hierarchical relationship with domestic judicial and legislative interpretive authorities.

International courts are different from quasi-judicial bodies because, in addition to interpretive authority, they also have adjudicatory authority. Adjudicatory authority enables human rights courts to deliver final judgments in individual cases and to authorise remedies for individual complainants, alongside offering an interpretation of human rights law that can have widespread consequences in the domestic context. Adjudicatory authority, by its very nature, must be final. Courts, however, do not enjoy absolute interpretive authority just because they also have adjudicatory authority. This means that while domestic authorities are under a legal obligation to award remedies to a particular individual with respect to a specific human rights law judgment, human rights courts do not automatically override domestic legislation or jurisprudence.

For practical purposes, one could argue that furnishing an interpretive authority with adjudicatory authority might have a positive spillover effect. This suggests that in the real world human rights courts are more likely to be deferred to than quasi-judicial interpretive bodies. There is, however, also a principled reason for combining interpretive authority with adjudicatory authority. Individual cases are important heuristic aids in the interpretation of human rights law, enabling interpreters to make sense of values in the light of changing circumstances. This principled view lends support to affording of adjudicatory powers to interpretive authorities, as does the more practical argument that courts are better respected than institutions with powers of recommendation.

7. Conclusion

This paper has focused for the most part on the correct point of departure in analysing the distribution of deference in interpreting international human rights treaties. I have argued that the place to start this analysis is the value of legitimacy in the context of human rights treaty interpretation in the international arena. The long-standing controversies surrounding legitimacy in the domestic context do not offer much guidance in analysing this international context. I have argued, therefore, that our conceptions of deference need to take into account the need for a qualified authority to facilitate the broad application of human rights principles and their development globally.

This interpretive move has enabled me to establish a standard with which to assess competing interpretations of legitimate authority.

Specifically, I have argued that the standard of distinct moral contribution to the advancement of a global human rights culture justifies an attitude of conditional deference towards the interpretive authority by domestic interpreters of all kinds. I have further argued that the international interpretive process facilitates a constructive dialogue about the best interpretation of human rights treaties, both through deference and rebuttal. In cases of principled disagreement, I have suggested that states should adopt an attitude of reconciliation rather than conflict when airing disagreements. Disagreement with the interpretive authority, therefore, should also be in the spirit of improving global interpretation of human rights law. My argument has not assumed a correct interpretive theory of human rights treaties. Rather, it has aimed to show that an attitude of deference on the side of domestic interpretive authorities offers a chance for such a theory to emerge and to establish a foothold globally.

The account of legitimacy I advance in this paper is sensitive to the circumstances of legitimacy. I do not argue that presumption of deference should be the basis of legitimacy at all times. Indirect instrumentalism is justified because global human rights treaty interpretation is in its early days: human rights protections are far from realised in most parts of the world, by domestic legislatures and judiciaries, let alone by governments. If these circumstances change, for example, if individuals participate in international institutions in more direct ways, rather than through their governments, or if concrete human rights interpretations are regarded as part of a solid overlapping consensus across all political communities in the world, a different theory of legitimacy might be more suitable, to reflect the changing purposes of these institutions.

Bibliography

Beitz, C., 2001. Human Rights as a Common Concern. *American Political Science Review* 95, 269–282.

Bellamy, R., 2007. *Political Constitutionalism: A Republican Defence of the Constitutionality of Democracy*, Cambridge University Press.

Benhabib, S., 2004. *The Rights of Others: Aliens, Residents and Citizens*, Cambridge University Press.

Buchanan, A., 2004. *Justice, Legitimacy and Self-Determination: Moral Foundations for International Law*, Oxford University Press.

2010. The Legitimacy of International Law. In S. Besson and J. Tasioulas eds. *The Philosophy of International Law*, Oxford University Press.

Çalı, B., 2009. On Interpretivism and International Law. *European Journal of International Law* 20, 805–822.

2012. Specialised Rules of Treaty Interpretation: Human Rights. In D. Hollis ed, *The Oxford Guide to Treaties*, Oxford University Press.

Coakley, M., 2011. On the Value of Political Legitimacy. *Philosophy and Economics* 10(4), 345–369.

Craven, M., 2000. Legal Differentiation and the Concept of a Human Rights Treaty. *European Journal of International Law* 11, 489–519.

Drzemczewski, A., 1998. *The European Human Rights Convention in Domestic Law: A Comparative Study*, Oxford University Press.

Dworkin, R., 2008. *Justice in Robes*, Cambridge: Harvard University Press.

Føllesdal, A., 2006. The Legitimacy Deficits of the European Union. *Journal of Political Philosophy* 14, 441–468.

2007. The Legitimacy of International Human Rights Review: The Case of the European Court of Human Rights. *Journal of Social Philosophy* 40, 595–607.

Freeman, S., 1990. Reason and Agreement in Social Contract Views. *Philosophy & Public Affairs* 19(2), 122–157.

Goldsmith, J. & Posner, E., 2005. *The Limits of International Law*, New York: Oxford University Press.

Hafner-Burton, E. M., 2012. International Regimes for Human Rights. *Annual Review of Political Science* 15, 265–286.

Hessler, K., 2005. Resolving Interpretive Conflicts in International Human Rights Law. *Journal of Political Philosophy* 13, 29–52.

Higgins, R., 1989. Human Rights: Some Questions of Integrity. *Modern Law Review* 52, 1–12.

Nickel, J., 2006. *Making Sense of Human Rights*, 2nd edition, Oxford: Blackwell Publishing.

Pellet, A., 2001. Droit de l'hommisme' et droit international. The Gilberto Amado Memorial Lecture, *Revue Droits Fondamenteux* at www.revue.dh.org accessed on 8 October 2012.

Rawls, J., 1955. Two Concepts of Rules. *The Philosophical Review* 64, 3–32.

1996. *Political Liberalism*, 2nd edition, New York: Columbia University Press.

2007. *Lectures on the History of Political Philosophy*, S. Freeman ed. Cambridge: Harvard University Press.

Raz, J., 2006. The Problem of Authority: Revisiting the Service Conception. *Minnesota Law Review* 90, 1003–1044.

Sen, A., 2004. Elements of a Theory of Human Rights. *Philosophy and Public Affairs* 32, 315–356.

Singer, P., 1973. *Democracy and Disobedience*, Oxford: Clarendon Press.

Sloss, D., 2009. *The Role of Domestic Courts in Treaty Enforcement*, Cambridge University Press.

Von Bogdandy, A. and Venzke, I., 2012. In Whose Name? An Investigation of International Courts' Public Authority and Its Democratic Justification. *European Journal of International Law* 23, 7–41.

Waldron, J., 2005. Foreign Law and the Modern Ius Gentium. *Harvard Law Review* 119, 129–147.

Wolff, R. B., 1970. *In Defense of Anarchism*, New York: Harper & Row.

6

Torture and the politics of legitimation in international law

IAN HURD

1. Introduction

All manifestations of political power eventually lead to questions about their legitimacy. The institutions of international human rights aspire to have power over governments and over individuals, and to the extent that they succeed the legitimacy of their authority is worth investigating. How and when can political authority be justified as legitimate, and what consequences follow from it? These questions are increasingly addressed to international law and organizations as a consequence of a perceived shift in the location of political power from the state to a more decentralized model of "governance without government" (Clark 2005; Hurd 2007; Lindseth 2010).[1] The institutions of domestic democratic governance are widely credited with providing legitimacy to the modern state, and the transfer of political authority from democratic states to nondemocratic international rules or bodies reopens the legitimacy problem anew.

Human rights laws and courts have seen tremendous growth since the 1980s. The power of these institutions leads directly to inquiries into their fairness, their accountability, and their foundation, all of which are in some form questions about legitimacy. However, most discussion of the connection between human rights rules and legitimacy has focused on the particularly narrow question of how legitimation might increase compliance. In other words, what institutional arrangements might be made in order to increase state compliance with the set of desirable human rights obligations? This is a question of institutional design and it is at the heart of much of the recent literature at the intersection of international law

[1] "Governance without government" in the international context comes from Rosenau & Czempiel (1992).

and political science (Hafner-Burton, Victor, & Lupu 2012; Koremenos, Lipson, & Snidal 2003; Simmons 2009).[2] It operationalizes legitimacy as a causal factor that might change state behavior toward compliance, and then seeks to manipulate it as a variable in ways that will contribute to higher levels of compliance. This leads to debates over which set of human rights can be seen as legitimate, and what institutional arrangements are legitimate in order to realize them.[3] The pursuit of international human rights through international law is premised on the idea that legitimation of the rules or human-rights institutions is a step toward better compliance by states.

The crucial link behind such thinking is the supposition that widespread belief in the legitimacy of an international rule will lead to greater compliance with that rule. This is a conventional assumption in literature on legitimacy in international politics and law – Thomas Franck, for instance, includes compliance in the definition of a legitimate rule – and yet it gets little attention, either empirical or conceptual.[4] This paper gives some reason to question this view of the link between legitimation and compliance. It examines the practical life of the antitorture regime in recent years and shows how the Bush administration in the USA constructed a pro-torture practice inside the antitorture legal institutions. The antitorture rules have a high degree of international legitimacy but the case shows that this does not preclude rule-violation. The legitimacy of the rules does indeed shape state behavior, and so it is consequential, but these consequences are not measurable in terms of changing state behavior from violation to compliance. The politics of legitimation around torture are more complicated: the Bush administration used the antitorture regime, accepting its legitimacy, to justify and authorize a policy of torture. It constructed ambiguity in the regime in order to fit its preferred policy within the rules. The legitimacy of the rules in the eyes of their audience was essential to making this work, since it shaped how violation was conducted and framed.

The problem that interests me is how legitimacy is conceived in social science scholarship. Legitimacy is widely defined in relation to rule

[2] On the existence of a "compliance gap" at the heart of international law and organization, see Luck & Doyle (2004).

[3] On the first, see for instance Benhabib (2008), on the second see for instance Christiano (2011).

[4] Franck says, "A partial definition of legitimacy adapted to the international system could be formulated thus: *a property of a rule or rule-making institution which itself exerts a pull towards compliance on those addressed normatively*" (Franck 1990: 16, emphasis in original).

compliance, as either a socializing force that induces actors to comply with a rule (Hurd 2007), or as a moral and psychological reason for an actor to choose to comply with a rule (Buchanan & Keohane 2006), or as an influence on costs and benefits that makes compliance the rational, profitable choice (Voeten 2005). These approaches leave no room to understand a case where rules appear to be widely accepted as legitimate and are also subject to noncompliance by those who believe in their legitimacy. In other words, these approaches deny agents the capacity to think, act, and choose in the presence of a legitimated rule or norm. To understand the politics of legitimation in such a case requires decoupling legitimacy from compliance, and therefore requires rethinking how legitimacy relates to rules, interests, and state behavior. These are the goals of this paper.

I divide the argument into three sections. The first examines the content of the legal regime against torture and its relevance to US behavior in the 2000s. This is largely contained in the Convention Against Torture (1984) and the Geneva Convention of 1949.[5] I make a case that these rules have a high level of legitimacy in the international community, including in the US government. Given the unmeasurable nature of legitimacy this case can only be tentative, but I believe it is nonetheless strong and more plausible than any alternative. The second section then discusses US behavior toward these rules under George W. Bush, emphasizing the effort to fit the practice of torture within the legal rules that forbid it. The legal arguments that they provided are elements in a politics of legitimation, and rest on the ability to use the rules instrumentally to legitimate a political choice – that is, it requires that legitimacy and agency exist simultaneously, and so cannot be understood in the conventional scholarly framing of legitimacy. The third section outlines an approach to international law and politics that can understand how legitimacy may coexist with rule-violation. States value being seen as complying with their international legal obligations, as evidenced by the widespread practice of using international legal arguments in public diplomacy. International law provides the resources out of which these justifications are made, and in this process it is inevitable that states will present competing and perhaps even irreconcilable understandings of the content of international law. Contested claims about compliance are endemic to international law, as they are to all law, and in the

[5] "Convention Against Torture and Other Cruel, Inhuman or Degrading Treatment or Punishment," 1984, at www2.ohchr.org/english/law/cat.htm. Geneva Conventions at www.icrc.org/eng/war-and-law/treaties-customary-law/geneva-conventions/index.jsp. Of special relevance below is the Third Convention: "Convention (III) Relative to the Treatment of Prisoners of War," 1949, at www.icrc.org/ihl.nsf/FULL/375?OpenDocument.

absence of a judicial institution they are likely to remain unresolved. The rule of law in world politics encompasses these controversies: states believe in the importance of rule-following even where they cannot agree on what actions constitute rule-following. In such a world, the power of the rules is evident in their use by states, independent of judgments regarding what constitutes compliance with them.

2. Torture in international humanitarian law

The universe of international human rights law and norms contains many prohibitions on torture. These vary in their legal status from the hortatory to the compelling. The Universal Declaration of Human Rights includes the very clear statement that "no one shall be subjected to torture or to cruel, inhuman or degrading treatment or punishment" (Art. 5). This was repeated in, among other places, the American Convention on Human Rights of 1969 and the International Covenant on Civil and Political Rights of 1976.[6] These are specific incarnations of the more general statement in the United Nations Charter that its member states "reaffirm faith in fundamental human rights."[7] However, none of these treaties frame their subject in terms of specific legal obligations that are binding on their signatories and so they are not of a type that can be complied with or violated – they describe what they see as the aspirations of the signatories.

The key documents for contemporary legal debate on torture are the Convention Against Torture and Other Cruel, Inhuman or Degrading Treatment (CAT), adopted in 1984 after negotiations in the UN General Assembly, and the Geneva Convention of 1949, particularly Article 3 on the treatment of people in non-international conflicts. The CAT defines torture as

> any act by which severe pain or suffering, whether physical or mental, is intentionally inflicted on a person for such purposes as obtaining from him … information or a confession, punishing him … or intimidating or coercing him …, when such pain or suffering is inflicted by or at the instigation of … a public official or other person acting in an official capacity.
>
> (Art. 1)

[6] "The American Convention on Human Rights," 1969, at www.oas.org/juridico/english/treaties/b-32.html/. The ACHR is open to members of the Organization of American States. "International Convention on Civil and Political Rights," 1976, at www2.ohchr.org/english/law/ccpr.htm.

[7] *Charter of the United Nations* Preamble, see also Article 56.

It requires that signatory states "take effective legislative, administrative, judicial or other measures to prevent acts of torture in any territory under its jurisdiction" (Art. 2) and "ensure that all acts of torture are offenses under its criminal law" (Art. 4).

The Geneva Conventions of 1949 prohibit "violence to life and person, in particular murder of all kinds, mutilation, cruel treatment and torture" (3rd, 3(i)a) and "outrages upon personal dignity, in particular, humiliating and degrading treatment" (3rd, 3(i)c). These apply in cases of declared war among contracting parties (Art. 2) as well as in conflicts of a noninternational character (Art. 3). This is the set of treaties that includes the three earlier Geneva Conventions (of 1864, 1906, and 1929) and adds a fourth, and has been ratified by every member of the United Nations – this makes it the centerpiece of international human rights law as it applies to behavior in the context of war and other armed conflict.

Both documents are in the form of an inter-state treaty, which means that the obligations that each contains are legally binding on the states that accept it and are not legally relevant to any other state or any other kind of actor. Public international law has traditionally been understood as having only states as its subjects and does not regulate the conduct of individual persons (though pirates may be seen as holding special status under international law). This is relevant in this context because it means that there is a gap between the international prohibition of torture and the legal position of the individuals whose conduct is presumably ultimately of interest to the law. To get from a public international law commitment against torture to an obligation that is binding on individuals as such, whether private or public officials, requires a bridge from public international law to either domestic law or international criminal law.

For the Convention Against Torture, this bridge is provided by its Article 4. By requiring that torture be made a criminal offense in the domestic law of its signatory states, the CAT exploits existing domestic legal regimes in order to impinge on the torturer as an individual. In this way, Article 4 of the CAT fills the legal gap between the domain of inter-state public international law and the regulation of the behavior of individual persons. For the Geneva Conventions, the gap is bridged by Article 1, which is common across all four of the conventions, and reads: "The High Contracting Parties undertake to respect and to ensure respect for the present Convention in all circumstances." This again is done with domestic legislation and military codes of conduct binding on the states' military personnel.

The operation of this domestic implication was recently explained for the CAT in the 2012 decision of the International Court of Justice (ICJ) in the case of *Belgium v. Senegal*.[8] The Court decided that Senegal committed a harm to Belgium by not prosecuting Hissène Habré for crimes covered under the Torture convention. Habré is the former president of Chad who has been living in Senegal for several years despite evidence of his responsibility for torture while in office. The ICJ reached several interesting conclusions in its decision: first, on jurisdiction, it found that the disagreement between Belgium and Senegal over how the CAT should be implemented was indeed a "legal dispute" and thus the Court's jurisdiction was activated; second, on substance, it found that Senegal's failure to act against Habré amounted to a violation of its promises to other CAT signatory states; and finally, it found that Belgium, as one of these states, had its international legal rights harmed by that violation and so was in a position to bring the matter to the ICJ in a contentious case. The judgment demands that Senegal use its domestic criminal institutions to prosecute Habré for torture, or that it extradite him in accordance with the CAT. The case shows the path by which the international obligation taken on by the government in signing the CAT is executed through changes in the domestic criminal codes, and also how this remains an international obligation over which the ICJ exercises oversight authority.

Other international human rights instruments can be compared on how they do or do not deal with this gap. The Genocide Convention, for instance, includes an obligation for domestic legal internalization. It requires that its States parties "enact, in accordance with their respective Constitutions, the necessary legislation to give effect to the provisions" of the Convention which criminalize genocide and set the terms for investigating and punishing those who commit it (Art. V). This puts the crime of genocide into the domestic criminal codes of all signatory states. The Rome Statute of the International Criminal Court is revolutionary because it relies on a very different means to bridge between international law and domestic individuals: it creates a new kind of international legal authority with "jurisdiction over natural persons pursuant to this statute."[9] The ICC treaty includes the promise by the States parties that they will consent to their citizens, as well as foreigners within their jurisdictions, being prosecuted by the ICC directly under certain conditions. This (arguably)

[8] *Questions Relating to the Obligation to Prosecute or Extradite* (*Belgium v. Senegal*), www.icj-cij.org/docket/files/144/17084.pdf.

[9] *Rome Statute of the International Criminal Court*, Article 25(1).

amounts to a new category of public international law where the subject is an individual person rather than a state. The ICC and the CAT can be contrasted with other instruments in which no effort is made to bridge between states' obligations to each other and the legal standing of individuals. For instance, there is nothing in the UN Charter or the ICCPR or the Universal Declaration of Human Rights that requires that individuals refrain from, or be punished for, acts of torture – in each of these instruments, the commitment against torture is made as a promise (or an aspiration) of states *inter se*.

The bridge between international law on torture and US domestic law is accomplished in several ways. For the Geneva Convention, this is done with the War Crimes Act of 1996, which makes grave breaches of the Conventions into federal crimes. In the domain of torture more broadly, the formal language of "torture" is used in US criminal law only to refer to acts committed abroad, while much of the substantive behavior that the CAT is concerned with within the USA falls under the Eighth Amendment to the US Constitution. The Criminal Code defines torture as "an act committed by a person under the color of law specifically intended to inflict severe pain and suffering" (18 US C. §2340), when the act was committed abroad. When committed inside the USA, these acts fall under the constitutional prohibition on "cruel and unusual punishments." The same acts committed by private actors without any connection to the purposes of the state (i.e., without "color of law" or "an official capacity") would be covered by general criminal laws against assault, murder, etc. Police brutality in Chicago, for instance, cannot be prosecuted as "torture" strictly speaking because it is domestic (Human Rights Watch 1998).

The antitorture regime represents an archetypal piece of traditional international law in the classical sense: these are explicit black-letter treaties that have effect as a result of state consent. It is relatively clear as treaty-law goes as it sets down what Liese considers to be a "non-derogable and absolute" prohibition (Liese 2009: 21). The purpose of these instruments is to induce compliance by government authorities, and they therefore fit into a very traditional frame in the legal architecture in world politics: public international law in the inter-state model. They are designed to change the costs and benefits that states face as they consider how they might use force against individuals in their custody, and specifically to increase the political costs of using torture. This is consistent with conventional accounts of the philosophy of international law, of how the international rule of law is generally understood, and with the "compliance model" of law in international relations.[10] The rules are also clearly designed for a nonideal world: the CAT treaty anticipates that violations will occur and sets rules about states' responses to instances of torture.[11] Most of its articles deal with the obligations of states when acts of torture are committed, either by their officials or against their citizens. These are rules that are grounded in the practical realities of inter-state relations.

The legitimacy of these rules also seems well established. Even accepting that it is impossible to measure legitimacy in international society with any confidence, several streams of evidence suggest that these rules are seen as highly legitimate by states and activists. For instance, both are among the most widely ratified human rights instruments: the Geneva Convention by 194 jurisdictions and the Convention Against Torture by 147. And even groups that are not qualified to ratify them (such as sub-state military forces) often make explicit statements about their commitment to the rules they contain – actors actively seek out affiliation with the rules, seeking no doubt some political legitimacy that they believe is attached to them.[12] There is little dissent from the idea that the rules are binding on the states that have accepted them and that they are both normatively and legally good; that is, they are accepted as important legal commitments by states, and they are endorsed as reflecting normative progress in world politics.[13] For instance, Louise Arbour, the UN High Commissioner for Human Rights, was likely speaking the majority opinion when she recently said that the "absolute ban on torture … [is] a cornerstone of the international human rights edifice."[14] When controversies arise over torture in international law, it is generally focused on how to make governments follow them more faithfully rather than whether they should exist or not. There is essentially no controversy over the rules themselves and no mobilization to abolish or limit them – all discussion is about their implementation, extension, or enforcement. The absence of controversy is unlikely to be "artificial" in the sense of being a result of either the exclusion of dissent

[10] On the international rule of law, see Chesterman (2008). On the "compliance model," see Howse & Teitel (2010).

[11] See the introduction to this volume on the importance of nonideal theorizing of international human rights.

[12] See for instance Interim Transitional National Council of Libya (2011).

[13] On antitorture rules as evidence of moral progress in world politics, see for instance Jolly, Emmerij, & Weiss (2009).

[14] Louise Arbour "On Terrorists and Torturers" (Statement by the UN High Commissioner for Human Rights, 7 December 2005) cited in Liese (2009).

by the imposition of political power or the fundamental irrelevance of the rules.[15]

Perhaps most telling among the evidence for the legitimation of antitorture laws is the fact that those who argue in favor of "coercive interrogation" or "exceptional measures" work hard to differentiate these from torture itself. Michael Ignatieff is representative of this position, with his argument that torture should be outlawed *and* (not "but") the government should be allowed to use coercive interrogation measures in certain circumstances or with special bureaucratic or political procedures (Forsythe 2011: Ch. 7; Ignatieff 2004). A different route to what might be the same outcome is taken by Alan Dershowitz who argues that torture is rightly outlawed in international law *but*, since it continues to be practiced by states, we should require that it be used only according to certain bureaucratic or political procedures (i.e., warrants to permit torture must be obtained first) so that the practice is accompanied by greater accountability (Dershowitz 2003). Both arguments begin with strong statements in defense of the illegality of torture, even though their consequent claims either endorse it in practice or are premised on its continuation. This supports the conclusion that the ban on torture is very nearly universally endorsed.[16]

All of these elements point to the conclusion that the obligations they contain are well legitimated among states, scholars, and activists, even if this conclusion can only be tentative and provisional.

3. Literature on legitimacy, and connection to compliance

The conventional understanding of legitimacy in social science would predict that this legitimacy should translate into faithful compliance with the rules. The scholarly literature maintains that legitimacy is naturally related to compliance: compliance is often modeled as a consequence of legitimacy (for instance, Hurd 2007; Voeten 2005), and legitimacy is often sought as a mechanism for increasing compliance or for reducing opposition (for instance, Bjola 2005; Buchanan 2007). This is evident across the spectrum of scholarship, and originates in the sociological literature from which the

[15] These are noted in the introduction to this volume as possible reasons (alongside legitimacy) for why a rule might exist without controversy.

[16] A case for its incompleteness could be premised on the following voices in US politics: *New York Times* (2011). However, much of the debate in American political discourse is over whether specific practices such as waterboarding constitute torture or not, which is distinct from the question of whether torture itself is permissible.

IR literature is derived: it is present in Max Weber's view of legitimacy, in Jürgen Habermas's model of communicative action, in John Gaventa's theory of acquiescence and social power, in consent theory, in democratic theory, and beyond. A rule that is legitimate is said to be more likely to induce compliance by actors.

The legitimacy literature in IR arrives at this conclusion by two distinct paths, reflecting competing visions of how to study legitimacy in social settings. A subjective tradition defines legitimacy as the belief by an individual that a rule or structure has rightful authority. This traces back to Max Weber's sociological theory of legitimacy, in a "descriptive" rather than "normative" attitude. It begins from the premise that legitimacy rests in the ideas held by an actor about their social surroundings. These ideas may be shared among many in a community, but it is reducible to an individual belief: because individuals behave differently toward rules that they believe are legitimate, the existence of a belief about legitimate rule has important consequences for aggregate social and political systems.[17] An objective tradition begins by asking what kinds of rules or structures are deserving of these beliefs, and it therefore posits external normative criteria, often derived from moral philosophy, to judge whether a rule or institution can be called legitimate. Common among these criteria are versions of democratic procedures or substantive goals such as fairness or respect for human rights. This view suggests that outside observers can judge the legitimacy of a rule by observing its content, or its genealogy, or its relationship to the governed.[18]

The subjective tradition has an affinity with behavioral studies in social science, and focuses on how people (or states) behave in the face of political authorities that they believe to be legitimate (or illegitimate). The objective tradition has more in common with normative philosophy, and has the power to second-guess people's own beliefs about the legitimacy of the institutions around them. For instance, Tom Tyler, following the subjective tradition, investigates when and why people in the USA obey laws and decisions that do not favor them (Tyler 1990). He finds that people are more likely to follow the law when they have faith in the legitimacy of the process that produced it. He does not ask whether these beliefs are justified. By contrast, Allen Buchanan suggests that a government should only be considered legitimate when it meets certain standards for the treatment of its citizens, regardless of how the population feels about it (Buchanan

[17] For instance, Gaventa (1982) on the behavioral consequences of the third face of power.

[18] For instance, Doyle (2011) on when preemptive force should be considered legitimate.

2007). This is characteristic of the objective approach – Buchanan posits a set of morally valuable criteria and then uses them to judge whether a government should count as legitimate.

The traditions coexist because each can illuminate the blind spots of the other. The objective approach is only as compelling as the moral criteria that it begins with, and these are endlessly contested in political philosophy. The subjective approach takes seriously people's beliefs about their political surroundings but provides no critical resources for assessing those beliefs; political leaders routinely try to legitimize their rule to their subjects, and they may succeed even if outsiders find the regime abhorrent. The two therefore mean very different things when they conclude that a rule or institution is legitimate, and these differences often keep the sides from talking clearly with each other.

They agree, however, that compliance is naturally connected to legitimacy. The objective tradition suggests that agents have a moral or political reason to comply with legitimate rules (a "duty to obey"), while the subjective tradition finds empirical evidence that they in fact do comply with them more than rules without legitimacy. Conversely, rule-violation is in this view evidence of the absence of legitimacy. As Schaffer, Føllesdal, and Ulfstein (this volume) note, "if a treaty ... fails to secure its objective to a certain minimum extent, it risks losing normative legitimacy: individuals and other actors may no longer regard themselves as bound to comply." Rules and institutions, it is said, lose their legitimacy and thus their power if they are routinely violated, just as law loses its bindingness through desuetude. Thus, increasing the legitimacy of a rule is said to increase the likelihood that it will be respected in the policy choices of states, which motivates the search for strategies of legitimation which might cause this to happen.

4. Legitimacy and the rules on torture: the US case

The laws on torture however do not fit this model. The rules apparently have a high degree of legitimacy in both the objective and subjective senses, and yet their near universal acceptance by states as rules that represent the "good" has not produced universal compliance. Many states that have accepted either or both of these treaties have nonetheless used torture in violation of their commitments. Torture remains an option that is used with some frequency by governments and their agents. It can be found in almost all settings of political power – it appears in the practice of all kinds of regimes, including democracies and dictatorships, and it is used in the pursuit of all kinds of political objectives, foreign policy, domestic, and other.[19] Of course, this is no different than many other international rules, perhaps all rules: we expect some degree of noncompliance by the parties. The question of interest in this article is how the apparent rule-breaking relates to the apparent legitimacy of the rules. The fact of the continuing and extensive practice of torture despite the antitorture legal regime might be evidence that the rules are in fact not seen as legitimate, or that the rules are not consequential, or that legitimation and compliance are distinct concepts without a natural affinity. This section pursues this third possibility – I suggest that international rules such as those on torture do gain power by being widely seen as legitimate but that this power cannot be gauged by its contribution to rule-following or compliance. Noncompliance of a type can coexist with legitimated rules without undermining the concept of legitimacy. The key is to take a more sophisticated approach to the relationship between agents and structures in social settings.

The tension between rule and practice in this case is notable for many reasons. Most importantly, the failure to forgo torture is a compelling humanitarian catastrophe for the victims and a political and legal disaster for the perpetrators (Center for Victims of Torture 2006). It also points to important questions about the weakness of international treaties and enforcement (Hathaway 2007). For the present article, I am interested in the relationship that it reveals between legitimacy and noncompliance. What does it mean for the politics of legitimation that a rule so apparently well legitimated is also violated at a nontrivial rate?

The US government under George W. Bush consistently maintained its claim to compliance with international law on torture. Mr. Bush famously said in 2005 "we do not torture." By way of explanation, he suggested that "there's an enemy that lurks and plots and plans to hurt America again. And so, you bet we will aggressively pursue them. But we will do so under the law" (Bush 2005). This reflects a deep-seated commitment to the idea of the rule of law in world politics, and to an important self-perception that US foreign-policy interests are naturally aligned with the demands of the rule of law. Similar claims to inherent rule-following are evident in other areas of US international policy, including the legality of killing Osama bin Laden (Holder 2011), the ban on aggressive war (Hurd 2011a), and the use of robots in war (ASIL 2010). In all these cases, the state appears certain of the legality of its behavior and provides an explanation for how the relevant international rules are coincident with its underlying interests.

[19] See for instance the CIRI Human Rights Dataset at ciri.binghamton.edu. Also Rejali (2009).

The tenure of George W. Bush as president of the United States is often characterized as being indifferent or hostile to the rules of international law, of "lawlessness" and of perpetrating an "attack on international law" or the "dramatic rejection of international legal constraints" (Liese 2009; Sands 2008; Slaughter 2008). And concomitantly, many have interpreted Barack Obama's presidency as including a "return" to international cooperation and international law (for instance, Kelly 2009). With respect to torture specifically, the Bush administration enacted policies regarding interrogation of prisoners in blatant violation of its international legal commitments.[20] It did this in secret at first, but continued under new political and legal justifications once it was exposed (Forsythe 2011; Mayer 2008). There is little doubt that these actions, and perhaps the policy-making that backed them up, constituted grave breaches of the Geneva Convention (assuming the USA was in a condition of war or armed conflict) and violations of the Convention Against Torture, meaning that those who approved and executed them put themselves in legal jeopardy under the war crimes provisions of the US criminal code and other US statutes.

However, it is equally true that the Bush administration invested heavily in explaining its behavior, and it used the existing international laws on torture as the framing around which it construed these explanations (Bradley 2009). These arguments have been widely rejected as legally unsound, but they are significant in the politics of legitimation of international human rights. The investment made in situating US policy within the law shows that the international legal architecture on human rights was indeed important to the Bush administration. The gap between law and practice in this case cannot be understood simply as a powerful state choosing to violate rather than comply with the rules. The naïve distinction between "rules" and "interests" that often characterizes debates about international law in IR is not sustainable.[21] The case therefore suggests a more nuanced view of the relationship between states, rules, and behavior.

As evidence of US torture became public, the US offered three kinds of legal arguments to substantiate its claim to rule-compliance: it said, first, that prisoners in US custody did not qualify for the legal protections of the

[20] This is documented in, among other places, Center for Constitutional Rights (2006); Forsythe (2011); Sands (2008). As I argue below, the US sought to create ambiguity over whether its actions qualified as torture as a matter of international law; this does not preclude acknowledging the existence of torture as a factual matter.

[21] For a classical statement of this distinction, see Keohane (1997) who posits norm-following as an alternative to interest-following. The same instinct to separate interests and norms as motivations for action underlies March & Olsen (2008).

antitorture regime set out above; second, that the particular practices of US interrogations, including waterboarding, did not satisfy the standard of "torture" in international and domestic law; and finally, that the US constitution allowed the President to supersede international law *in extremis*. These arguments used the resources of the international legal regime on torture in order to construct explanations and justifications for American policy that would reconcile US behavior and the rules. It represents an appeal to international law in general, and a reinvestment in the rules prohibiting torture in particular, done in the service of avoiding legal responsibility for rule-violation. The case helps to show in conclusion that the practice of international law is at once constraining on states and irrevocably political.

The first claim was essentially about jurisdiction, and rested on the argument that the individuals that the USA was holding as a result of its "war on terror" were not of the types described as qualifying for protection under any of the Geneva Conventions. This argument was developed by the now-notorious legal team in the Office of Legal Counsel at the Department of Justice in 2002, who wrote advice for the President in January 2002 which the President adopted in February of that year (Bush 2002). It said that conflict with al-Qaeda was outside the scope of the Geneva Conventions because it was neither inter-state nor noninternational, and so the legal terms in the Third Geneva Convention were not relevant to prisoners captured in that conflict. No American behavior toward these people could violate the rules because the individuals were not within the jurisdiction of the rules. Further, it argued that while the war in Afghanistan *was* within the terms of the Third Convention, individuals fighting against the USA there did not qualify as prisoners of war under the Convention – they were not organized as a militia, with uniforms and command structure, and they did not themselves abide by the laws of war, said the USA (Bradley 2009: 63). To accommodate both sets of people, then the US created the new category of "illegal enemy combatant." It understood this new category as excluded from both the Geneva Convention protections guaranteed to combatants in inter-state war and those guaranteed to "irregulars" and fighters in non-international wars. There was therefore no legal requirement, they said, to follow any particular course of protection for their rights.

The second claim arose from close readings of the Convention Against Torture, the US Criminal Code, and other regulative documents on torture. The argument here was that the behaviors of interest to the USA, including beating, waterboarding, mock execution, and animal threats, were not encompassed by the term "torture" in these legal instruments. The content of "torture" was instead said to be limited to those acts which produce pain "equivalent in intensity to the pain accompanying serious physical injury, such as organ failure, impairment of bodily functions, or even death," or produce mental harm that persists for months (Bybee 2002). At the same time, the US took the view that to qualify as torture, the torturer had to "have the intent to inflict severe pain or suffering," as opposed to inflicting pain incidental to the intent to acquire information. For US domestic law, Justice Antonin Scalia of the Supreme Court later offered the view that these might not constitute violations of the Eighth Amendment either since they were not primarily intended as "punishments" relevant to that Amendment (BBC News 2008). Thus, one by one the behaviors of interest to the USA were identified and excluded from operative legal definitions of torture for US personnel, and then bundled under the heading of "enhanced interrogation techniques."

Finally, the administration maintained that under some circumstances the US President was not bound by the international legal commitments taken on by the United States. The Bybee memo suggested that the President was essentially unregulated by Congress or by international law in his commander-in-chief duties such that the treatment of detainees in the "war on terror" was at his discretion (Bybee 2002; Yoo 2006).[22] This also applied, it said, to the behaviors of subordinates to the President who were acting on his instructions. The constitutional position of the President relative to other legal institutions meant that the torture prohibitions were not constraints on his authority nor on the behavior of his agents. This has generated a great deal of discussion among scholars of US constitutional law, overwhelmingly critical (for instance Koh 2006). However, its function in the political debates over torture was to find space within the rule of law where that which was banned by the rules could be practiced without violating them.

Each of the arguments has met with fierce criticism in the USA and elsewhere. Each fails in the face of either logic or law, and none is currently the operative position of the US government. But this does not mean they are unimportant – as Abbott and Snidal note, "legalization entails a specific form of discourse, requiring justification and persuasion in terms of applicable rules and pertinent facts" (Abbott & Snidal 2000: 429). The

[22] This is different than the argument about a kind of "state of exception" in which the President is given discretion to violate the law. For instance, Jack Goldsmith defended the proposition that torture could be legal in situations "in which the President believed that exceeding the law was necessary in an emergency." Goldsmith, *The Terror Presidency*, 2007: 148, cited by Scharf (2009: 349).

American government in this case was committed to remaining within the framework of "legalized" politics in this sense. In what follows, I am interested in how these arguments made use of the international regime on torture, and in their cumulative effect in the politics of legitimation. This is distinct from the legal persuasiveness of the arguments themselves, and shows why we should not dismiss these arguments as merely self-serving gloss on self-evidently illegal behavior. It is true that they constituted self-serving justifications overlaid on rule-breaking, but this cannot be used to dismiss their political impact: they have important social consequences precisely because of how they invoke legal resources in the service of political ends.

The various legal defenses of torture generated by the Bush administration all present US behavior as consistent with the legal framework of international society. Together, they constitute a pattern in which individuals who are highly motivated to avoid the constraints of international law find it appealing to appear committed to operating within the constraints of international law; this might be a matter of superficial strategic calculation, or a deep-seated self-image as a rule-following agent, or some other combination of motivations. Regardless of the motivation, the observable consequence is a stream of rule-following justifications around apparently rule-breaking behavior. It constructs new ambiguity about the meaning of compliance within the legitimated norms and institutions of international human rights. The US-torture case takes a stark example of apparent non-compliance and sees in it the pervasive power of rule-compliance and a generalized rule-of-law ideology.

5. Implications

Three things are evident in the practice of the United States toward torture under George Bush.

First, it is clear that the leading voices in the Bush administration wanted US officials to be unlimited in their freedom to treat the prisoners as they wanted (Sands 2008; Scharf 2009). They were highly motivated to use physical violence against people under their control. But they also appear to have believed that this desire could be consistent with the legal framework around the treatment of detainees. They endorsed the prohibition on torture at the same time that they wanted US torture to be legal.

The international laws on torture gave them the tools to construct a legal space within the antitorture regime in which torture would be legal. The laws were being used as an instrument to insulate behavior from legal responsibility, in reverse of how law is usually understood. The more conventional model of the rule of law suggests that the law defines acceptable behavior and that actors should (though may not) modify their conduct to suit. In the torture case, the meaning of compliance was shaped around the policy – I argue elsewhere that this is in fact the normal condition for the rule of law in world politics (for instance, Hurd 2011a and 2012). The torture case supports the point made by Scott Veitch, that law organizes irresponsibility for harm as much as it does responsibility for harm. It "facilitate[s] the dispersals and disavowals of responsibility that together may be seen to constitute the practices of irresponsibility" (Veitch 2007: 3). The law in the torture case was used to create categories that insulated behavior from legal responsibility. This may well have been in part motivated by the desire to protect the decision-makers themselves and others from criminal liability in the USA or elsewhere – the legal justifications were preemptive in that they could answer any later complaint about criminal behavior. They were also intended to place US foreign policy and national interests within the frame of rule-following for international politics.

Second, it shows the pervasive power of the rule of law as an ideology in international affairs. The idea that foreign policy is and should be organized according to known rules is a central piece of the narrative of contemporary international politics. For but one example, Barack Obama said in his Nobel speech, "Where force is necessary, we have a moral and strategic interest in binding ourselves to certain rules of conduct … [E]ven as we confront a vicious adversary that abides by no rules … the United States of America must remain a standard bearer in the conduct of war. That is what makes us different from those whom we fight. That is the source of our strength" (Obama 2009). John Ikenberry has argued that the post-WWII international order is characterized by its commitment to international rules rather than bare power politics: it is a rules-based system, a fundamental change from previous eras (Ikenberry 2011).

The rule of law rests on the idea that the rules are fixed and known, and can therefore be used to differentiate between lawful and unlawful conduct (for instance Tamanaha 2007). Its premise is that the gap between rule-following and rule-breaking is knowable, either because it can be read directly from the rules themselves or because it is authoritatively decided by a judicial institution. Knowing that gap then makes it possible to make judgments about the behaviors of actors: the rule of law is what makes it possible for Madeleine Albright, among others, to distinguish "law-abiding" countries from "rogue states" and "terrorists" (Albright 1997).

The torture case provides an example of a situation where the difference between compliance and noncompliance is not knowable in the way that is necessary for the rule of law idea to work in its traditional form. In this case, and in other instances where the difference between compliance and noncompliance is contested in international relations, all actors can unite around the importance of rule-following and all can claim their own behavior as compliant, but the rules are insufficient to resolve the differences over these claims. The rules themselves may be thoroughly legitimated and may have been internalized by a wide range of states, and yet state behavior may frequently not match the rules. The "problem" in such cases is not an insufficient amount of legitimation or socialization,[23] nor the triumph of "interests" over "norms" (for instance Guzman 2008), but instead the fact that the legitimation of the rules does not in itself imply or create consensus over the meaning of compliance. States do not agree on what constitutes a violation of the rules and the system of international law is not able to resolve their disagreements. The study of international law needs therefore to consider the impact of law outside of the "compliance" paradigm.[24]

States continue to invest in showing that they are complying with the rules rather than violating them. They appear to believe that there are social rewards from rule-following, and this suggests that the rules are powerful even when the meaning of compliance is contested. The rules on torture have evident power over states, and their legitimacy is fundamental to that power, but neither the power of the rules nor the difference that legitimation makes can be assessed by examining compliance by states because it is the meaning of compliance that the parties are arguing over. Instead, the legitimacy of the rules is evident in how states explain and understand their behavior. It shapes the justifications that states make about themselves and their interests. This is a significant manifestation of legal power, distinct from debates over the meaning of compliance.

This leads to the third implication, which deals with the issue of what international law is for. The standard answer is that it distinguishes rightful conduct from forbidden conduct, as suggested by the rule of law model in domestic legal theory (Bingham 2010; Chesterman 2008; Tamanaha 2008). This view is traditional in IR and international legal scholarship (for instance Hafner-Burton, Victor, & Lupu 2011), and in this spirit

23 On socialization, see Checkel (2007).

24 For suggestions in this direction see Howse & Teitel (2010); Hurd (2011b).

Hedley Bull said that the job of the international lawyer is to "state what the rules of international law are" to her government (Bull 1977: 150). This may be possible in settings where there exist institutions that provide definitive rulings on rule-breaking and rule-following, for instance in a dispute heard by the International Court of Justice where the court's decision is decisive.[25] But it cannot be the case for the antitorture regime, and many other questions of international law, where disagreements about the meaning of legal terms will not be decided by a competent authority. In such settings, the parties will disagree on the meaning of compliance and their interpretations are inseparable from their preferences over the substance of the dispute. The strategic use of international law as a legitimating device is likely to occur wherever powerful political interests intersect with the categories of international law and there are no authoritative judicial institutions with jurisdiction to resolve conflicts. The list of substantive disputes that have this feature is long – for instance: debates over the legality of the use of force, either for self-defense or for humanitarian purposes (Hurd 2011a); the self-serving efforts by the USA to construct a legal regime that will permit its practice of using aerial drones against individuals;[26] the competing arguments around the legal effects, if any, of the doctrine Responsibility to Protect (Bellamy, Davies, & Glanville 2010). In these cases, disparate elements of law and of state practice are advanced by competing activists in support of their positions, all pursuing the legitimation that comes from being seen as compliant with international law. These practices show the importance that states attach to compliance with their legal obligations, and at the same time show that disagreement will be endemic over the meaning of compliance, the interpretation of state behavior, and the connection between the two.

The public nature of international legal resources means that claims regarding compliance by a state are met by counter claims also built from these resources. For most disputes, there is no authoritative body to reconcile them and so the diplomatic interaction over it does not produce greater consensus over the rules.[27] The literature on argumentation and persuasion

[25] This does not require that we believe that the court resolves all ambiguity – clearly that is not possible. All it requires is that the court be in an institutional position of authority to provide interpretations of legal questions that are legally final.

[26] See for instance Mazzetti (2012) and the subsequent debate at www.lawfareblog.com/tag/mark-mazzetti/.

[27] Hurd (2011b) argues that international diplomacy consists of competing legal arguments that do not necessarily lead to consensus.

through law tends to assume that these interactions will contribute to reducing the amount of disagreement over the question.[28] The process of deliberation and discussion is a problem-solving device, it is said, because it causes the parties to narrow their differences. The torture case contradicts this assumption, both in practice and in theory: in practice, it shows how a great deal of high-stakes diplomacy can go on around a legal controversy without the underlying issues being resolved, and the importance of the process is not contingent on the development of a consensus over the matter; in theory, the case shows how the USA used legal argumentation as an instrument to legitimate a highly controversial policy, and its strategy depended on the availability of competing interpretations of the law. Neither in practice nor in theory is a consensus over the core question the logical outcome of the process.

The role of international law must be understood without presuming a consensus over the content of "compliance" and "noncompliance." In this vein, Peter Lindseth has said of EU law that "the very nature of public law has itself deeply evolved. It has become less a system of rules marking seemingly clear lines between 'valid' and 'invalid' exercises of authority, as classical understandings of … the rule of law might have demanded. Instead, public law has evolved toward something more focused on 'the allocation of burdens of reason-giving,' or … 'accountability' " (Lindseth 2010: 21–22). The role of international law is best described in terms from Harold Koh: "by imposing constraints on government action, law legitimates and gives credibility to government action" (Koh 2010). Law legitimates, even if we can't agree on its content.

The instrumental use of law is analogous to how "science" is often used as a political instrument in environmental politics. Charlotte Epstein, for instance, has argued that controversies over whale hunting are often fought on the terrain of claims about science at the International Whaling Commission. The pro- and anti-whaling members of the IWC reach for data on whale stocks and movement as resources to construct justifications for their policies. Both sides behave as if "the provision of perfect scientific knowledge will resolve all remaining disagreements, because it will unequivocally reveal the appropriate, rational course of action with regard to a natural resource and the environment at large" (Epstein 2008; Hurd 2012). In Epstein's case, science is a tool in the politics of legitimation, much like law is a tool to justify or criticize behavior around the

[28] See for instance Johnstone (2011), following Habermas.

antitorture regime. Both law and science can be powerful legitimating devices when they are put to work in defense of a political position.

6. Conclusions

In this paper I use recent American behavior around the rules on torture to examine the politics of legitimation. In doing so, I contribute to a better understanding of the relationship between international law, human rights, and legitimation. When the USA was breaking the rules on torture, it also did two other things: it claimed that it was not breaking the rules, and it provided an interpretation of international law with which it sought to substantiate its claims. The first reaffirmed its commitment to the rule of law in world politics in general and the importance of compliance in specific, while the second argued that terms of compliance with the rule on torture should be understood in such a way that US behavior was not a violation. International law in this case was a tool used in legitimation contests among political actors. All sides claimed to be operating within the international rule of law, and this caused their disagreement to be framed as a fight over the meaning of compliance. The case shows why legitimacy cannot be equated to compliance – since compliance is essentially contested – and how the distance between the two concepts makes it possible to see the political power that is carried by the instrumental use of international law.

The behavioral output of a legitimated human-rights treaty is not necessarily respect for its substantive terms. This is at one level a depressing conclusion, since it means that the strategies of legitimation argued over by activists and scholars may not be reliable devices for improving the situation of those who might become victims in the future. However, it sustains the view that the laws are indeed powerful, even over powerful states and over nonaccountable leaders – the need to justify oneself according to the rules makes those leaders dependent on those rules and on their self-serving legal arguments about compliance. This dependence makes them vulnerable. Their arguments can be met with counter-arguments drawn from the same resources, and the political (and legal) costs of being seen to lose this argument can be high. Where there exist institutions to organize this accountability, such as the ICC or national criminal courts willing to claim jurisdiction, the practical life of international rules can be compelling on individuals. This is not impeded by the fact that even well-legitimated rules contain within them the possibility of endless competing interpretations of compliance and noncompliance.

Bibliography

Abbott, K. W. & Snidal, D., 2000. Hard and Soft Law in International Governance. *International Organization*, 54(3), 421–456.

Albright, M., 1997. Building a Bipartisan Foreign Policy. Address at Rice Memorial Center, Rice University, Houston, Texas: February 7, 1997. Available at: www.womenspeecharchive.org/files/Building_a_Bipartisan_Foreign_Polic_D3FED68BA927D.pdf [Accessed February 11, 2013].

American Society of International Law (ASIL), 2010. US State Dept. Legal Advisor Lays Out Obama Administration Position on Engagement, "Law of 9/11," Press Release, March 25, 2010.

BBC News, 2008. US Judge Steps in to Torture Row, February 12, 2008. Available at: http://news.bbc.co.uk/2/hi/americas/7239748.stm [Accessed February 6, 2013].

Bellamy, A. J., Davies, S. E., & Glanville, L., 2010. *The Responsibility to Protect and International Law*, Leiden: Brill.

Benhabib, S., 2008. The Legitimacy of Human Rights. Daedalus, Summer: 94–104.

Bingham, T., 2010. *The Rule of Law*, London: Penguin.

Bjola, C., 2005. Legitimating the Use of Force in International Politics: A Communicative Action Perspective. *European Journal of International Relations*, 11(2), 266–303.

Bradley, C. A., 2009. The Bush Administration and International Law: Too Much Lawyering and Too Little Diplomacy. *Duke Journal of Constitutional Law and Public Policy*, 59, 57–75.

Buchanan, A., 2007. *Justice, Legitimacy, and Self-Determination: Moral Foundations for International Law*, Oxford University Press.

Buchanan, A. & Keohane, R. O., 2006. The Legitimacy of Global Governance Institutions. *Ethics and International Affairs*, 20(4), 405–437.

Bull, H., 1977. *The Anarchical Society: A Study of Order in International Politics*, New York: Columbia University Press.

Bush, G. W., 2002. Memorandum from President George W. Bush to Vice President Dick Cheney et al., Humane Treatment of al Qaeda and Taliban Detainees, February 7, 2002.

2005. News conference, Panama City, Panama, November 7, 2005.

Bybee, J. S., 2002. Memorandum from Jay S. Bybee, Assistant Attorney General, to Alberto Gonzales, Counsel to the President, RE: Standards for Conduct for Interrogation, August 1, 2002. Available at: www.justice.gov/olc/docs/memo-gonzales-aug2002.pdf [Accessed February 6, 2013].

Center for Constitutional Rights, 2006. Report on Torture and Cruel, Inhuman and Degrading Treatment of Prisoners at Guantanámo Bay, Cuba. Available at: http://ccrjustice.org/files/Report_ReportOnTorture.pdf [Accessed February 6, 2013].

Center for Victims of Torture, 2006. Project Bibliography. Available at: http://cvt.hutman.net/files/pg46/BIBLIOGRAPHY_website_Aug2006.pdf [Accessed February 6, 2013].

Checkel, J. T., 2007. International Institutions and Socialization in Europe: Introduction and Framework. In J. T. Checkel ed. *International Institutions and Socialization in Europe*, Cambridge University Press.

Chesterman, S., 2008. An International Rule of Law? *American Journal of Comparative Law*, 56(2).

Christiano, T., 2011. Is Democratic Legitimacy Possible for International Institutions?, Working paper, University Center for Human Values, Princeton University.

Cingranelli–Richards (CIRI) Human Rights Dataset. Available at: ciri.binghamton.edu [Accessed February 6, 2013].

Clark, I., 2005. *Legitimacy in International Society*, Oxford University Press.

Dershowitz, A. M., 2003. The Torture Warrant: A Response to Professor Strauss. *New York Law School Law Review*, 48(1–2), 275–294.

Doyle, M. W., 2011. *Striking First: Preemption and Prevention in International Conflict*, Princeton University Press.

Epstein, C., 2008. *The Power of Words in International Relations: Birth of an Anti-Whaling Discourse*, Cambridge, MA: MIT Press.

Forsythe, D. P., 2011. *The Politics of Prisoner Abuse: The United States and Enemy Prisoners after 9/11*, Cambridge University Press.

Franck, T., 1990. *The Power of Legitimacy Among Nations*, Oxford University Press.

Gaventa, J., 1982. *Power and Powerlessness: Quiescence and Rebellion in an Appalachian Valley*, Champaign: University of Illinois Press.

Gilligan, M. J. & Nesbitt, N. H., 2006. Do Norms Reduce Torture?, Working paper.

Guzman, A. T. 2008. *How International Law Works: A Rational Choice Theory*, Oxford University Press.

Hafner-Burton, E. M., Victor, D. G., & Lupu, Y., 2011. Political Science Research on International Law: The State of the Field, *American Journal of International Law*, 106, 47–97.

Hathaway, O., 2007. Why Do Countries Commit to Human Rights Treaties?, *Journal of Conflict Resolution*, 51(4), 588–621.

Holder, E., 2011. US Attorney General, testimony to US Senate May 4, 2011.

Howse, R. & Teitel, R., 2010. Beyond Compliance: Rethinking Why International Law Really Matters, *Global Policy*, 1(2), 127–136.

Human Rights Watch. 1998. Shielded from Justice: Police Brutality and Accountability in the United States. Available at: www.hrw.org/legacy/reports98/police/uspo53.htm [Accessed February 6, 2013].

Hurd, I., 2007. *After Anarchy: Legitimacy and Power in the UN Security Council*, Princeton University Press.

2011a. Is Humanitarian Intervention Legal? The Rule of Law in an Incoherent World, *Ethics and International Affairs*, 25(3).

2011b. Law and the Practice of Diplomacy, *International Journal*, 66(3), 581–596.

2012. Almost Saving Whales: The Ambiguity of Success at the International Whaling Commission, *Ethics and International Affairs*, 26(1).

Ignatieff, M., 2004. *The Lesser Evil: Political Ethics in an Age of Terror*, Princeton University Press.

Ikenberry, G. J., 2011. *Liberal Leviathan: The Origins and Transformation of the American World Order*, Princeton University Press.

Interim Transitional National Council, 2011. Press Release, March 25. Benghazi, Libya.

Johnstone, I., 2011. *The Power of Deliberation: International Law, Politics and Organizations*, Oxford University Press.

Jolly, R., Emmerij, L., & Weiss, T. eds., 2009. *UN Ideas that Changed the World*, Bloomington: Indiana University Press.

Kelly, M. J., 2009. Charting America's Return to Public International Law Under the Obama Administration, *Journal of National Security Law and Policy*, 3(2), 239–262.

Keohane, R. O., 1997. International Relations and International Law: Two Optics, *Harvard International Law Journal*, 38, 487–502.

Koh, H. H., 2006. Can the President be Torturer in Chief? *Indiana Law Journal*, 81, 1145–1167.

2010. Statement to American Society of International Law, March 25, 2010. Available at: www.state.gov/s/l/releases/remarks/139119.htm [Accessed February 6, 2013].

Koremenos, B., Lipson, C., & Snidal, D. eds., 2003. *Rational Design of International Institutions*, Cambridge University Press.

Liese, A., 2009. Exceptional Necessity: How Liberal Democracies Contest the Prohibition of Torture and Ill-Treatment when Countering Terrorism, *Journal of International Law and International Relations*, 5(1), 17–47.

Lindseth, P., 2010. *Power and Legitimacy: Reconciling Europe and the Nation-State*, Oxford University Press.

Luck, E. C. & Doyle M. W. eds., 2004. *International Law and Organization: Closing the Compliance Gap*, Lanham, MD: Rowman and Littlefield.

March, J. G. & Olsen, J. P., 2008. The Logic of Appropriateness. In M. Moran, M. Rein, & R. E. Goodin eds. *Oxford Handbook of Public Policy*, Oxford University Press.

Mayer, J., 2008. *The Dark Side: The Inside Story of How the War on Terror Turned into a War on American Ideals*, New York: Doubleday.

Mazzetti, M., 2012. The Drone Zone, *New York Times*, July 6.

New York Times, 2011. The Torture Candidates, November 14. Available at: www.nytimes.com/2011/11/15/opinion/the-torture-candidates.html [Accessed July 12, 2012].

Obama, B. H., 2009. Nobel Lecture by Barack H. Obama, Oslo, December 10, 2009. Available at: www.nobelprize.org/nobel_prizes/peace/laureates/2009/obama-lecture_en.html [Accessed February 6, 2013].

Rejali, D., 2009. *Torture and Democracy*, Princeton University Press.

Rosenau, J. N. & Czempiel E.-O., 1992. *Governance Without Government: Order and Change in World Politics*, Cambridge University Press.

Sands, P., 2008. *Torture Team: Rumsfeld's Memo and the Betrayal of American Values*, Basingstoke: Palgrave Macmillan.

Scharf, M. P., 2009. International Law and the Torture Memos, *Case Western Reserve Journal of International Law*, 42, 321–358.

Simmons, B., 2009. *Mobilizing for Human Rights: International Law in Domestic Politics*, Cambridge University Press.

Slaughter, A-M., 2008. ASIL Leaders' Views, *American Society of International Law*. Available at: www.asil.org/slaughter-leaderview.cfm [Accessed February 6, 2013].

Tamanaha, B., 2007. A Concise Guide to the Rule of Law, St. John's University School of Law working paper, #07–0082.

2008. *On the Rule of Law: History, Politics, Theory*, Cambridge University Press.

Tyler, T., 1990. *Why People Obey the Law*, Princeton University Press.

Veitch, S., 2007. *Law and Irresponsibility: On the Legitimation of Human Suffering*, London: Routledge-Cavendish.

Voeten, E., 2005. The Political Origins of the UN Security Council's Ability to Legitimize the Use of Force, *International Organization*, 59(3), 527–558.

Yoo, J., 2006. *War by Other Means: An Insider's Account of the War on Terrorism*, New York: Grove/Atlantic.

7

Legitimacy, institutional power, and international human rights institutions: a conceptual enquiry

LYNN DOBSON

1. Introduction

Our twenty-first-century world contains a variety of international institutions – treaty bodies, commissions, courts – claiming interpretive or adjudicative authority over fundamental human rights (Steiner, Alston, and Goodman 2007). As is adumbrated in the Introduction to this volume the irruption of these claims into domestic contexts, and especially into states confident in their own institutional and normative capability to support human rights, has provoked worry about the legitimacy of the international human rights institutions making them (which for terminological ease I'll refer to collectively as IHRIs henceforth). Political legitimacy is a hoary old topic in political theory. In many ways IHRIs' rule-making and norm-setting powers lead them into territory we have been used to considering the preserve of political institutions, and the legal reach of IHR courts in particular is becoming increasingly politically controversial in modern liberal democracies. Thus it may be worth seeing what an approach from a position drawing on political theory might bring to the debates. We await a fully formed normative theory of political legitimacy able to address the problem of international institutions convincingly, and one is not ventured in this chapter. As a preliminary, some discussion of the purpose and implications of the present enquiry may help to clarify what is at stake.

This work was begun under the aegis of the Norwegian Academy of Science and Letters' research project 'Should States Ratify Human Rights Conventions?' 2009–2010, led by Professors Føllesdal and Ulfstein. I owe thanks for the Academy's support, including the wonderful facilities afforded me during a period of residency at the Centre for Advanced Studies in Oslo.

When we ask whether IHR institutions (qua organisations), as distinct from human rights, or human rights laws, are legitimate, what exactly is it that we are asking? That is the subject-matter of this chapter.

2. Legitimacy – the concept

2.1 Legitimacy is not justification, morality, or justice

In everyday speech we often use 'legitimate' where we might otherwise say 'justified' or 'acceptable', or even 'appropriate', as in the sentence 'the gambler thought that buying a round of drinks was a legitimate use of his winnings'. But outside such colloquial usage, legitimacy is not synonymous with justification. If justification is the genus, then legitimacy is a species of it. Other species of justification relevant to political institutions are morality, performative criteria (such as effectiveness), and justice, to name a few. All of these can be linked, and theories of one of these usually have a place for the others (so, modern theories of political legitimacy usually have a place for justice, for example) but a major task of any theory is precisely to elaborate those links. In advance of that theoretical work, we must not beg the question by assuming that these separate justifications necessarily have anything at all to do with each other – the literature is already bedevilled by the conflation of legitimacy and justice (Peter 2010). Initially at least the concept of legitimacy needs to be grasped in its distinctiveness, as a form of justification independent of other forms of justification. The Council of Ten of the Venetian Republic enjoyed political legitimacy, but could hardly be said to have been just; assorted rulers across space and time have been accounted politically legitimate irrespective of their ineptitude or immorality.

In political theory the most fundamental concept is (political) power. Questions about the legitimacy of a body making collective rules are questions about the bases of justification of its power to do so. The objects of interest in political legitimacy are usually particular bodies rather than their decisions or norms or practices; the capacity to wield power, rather than manifestations of its exercise, is what is examined. In appealing to legitimacy to uphold its claim to power over the claims of its rivals, a political body appeals to a specific form of justification that is directly political rather than directly moral or directly ethical. The kind of justification embodied in 'legitimacy' is distinct from the kinds of justifications embodied in 'just' or 'good'. In asking whether a body is politically legitimate we don't ask whether it acts justly (if we wanted to know that, we would ask whether it acts justly). Instead we ask whether it has the rightful power it claims to have. Only once we have a theory of legitimacy in hand to motivate our inert concept of legitimacy and tell us what conditions must be met before the power can count as 'rightful' can we ascertain what role, if any, justice and other values should play in attributing political legitimacy to the body in question. There are of course complex links between legitimacy on the one hand and other important values on the other. But prior to their theoretical elaboration, the point being made is that political legitimacy invokes a distinct type of justification, not to be confused with other types, and pertains to the wielding of certain kinds of power by specific bodies. It might be wondered what therefore the point of attributing political legitimacy to an institution is, if it is not in the first place a pronouncement on the institution's justness or goodness etcetera. Succinctly, to invoke the concept of political legitimacy in relation to an institution directs our attention to claims about its powers, rather than to claims about its virtues, and the relevant power-related claims are two: (a) it has a right to rule, and (b) its subjects are under a political obligation to it.

2.2 Legitimacy: the right to rule

In respect of (a), to rule is to provide those subject to the rule with content-independent reasons for action. Prior to a command prohibiting me from *x*-ing, I may already have content-dependent reasons not to *x*, stemming from morality or ethics (to *x* is to commit a wrong), from prudence (*x*-ing has unpleasant consequences), or from self-interest (my interests are served by refraining from *x*-ing). The command not to *x* produced by the legitimate body embodies a first-order claim that I should not *x*, and a higher-order claim that the fact of the command itself is a sufficient reason to act in compliance with the first-order claim. To adopt a Razian formulation, the command claims to be peremptory, and pre-emptive in being exclusionary (Raz 1979; 1986: 42–45, 57–69; 1994).[1] If this higher-order claim succeeds,

[1] This part draws loosely on some ideas and terminology made famous by Raz, and does so primarily for their utility in articulating ideas implicit in relevant political theory. Their usage is inspirational and opportunistic only and certainly not intended as a presentation or application of or comment on Raz's thinking. Any of these tasks would call for more careful and systematic treatment than is given here. In particular, my employment of the idea of content-independent higher-order pre-emptive reasons does not imply my acceptance of Raz's service conception of authority (which in fact I reject).

I need not myself enquire into and carefully evaluate the content-relevant arguments for and against *x*-ing. All I need to do is to comply with whatever the rule tells me to do or to refrain from doing. An important difference between rule that is effective although not legitimate and rule that is legitimate lies in whether or not the sovereign's higher-order claim – that the fact of the command itself is a sufficient reason to act – is accepted. A command to *x* made by an effective but not legitimate ruler may secure my compliance, but only insofar as I am motivated to comply for reasons I already had, for example because *x*-ing is good or just or serves my interest, or because failing to *x* will bring about bad consequences for me.

By contrast, in virtue of the command of a legitimate ruler, I have an additional, and this time content-independent and sufficient, reason to be added to any of these prior content-dependent reasons already moving me to refrain from *x*-ing: I have been commanded not to *x* by a body having the right to command me in this way, and the fact of its having that right is a sufficient reason for me to refrain from doing whatever it is that its command prohibits. Note that all that is required for legitimacy is that I accept the higher-order claim as an independent reason for action. In many cases the reason for action provided by the fact of (legitimate) command itself will be not only additional but also redundant.

2.3 *Political obligation: the other side of the coin*

In respect of (b), a legitimate political body's expectation of its commands providing sufficient content-independent reasons for action implies some correlative responsiveness on the part of those to whom commands are addressed, and this has traditionally been known in the literature as 'political obligation' (Horton 1992; Peter 2010; Simmons 1979). Just as legality and morality are kinds of justification distinct and separable from legitimacy as a kind of justification, so legal and moral obligation are distinct and separable from political obligation (Gewirth 1982) though, similarly, the different kinds of obligation interlink in often intricate ways. On a narrow reading, political obligation is understood to be the general duty to comply with the laws of one's state. A broader reading involves a more diffuse concern for the *res publica* or the common good, and extends into duties such as military service, jury service, and public-spirited activity not captured by the idea of obedience to laws.

Many authors use the terms 'obligation' and 'duty' interchangeably. Of the rest, some hold duties to be general while obligations are always specific; others hold duties to be natural while obligations are always acquired. In the absence of consensus, I adopt 'obligation' here to mean generally that one stands in a relation to another such that the relation generates indeterminate duties (Brandt 1964; Hart 1955, 1961). 'Obligation' denotes that relationship. The specific content of the obligation itself is dispositional, to hold oneself in a state of prima facie readiness to fulfil duties that the obligation engenders or supports, and because that is what constitutes the relationship. No other specific performance than this can fulfil an obligation, while the performance that fulfils any duty is specified by that duty. Obligation also bears on potential acts which are not duties properly speaking, since they do not have binding force, but its effect is to shift the burden of justification from the side on which it would normally lie. If I have no obligation to you, and you request a (morally underdetermined) favour of me, my turning you down does not call for any explanation. I might offer an excuse for the sake of courtesy, but neither of us is likely to feel that I ought to justify my refusal. If we by contrast stand under an obligation to each other my refusal to help you does call for an explanation, even if only of a weak sort ('I'm afraid I'm already running late for an important appointment'). In this way obligation makes even acts that are not properly regarded as duties into 'oughts' that are duty-like in their relation to justification. On the view that I am developing here, the structure of obligation mirrors the structure of legitimacy – it provides an additional content-independent reason for action, additional to any other reasons one may already have for undertaking those acts and omissions comprising the content of the duties generated under the obligation.

Political obligation then is the idea that subjects (citizens and groups) stand in a relation to the legitimate institution such that they each owe it a dispositional readiness to accept its claims to provide sufficient content-independent reasons for action. If the ruler is not legitimate, it does not follow that subjects have no good reason or indeed no duties to do whatever it is that the legitimate body enjoins: subjects may still each have duties to do *x*, *y*, and *z* – duties of legality, morality, or justice, for example – but they have no political obligation to do those things, meaning that they have no reason to accept the fact of the ruler's having commanded *x*, *y*, or *z* as a reason sufficient in itself to do *x*, *y*, or *z*. By definition, then, where there is no political legitimacy, there can be no political obligation; where there is no political obligation, there can be no political legitimacy. Where political obligation does hold, then out of it duty-like norms will arise and, regardless of whatever other reasons subjects may have to do these things, if the legitimate body commands subjects to do them, then that command is a (sufficient) reason to do them.

From hereon I will use terms such as 'legitimate' and 'obligation' as specified above.

2.4 Legitimacy, obligation, and coercion

Coercion (understood widely to include restraint) is not intrinsic to the concept of legitimacy though it may feature contingently in its conditions, for example if political effectiveness were to be a condition of a body's legitimacy. The argument that might be put for effectiveness to be a condition of legitimacy is the same argument that could be put for it to be a condition of rule more generally: namely, it must be the case that the body's commands are effective. A sovereign whose commands are ignored or are complied with only as convenience dictates is not a sovereign capable of solving assurance problems. And since individuals and groups have an incentive to free-ride on others' compliance where they can get away with it, and some will act on that incentive if no countervailing disincentive to do so is provided, the sovereign must be able to enforce its commands coercively. All these propositions stand in the absence of legitimacy. On the other hand, one can imagine accepting a body's claim to produce the reasons that constitute it as legitimate and entail our obligation to it, even where it does not coerce, and even where that failure to coerce leads to its being ineffectual.

The normative force of an attribution of legitimacy and its obligation is that it provides grounds on which an actor ought to be moved to comply or be under pain of explaining or justifying why not. Its significance is less in supporting coercion than in raising a need for justification where that might otherwise be absent or only weakly motivated. Legitimacy's purchase then is in situations where other reasons for action are incompletely determinative. It shifts the burden of justification. So coercion is detachable from legitimacy and political obligation, but belongs to rule generally. Conversely, although coercion may contingently be justified on the grounds of legitimacy, it may also be justified on other grounds too – for example, and non-contingently, to ensure we act in accordance with our moral duties.

2.5 Context of problematisation no. 1: measurement versus selection

It is a truism that 'we are most likely to ask questions about the legitimacy of a system only when things appear to be going wrong' (Clark 2003: 75). Legitimacy tends to emerge as a topic for enquiry when one or both of the following situations arise: (a) we are unsure whether a body meets the threshold conditions for legitimacy; (b) there are competing contenders staking claims to the constitutive powers of legitimacy over the same terrain and we are unsure which one of them, if any, to deem legitimate. Legitimacy functions not only as measure, supplying standards against which we can assess a political body, but also – and historically this second function has been the most important – as a way of picking out which of the several 'pretenders to the throne' is to be the one whom, henceforth, will be deemed to provide content-independent reasons for action. Much ink has been spilled on the former aspect of the legitimacy problem, whereas the latter has received scant attention. However, it is this second aspect motivating the current enquiry into the legitimacy of IHRIs and indeed current debates on the legitimacy of international institutions generally. We are puzzled because these bodies lay claims to rule-making and other powers that we are accustomed to accord to the state and its organs, in a context where the state is not only very much alive and kicking but still exercising powers in the same areas of activity in which the international bodies lay claim to like powers. With conditions of legitimacy in hand we can ascertain whether a particular institution meets them in whole or in part or not at all, and whether or not it gets over some vital threshold; but where rivals are equivalent in this respect conditions for legitimacy by themselves may not serve to identify which of them will be found legitimate.

In wider debates about the role of international institutions 'legitimacy' is frequently treated as shorthand for normative justifiability, understood as a kind of scale with a bar above which an institution could be said to be legitimate and below which it could not. The purpose of an attribution of legitimacy on this reading is to indicate an institution's passing some threshold of normative acceptability. On this understanding it is perhaps unsurprising that the resources of the concept of justice have been put to work to produce an account of legitimacy (Buchanan 2004). Surely, some might feel, if a political institution is just, then it is legitimate, and vice versa? The problem with this heuristic is that it cannot address the underlying problem that prompted the flight to the notion of legitimacy in the first place. Typically, we reach for the idea of legitimacy when we have competing candidates for a domain of power that in principle (even if matters are not quite so straightforward in practice) ultimately admits only one holder, and where each of those candidates is at least on the face of it a credible candidate. A serious defect attending the conflation of legitimacy and justice, therefore, is that it fails to help in selecting between rivals in those circumstances where of the universe of institutions more than one manages to cross the threshold on the scale of 'justness'. (And this is precisely the problem at stake, for example, in the question of authority between the European Court of Human Rights and the democratic states growing increasingly restive with its powers of interpretation.) Conflating legitimacy with justice tells us that unjust institutions should be regarded as illegitimate and are therefore normatively unjustifiable, but since on the way to reaching that conclusion we would already have had to conclude that unjust institutions are normatively unjustifiable on the grounds of their being, well, unjust, nothing worthwhile has been added to any general normative evaluation by introducing the notion of legitimacy into the discussion.

Of course an attribution of legitimacy implies threshold condition(s), and one or more of these may be basic moral conditions like justice, but its main function – to select this body rather than that body as sovereign in the domain of decision at stake – is at least as important, and concealed by approaches substituting considerations of justice for analyses of political right. Indeed, one of the merits of the concept of legitimacy as a form of justification is its ability to step into the gaps left by the concept of justice as a form of justification. This comes through clearly in the debate between Rawls and Simmons on the idea of just institutions (Rawls 1973: 114–117, 333–337; Simmons 1979: 147–152). According to Rawls, we each have a natural moral duty to support just institutions. The duty is universally held by each person qua moral agent, and is owed universally to every just institution. Simmons doesn't deny such a duty; instead, he points out that it cannot explain why it is we might owe duties to 'our' state's just institutions that we do not owe to the just institutions of other states (political obligation), and why the 'right to rule' of the just institutions of 'our' state are circumscribed to us qua citizens and do not extend over all persons qua moral agents (political legitimacy). In other words, Simmons's charge is that even granting Rawls's propositions, viz. that we each have universal moral duties with respect to just institutions, those propositions do not amount to an account of political legitimacy.

Furthermore political institutions have wide responsibilities, and support and promote justice while at the same time being required to uphold other values. Justice is less than fully determinative and often an array of potential determinations is consistent with it. Morality-conforming and justice-realising outputs often have to be weighed against other principles and social values as well as each other. An appeal to the concept of justice to explicate why this body's power of authoritative interpretation must prevail over that body's claim to the power of authoritative interpretation will be bound to fail, because the concept of justice is both universal and incompletely determinative. If we want to know which of *w*, *x*, and *y* we should regard as the producer of pre-emptive reasons (i.e. holding politically legitimate authority) for action in domain of activity *z*, where each of them is claiming to hold that authority, it will not help us to know that they are all just. At best, knowing they are all just merely tells us that none is excluded from the possibility of being deemed legitimate by dint of its being unjust. It tells us they are all just, but doesn't tell us which of them (if any) is legitimate as well as being just. For that we must reach beyond the idea of justice.

Earlier in the discussion of legitimacy's use as a measure I described it as a threshold, giving rise to an 'either/or' assessment of legitimacy; but also as a set of conditions or criteria which might be met in whole or in part, and so permit 'more or less' assessments. And, of course, these could operate together, so as to produce complex accounts. But I also suggested in the discussion of legitimacy's selection function that it selects from among competing and mutually exclusive claimants to legitimacy, and selects one only. This claim should be qualified somewhat, but not wholly abandoned. The argument for an ultimate authority able to adjudicate conflicts are well-rehearsed: first, so that conflicts are not in principle irresolvable due to each party being judge and jury in its own case (Waldron 1999), and second, to solve assurance problems (Hobbes 1968). In reality the exercise of politically legitimate norm-setting and rule-making has been neither as monolithic nor as insulated from internal and external pressures as a theoretical insistence on the exclusive and singular nature of political legitimacy might suggest (Krasner 1999). Our paradigm instance – the state – is itself an assemblage of institutions some of which may be able to call on their own sources of legitimacy different to, and perhaps even older than, the modern state itself, while the ideas of delegated and pooled sovereignty alert us to the complexity and porosity of the real-world environment in which our theoretical characterisations of legitimacy take their place. Thus, in practice even the selectivity of the concept of legitimacy has operated at least at the margins in a 'more or less' rather than a starkly 'either/or' fashion.

Still, there is no getting away from the problem that when rule-making, -interpreting, or -adjudicating bodies contest the same norm-setting terrain, the need is felt (theoretically and practically) for some kind of an ultimate authority – whether organisation, hierarchy of norms, decision-procedure – to settle the dispute. Practically speaking, that in essence is what prompts the current enquiry. Did we but know how to satisfactorily intercalate the various overlapping or conflicting powers of national and international bodies, our thoughts would not turn to questions of legitimacy. Theoretically speaking, it is not possible with respect to any particular rule-setting domain to have more than one institution able to provide exclusionary reasons of the type constitutive of legitimacy (by definition, any claims provided by a rival are pre-empted and excluded). Its exclusionary power excludes *ex hypothesi* the possibility of being undermined or confounded by a countermanding power.

However, unqualified recourse to the idea of a sovereign à la Hobbes is unlikely to be fruitful since it is precisely the transformation of the world in which and for which their theories of legitimate power were developed that presents us with our current crop of legitimacy puzzles. So what are the theoretical alternatives to rightful powers that are (in principle) singular and exclusive? Three spring to mind. First, institutions' self-regulation: their collective pre-commitment to some kind of institutional-normative algorithm the employment of which would allow them to settle matters themselves. However this would require supervision and enforcement, so rather than solving the problem this alternative simply moves it up a level. Second, institutions contesting matters between them, until one prevails and is acknowledged as final authority. But this looks like a theory of might making right, so should be dismissed as normatively unattractive. Third, radical pluralistic undecideability: institutions engaging in inconclusive case-by-case skirmishes to provisional truces guaranteed only to hold until the next agonistic bout. This has a reassuring air of radical chic but might mean uncertainty for addressees, instability of the system, diversion of attention and other institutional resource into inter-institutional battles to the detriment of wider public concerns, and possibly erosion of the bases for legitimacy. Hence, theoretical consistency and coherence support singularity of power to produce pre-emptive content-independent higher-order reasons, while a consideration of non-ideal theory and political practicalities leads me to conclude that acceptance of the singularity and exclusivity of political legitimacy is the least bad option.

2.6 *Context of problematisation no. 2: legitimacy and obligation are triadic*

If we construe: 'are international human rights institutions legitimate?' as a query about measurement, in effect asking whether such institutions meet threshold conditions for political legitimacy, the question makes sense, albeit is defective (for a start, in that it conflates an attribution of legitimacy with an attribution of compliance with its conditions). But if we construe it instead either as a query about which of competing institutions is the legitimate one, or as a wholesale query taking into account both the measuring and the selection aspects of the concept, then the question 'are international human rights institutions legitimate?' lacks enough information to make it meaningful, because there is no such thing as legitimacy *sub specie aeternitatis*. Attributions of legitimacy have always to be contextual, and specify which institution is legitimate for whom over what. A complete statement looks like this: body *x* is legitimate for agent *y* in respect of activity *z*. (Or to deal with types rather than tokens: set of bodies *x* is legitimate for agents *y* in respect of set of activities *z*.) On the reading of political obligation I presented earlier, its relations are similarly triadic: in respect of activity *z*, agent *y* binds her- or himself to accept body *x*'s rules as presumptively sufficient reasons for action (or, in respect of set of activities *z*, agents *y* bind themselves to accept set of bodies *x*'s rules as presumptively sufficient reasons for action).

In the debate between Rawls and Simmons invoked above, Simmons brings forcefully to our notice this feature of legitimacy: it is always particularistic. While a just institution if it is indeed just must be just from every person's viewpoint, a legitimate institution is legitimate only from some particular perspective. If legitimacy is the right to rule, and the UK government is legitimate, it is so only in relation to those whom its right to rule extends over. That is, to advert to my larger argument as to the meaning of the concept, if the fact that the UK government tells UK residents that they must do jury service was taken by them to be a sufficient reason to do so that would not be surprising, but we would not expect residents of Singapore to believe themselves under an obligation to do jury service in the UK *for the same reason*.[2] Conventionally the parties to this particularising relationship (of legitimacy and obligation) are assumed to be states' governments on the one hand and their citizens on the other. The example in the preceding sentence traded on that assumption. But this is an essentialising assumption that is not necessary to the conceptual apparatus of legitimacy and obligation per se. The rubric 'body *x* is legitimate for agent *y* in respect of activity (or set or domain of activities) *z*' is open to differing possibilities when it comes to replacing abstract *x* and *y* with real place-holders. As to *z*, conceptually legitimacy is particularistic not only in applying to particular institutions, persons, or populations, but also to

[2] Given constraints of time and purpose I can only make the point broadly and briefly here. A full theory of legitimacy would address quirks and apparent exceptions – for example, the position of legitimate governments in relation to their citizens who reside abroad and to non-citizens resident on their territory, and the position of third parties – who may well have duties to support legitimate governments even when they are not legitimate in respect of them. See Waldron (1993: 8–9).

particular domains of activity. If we agreed the International Postal Union was the legitimate authority in respect of the coordination of international postal services, it would not follow that we have content-independent reasons for complying with any command it might make that we declare war on North Korea.

2.7 Conditions for legitimacy and obligation: putting the concept to work through theory

What distinguishes legitimate political power from raw political power is its 'rightfulness' – a legitimate political body rules not through the exercise of power *simpliciter*, but 'by right'. So what conditions must be met before rule counts as 'by right'? On this question there has historically been much variation (Beetham 1991). In today's liberal democracies battle honours, being first-born son, or having unique access to the sacred, are no longer credible conditions for legitimacy, whereas conditions like protection of human rights, equality, mutual respect, due process, consent, and identity might be, depending on which theory one adopts. Whatever set of conditions out of the potential array applies, a body claiming legitimacy has the right to rule and can expect the obligation of subjects if and only if the conditions of having the right are met. If the conditions are met, the body is legitimate. (The conditions also explain how a particular body comes to be legitimate, by allowing the construction of a narrative – theoretical or empirical, often historical – grounding the legitimacy of that body in its meeting of the relevant criteria.)

It is at this point in the enquiry that normative theory is needed to breathe life into the concept of legitimacy, because a normative theory will elaborate a structured argument showing what conditions and criteria matter, and how they should relate to each other, especially when they conflict. In doing so normative theory also addresses the crucial matter of how legitimacy relates to morality, including that part of it we call 'justice'. Modern theories posit 'justness' to be a condition of legitimacy (so that a systematically unjust government, for example, has no claim to legitimacy); they also accommodate subjects' possibilities to reject, on morally principled grounds, compliance with legitimate political institutions (as in theoretical debates on civil disobedience, for example). Theories of legitimacy are also at the same time theories of resistance (Baumgold 2005), since by setting out the conditions institutions must meet to mount claims to legitimacy and ensuing obligation they also set out the limits of the right to rule and the grounds for its overthrow. This means that legitimacy and obligation are neither absolute nor fully determinative. Just as we may have content-dependent reasons that would in any case move us to do whatever it is that the legitimate body prescribed irrespective of its prescription, so we may have content-dependent moral reasons to refrain from doing what it prescribes; and on some occasions – specified by the theory we adopt – those moral reasons may well negate and override the exclusionary force of the content-independent reasons we have for complying with the ruler's demands. So not only is it the case that we may have good or even compelling reasons to conform to the commands of an institutional body that is not legitimate with respect to us, as I remarked earlier, but we may also have sufficiently strong reasons not to conform to the commands of an institutional body that is legitimate with respect to us. Our conferral of legitimacy on a body is neither absolute nor unconditional, unless we surrender the possibility of maintaining status as moral agents.

3. International human rights institutions and legitimacy/obligation

From the perspective outlined in Section 2, the question of the legitimacy of IHRIs is not a question about their justification or normative acceptability in any general sense, nor is it a question about their justice or their morality or their goodness or their effectiveness etcetera. Also, the question of their legitimacy is a question about their status (as claimants of certain powers) and is distinct from any questions we might have about the ways in which those powers might be exercised, or what the fruits of such exercise might turn out to be in the way of norms, policies, rules and regulations, laws.[3] Instead, we ask either a general kind of question: are IHRIs legitimate for states[4] in respect of fundamental human rights 'rules'?[5] or a specific question, something like: is the ICCPR[6] Human Rights Committee legitimate for state parties to the ICCPR in respect of the matters it claims authority

[3] In practice these are not entirely separate, since both in theory and in practice at the margins we should expect systematic serious failures – bad procedures and/or outputs – to undermine the bases of legitimacy. But there is quite a lot of slack to take up both in theory and in practice before reaching those limits.

[4] Of course states are not the only potential addressees, since other organisations and individual persons might also be relevant here. Any theory of legitimacy aiming to tackle this topic would need to elaborate which agents matter and the relations between them.

[5] The inverted commas indicate the loose usage here, as shorthand for the body's product: norms, laws, commands, interpretations, and so on.

[6] International Covenant on Civil and Political Rights, one of the United Nations' chief human rights treaties.

over? And the meaning of 'legitimate for' in these formulations involves the acceptance of IHRIs' or the ICCPR Human Rights Committee's content-independent higher-order pre-emptive reasons for action, reasons in other words cashed out in terms of institutional power rather than human rights.

Considering these questions entails also considering whether, generally, in respect of fundamental human rights rules states (and perhaps others) are politically bound – not legally bound or morally bound, but politically bound – to accept IHRIs' rules as presumptively sufficient reasons for action independently of their merits; or, specifically, whether state parties to the ICCPR are politically bound to accept the ICCPR Human Rights Committee's Concluding Observations and General Comments as presumptively sufficient reasons for action (again, pre-empting and excluding consideration of those observations' and comments' merits). The 'binding' here is that of obligation rather than duty. The thought is about the kind of relationship the parties are embroiled in, not any of the specific imperatives it motivates.

The relationship is about power, and so it is political. Though the duties it motivates may not be political, the obligation is. Doubtless important legal and moral duties are also at stake here given that our topic is that of law and the protection of vital and basic human interests, and if our task was to arrive at some kind of overall normative assessment of these bodies – an assessment, that is, of which an examination of their legitimacy would form only a part – it would be remiss not to take into account in our assessment these legal and moral dimensions too. But in advance of a theory elucidating whether (and if so, how) legal or moral obligation and their duties are relevant to issues of legitimacy and obligation of the type under discussion here, our focus must remain laser-like on their conceptual core: the status of the bodies and their claims to power on the one hand, and the status of the normative compulsion embraced by their putative subjects on the other. In thinking about how the concept of legitimacy as parsed here might relate to IHRIs, difficulties emerge in relation to the contextual points and the way they interact and in arriving at a set of conditions for the legitimacy of IHRIs and correlative obligation in respect of them that are plausible and attractive theoretically, normatively, and practically.

One line of argument might hold 'legitimacy talk' of this kind to be altogether misplaced. Because international institutions' powers of coercion are not analogous to those of the state, the adoption of strong concepts of legitimacy and obligation are a kind of category mistake, the objection might run. It is true that the analogy is stretched, but international institutions as a class are not entirely deficient in coercive power and IHRIs in particular are not toothless. IHRIs' powers range from hortatory to judicial, and 'enforcement' spans a range from recommendation to sanctions like fines or suspensions of voting rights. But in any case, as noted in the previous section, the concept of legitimacy per se neither requires nor implies coercive power (although any theory of legitimacy, by contrast, might), and even were we not to hold an IHRI legitimate it is not impossible that coercion to enforce compliance with its rules would be justified on some ground other than that of legitimacy.

It is not a capacity for coercion that makes legitimacy consequential; rather, it matters because it shifts the burden of explanation and justification. That burden might involve penalties that are more or less onerous. A state that has made explicit its refusal to regard an IHRI as an authoritative producer of pre-emptive reasons can escape censure for any flagrant disregard of that body's interpretations in a way that a state which has acknowledged or apparently acknowledged the IHRI's legitimacy will find harder (though of course that recalcitrant state might well face condemnation for its non-compliance with a specific interpretation on other grounds). The availability or non-availability of coercion makes no real difference to the attribution of legitimacy and expectation of obligation except insofar as it affects the conditions attaching to them as specified in a normative theory (we might expect the conditions to be more demanding and harder to meet the greater the coercive power available).

Since we use the concept of legitimacy to select among actual or potential contenders it is always comparative, and in evaluating and ascribing legitimacy to a body we do so against a backdrop populated by alternatives (including hypothetical institutions as yet to be actually created). In effect the concrete question about IHRIs' legitimacy boils down to: under what conditions should states defer to the content-independent authority of other bodies? In particular, under what conditions should states that believe their own institutions (their elites, bodies, rules, practices) adequate to the task of making, interpreting, and adjudicating with respect to fundamental human rights, defer to other bodies in these respects? For part of an answer to this it might be possible to appeal to the importance of states not being in a position to be sole judges and juries in their own cases in certain areas of activity, and make a case that fundamental human rights protection is one such area. But notice that – at best – this is a moral argument that states ought to confer legitimacy with respect to human rights on a non-state body; it does not help to identify which of the potential and actual contenders any state should confer legitimacy on. And a sceptic might still remain unconvinced that states need to regard any other institution as legitimate in the strong sense developed in this chapter. It could be argued that states that are themselves assemblages of institutions incorporating opportunities for contestation (Bellamy, this volume) are no more vulnerable to the *nemo iudex in sua causa* point than would be any IHRI that might supplant them.

Political legitimacy as applied to an IHR body is the same as that applied to a state: that its pronouncement embodies a first-order claim (recommendation, interpretation, adjudication) *x*, together with a higher-order claim: the claim that simply the fact that it has pronounced is a sufficient reason to act in compliance with that first-order claim. What makes for legitimacy rather than merely effectiveness is that this higher-order claim – to wit, that the pronouncement itself is a sufficient reason to act – stands. However, its contextual constraints (that legitimacy is always of some institution for some addressees in respect of some action-set) bring out an important asymmetry. States and IHR bodies are different types of institutions. States' peremptory and exclusionary reach is formally all-encompassing. A state formulates rules in any area of activity within its political jurisdiction from a perspective of oversight of all areas, and thus is able to develop rules for any one area that take into account those rules' implications for any or all other areas; moreover, it can do this in accordance with priorities guided by political choice anchored within socially accepted (consultative or democratic) processes.

By contrast, the compass of IHRIs is formally narrow (being confined to human rights) and indeed its being so is accounted a virtue. Nonetheless, while that compass might be formally narrow it is substantively all-pervading, because it disposes over very fundamental human needs that manifest in all areas of human activity. Additionally, the rights in most and perhaps all cases are susceptible to minimalist or maximalist interpretations along a spectrum that can be very wide. As a result a rule produced by an IHRI to motivate action within a state will very likely have impacts across a number of areas otherwise regulated in accordance with social orderings of value. In effect, a state's acceptance of an IHRI's powers to produce pre-emptive reasons with respect to human rights will lead incidentally to its having to accept such pre-emption to some degree at least with respect to other areas of policymaking and political choice. Suppose the impact of a state's Interpretation A of right *x* in policy area *a* were less detrimental to important and socially decided values and rights in policy areas *b*, *c* and *d* than an IHRI's Interpretation B of the same right *x* in policy *a* would be on those same values and rights in those same policy areas. Under what conditions should that state be bound to accept the IHRI's claim to hold superior powers over the interpretation of right *x* and consequently be bound to accept what from its point of view is an interpretation that is sub-optimal in multiple dimensions?

At this stage normative theory could usefully make its appearance, because it is possible that the conditions it specifies for legitimacy could be put to work to decide the question. Currently, what kinds of conditions might be proposed as appropriate for IHRI legitimacy and what thresholds ought to apply are under-theorised. Beyond a universal if tacit agreement that those who sit on such bodies ought to be adequately professionally qualified, the debate has not yet coalesced around suitable criteria or the theoretical resources from which they might be inferred. Still, possibilities are emerging.[7] For example, anyone disposed to accept Raz's normal justification thesis has an answer to the problem of conflicting claims to legitimate authority to hand: 'whether a given authority's power extends to exclude the authority of another is to be judged in the way we judge the legitimacy of its power on any matter, namely, whether we would conform better to reason by trying to follow its directives' (Raz 2006: 1021). His normal justification thesis provides theoretical propositions about the conditions of legitimacy, and consequently a means of selecting which contender is – in accordance with those conditions – the legitimate one. Note that this result is consistent with my conceptual analysis; Raz does not dispute the contention that with respect to the same set of activities (i.e. my third triadic term) there can be only one holder of pre-emptive power.

But even with a theory ready to deploy, given this conceptual structure it seems the best that could be managed would be an articulation of why either the state or the IHRI was the legitimate power (legitimate, to recap, in being able to exclude the other's power to reason toward a conclusion). While theoretically neat, there's something unsatisfying about the practical implications of this. After all, if the power of the state to reason exclusively about human rights protection within state jurisdictions was unproblematic, there would have been no reason for international human rights regimes to emerge in the first place; while if the power of IHRIs to reason exclusively about human rights protection within state jurisdictions was unproblematic, we would not be undertaking the present debate. We

[7] In this volume see Besson and Wheatley on Raz's service conception of authority, Besson and Hessler on Buchanan's notion of reciprocal legitimation, Schaffer on consent, and Çalı's instrumentalist argument.

appear to be caught on the horns of a dilemma. Either we are destined to arrive back at the same practical tension (state or IHRI?) after an extensive theoretical detour, so that at best we will now know why whichever one of those two it is that we deem legitimate in this matter, is so deemed. If so, we will have solved the theoretical puzzle but without removing the intuitive unease about real-world implications that gives the theoretical puzzle its point. Or we must abandon the conceptual structure tying together the right to rule (cashed out in terms of pre-emptive reasons) and the obligation to comply (cashed out in terms of accepting claims to pre-emption), but then it is not evident what might take its place other than the adoption of the term 'legitimate' to mean 'just' or 'good' or some other as-yet under-specified sense of normative acceptability (which would render the term otiose).

3.1 *Revisiting the concept: three levels of reasons for action?*

Instead, and to conclude, I want to briefly canvass the possibility of a different approach, one that digs into the idea of pre-emption and examines the conceptual room for manoeuvre within it. Earlier it was contended that a legitimate body is so because its first-order claim (do *x*) is accompanied by a higher-order claim (to the effect that it has the power to produce pre-emptive reasons), and the acceptance of this latter claim by its addressees confers legitimacy on the claimant. This is a two-tier structure of reasons for action. However, let me now propose that we should understand legitimacy as normally incorporating a three-tier structure of claims, looking like this:

First-order (1): Do *x*;
Second-order (2): Act so as to give effect to our first-order commands;
Third-order (3): Acknowledge our pre-emptive power to give second-order commands over set of activities *y*.

Call this the 'standard' or 'default' structure, familiar from our formal thinking about the state. But now let us abstract from the second-order claim and substitute a placeholder, as follows, so that what the addressee is enjoined to do with respect to first-order claims is under-determined:

First-order (1): Do *x*;
Second-order (2): Act so as to ϕ with respect to our first-order commands;
Third-order (3): Acknowledge our pre-emptive power to give second-order commands over set of activities *y*.

Making this change to the second-order claim allows a shift away from the command 'give effect to', towards a more amenable injunction. What exactly that might be would be open to debate, since it is open to differing possibilities. As well as varying the content of the replacement injunction, we might also vary its scope. Previously the formal asymmetry in terms of scopes of jurisdiction between states and IHRIs was noted, as was the way in which the nature of the domain over which IHRIs have formal power is such as to informally undercut states' powers over the remaining domains. This asymmetry touches directly on the third-order claim above. But the move I suggest now is that we consider the scope of the second-order claim to be similarly liable to truncation, so that it too has a narrower compass than the comprehensive 'give effect to'.

A loosely sketched example might help to illustrate. Imagine that we are persuaded by Scanlon's (moral) theory, according to which we as rational agents are motivated to act vis-à-vis each other in ways we could justify to each other, and so ought to treat each other in terms of principles we each could not reasonably reject (Scanlon 1998). Then let the 'ϕ' in the revised second-order claim stand for some well-formulated injunction incorporating ideas such as 'fully and carefully reflect on and consider giving effect to, do not unreasonably reject, be accountable for your decision, offer justifications for it using forms of reasoning no other party could reasonably reject', and so on. This second-order injunction could be constructed so as to preclude the addressee's acting arbitrarily, move incentives heavily against non-compliance, and put a strong burden of justification firmly and clearly on the addressee.

Now let us characterise two kinds of entity in international life: functionally comprehensive associations (such as states and regional associations like the European Union), and functionally specific institutions (such as belong to human rights, or climate change, regimes). In this universe a functionally specific institution has standing as the representative and embodiment of the relevant technical and professional expertise, and as the repository of comparative knowledge about both the pertinent principles (in an 'ideal-theory' sense) relevant to the functional area and their normative interpretations and approximations across the social settings served by the association. It knows only about one thing, but it knows about that one thing over many geographical and cultural and organisational contexts. By contrast, the attention of any functionally comprehensive association is more concentrated geographically and culturally and organisationally, but spread thinly across many different functions. In its own small realm of expertise, let us suppose, the functionally specific institution has an overview enabling it to know better than any comprehensive association the state-of-the-art in development of (relevant) principles and in development of the practical reasoning about those principles taking place within comprehensive associations. The functionally specific institution is a kind of Panopticon, and a point of international convergence of norms – norms, perhaps, about the interpretation of certain rights. As an ideal-type it embodies group wisdom, and it is the institutional space within which mutual adaptation by comprehensive associations can occur.

On this construal, the import of legitimacy and obligation is that the IHRI has powers to exclude certain kinds of reasons for the state's preferring of its own interpretation. Instead, the state is obliged to reflect on its compliance with the IHRI's interpretive claims, and offer reasons for any deviations – reasons couched in terms that other parties could not reasonably reject (not, for example, 'that's just the way we do things around here') and carried in forms of reasoning that others could not reasonably reject (not, for example, appealing to divine revelation). This accountability and the need to address justification to the IHRI are motivated by the IHRI's role as proxy for the group wisdom of the international community on the interpretation of principle. (On the question of commitment to principle itself, our moral theory assumes (a) all persons have non-consensual duties to protect human rights, and derivatively states have such duties, (b) parties are motivated to find agreement, and (c) promises should be kept, or *pacta sunt servanda*. Our pragmatic analysis points to the fact of consent to the existence and importance of human rights as shown in states' having actually acceded to relevant treaties.)

Obviously all I am doing here is gesturing towards a way of refining the concept, and trying to illustrate it by importing into it some fragments of normativity plundered from a larger theory. A persuasive argument tying together the idea of legitimacy and Scanlon's test of reasonable rejection, or indeed any other theory supplying the building materials for the construction of the second-order claim in the three-tier structure of legitimacy advanced in the present work, would need a very much longer treatment all to itself. But even in the absence of such explication I hope it is evident that an international institution's claim to legitimacy, if it were to resemble the revised structure set out above, would be less comprehensive and less hard-nosed than is the standard claim to legitimacy than we are familiar with. A claim to hold legitimate power would still be a claim to a kind of pre-emption, but the force of that pre-emption would be narrower: it would be dialogically prescriptive rather than prescriptive over a comprehensive schedule of acts-in-accordance-with. With legitimacy understood in this light IHRIs' powers would only indirectly be to tell states 'what to do'; their direct effect would be to enforce mutual accountability in that states would have to provide strong explanations and justifications for deviation from first-order commands.

Bibliography

Baumgold, D., 2005. Hobbes's and Locke's Contract Theories: Political not Metaphysical, *Critical Review of International Social and Political Philosophy*, 8 (3), 289–308.

Beetham, D., 1991. *The Legitimation of Power*, Basingstoke: Palgrave Macmillan.

Brandt, R. B., 1964. The Concepts of Obligation and Duty, *Mind*, 73, 374–393.

Buchanan, A., 2004. *Justice, Legitimacy, and Self-Determination*, Oxford University Press.

2011. Reciprocal Legitimation: Reframing the Problem of International Legitimacy, *Politics, Philosophy & Economics*, 10 (1), 5–19.

Clark, I., 2003. Legitimacy in a Global Order, *Review of International Studies*, 29, 75–95.

Føllesdal, A., 2000. Liberal Nationalism – Defending the Very Idea, ISSEI 2000. Available at: www.follesdal.net/publ.htm. Accessed 6 February 2013.

Gewirth, A., 1982. Obligation: Political, Legal, Moral. In A. Gewirth, *Human Rights: Essays on Justification and Applications*, University of Chicago Press, 256–289.

Hart, H. L. A., 1955. Are There Any Natural Rights?, *The Philosophical Review*, 64 (2), 175–191.

1961. *The Concept of Law*, Oxford: Clarendon Press.

Hobbes, T., 1968. *Leviathan*, C. B. Macpherson (ed.), London: Penguin Books.

Horton, J., 1992. *Political Obligation*, Basingstoke: Palgrave Macmillan.

Krasner, S. D., 1999. *Sovereignty: Organized Hypocrisy*, Princeton University Press.

Peter, F., 2010. Political Legitimacy, *The Stanford Encyclopedia of Philosophy (Summer 2010 Edition)*, Edward N. Zalta (ed.). Available at: http://plato.stanford.edu/archives/sum2010/entries/legitimacy/. Accessed 6 February 2013.

Rawls, J., 1973. *A Theory of Justice*, Oxford University Press.

Raz, J., 1979. *The Authority of Law*, Oxford University Press.

1986. *Morality of Freedom*, Oxford: Clarendon Press.

1994. *Ethics in the Public Domain: Essays in the Morality of Law and Politics*, Oxford University Press.

2006. The Problem of Authority: Revisiting the Service Conception, *Minnesota Law Review*, 90, 1003–1044.

Scanlon, T. M., 1998. *What We Owe to Each Other*, Cambridge: Harvard University Press.

Simmons, A. J., 1979. *Moral Principles and Political Obligations*, Princeton University Press.

Steiner, H., Alston, P., & Goodman, R., 2007. *International Human Rights in Context: Law, Politics, Morals*, 3rd edn, Oxford University Press.

Waldron, J., 1993. Special Ties and Natural Duties, *Philosophy and Public Affairs*, 22 (1), 3–30.

1999. *The Dignity of Legislation (The Seeley Lectures)*, Cambridge University Press.

8

Legitimacy, global governance and human rights institutions: inverting the puzzle

JOHAN KARLSSON SCHAFFER

1. Introduction

In this chapter, I draw on recent scholarship on the alleged legitimacy deficits in global governance institutions, seeking to engage the notions of legitimacy this literature suggests with the intriguing case of international human rights institutions. First, I reconstruct how this literature views the problem of legitimacy in global governance, a view that relies on a particular notion of international institutions which both explains and justifies global governance institutions in terms of the collective goods they help states obtain. The puzzle of legitimacy, on this view, lies in offering citizens valid reasons to obey, support or refrain from interfering with global governance institutions – reasons that include certain procedural, epistemic and substantive elements, which together comprise a complex, hybrid standard of legitimacy.

Second, I explore to what extent this view of legitimacy problems with global governance institutions can be applied for analyzing corresponding legitimacy problems with international human rights institutions, which constitute a different kind of political entity than typical global governance institutions. Uniquely, international human rights institutions normally do not help states obtain joint benefits in their external affairs, but regulate the internal relation between a government and individuals under its jurisdiction, and, to the extent that they are effective, chiefly rely on

For valuable comments on earlier versions of this chapter, I am grateful to my co-editors and the contributors to this volume; to Göran Duus-Otterström, Lennart J. Lundqvist, Marie Demker, Bengt Brülde and other participants at the Research Seminar in Practical Philosophy and Political Theory, University of Gothenburg, March 8, 2012; and to Thomas Christiano, André Nollkaemper, Michael Zürn and others who attended the MultiRights Startup Conference at the University of Oslo, September 9–10, 2011.

domestic mechanisms of enforcement. This crucial difference between the two kinds of international institutions, in turn, changes the authority relation and the legitimacy puzzle involved. In the human rights area, the problem of legitimacy is to give reasons to governments why they should accept their obligations under international human rights law, in light of the benefits or opportunities human rights treaties provide for citizens or individuals. In the third section, I draw out the implications of this analysis for finding such reasons. While the complex, hybrid standards of legitimacy suggested for global governance institutions need to be substantially reworked in order to apply to international human rights institutions, the often discarded notion of state consent provides an essential component of legitimacy for the human rights area. Finally, I discuss whether the notion of international institutions discussed in the chapter may have implications beyond the human rights area.

2. Global governance institutions and problems of legitimacy

Over the past couple of decades, scholars from various fields – international law, political philosophy, international relations, European studies, etc. – have produced a burgeoning literature on the legitimacy of the institutions of global governance. Most, if not all, seem to agree that there is an expanding gap between, on the one hand, the number, the scope and the power of international institutions, and, on the other hand, the justification of their right to govern, which cannot merely, or at all, be based on the consent of the states that have created them and delegated authority to them. And while some doubt that this gap could be overcome, most seem to think of it as one of the most urgent contemporary global political matters. In short, a broad international academic literature seems to agree that we are witnessing an impending legitimacy crisis in global governance (Clark 2004; Keohane 2003; Scholte 2004; Zürn 2004; Zürn & Stephen 2010).

In this chapter, I shall draw on a particular line of scholarship that has addressed problems of legitimacy in global governance. I shall refer to it as *cosmopolitan functionalism*, for it combines an attempt to explain and justify international institutions in terms of the benefits they help states obtain – a functionalist argument – with a commitment to liberal cosmopolitanism; the idea that human beings are equally the ultimate units of moral concern for everyone (and that states, consequently, are at most of derivative value). As another characteristic trait, cosmopolitan functionalism rejects state consent, global democracy and global justice as normative conceptions of international institutional legitimacy, and instead suggests that a proper theory of legitimacy for global governance must be complex, taking into account both procedural, epistemic and substantive elements. Admittedly, I take certain liberties here, since the theorists whose arguments I group together under this label may perhaps not think of themselves as members of the same family, nor be comfortable with the label, and their accounts of legitimacy differ in some respects.

In general, however, cosmopolitanism and functionalism are not improbable allies. For instance, recently burgeoning literatures on political cosmopolitanism and global justice (e.g. Held 2006; Kuper 2006; Pogge 2002) often rely on functionalism in order to justify a cosmopolitan political order: many pressing contemporary societal problems transcend the borders of stats and therefore call for corresponding cross-border, functional, multi-level and multi-sited governance institutions, rather than the current order of sovereign states or a rigid world state, in order to approximate cosmopolitan ideals (Karlsson 2008, chap.5).

The object of study for the literature on legitimacy in global governance is increasingly influential international organizations, such as the International Monetary Fund, the World Trade Organization, the International Criminal Court, or the United Nations and its various organs and agencies. A key reason for focusing on such institutions is the political power or authority they exercise, but it is a type of authority that distinguishes them from other political entities, most notably states, and may therefore require evaluation according to different notions of justification and legitimacy. Akin to states, global governance institutions issue rules and claim the authority to sanction those who fail to comply with those rules (Buchanan & Keohane 2006). By the rules they set, institutions may constrain the choices facing societies and impact on many persons' fundamental interests, which makes them distinctly political institutions (Caney 2009). In contrast to states, however, global governance institutions have a restricted remit rather than comprehensive authority; they do not claim a Weberian monopoly of violence, and they rely for their implementation chiefly on the consent of states that delegate authority to them (Buchanan & Keohane 2006). Moreover, compared to a state, a global governance institution usually by definition faces greater cultural pluralism and people do not identify with it in the way that they identify with their states and nations. To conclude, global governance institutions are *sui generis*, which sets the terms for assessing them normatively (Caney 2009, p.111).

What justifies the existence of such institutions? From a cosmopolitan functionalist perspective, we may think of three kinds of instrumental justifications for international institutions: they provide joint benefits, prevent abuses of power and promote global justice. The first set of arguments, which reflects neoliberal institutionalist theories of international cooperation, focuses on the short-term and fairly concrete benefits international institutions provide by helping states overcome collective action and coordination problems that result from the anarchical condition of the international system. Institutions enable states, as self-interested as they are, to construct regulatory frameworks and establish mutually beneficial welfare-enhancing cooperation that they cannot otherwise obtain. Typical examples of such cooperation are regulatory regimes that promote free trade, regulate financial markets or curb border-transgressing environmental degradation. Another set of arguments, drawing, perhaps, on federal-republican international theory, suggests that in an international system characterized by immense power asymmetries, international institutions play an important constraining role, as a system of checks and balances on sovereign states, preventing powerful states from abusing their power and protecting weak powers from domination (Deudney 2007; Ikenberry 2001). In that sense, international institutions, built on strategic restraint, by which the great powers make concessions to smaller states in exchange for compliance, may advance a nascent liberal, constitutional order. A third set of arguments, which mirrors more idealist notions assuming international cooperation to serve a harmony of interests, suggests that global governance institutions serve a greater purpose of the common good, such as promoting world peace or global justice. Eventually, global governance institutions will play an important part in a functional division of labor in the pursuit of global justice or in developing a cosmopolitan political order, and they may help to ensure that otherwise unwilling states comply with cosmopolitan aims and principles. That is, not only would multilateral institutions ameliorate an anarchic system of sovereign states; institutions may potentially, in the long run, lead the international order to transform into something qualitatively different (Jacobson 2000) – possibly some sort of cosmopolitan world order.

While not necessarily mutually coherent (nor exhaustive), these three sets of arguments – joint benefits, checks and balances and global justice – supposedly answer the question why international institutions exist in two related but distinct ways. First, they offer *normative justifications* of international institutional authority: global governance institutions may hold a *prima facie* presumption of normative justification to the extent that they fulfill certain functions and promote certain ends. Hence, these justifications are instrumental or functional, as they do not seek to justify international institutions in terms of some innate virtue or inherently fair procedures, but in terms of the outcomes they help bring about. Such instrumentalism may seem the obvious way to justify international institutions, but one may think of corresponding justificatory theories of the state to see why instrumentalism does not exhaust the possibilities (cf. Zürn & Stephen 2010). Second, these arguments may also read as *functional explanations* of why international institutions exist: the agents of world politics create international institutions in order to solve collaboration and coordination problems in the provision of certain collective goods, such as a clean environment, world peace or international order. As explanatory accounts of international institutions, then, these arguments seem consistent with a rationalist-functionalist account of international institutions. The justificatory aspect dovetails with the explanatory aspect, showing to the potential skeptic why international institutions in general are both desirable and feasible.

However, while the provision of such public goods may justify the existence of global governance institutions, it does not obviously legitimate their authority. To the extent that one explains or justifies international institutions in terms of the collective goods they provide, one also needs to clarify who constitutes the collective that may enjoy the good: *cui bono*? While some of these collective goods are pure public goods – in the sense that anyone, and not just the contracting states, could enjoy world peace – others are less purely public, as the contracting states are the primary or only direct beneficiaries, and may not automatically translate into a collective good for the populations of those states. Moreover, even if a good or service is strictly and wholly public in consumption, it remains private in production; even when everyone can enjoy the good, someone must pay the price of providing it (Filippov et al. 2004, p.51). David Lake, who theorizes international authority defined in terms of a social contract, points out the distributional effects of creating an authoritative institutional order:

> As a negotiated compact, authority must benefit on average the members of the relevant society … But even if everyone in society benefits from having a social order in general, some always benefit more than others. These beneficiaries, in turn, have incentives to support the creation of particular authorities in the first place, and, once vested in that authority, have especially strong reasons for supporting the governor and its corresponding political order.
>
> (Lake 2010, p.593)

Thus, any authoritative institutional order may have profound influences on the distribution of social, economic and political success and failure within a community (Bohman 1999). Moreover, what is rational for governments representing states to agree upon (even if they were somehow perfectly representative of their respective citizens' interest) is not the same as what is rational if the interest of each and every citizen were directly taken into account (Kuper 2006, p.16f). For our present purposes, distinguishing between beneficiaries and benefactors is important in order to understand why the authority exercised by global governance institutions, in spite of the benefits that explain and justify their existence, may open for important legitimacy problems.

Second, while we may quite convincingly justify international institutions generally in terms of the public goods they provide to governments, to states and their citizens, or to humanity as a whole, such arguments seem insufficient to ground the legitimate exercise of authority by particular international institution over its particular subjects. In fact, it is not obvious that the mere unsolicited provision of benefits would ground any right to rule at all (Simmons 1999). Thus, like firms and states global governance institutions solve certain problems of collective action, and their existence may therefore be desirable and justified, compared to anarchy, but they do not acquire any right to rule over unwilling persons simply by virtue of being useful.

2.1 International institutional legitimacy: problems and solutions

Having thus reconstructed a cosmopolitan functionalist account of what global governance institutions are (as distinct from other types of political institutions) and why they are justified in general, let us proceed to discuss the ways in which they give rise to legitimacy problems. Global governance institutions may be a good thing to have in the world in virtue of promoting joint benefits, checks and balances and global justice, but in order for such institutions to provide those goods efficiently, people must perceive the institutions to be legitimate. As Buchanan & Keohane (2006; cf. 2011) put it, "[t]he perception of legitimacy matters, because, in a democratic era, multilateral institutions will only thrive if they are viewed as legitimate by democratic publics." However, in recent years, people – typically, citizens of Western, liberal democracies or an emerging transnational civil society – have increasingly started to question and dispute the authority exercised by international institutions, a development which may portend an impending crisis of legitimacy (cf. Clark 2004; Zürn et al. 2012), most theatrically indicated, perhaps, by violent protests at various international summits. In terms of *descriptive* or *subjective legitimacy*, many people increasingly seem to believe that these institutions, or the broader political order that they comprise, do not live up to their normative expectations of a decent political order, and, as people act on such beliefs, international institutions will increasingly have difficulties providing the public goods that justify their existence (Zürn 2004). Further, these beliefs about a lack of legitimacy may be correct. In *normative* or *objective* terms, international institutions fail to meet the appropriate standards of legitimacy, but people's subjective beliefs about the illegitimacy of an institution may also have normative implications: whether an institution has the objective right to exercise power may depend in part on whether people subject to its authority find it legitimate.

Thus, we could say that following this view, and admittedly much simplified, the problem of legitimacy in global governance involves three sets of entities: international institutions, governments (and their various agencies) and citizens. We may call this the *authority relationship*, which is the object of legitimacy – the circumstance that may need normative legitimation and social acceptance (cf. Lake 2010). For governments, who on average are the primary beneficiaries of the collective goods an institution provides, to be able to obtain those goods may seem sufficient justification, in line with their rational self-interest. Legitimacy crises arise when citizens distrust international institutions to the extent that they can no longer provide the collective goods for which they were set up. The puzzle lies in offering individuals reasons, short of justice and self-interest (Buchanan & Keohane 2006), to accept the authority of international institutions even though they are far from just and even though individuals are not necessarily their net beneficiaries. And the fact that institutions provide one class of agents (governments or states) with certain joint gains may seem an insufficient reason for another class of agents (citizens) to accept the authority of that institution, and to bear the costs, directly or indirectly, of providing those benefits (Peter 2010; Waldron 1987). Of course, this is not to deny that global governance institutions may imply benefits or opportunities for individuals, or imply costs or constraints for states. Governments of developing countries may, for instance, find international economic multilaterals such as the International Monetary Fund or the World Trade Organization to be to their net disadvantage, and yet find no other option but to participate. But the legitimacy crisis of global governance typically arises when governments need to convince citizens that they should carry the burdens of having their state participate in such institutions, even if it is not to their direct advantage. In such situations, citizens may plausibly find the standard justification of global governance institutions – the promotion of certain otherwise unobtainable public goods – an insufficiently legitimating reason.

The question then is: under what circumstances should citizens obey, support or at least abstain from interfering with international institutions? In other words, what criteria should international institutions fulfill in order to be legitimate? Cosmopolitan functionalist contributions to the literature on legitimacy in global governance tend to share a few commonalities: rejecting theories that point to global democracy, global justice or state consent as conditions of legitimacy, they instead present theories of normative legitimacy which bring in a diverse set of elements into complex or hybrid standards or principles according to which international institutional legitimacy can be objectively assessed. Thus, for instance, Allen Buchanan & Robert Keohane (2006) present a *complex standard* of legitimacy, whereby a global governance institution is legitimate – and thus deserves that those who are subject to it treat the rules that it issues as worthy of compliance, regardless of the content of those rules – to the extent that it (a) enjoys the ongoing consent of democratic states; (b) meets certain substantive criteria, such as not violating basic human rights and actually meeting the objectives in terms of which it justifies its existence; and (c) provides outside epistemic agents, such as NGOs, opportunities to engage in monitoring what it does and to participate in revising its goals and procedures.[1] Simon Caney (2009, p.117) offers a shorter but similar *hybrid model*, which combines a substantive and a procedural component: "international institutions should be designed so that (i) persons' most fundamental rights are upheld … and, then, (ii) over and above that they provide a fair political framework in which to determine which principles of justice should be adopted to regulate the global economy" (he focuses on institutions of economic governance). Based on the hybrid model, he suggests reforms to global governance which focus on improving participation, representation, transparency, accountability and public justification.[2] Finally, Matthias Kumm (2004) presents a constitutionalist model for analyzing the legitimacy of international law as a form of global

[1] More recently, Buchanan & Keohane (2011) exclude the element of democratic state consent from their complex standard of legitimacy.

[2] While Caney does not explicitly reject Buchanan & Keohane's complex standard, he does criticize a modified version of state contractarianism ("SCIII") that incorporates elements similar to their procedural, substantive and epistemic elements. Against SCIII, Caney (2009, p.109) argues that while incorporating a democracy criterion of membership may contribute

governance. He suggests that while international law has a *prima facie* justification in virtue of the public goods it promotes, that formal principle of legality must be weighed against a jurisdictional principle of subsidiarity, a procedural principle of adequate participation and accountability, and a substantive principle of achieving outcomes that do not violate fundamental rights and are reasonable.

There are certain important differences between these authors in how they conceive of normative legitimacy. Buchanan & Keohane (2006, p.405) define legitimacy as a right to rule, but in their conception that right is not limited to a right to coercively enforce rules against noncompliers; rather, in their wide definition, ruling "includes promulgating rules and attempting to secure compliance with them by attaching costs to non-compliance and/or benefits to compliance." Neither does the right to rule correspond to a duty to comply on the part of subjects; legitimacy establishes content-independent reasons for governments to comply with the regulations of a global governance institution and, for citizens, to support it, or at least not to interfere with or seek to overthrow it. A conception of legitimacy that includes a duty to obey and a right to coerce, they suggest, is "too strong for global governance institutions, which generally do not wield coercive power or claim such strong authority' (Buchanan & Keohane 2006, note 11; cf. Buchanan 2010, p.81ff). In some cases, of course, an international institution may claim authority in a stronger sense (a right to rule exclusively, to be obeyed and to coerce noncompliers), but, they claim, we can still ask whether a global governance institution that only claims weaker forms of authority is legitimate and whether, for instance, citizens, who are not subjects of the institution's attempt to impose duties, have content-independent reasons for supporting the institution.

Kumm, by contrast, asserts that legitimacy entails a duty to obey, suggesting that "the very idea of legitimacy develops clearer contours when connected to questions of obedience. Only if and to the extent that international law is legitimate is there a moral duty to obey international law. Such a duty, to the extent that it exists, is of central concern for citizens governing themselves through the framework of a national constitution" (Kumm 2004, p.908). However, Kumm says less on whether legitimacy also entails a right to rule and to sanction noncompliers, and, if so, what institutional agent has that right. Indeed, part of the problem of legitimacy,

to the legitimacy of an international institution vis-à-vis the citizens of democratic member states, it fails to legitimate the institution's inescapable coercive impact on members of non-democratic states (a point also acknowledged by Buchanan & Keohane).

on his view, is the lack at the international level of authoritative institutions comparable to the legislative bodies at the state level. It is part of his description of international law as governance that international treaty-bodies may increasingly have the authority to specify state obligations, which may in turn constrain the choices available to the democratic citizenry. Furthermore, the international legal order "exerts influence" on domestic processes and "exerts pressure" on noncompliers. It is unclear, however, whether such authority also entails a right to enforce, to coerce. Like Buchanan & Keohane, then, Kumm seems to understand authority chiefly as a form of coordination, by which power is exercised via incentive structures and normative frameworks, rather than via coercive force.

While such softer notions of authority may seem to fit the current structure of global governance, they may cause two problems for the argument. First, they may appear to imply that we contrast the flat, networked nature of global governance with a caricatured notion of the state, but the enforcement repertoire of modern states is hardly limited to physical coercion. Beyond the simple dichotomy of coercion and coordination and beyond the ideal-types of "the state" and international institutions, the difference in hierarchy between the domestic and the international sphere may be conceived as a matter of degree, where the extremes are seldom approximated (Lake 2009). Second, conceiving of authority as coordination may also seem to downplay the problem of legitimacy and to depoliticize the power exercised by global governance institutions. Even when institutions govern via incentive structures and normative frameworks, rather than via commands and coercion, they may significantly constrain the freedom of the agents over which they exercise authority (cf. von Bogdandy et al. 2008).

Caney (2009) rather emphasizes the political power that international institutions exercise, which helps him to dismiss varieties of state consent as morally inadequate notions of legitimacy. The tremendous regulatory, coercive impact these institutions have over states, and thereby over people's lives and choices, make them explicitly political, he argues. Caney descriptively asserts international institutions' *de facto* power, which he defines in general Dahlian terms as influence (Lukes 1974). Insofar as such institutional power fulfills the criteria of normative legitimacy, I think we might understand it as a right to rule, to be obeyed and to coerce noncompliers: international institutions issue binding rules and have coercive impact, on Caney's view, which is why he thinks they need legitimation. Hence, although Caney does not explicitly relate legitimacy to authority, his view comes closest to include all three elements of a strong notion of legitimacy.

Yet, these conceptions of international institutional legitimacy share certain commonalities. They suggest that legitimacy results from fulfilling not a single value or property, but a mixture of procedural, epistemic and substantive components. While the conceptions may differ in their weighting of these elements, their common key *substantive* concern is that an international institution cannot be legitimate if it violates basic human rights, assuming that such rights provide a standard for minimal moral acceptability to which most people would agree, while the *procedural* components call for channels through which a select group of actors – democratic states and nongovernmental organizations – can express their consent, monitor and hold to account. In that sense, they reflect a nuanced, pluralist idea of what may contribute to enhance the legitimacy of global institutions and avert potential crises of legitimacy.

Now, what are we supposed to do with these standards? One might understand them as operationalizations of normative concepts of legitimacy for empirical research. Hence, we could, presumably, apply the standards to real existing international institutions in order to compare their legitimacy, perhaps quantifying and ranking them according to a legitimacy index. We would face certain epistemic problems of reliability and validity, such as how to weight the various components and how to quantify from qualitative observations. For instance, when assessing whether an institution fulfills the criterion of ongoing consent of democratic states, should the consent of India and Iceland count the same, or rather in proportion to their population? And where along the continuum between a simple majority and full consensus would the criterion be fulfilled? Determining such issues is difficult, but manageable, as for any empirical study of the kind (cf. Buchanan & Keohane 2011). Such an index might be useful, for instance for testing whether international institutions that score high on the normative legitimacy index, or on its various components, also meet higher social acceptability among states or other key groups.

However, another way to understand these normative standards of legitimacy rather sees them as providing guidance for political action. As individuals, policy-makers or citizens, we ought to take these principles to heart and act on them by giving our support to institutions that fulfill the standards, while working to reform those that fall short. Understood in this way, the complex, hybrid standards are part of a theory about the conditions under which citizens of Western, liberal democracies have a moral duty to obey international law in their exercise of constitutional government (to speak with Kumm) or have content-independent reasons to support or at least not interfere with global governance institutions (on

Buchanan & Keohane's view), or the standard may indicate principles that citizens or policy-makers of such states should adhere to when designing or reforming international institutions in order to improve their legitimacy (which seems to be Caney's intention).[3] I take it that these authors conceive of their standards as guiding action and policy in this sense, or perhaps they would dispute the distinction between a standard for empirical research and one for political action (on action-guidance, see Sangiovanni 2009). However, if we take the standards to guide individual action, we encounter epistemic and practical problems considerably more difficult to surmount than are the difficulties of operationalizing the standards for empirical research.

First, to the extent that the standards are intended to help individual citizens or policy-makers decide what to do, the more complex and unclear the standard, the more difficult it will be to act upon. For instance, judging whether an institution deserves our obedience, support or noninterference may require that we gather information about whether democratic states express consent for the institution on an ongoing basis, about the extent to which the institution impacts on fundamental human rights, is comparatively beneficial and fulfills its constitutive purposes and about whether the institution allows external agents to participate in revising its objectives and procedures. While such epistemic problems in assessing the standard may be manageable within a scientific study, many individuals will find it difficult to gather and assess such information, even when the institution readily provides it to outsiders (a criterion included in Buchanan & Keohane's standard). Such epistemic difficulties may not seem to undermine the normative validity of a conception of legitimacy, but they reduce its potential to guide political action. We cannot expect individuals to act on principles that they find unintelligible, opaque or equivocal, especially not as a requirement of legitimacy (Waldron 1987).

Second, even if citizens could reliably gain the knowledge about international institutions they would need, how are they supposed to act upon that knowledge so as to conform to the demands of legitimacy? Put differently, what does it mean for citizens, in Kumm's words, to obey or disobey international law when they collectively exercise constitutional government or design domestic political and legal institutions? What does it require

[3] "We advance the Complex Standard as a proposal for criteria that individuals and groups can use to determine whether particular global governance institutions ought to be regarded as authoritative in their domains of operation … as a reasonable basis for a valuable practice" (Buchanan & Keohane 2011, p.45).

for citizens to act on their content-independent reasons, on Buchanan & Keohane's view, to support or at least not interfere with or overthrow legitimate global governance institutions? Citizens in modern, democratic states mainly participate in constitutional government by electing representatives. It seems hard to tell what it means for citizens to obey international law or to support international institutions when they cast their vote for a party or a candidate (or occasionally a referendum proposal). Any person's individual impact on global governance is so attenuated, and may be offset by a range of other pertinent, salient concerns, so as to be practically meaningless, most of the time.[4] Moreover, it seems close to a category mistake to require of citizens that they obey international law in their exercise of their democratic rights, since they are rarely subjects of international authority in the way that the states they inhabit and the governments they elect may be, even taking into account the blurring of the distinction between national and international law described by Kumm. As an official or agency of the international law system (cf. Waldron 2011), a government (and, in turn, its officials and agencies) seems a more plausible candidate for holding a duty to obey international law in its collective exercise of constitutional government, and it is also more likely than citizens to have the epistemic capacity to exercise such a duty in a meaningful way.

A third problem with these complex standards is whether the components they embody really are of the kind that would grant an institution the right to rule and to be obeyed by those subject to its authority. Take Buchanan & Keohane's standard as an example: the fact that an institution receives the ongoing consent of democracies, meets its own objectives and refrains from violating basic human rights, and allows outside agents to monitor and to hold it to account may show – to paraphrase A. John Simmons – that it is good (or, at least, not bad) in certain ways, but it does not obviously show that it has the kind of special moral relationship with any particular subjects that gives it a right to rule over them, to be obeyed by them and to sanction noncompliers (Simmons 1999, p.748). Of course, Buchanan & Keohane do not actually suggest that individuals have a duty to obey the directives of an institution that appropriately fulfills their standard, only that they have reason to refrain from interfering

[4] When Buchanan & Keohane (and similarly Caney) reject democratic state consent as a sufficient criterion of legitimacy for international institutions, they point to the "problem of diluted authorisation" in long, stretched chains of delegation. But if citizens' impact on international institutions (via elections) is too weak to legitimate global governance institutions, is their electoral activity still significant enough to be constrained by normative concerns over how they affect international institutions?

with, or even positively support, such institutions – to reform them, and not overthrow them (Buchanan & Keohane 2011, p.43). But this more modest demand on individuals indicates that their standard actually is not so much part of a theory of the legitimacy of international institutions, but of their justification. Similarly, Caney (2009, p.118) concludes that "international institutions possess legitimacy to the extent that they uphold fundamental rights and provide a context for the fair adjudication of competing visions of how to govern the global economy." But what rights to rule (and to coerce) follow from the fact that an institution possesses legitimacy in that way? What duties to obey – or else adjust their action – fall on the agents subject to such legitimate authority? Caney indicates that legitimate international institutions would have "the powers necessary" to uphold certain fundamental rights, which, presumably, might include rather extensive coercive means. But a theory of legitimacy may seem incomplete unless it can account for how such powers may (and may not) be wielded so as to coerce disobedient individuals. In fact, the cosmopolitan functionalist standards seem to elaborate further reasons in terms of which international institutions may be justified and may command a certain general respect from individuals: the criteria specify a type of institution that is morally acceptable, seeking to convince the hypothetical anarchist that having institutions of this type, as flawed as they may be in practice, is preferable to the *status quo ante* (Buchanan & Keohane 2011, p.49). But such justificatory arguments in fact say little about the grounds of legitimate authority: the right of an institution to rule over and to be obeyed by its subjects and to coerce those who fail to comply.

Thus, taken together, for both epistemic, practical and conceptual reasons, the complex, hybrid notions of legitimacy seem inadequate as requirements on the political choices and actions of individuals or citizens. As normative demands, the standards fall short of the "ought implies can" requirement. Of course, the standards could still fulfill other important purposes, not least by offering an operationalization of normative legitimacy for empirical research, perhaps forming part of an explanatory theory of social legitimacy, hypothesizing that the more institutions approach these objective criteria, the less societal resistance and critique they will face from the pertinent political actors. The outcome of such research, in turn, may inform public debates about international institutions, and so influence indirectly the choices of citizens (a reasonable interpretation of Buchanan & Keohane's view).

Still, while these standards may be difficult to act upon, the important point is that taking them to guide action for citizens, rather than just to operationalize a normative concept of legitimacy for empirical research, also clarifies how this literature understands the legitimacy problem of global governance institutions: the problem entails giving citizens reasons to accept the authority of international institutions, even though the benefits such institutions provide are mainly enjoyed by states. In order to solve this impending legitimacy crisis, cosmopolitan functionalism suggests combining procedural, epistemic and substantive elements into a complex, hybrid standard of legitimacy, which may then be used to assess whether citizens should obey, support or abstain from interfering with institutions that live up to such complex measures. Now, in the next section, I shall explore how we need to modify this understanding of international institutions, and of the problems and solutions of their legitimacy, in order to make sense of the peculiar case of international human rights institutions.

3. Why international human rights treaties are different

Now, could we apply or transpose the notions of legitimacy in global governance to the case of international human rights institutions? I shall suggest that the peculiar nature of international human rights institutions recasts the problem of legitimacy in ways that have important repercussions for how to assess and address their legitimacy in normative terms. Detailing how international human rights institutions differ from other international regulatory regimes or global governance institutions will help us understand better the problem of their legitimacy, which in turn will help us better grasp solutions to that problem. Thus, this section serves to present an idea about how international human rights institutions have an impact on politics, what sort of difference they make and what kind of authority they hold over whom. That idea will then serve as the basis for an argument about how to understand the problem of their legitimacy. Moreover, this exercise may also help us determine the proper scope of cosmopolitan functionalism as a general approach to international institutional legitimacy.

What is so special about international human rights treaties? A number of international relations scholars have noted how international human rights regimes present something of an anomaly for mainstream theories of international relations. Some scholars have sought to analyze international human rights regimes as yet another case of global governance – a regime similar in kind to those regulating other issues areas (Donnelly 1986; Montgomery 1999; Nickel 2002). However, international human rights law and the mechanisms for its enforcement diverge in important respects from most forms of international institutions that seek to regulate interactions among states, as Andrew Moravcsik points out:

> Unlike international institutions governing trade, monetary, environmental, or security policy, international human rights institutions are not designed primarily to regulate policy externalities arising from societal interactions across borders, but to hold governments accountable for purely internal activities. In contrast to most international regimes, moreover, human rights regimes are not generally enforced by interstate action. Although most arrangements formally empower governments to challenge one another, such challenges almost never occur. The distinctiveness of such regimes lies instead in their empowerment of individual citizens to bring suit to challenge the domestic activities of their own government.
>
> (Moravcsik 2000)

Hence, international human rights regimes constitute a special case of international institutions because they constrain government behavior towards citizens, rather than inter-state behavior. Furthermore, unlike other regimes, international human rights regimes do not necessarily represent any mutual gain for contracting states (Landman 2005).

Conventional approaches to international politics seem to have difficulties making sense of these peculiar aspects of international human rights regimes. Beth Simmons (2009, p.114) suggests that international relations scholars have been overly pessimistic about the political impact for international human rights treaties because they have been looking in the wrong direction: "outward at interstate relations rather than inward at state-society relations." Evaluating existing accounts that seek to explain states' compliance with international human rights treaties as a matter of inter-state politics, Simmons argues that the realist skeptics are mostly correct and that rationalist-functionalist theories largely miss the mark. Realists are accurate in their claim that governments are unlikely to comply with international human rights treaties unless it is in their interest to do so. Moreover, the family of rationalist-functionalist theories, analyzing international institutions in terms of self-enforcing agreements and credible commitment, "is simply an uncomfortable fit for explaining human rights compliance" (Simmons 2009, p.123). Simmons indicates at least three ways in which such theories have difficulties explaining why states comply with international human rights treaties: in the human rights area, there are no *joint benefits*, since a state can generally realize the level of rights protection it desires without the cooperation of other states; there is no *reciprocal enforcement*, as a government is unlikely to alter its own rights practices in order to reciprocate for abuses elsewhere; and there are no significant *reputational costs*, since, compared to other areas, it is hard to identify consequences of a bad reputation with respect to human rights treaty compliance.[5] Similarly analyzing the limits of international action as a mechanism of human rights enforcement, Jack Donnelly (2002, p.178f) suggests that other states are unlikely to find it in their self-interest to reciprocate or retaliate abuses by a government against the human rights of its own citizens. Retaliatory inter-state action is costly, because leverage must be imported from other areas, such as trade or aid; difficult to legitimize, since such means of retaliation are only indirectly tied to the violations; and risky, since it is so much easier to produce great harm than great benefit through international interventions and sanctions. Thus, because of their peculiar nature, international human rights treaties give rise to, rather than help solve, problems of collective action among states.

And yet, international human rights treaties do have a political impact – it just occurs in another political domain than where students of international relations and international law have been prone to look: in the domestic realm. Scholars providing such second-image explanations argue that international human rights treaties can have important effects on domestic politics, by empowering individuals and groups domestically and, correspondingly, by restricting the political discretion of governments.

What domestic factors can account for the fact that states willingly restrict their sovereignty by binding themselves by international human rights treaties? In his case study of the European human rights system, Moravcsik (2000; cf. 1995) argues that governments commit to international human rights institutions, with independent jurisdiction and private access, just as they commit to independent domestic institutions, as "self-interested means of 'locking in' particular preferred policies – at home and abroad – in the face of political uncertainty." This tactic is particularly useful for newly established democracies, for which the benefits of stabilizing the domestic political status quo against anti-democratic threats outweigh the sovereignty costs of membership. Hence, by alienating sovereignty to an independent international authority and binding

[5] Obviously, a government may face certain costs if it builds a reputation of being a systematic human rights violator, but it is less clear that a reputation for being an unreliable treaty partner in the human rights area would make a government an unreliable trading partner or military ally, and reputational enforcement gives rise to inter-state collective action problems, so reputation works, at best, as a weak mechanism enforcing compliance (Simmons 2009, p.123ff).

itself to an international human rights treaty, a government may seek to preserve its favored domestic policies and insulate itself from the actions of future governments. Relatedly, Simmons (2009) proposes that governments primarily commit to international human rights treaties because they believe that they can and will live up to the treaty's provisions. Of course, some governments may ratify insincerely, for strategic reasons or because of peer pressure, whereas other governments who share the treaty's values still fail to ratify because domestic legal traditions, ratification procedures or decentralization influence the treaty-acceptance process. At any rate, once governments have publicly committed to a treaty, it also constrains them by focusing expectations on certain accepted and proscribed behaviors.

International human rights treaties not only serve to constrain domestic governmental discretion, however, but also provide opportunities for political action, by allowing individuals and groups new means by which to pursue their interests vis-à-vis their governments. In order to explain why states comply with international human rights norms, Simmons (2009) suggests three mechanisms by which international human rights treaties may have an impact on domestic policies and in turn on human rights practices: treaties may *effect elite-initiated agendas*, by raising questions of ratification and implementation, and thus insert topics into domestic politics that would not otherwise have been there. Further, treaties may *support litigation*, by rights claimants and lawyers, especially where treaties have the status of domestic law and where courts are relatively independent from political power. Finally, treaties may *spark mobilization* by providing crucial political, legal and social resources to individuals and groups whose goal is to hold governments to their promises. Whether such mechanisms are effective depends crucially on the institutional features of the domestic political and legal system, and on the nature of the human right in question, and changes are often subtle: "They involve changes that give relatively weak political actors important tangible and intangible resources that raise the political costs governments pay for foot-dragging or for noncompliance" (Simmons 2009, p.15).

Summarizing her argument, Simmons suggests that international human rights treaties constitute a unique class of international agreements:

> International human rights treaties have a singularly unusual property: They are negotiated internationally but create stakeholders almost exclusively domestically. In the human rights area, intergovernmental agreements are designed to give individuals rights largely to be guaranteed and respected by their governments. Treaties of this kind have a potentially

> dramatic impact on the relationship between citizens and their own government, creating a huge pool of potential beneficiaries if the treaty is given effect … By sharp contrast, international human rights treaties engage practically no important interests among states *in their mutual relationships with each other*. Most of these agreements simply do not have the capacity to alter international politics in important and predictable ways. The same is not true of politics at home.
>
> (Simmons 2009, p.125, original emphasis)

In order to see why it is not trivial to rethink international human rights regimes in this way, we may contrast it to conceptions of the practice of human rights offered in certain recent philosophical theories of human rights. Many philosophers seeking to provide a political notion of human rights (as distinct from ethical or metaphysical notions of human rights) seem to understand the international human rights regime mainly as an international agreement among liberal states, which specifies the standards that determine when the international community of states should accept a government of a sovereign state as a legitimate member; when other states should tolerate a government, even if it pursues certain illiberal practices; and, conversely, when external agents, individually or acting in concert, may permissibly intervene against a government that engages in gross violations of human rights (for overviews, see Baynes 2009; Ingram 2008; Nickel 2006; Tasioulas 2009; Valentini 2012). That is, these philosophical conceptions mainly regard human rights as a matter of inter-state politics, as a reason for action for governments to take into account in their exercise of foreign policy in bilateral and multilateral relations. However, they have less to say about the role international human rights norms and institutions may play in political struggles within states, where individuals and groups appropriate and apply international human rights norms, and bring them to bear on their government, seeking to improve their own situation. If this is how international human rights have their real significance, rather than serving as standards for membership and conduct in the inter-state domain, it also deserves more attention in normative philosophical accounts of international human rights (cf. Benhabib 2011). For present purposes, suffice it to say that the way we conceive of international human rights institutions generates quite different expectations about the authority relationships and the legitimacy puzzles involved.

Now, if, as a matter of empirical fact, international human rights institutions have their effects on politics not by promoting mutual benefits in inter-state politics, but by restricting governmental discretion and enabling individuals and groups to pursue their interests vis-à-vis their government, what sort of normative problems of legitimacy follow? Notably, these second-level theories are not explicitly normative, but as ontological and explanatory accounts of what international human rights institutions are and why they make a difference to politics, they describe an authority relation between states, persons and international institutions that may need a special kind of normative legitimation.

3.1 *The legitimacy puzzle of international human rights institutions*

If legitimacy is about morally evaluating the exercise of authority, any theory of legitimacy must offer an account of who holds authority over whom, to whom justification may be owed. That is, before we can justify an institution's exercise of power, we must specify what its political significance is, and over whom. If international human rights institutions are dissimilar to global governance institutions in general, since they cannot meaningfully be construed in terms of mutual advantages and reciprocal enforcement in the external relations among states, but rather have their prime political effects in altering the internal relation between a government and its citizens, then they comprise an altogether different legitimacy puzzle as well. First, while global governance institutions may claim *prima facie* justification in terms of providing states with certain collective goods or joint benefits, international human rights institutions would rather claim a baseline justification in terms of providing certain advantages or opportunities to individuals and groups. Second, the provision of such advantages typically fall not on citizens, but on governments, who relinquish domestic political discretion to an independent international treaty-body and commit to norms and policies that may be turned against them or their future successors.

Thus, compared to global governance institutions, international human rights institutions invert the legitimacy puzzle. In the area of human rights, the problem of legitimacy is rarely to offer citizens content-independent reasons to refrain from interfering with or actively supporting international human rights courts, or to show that individuals-qua-citizens have a duty to obey international human rights law when they participate in politics. Rather, the problem of legitimacy is to offer such reasons to states – to governments, parliaments, courts, the police, and other institutional agents of the state who are supposed to commit to and comply with the norms of international human rights treaties. As in global governance, there is a triangular authority relation that may need legitimation, but it points in another direction. Here, the question of legitimacy is not, as in global governance, why individuals should comply, in spite of tangible net costs, with rules or institutions which provide states with certain net benefits they could not otherwise obtain, but rather why governments should comply with human rights norms in spite of the tangible costs (and usually meager benefits) they impose on states, assuming that those norms hold a *prima facie* claim to justification in light of the advantages and opportunities they provide to individuals and groups.

Like the three sets of arguments offered to justify and explain global governance institutions, similar functional and instrumental arguments suggest themselves for human rights institutions. They may improve the human rights behavior of states by offering alternative channels and practical tools by which individuals and groups can seek to pursue their interests, in addition to the channels and tools already offered by state and civil society institutions.

3.2 *The usefulness of state consent*

Now, if the legitimacy puzzle of international human rights institutions involves offering states or governments reasons to carry the costs or constraints they entail, the benefits or opportunities those institutions provide for individuals will seem insufficient reasons, just as joint benefits for states may seem insufficient reasons for individuals to accept the authority of global governance institutions. So in terms of what could the authority of international human rights institutions over states be legitimated? Here, I shall suggest that the legitimacy problems of international human rights institutions seem to require different standards of legitimacy than the corresponding problems of global governance institutions.

Many normative theorists of international institutional legitimacy, including those whose family resemblance I have earlier referred to by the term cosmopolitan functionalism, reject state consent: the notion that international law or institutions derive their legitimacy from the fact that states have consented to them, Buchanan & Keohane (2006, p.413) claim, reflects an outdated, or even immoral, conception of international order "that fails to impose even the most minimal normative requirements on states." Kumm (2004, p.914), similarly, claims that state consent today has lost its legitimating function: international treaties today increasingly delegate powers to quasi-judicial treaty-bodies, which often engage in expansive interpretation of the terms of their own treaties, and modern customary international law "discounts the requirement of general and consistent state practice." Caney (2009, p.107), likewise, argues that "state-centric contractarianism" – the view that international institutions possess legitimacy to the extent that they have been properly authorized by states – is unable to provide an adequate account of political legitimacy.

However, given that international human rights institutions turn the problem of legitimacy on its head, might state consent in fact offer a basic component of their legitimacy? I think it does. As the puzzle now is why states (not citizens) should accept the authority of international human rights institutions, although they have little to gain from it, the fact that states actually and voluntarily have ratified human rights treaties seems to provide one compelling reason (if not the only one) for why they should also comply. Applied to the peculiar case of international human rights institutions, moreover, state consent seems to withstand at least some of the standard criticism.

For instance, both Buchanan & Keohane (2006) and Caney (2009) attempt a *reductio* against state consent, arguing that this notion of legitimacy presupposes that legitimacy can be delegated, so that global governance institutions inherit their legitimacy from legitimate states consenting to them. However, their objection goes, many states do not have any legitimacy to pass down the line, because they mistreat their own citizens (and foreigners) and because they lack procedures guaranteeing democratic accountability. Thus, illegitimate states cannot transfer any legitimacy to international institutions. This might seem a plausible objection, given the way we construct the legitimacy puzzle for global governance institutions. The fact than an oppressive government has consented to a global governance institution should have little significance for citizens, subjects of that government or another, who ponder whether or not to give the institution their support, let alone obey it.

But in the context of international human rights treaties, dismissing state consent on these grounds would have the equally absurd implication of absolving oppressive, nondemocratic governments of their human rights obligations. Consider a state such as Eritrea, which has ratified or acceded to a range of key international human rights conventions, including the ICCPR, the ICESCR, the CRC and the ACHPR. Eritrea's government cannot claim any credentials in terms of electoral accountability, having refused to implement a democratic constitution ratified in 1997, and it persistently violates even the most basic human rights of the vast majority of its citizens (and thus also violates the terms of those treaties) by jailing political opponents, independent journalists and believers of minority religions; by systematically drafting youth to forced labor under the indefinitely extended military service; and by keeping the majority of its population just on the brink of starvation. Obviously, these established facts of oppression and tyranny cannot imply that Eritrea's government could not be held to the international human rights treaties it has ratified. But in the human rights area, the *reductio* objection to state consent ironically may seem to serve to relieve oppressive governments of their international human rights commitments and obligations toward their own populations: illegitimate regimes cannot be bound by human rights conventions, since they cannot legitimately make international treaties. As that conclusion seems counterproductive, we may grant that at least in the human rights field, the fact of internal illegitimacy does not absolve a government from its international obligations.

Moreover, only some form of actual consent seems necessary to establish an authority relationship between an international human rights regime and the state governments subject to its authority. While the general virtues or benefits of having international institutions of this kind may well be taken as a reason for both individuals and governments to support them in general (or, at least, not to interfere with them), that general goodness or fairness of an institution cannot in itself ground a particular duty to comply with its directives. Put differently, a government may well accept or even support the existence of international human rights regimes, in terms of the benefits they help bring about, and yet find those general benefits to be an insufficient reason to comply with the regime in particular instances.

Of course, one might respond that the way in which the government of Eritrea treats its own citizens is plainly wrong, and that establishing the legitimate authority of the human rights treaties it has ratified (yet violates) adds no weight to the moral condemnation of its oppressive practices. But in the human rights field, state consent seems crucial for pragmatic reasons, offering a useful additional resource for justifying why governments should accept to be held to human rights standards: because they have consented to them. We should not underestimate how useful state consent is in this regard. Buchanan & Keohane (2006, p.413) suggest that "those who take human rights seriously" cannot accept "the fiction that all states – regardless of whether they respect the basic rights of their own citizens – are moral agents worthy of respect." Unpacking this double-barreled claim, one could regard states as *moral agents* – that is, as agents with a capacity for moral deliberation and action, who can bear the moral burdens of duty and blame (Erskine 2008) – without thinking them *worthy of respect* regardless of what they do, for instance, regardless of how they treat their own citizens. And even if states' moral agency might be shrugged off as a fiction (or states' corporate agency more generally, following the dominant instrumentalist methodological individualism in mainstream international theory), it might still be a fiction useful precisely to those who take human rights seriously (cf. Wendt 2004). Indeed, much of the work done by the international human rights community and transnational advocacy networks, which engage in naming and shaming of governments that fail to live up to their international human rights commitments, seems to rest on the assumption that states, or governments representing them, are moral agents, who deserve blame or praise depending on whether they respect the basic rights of their own citizens and others subject to their authority (Nickel 2006; Risse et al. 1999). Likewise, the assumption that governments could and should be held to their commitments is a key precondition for international human rights to have domestic impact – in changing elite agendas of executives and legislatures, in supporting litigation by rights claimants and lawyers, and in sparking mobilization by individuals and groups with a stake in compliance: "Key here is the legitimating function of an explicit public commitment to a global standard. That commitment is used strategically by demandeurs to improve the rights in which they have an interest" (Simmons 2009, p.15).

Hence, in the human rights area, state consent may offer a necessary component of a normative notion of legitimacy. While we might also think of other reasons suggesting why governments should comply with their human rights obligations – because it is morally right or in their self-interest to do so – such reasons are not content-independent reasons of legitimacy. Moreover, alternative components such as the ongoing consent of *democratic* states, proposed by Buchanan & Keohane as a necessary element of legitimacy in global governance institutions, seems to offer little added weight in the case of international human rights institutions. Certainly, democratic governments have been the most avid supporters of international human rights treaties, ratifying optional protocols that expose them to even further scrutiny by allowing individuals to file complaints about violations to international authoritative bodies, but that enthusiasm in itself offers no additional reason why states should regard themselves as legitimately bound by those treaties, especially not for non-democratic states. Rather, one would suspect that making the legitimacy of international human rights institutions depend on the consent of democratic states would not enhance their legitimacy in many corners of the world, but rather raise fears of Western bias, parochialism and even imperialism. Additionally, for individuals and groups who seek to hold governments to their international human rights commitments, the democratic credentials of the government seems to offer little extra leverage.

And as an action-guiding notion of legitimacy, state consent offers a simpler criterion than democratic state consent, by avoiding some of the weighting and threshold problems and by being premised on the idea that sovereign states are formally equal. Moreover, state consent improves clarity: while states and other agents may often dispute the interpretation of human rights treaties, treaties have become the preferred format of international agreement precisely because they sharpen the focus on particular accepted and proscribed behaviors: 'Treaties constrain governments because they help define the size of the *expectations gap* when governments fail to live up to their provisions.' (Simmons 2009, p.14) Hence, the notion of state consent, indicated through ratification of a human rights treaty, provides a clear and therefore also feasible, action-guiding criterion of legitimacy.

If state consent provides a necessary element of legitimacy of international human rights institutions, what else is needed? The complex, hybrid standards comprise procedural, epistemic and substantive elements that supposedly add to the legitimacy of global governance institutions. Similarly, an epistemic component may improve the acceptability of international human rights institutions to states. Allen Buchanan (2008) argues that international human rights institutions perform crucial epistemic functions that may contribute to their legitimacy, such as assessing relevant empirical information when specifying and applying human rights norms and when formulating new norms in specialized conventions. Moreover, institutions may help to resolve conflicts of interpretation, and thus help states (and groups and individuals) determine what respect for human rights requires of governments. In the particular case of international human rights institutions, such epistemic mechanisms may suggest further reasons for states to accept that form of international authority, providing a safeguard against the suspicion of parochialism and bias in the continuously developing exercise of that authority. In order to secure that function, drawing on information provided by independent experts or third parties may be useful. Hence, an epistemic element may belong on a standard of legitimacy in the human rights area, but with states as the subjects of legitimacy, it serves a different purpose than in the case of global governance institutions.

Finally, the substantive elements emphasized in cosmopolitan functionalist theories of international institutional legitimacy suggest that in order to hold legitimate authority over citizens, a global governance institution should respect generally accepted basic human rights and meet the goals in terms of which it justifies its existence. Would that element also have a place in offering states reasons to accept the authority of international human rights institutions as legitimate? The substantive elements express a concern that citizens should regard a global governance institution as legitimate only if it actually contributes to realize the sort of short and long-term values in terms of which cosmopolitan functionalists may both justify and explain its existence – such as joint benefits, checks and balances and global peace or justice. Even as an institution may at times fail to fulfill those values, it should openly demonstrate that it strives towards the goals and have procedural mechanisms that increase the likelihood that it realizes its goals relatively efficiently and effectively, although assessing the performance of international organizations is an inherently difficult task (Gutner & Thompson 2010). It seems uncontroversial that citizens should not accept a duty to obey, support or abstain from interfering with an institution that violates basic human rights, or that repeatedly fails to solve the inter-state problems for which it was created. In the case of human rights institutions, the two substantial elements collapse into one: promoting the respect for human rights is the goal in terms of which such institutions may justify their existence.

However, if we want to pursue the inverted legitimacy puzzle, so that the subjects of legitimate authority in this case are not citizens, but governments, what sort of outcomes might constitute valid reasons for governments to regard an international human rights institution as illegitimate? The notion of minimal moral acceptability has no clear analogy in the case of human rights institutions. States sometimes justify flouting their human rights obligations in terms of threats to sovereignty (or popular sovereignty), but international human rights treaties rarely have such existential effects. Generally, international human rights law is not just consistent with but premised on state sovereignty (see Nagano 2006). Treaties may constrain the domestic political discretion of governments by inserting issues on elite agendas, by offering lawyers new tools and by providing resources for social groups to mobilize, but such effects are subtle and never spell the end of sovereignty. However, if a particular international human rights institution were to persistently fail to contribute to improving the human rights situation within the contracting states generally or if it would stray too far from the core values of the treaty, such negative outcomes may provide valid reasons for states to dispute the authority of the institution.

Hence, in the human rights area, the problem of legitimacy entails defending the authority of international human rights institutions over states, in light of the benefits they provide for individuals and groups within states. If we construe the problem in this way, state consent may not only withstand some of the objections raised against it, but it may offer a necessary element of legitimacy. Of course, this is not to say that state consent is a sufficient criterion of legitimacy in the human rights area, nor to suggest that it is generally a necessary condition for the legitimacy of global governance institutions, but rather that we should appreciate the usefulness of this notion of legitimacy. Moreover, if we think of states as the primary subjects of legitimacy – that is, as the agents to whom legitimation is owed – in the human rights area, epistemic and substantive elements of legitimacy may well have their place, but for different reasons than in the case of global governance institutions.

4. Conclusion

I have emphasized that human rights institutions are inherently different than global governance institutions because they entail a different – indeed inverse – relation of authority. Turned upside down, the problem is not why citizens should accept the authority of institutions that help states obtain certain collective goods, but rather why states should accept the authority of international institutions that help individuals secure their rights and interests vis-à-vis their governments. I believe these two differently structured legitimacy problems also mirror political debates about international institutions in many countries. While some suggest that the so-called legitimacy deficit of global governance institutions is indicated by the resistance such institutions and governments face from a host of civil society groups and non-governmental organizations, such groups rarely voice resistance against international human rights treaties and their sometimes expanding authority. In the human rights area, reluctance and resistance rather comes from executives, legislatures, judiciaries and bureaucracies – the institutional agents of the state who will have to bear the costs of implementing an international treaty with a potential to restrict their discretion and change domestic politics in subtle but unforeseeable ways.

While I have restricted my argument to international human rights treaties, as a special class of international institutions, could it be generalized beyond that case? An ontological notion of international institutions – what they are, why they come about, what their impact is and on whom – sets the terms for analyzing problems of their justification and legitimacy. And compared to other kinds of international institutions, international human rights institutions are *sui generis*: they do not entail any joint benefits among states and are not enforced through reciprocal action. They are negotiated among states, but create stakeholders in domestic societies, who can use the rights specified in international treaties as resources to hold their governments to account. Of course, this depiction of two species of international institutions is ideal-typical: an abstraction, for analytical purposes, from the complexity of reality. To the extent that institutions in other issue-areas resemble international human rights institutions, the conceptions of legitimacy I have suggested here may have a more general validity. Andrew Moravcsik (2000) argues that other kinds of international agreements may be explained not just as inter-state bargains, but as independent institutional constraints governments use to increase domestic policy predictability, for instance some trade agreements. Michael Zürn (2004) suggests that new types of complex policy issues have changed the role of global governance: whereas the institutions established after World War II addressed states in the predictable regulation of inter-state problems, new types of institutions, such as global governance regimes in the environmental area, rather target intra-state issues and rely on the compliance of domestic actors for their successful implementation. Similarly, Matthias Kumm (2004) describes how international law has expanded into what was previously considered domestic affairs, thus blurring the distinction between international and national law. Moreover, some international regimes may be of a mixed kind. For instance, international regulations on trafficking in persons both seek to address coordination and collective action problems among states and detail a set of rights for individuals to claim against those states. Such cases may seem to transcend the simple ideal-typical notions of international institutions employed here, and indicate a need for even more hybrid standards of legitimacy that are able to address such mixed authority relations. Yet, international human rights institutions uniquely empower individuals and groups to pursue their rights vis-à-vis their governments, a singular feature that has important, if subtle, political effects, and which may call for a special notion of legitimacy.

Bibliography

Baynes, K., 2009. Discourse Ethics and the Political Conception of Human Rights. *Ethics & Global Politics*, 2(1). Available at: www.ethicsandglobalpolitics.net/index.php/egp/article/view/1938 [Accessed November 16, 2010].

Benhabib, S., 2011. *Dignity in Adversity: Human Rights in Troubled Times*, Cambridge: Polity Press.

von Bogdandy, A., Dann, P. & Goldmann, M., 2008. Developing the Publicness of Public International Law: Towards a Legal Framework for Global Governance Activities. *German Law Journal*, 9(11), 1375–1400.

Bohman, J., 1999. International Regimes and Democratic Governance: Political Equality and Influence in Global Institutions. *International Affairs*, 75(3), 499–513.

Buchanan, A., 2008. Human Rights and the Legitimacy of the International Order. *Legal Theory*, 14(01). Available at: www.journals.cambridge.org/abstract_S1352325208080038 [Accessed July 29, 2011].

2010. The Legitimacy of International Law. In S. Besson & J. Tasioulas, eds. *The Philosophy of International Law*. Oxford University Press, pp. 79–96.

Buchanan, A. & Keohane, R. O., 2006. The Legitimacy of Global Governance Institutions. *Ethics & International Affairs*, 20(4), 405–437.

2011. Precommitment Regimes for Intervention: Supplementing the Security Council. *Ethics & International Affairs*, 25(01), 41–63.

Caney, S., 2009. The Responsibilities and Legitimacy of Economic International Institutions. In L. H. Meyer, ed. *Legitimacy, Justice and Public International Law*. Cambridge University Press.

Clark, I., 2004. Legitimacy in a Global Order. *Review of International Studies*, 29(S1), 75–95.

Deudney, D., 2007. *Bounding Power: Republican Security Theory from the Polis to the Global Village*, Princeton University Press.

Donnelly, J., 1986. International Human Rights: A Regime Analysis. *International Organization*, 40(3), 599–642.

2002. *Universal Human Rights in Theory and Practice*, Ithaca: Cornell University Press.

Erskine, T., 2008. Locating Responsibility: The Problem of Moral Agency in International Relations. In C. Reus-Smit & D. Snidal, eds. *The Oxford Handbook of International Relations*, Oxford University Press, pp. 699–707.

Filippov, M., Ordeshook, P. C. & Shvetsova, O., 2004. *Designing Federalism: A Theory of Self-sustainable Federal Institutions*, Cambridge University Press.

Gutner, T. & Thompson, A., 2010. The Politics of IO Performance: A Framework. *The Review of International Organizations*, 5(3), 227–248.

Held, D., 2006. Reframing Global Governance: Apocalypse Soon or Reform! *New Political Economy*, 11(2), 157–176.

Ikenberry, G. J., 2001. *After Victory: Institutions, Strategic Restraint, and the Rebuilding of Order after Major Wars*, Princeton University Press.

Ingram, J. D., 2008. What Is a "Right to Have Rights"? Three Images of the Politics of Human Rights. *American Political Science Review*, 102(04), 401.

Jacobson, H. K., 2000. International Institutions and System Transformation. *Annual Review of Political Science*, 3(1), 149–166.

Karlsson, J., 2008. *Democrats Without Borders: A Critique of Transnational Democracy*. Doctoral dissertation. Gothenburg: University of Gothenburg. Available at: http://gupea.ub.gu.se/dspace/handle/2077/18348 [Accessed August 19, 2010].

Keohane, R. O., 2003. Global Governance and Democratic Accountability. In D. Held & M. Koenig-Archibugi, eds. *Taming Globalization: Frontiers of Governance*. Cambridge: Polity, pp. 130–159.

Kumm, M., 2004. The Legitimacy of International Law: A Constitutionalist Framework of Analysis. *European Journal of International Law*, 15(5), 907–931.

Kuper, A., 2006. *Democracy Beyond Borders: Justice and Representation in Global Institutions*, Oxford University Press.

Lake, D. A., 2009. Relational Authority and Legitimacy in International Relations. *American Behavioral Scientist*, 53(3), 331–353.

2010. Rightful Rules: Authority, Order, and the Foundations of Global Governance. *International Studies Quarterly*, 54(3), 587–613.

Landman, T., 2005. The Political Science of Human Rights. *British Journal of Political Science*, 35(3), 549–572.

Lukes, S., 1974. *Power: A Radical View*, London: MacMillan.

Montgomery, J. D., 1999. Fifty Years of Human Rights: An Emergent Global Regime. *Policy Sciences*, 32(1), 79–94.

Moravcsik, A., 1995. Explaining International Human Rights Regimes: Liberal Theory and Western Europe. *European Journal of International Relations*, 1(2), 157–189.

2000. The Origins of Human Rights Regimes: Democratic Delegation in Postwar Europe. *International Organization*, 54(2), 217–252.

Nagano, T., 2006. A Critique of Held's Cosmopolitan Democracy. *Contemporary Political Theory*, 5(1), 33–51.

Nickel, J. W., 2002. Is Today's International Human Rights System a Global Governance Regime? *The Journal of Ethics*, 6(4), 353–371.

2006. Are Human Rights Mainly Implemented by Intervention? In R. Martin & D. A. Reidy, eds. *Rawls's Law of Peoples: A Realistic Utopia?* Oxford: Blackwell, pp. 263–277.

Peter, F., 2010. Political Legitimacy. In E. N. Zalta, ed. *Stanford Encyclopedia of Philosophy*. Available at: http://plato.stanford.edu/entries/legitimacy/ [Accessed October 22, 2010].

Pogge, T. W., 2002. *World Poverty and Human Rights: Cosmopolitan Responsibilities and Reforms*, Cambridge: Polity.

Risse, T., Ropp, S. C. & Sikkink, K., eds., 1999. *The Power of Human Rights: International Norms and Domestic Change*, Cambridge University Press.

Sangiovanni, A., 2009. Normative Political Theory: A Flight from Reality? In *Political Thought and International Relations: Variations on a Realist Theme*. Oxford University Press, pp. 219–239.

Scholte, J. A., 2004. Civil Society and Democratically Accountable Global Governance. *Government and Opposition*, 39(2), 211–233.

Simmons, A. J., 1999. Justification and Legitimacy. *Ethics*, 109(4), 739–771.

Simmons, B., 2009. *Mobilizing for Human Rights: International Law in Domestic Politics*, Cambridge University Press.

Tasioulas, J., 2009. Are Human Rights Essentially Triggers for Intervention? *Philosophy Compass*, 4(6), 938–950.

Valentini, L., 2012. In What Sense Are Human Rights Political? A Preliminary Exploration. *Political Studies*, 60(1), 180–194.

Waldron, J., 1987. Theoretical Foundations of Liberalism. *The Philosophical Quarterly*, 37(147), 127–150.

2011. Are Sovereigns Entitled to the Benefit of the International Rule of Law? *European Journal of International Law*, 22(2), 315–343.

Wendt, A., 2004. The State as a Person in International Theory. *Review of International Studies*, 30(2), 289–316.

Zürn, M., 2004. Global Governance and Legitimacy Problems. *Government and Opposition*, 39(2), 260–287.

Zürn, M. & Stephen, M., 2010. The View of Old and New Powers on the Legitimacy of International Institutions. *Politics*, 30, 91–101.

Zürn, M., Binder, M. & Ecker-Ehrhardt, M., 2012. International Authority and its Politicization. *International Theory*, 4(01), 69–106.

9

The democratic legitimacy of international human rights conventions: political constitutionalism and the Hirst case

RICHARD BELLAMY

1. Introduction: democracy, international human rights conventions and the Hirst case

Prisoners serving custodial sentences within the UK are currently disenfranchised by section 3 (1) of the Representation of the People Act 1983.[1] The disqualification does not apply to those imprisoned for contempt of court or following default for non-compliance with a noncustodial sentence, such as payment of a fine, or – since the passage of the Representation of the People Act 2000 – prisoners held on remand. Mr Hirst, who had pleaded guilty to manslaughter due to diminished responsibility and been sentenced to discretionary life imprisonment in February 1980, challenged this provision as being incompatible with the Human Rights Act (HRA), which incorporates the European Convention on Human Rights (ECHR) into domestic British law. At issue was Article 3 Protocol 1, whereby the High Contracting Parties undertake to hold 'free elections at reasonable intervals by secret ballot, under conditions which will ensure the free opinion of the people in the choice of the legislature'. His application was heard before Lord Justice Kennedy in the Divisional Court in March 2001

Earlier versions of this paper were delivered at the universities of St Andrews, Oslo, Hannover, Glasgow Caledonian, Geneva, Minho, Montreal, and the Hebrew University in Jerusalem, the ECPR General Conference at Reykjavik, and as the Statute Law Society Lecture and the Plenary Lecture of the Association for Social and Legal Philosophy Annual Conference in Belfast. I am grateful to the audiences on all these occasions for their helpful comments and especially Marco Goldoni, Stephen Gardbaum, Janet Hiebert, Annabelle Lever, Peter Niesen, Philip Pettit, Justice Philip Sales, Johan Karlsson Schaffer, Mark Tushnet and my colleagues Cecile Laborde, and Albert Weale.

[1] For a summary of the position pre- and post-Hirst, see I. White, 'Prisoners' Voting Rights', House of Commons Library, Standard Note SN/PC/01764 11 December 2012.

and rejected. An application for appeal was refused. He took his case to the European Court of Human Rights (ECtHR), where it was heard in December 2003. The Chamber held unanimously that there had been a violation of Article 3 Protocol 1.[2] The UK government requested the case be referred to a Grand Chamber, which in October 2005 ruled by 12 votes to 5 in favour of the applicant, the British judge voting with the majority.[3]

The judgment was ambiguous. It included two concurring opinions qualifying the view of the majority as well as two dissenting opinions from the minority. As a result, views on what was necessary to comply with the judgment differed widely. Some held the right to vote had been deemed a core human right and that any ban was inadmissible except possibly for offences related to electoral malpractice, others that it might be imposed in exceptional circumstances by the sentencing judge as appropriate in a given case, still others argued that the Court's objection only related to a blanket ban on all prisoners, with a ban that affected only those prisoners convicted of more serious crimes being allowable, while a few believed the main objection related to Parliament's supposed failure to debate the issue adequately and justify its stance when framing the legislation. This range of views reflects the current situation across Europe, where a minority of countries either include or exclude all prisoners from the vote, with the majority either allowing judges to remove this right when sentencing and/or restricting this penalty to a variety of specified crimes. The then Labour government undertook a consultation on how the law might be changed but had taken no action by the time of the 2010 general election, leading to a rebuke from the Council of Europe's Committee of Ministers. On 20 December 2010, the new Conservative-Liberal Democrat administration announced that offenders sentenced to less than four years would be allowed to vote in Westminster and European elections.[4] This proposal was deemed to answer the proportionality issue raised by the ECtHR's judgment, removing an element of arbitrariness whereby many prisoners sentenced to less than four years only lost their vote if an election occurred during their incarceration. Even so, the House of Commons Committee on Political and Constitutional Reform remained unsure it would satisfy the Court given the ambiguities in the judgment. Nevertheless, the proposal aroused considerable parliamentary opposition among MPs

[2] *Hirst v United Kingdom (No. 2)* (74025/01) Fourth Section Judgment 30/03/2004.

[3] *Hirst v United Kingdom (No. 2)* (74025/01) Grand Chamber Judgment 06/10/2005.

[4] HC Deb 20 December 2010 c151WS.

from all parties and prompted a backbench debate initiated by Jack Straw, a former Labour Minister of Justice, and David Davies, a former Conservative Shadow Home Secretary. They tabled a joint motion noting that the ECtHR had 'held that there had been no substantive debate by members of the legislature on the continued justification for maintaining a general restriction on the right of prisoners to vote' and asking the House to 'acknowledge the Treaty obligations of the UK' and endorse the opinion 'that legislative decisions should be a matter for democratically elected lawmakers' and support 'the current situation in which no prisoner is able to vote except those imprisoned for contempt, default or on remand'.[5] Their motion passed by 234 to 22 votes on 10 February 2011. Given Grand Chamber decisions cannot be appealed, the government appeared trapped in an impasse, caught between its international obligations to the ECtHR, on the one hand, and to Parliament, on the other.

The Court's latest decision – a Grand Chamber judgment of 22 May 2012 in *Scoppola v Italy (no. 3)*, to which the UK government was allowed to submit comments as a third party – raises a further set of issues. The Court backtracked from an earlier post-Hirst decision, *Frodl v Austria*, which appeared to allow for no discretion in this area, confirming that a 'margin of appreciation' existed as was apparent from the wide range of laws limiting prisoners' voting rights among the contracting States. As such, it demonstrated a willingness to respond to objections from legislators and governments as well as domestic courts and to accommodate differences regarding certain rights. However, it reaffirmed another post-Hirst decision in *Greens and M.T. v the United Kingdom* that a blanket ban on all prisoners was unacceptable in not allowing for any degree of proportionality between the loss of the vote and the severity of the sentence. Yet, many favourable to granting prisoners the vote would regard the Italian regulations as worse than the disputed UK measure. For although prisoners sentenced to less than three years retain the vote in Italy, those receiving sentences between three and five years are disenfranchised in prison and for up to five years following their release, while habitual offenders and those, like Mr Scoppola, sentenced to terms of five years or more receive a lifetime ban from public office and lose 'the right to vote or stand for election in any electoral body and all other political rights'.[6] Meanwhile, the UK government remains opposed to granting prisoners the right to vote but in compliance with the judgment published a draft Bill on 22 November 2012

[5] HC Deb 10 February 2011 c 493–584.

[6] Italian Criminal Code Articles 28 and 29.

that proposes offering legislators three options – disenfranchisement for prisoners sentenced to four years or more, disenfranchisement for prisoners sentenced to six months or more, or the present total ban. While the Committee of Ministers has welcomed the legislative proposals it has signalled the third option would be incompatible with the ECHR.[7]

The Hirst judgment raises the issue of the democratic legitimacy of International Human Rights Courts. On the one hand, it struck down the decision of a democratically elected legislature, possibly undermining democracy; on the other, it upheld the democratic right of prisoners to vote, arguably reinforcing it. A standard view holds the latter action validates the former, with 'strong' review by an international court being justified to defend democracy against itself. At most, such systems require endorsement in a popular referendum to have democratic legitimacy. This chapter challenges that analysis. It proposes a way of conceiving international human rights regimes consistent with treating domestic democratic legislatures as final arbiters on human rights – including those entailed by the democratic process. These regimes can be construed in analogous terms to parliamentary bills of rights as issuing from and being controlled by an association of democratic states, and involving only 'weak' review. Democratic states have good reasons to establish such regimes, which add to rather than detract from their democratic legitimacy. In key respects the European Convention on Human Rights corresponds to this model, as does the Hirst judgment, while their departures from it largely underscore the advantages of the proposed scheme.

The concern of this chapter, therefore, is neither to adjudicate on the legal merits of the Court's decision, nor – other than peripherally, as part of a broader argument – to explore the substantive issue of whether prisoners have a human right to vote. Rather, it deploys the Hirst case to examine, from a normative perspective, the legitimacy of such interferences by international human rights courts (IHRCts) with the legal and political decisions and processes of well-established national democracies. On most measures the UK qualifies as a well-functioning democracy with a good record of human rights protection. It has incorporated the ECHR into domestic law and has rigorous parliamentary and judicial mechanisms for ensuring domestic legislation is rights compliant, including by reference to the relevant jurisprudence of the ECtHR. Yet, the Hirst judgment sets aside the arguments of both parliament and the domestic courts,

[7] Decision of the Committee of Ministers 4–6 December 2012.

attracting criticism on grounds of democratic legitimacy. What follows explores how this criticism might be met.

Andrew Moravcsik has observed that the ratification and support for International Human Rights Conventions (IHRC) by well-functioning democratic regimes poses something of a puzzle (Moravcsik 2000: 219). As with the Hirst case, the prime focus of such instruments is generally the domestic policies and arrangements of the signatory states. However, it is not obvious why IHRC and the bodies that uphold them should be regarded as more legitimate than the domestic conventions, constitutional courts and legislatures of these states, whose decisions they may censure and even require to be changed. Prima facie, these domestic arrangements seem to possess a greater degree of democratic legitimacy than most international arrangements. They enjoy both democratic authorisation and enshrine democratic accountability. In many cases, state constitutions have been subject at some point to democratic approval by a majority or super-majority of either the people themselves or their elected representatives. Moreover, not only are legislatures and executives democratically accountable for their decisions but also, indirectly, so are domestic courts – be it through the selection process of the judges, the influence of public opinion, which can exert rather greater sway in the domestic than in the international arena, or – in some jurisdictions – because of democratic procedures, such as referenda or a parliamentary vote, that allow court decisions to be overridden. By contrast, many IHRC involve states whose democratic credentials are doubtful. Even among those parties that are democracies, they enjoy at best the indirect democratic legitimacy of having been entered into by their elected representatives, with little or no electoral or legislative scrutiny of these undertakings.

It might be objected that democracy and rights provide distinct criteria for assessing the legitimacy of a given system, and scoring high or low on the first is immaterial to the assessment of its performance with regard to the second. Supporters of judicial review typically advocate the independence of the judiciary from democratic pressures. They claim independence enhances the impartiality of courts and is central to their defence of individual rights against prejudiced or myopic majorities or the intemperate actions of elected executives and their agents. As a result, they view the greater distance and independence of international tribunals from such democratic influences as an advantage. As Judge Caflisch put it in his concurring opinion in *Hirst (2)* para 4, 'the decisions taken by this Court are not made to please or indispose members of the public, but to uphold human rights principles'. However, such a sharp distinction between rights and democracy proves too neat. Empirically, a strong instrumental link exists between democratic systems that enshrine political equality and popular accountability and respect for rights (Christiano 2011). Democratic states offer reliable protection for basic rights, while non-democratic states just as reliably endanger them. Normatively, some theorists argue that there is an intrinsic link between rights and democracy – that either the one entails the other (Habermas 1996), or that democracy rests on the self-same moral considerations as rights in stressing the need to show individuals equal concern and respect as autonomous reasoners (Waldron 1999). Less contentiously, most rights theorists would acknowledge that democracy possesses a moral force of its own. If rights can accommodate and benefit from democratic endorsement, therefore, that can be welcomed as adding to their legitimacy.

Thus, there are both pragmatic and principled reasons to take the democratic legitimacy of IHRC seriously and not to rely for their legitimation on the normative authority of rights-based arguments alone. Indeed, one can conjecture that IHRC are more likely to be upheld and identified with the more democratically legitimate they manage to be, and rejected to the extent that they appear less democratically legitimate than similar domestic arrangements. That supposition appears confirmed by Moravcsik's finding that mature democracies prove unenthusiastic promoters of such conventions (Moravcsik 2000). If he is correct in considering the prime motivation for democracies to support these instruments is to boost democratisation in non- or newly democratic states, one might expect the strains to increase over time and enthusiasm for such conventions to wane the more secure the democratic systems of the signatory states become – a hypothesis that the reaction to *Hirst (2)* arguably confirms (see too Simmons 2009). In this case, exploring whether there are good democratic arguments beyond the stabilising of democracy that might legitimise such international rights regimes may be of more than mere academic interest. For such arguments may be integral to their obtaining the continued support of established democratic states. Alternatively, if no additional democratic reasons can be given, it could be that they are best viewed as transitionary arrangements destined to wither away in a more democratic world rather than, as is sometimes maintained (Buchanan 2004), the basic components of a post-statist, possibly less democratic, but a more just and rights-compliant cosmopolitan international order.

Such considerations should carry weight even with 'legal constitutionalists' (e.g. Dworkin 1996), who support forms of constitutional democracy that circumscribe democratic mechanisms within legal, rights-based constraints that are upheld by constitutional courts. For the domestic constitutional courts of a well-functioning constitutional democracy may have as much reason to question the legitimacy of an international court as a democratically elected legislature if they regard their authority as emanating from domestic legal sources such as 'we the people'. As a result, even this position can grant that accession to such conventions will benefit from democratic authorisation (Buchanan & Powell 2008). However, in this paper I wish to explore this issue from the perspective of 'political constitutionalists' (Gee & Webber 2010), who regard the very processes of 'actual existing democracy' – namely, a system involving regular, free elections between competing parties of representatives for the legislature and executive on the basis of one person, one vote and majority rule – as possessing constitutional qualities that ought not to be subordinated to control by a constitutional court.

There are two main reasons for doing so beyond the fact, relevant to the Hirst case, that the UK has traditionally been regarded as having such a political constitution (Griffith 1979) – even if that view has become increasingly controversial since the passing of the HRA.[8] First, even within constitutional democracies there is an ongoing debate about the democratic legitimacy of rights-based judicial review by constitutional courts and disputes about the accuracy of portraying constitutional law as simply the creature of courts rather than part of ongoing democratic politics (e.g. Dahl 2003; Devins & Fisher 2004; Kramer 2004; Tushnet 1999 on the USA). Arguments that take the legal constitutionalist stance as given, or that view democratic legitimacy as restricted to exceptional moments of democratic endorsement, such as referenda, fail to do justice to this democratic critique. The political constitutionalist position seeks to capture these democratic concerns and insights without denying the importance of rights or other constitutional values, such as the rule of law (e.g. Bellamy 2007; Waldron 1999). Consequently, this perspective allows for a fuller consideration of the compatibility of such instruments with the legislative authority of the democratic process. If there is a way of reconciling IHRC with political constitutionalism, then that solution may also prove relevant for constitutional democracies given that worries about the democratic legitimacy of rights-based judicial review persist within such regimes and they often contain significant political constitutionalist elements. Second, I shall argue that political constitutionalism offers an alternative, democratic, view of the purpose and functioning of IHRC. As I noted, there has

[8] E.g. Bogdanor (2009), although see Bellamy (2011) and Tomkins (2005).

been a tendency to view these mechanisms as promoting legal constitutionalism on a global scale, prompting some at least to believe that they would only be compatible with democracy if that was likewise institutionalised at the global level (Buchanan 2004). However, such proposals risk being regarded as utopian. Moreover, they do not address the immediate problem of a growing critique of IHRC by the very states one might expect to be their most fervent champions.[9] By contrast, a political constitutionalist account seeks to meet such criticisms by taking seriously the origins of international human rights practice in agreements among democratic states.

This chapter does not offer an explicit defence of the political constitutionalist position or a critique of legal constitutionalism (see Bellamy 2007 for such a defence and critique). Rather, it takes political constitutionalism as a starting point on the grounds that it expresses certain common democratic complaints about IHRC to be found even within established legal constitutionalist systems. The aim is to investigate the implications of such democratic arguments and see if they are in any way compatible with a role for such bodies. I begin by outlining the main premises of the political constitutionalist position. I argue that these are not satisfied by permitting periodic constitutional referenda but are compatible with both a statutory bill of rights and a form of 'weak review' by courts, only excluding the 'strong review' typically associated with legal constitutionalism.[10] I then consider the implications of this argument for the organisation and role of international courts. Whereas it rules out certain common arguments for such bodies, which I group under the heading of being 'judge in one's own cause', I contend that their exercise of 'weak review' is legitimate. However, as with domestic courts, this practice is only possible in the context of a judicial system that is democratically dependent even if judges are independent when deciding individual cases. Whereas global democracy would be unlikely to possess the requisite constitutional qualities to provide the democratic context for international courts, a system of international democracy that results from voluntary agreements between democratic and democratising states can do so. I conclude that this model offers a plausible picture of how we might understand the ECHR and ECtHR and many, if not all, features of the Hirst judgment.

9 For example, see the analysis of recent criticisms of such bodies in Nordic countries in Føllesdal & Wind (2009).

10 For this distinction see Waldron (2006) at 1354–1355.

2. Political constitutionalism: democracy, human rights and weak judicial review

The political constitutionalist argument rests on the view that what might be called 'actually existing' democracy – that is, a political system involving regular elections for the legislature and executive between competing parties on the basis of one person, one vote and majority rule – offers the most legitimate mechanism for promoting rights (Griffith 1979). According to the political constitutionalist, the legitimacy of these democratic processes derives from their intrinsic and instrumental merits in ensuring the collective policies of the polity, which give form to the rights of citizens and structure the ways they lead their lives and interact, treat all fairly and give equal consideration to their interests. The intrinsic merit lies in according each individual equal respect as a source of reasons about rights, whose views ought to be placed on a par with those of everyone else – especially given the presence of reasonable disagreements about rights (Waldron 1999). The instrumental merit follows from this intrinsic aspect and derives from the way an equal vote within such a process indicates in a public way that the rights of all are treated with equal concern (Bellamy 2007: Ch. 6). The complexity and openness of modern societies renders even the most conscientious and professional politician, official or judge cognitively partial in their judgments, inevitably favouring positions that reflect their own experience and preferences. Given this context of biased disagreement, democracy offers an impartial mechanism for citizens to protect and promote their interests in an equitable manner (Christiano 2008).

These arguments will not be defended here (see Bellamy 2007: Chs. 4–6). It suffices for present purposes to note how they ground accounts of democratic legitimacy. For example, they figured prominently in the parliamentary debate of the Hirst judgment (Nicol 2011a). The aim is to see whether these arguments are compatible with international human rights regimes, and if so in what ways. The rest of this section explores three issues relevant to this investigation: i) the adequacy from this perspective of constitutional referenda or some other form of popular endorsement as mechanisms for giving democratic legitimacy to an entrenched and judicially protected domestic or international convention on rights; ii) the consistency of political constitutionalism with a legislative bill of rights and iii) the acceptability of judicial review based on such a bill. This analysis will show that for IHRC and IHRCts to possess democratic legitimacy they must be products of and controlled by an international system of normal democracy grounded in and compatible with the domestic systems of the contracting states, provide international versions of a legislative bill of rights and only involve the exercise of 'weak' review. Subsequent sections will then indicate how such a system proves possible.

It is sometimes argued that a system of strong rights-based judicial review could be democratically legitimated by way of a constitutional referendum (Buchanan & Powell 2008). However, such referenda prove deficient with regard to both the intrinsic and instrumental qualities political constitutionalism associates with the normal democratic process. Normal democracy creates incentives for politicians to propose policies with broad appeal that reflect the relative weighting of the views and interests of citizens across the whole range of public policies. It looks at rights in the round and with regard to how they impact upon each other with regard to different policy proposals. It also does so in an ongoing way, responding to past mistakes and changing circumstances and opinions – not least due to the continuous criticisms of opposition parties offering alternative programmes of government to the incumbent office holders.

By contrast, referenda tend to be exceptional and relate to a single issue. There is no weighing of the relative importance of the issue being considered vis-à-vis other issues. They can also be 'second-order' votes registering approval, or more often dissatisfaction with, the incumbent administration rather than an assessment of the popularity of the constitutional measure in question. Moreover, once the vote is taken, it becomes harder to change, with its evolving meaning often handed over to a non-democratic agency, such as an IHRCt, which may come to interpret the measure not just in a very different way to what the citizens who voted for it intended, but also to how current voters understand it. Therefore, such referenda doubly offend political equality. On the one hand, they fail to show equal concern and respect to the various concerns of citizens by unduly narrowing the range of views and issues that can be considered and through being periodic, often with a high threshold for change, thereby favouring a potentially less just status quo. On the other hand, they give the specification of rights to an anti-egalitarian body that is liable, due to lack of relevant information and cognitive bias, to make decisions that fail to treat all as equals.

That does not mean that political constitutionalists do not think that rights are particularly important and merit special consideration or that courts should play no role in their protection. However, they believe that the specialness of rights can be indicated by the special way they are treated by politicians rather than through their not being handled by politicians at all, and that courts should be a part of, and ultimately defer to, this special political process. For example, although the UK Human Rights Act (HRA) is an ordinary statute which can be repealed or amended like any other piece of legislation, it does enact particularly rigorous procedures for ensuring all other legislation takes rights into consideration (Bellamy 2011). Under section 19 of the HRA, Ministers must accompany all legislative proposals with a declaration of compatibility with the Act, or if necessary explain why they believe it is justified in not being compatible. These declarations are informed by a scrutiny of the legislation by a special committee of both houses of parliament, the Joint Committee on Human Rights. The JCHR reports inform subsequent debate of the legislation in Parliament and Explanatory Notes on rights compliance are now published with every government bill. Other jurisdictions which prioritise parliamentary over judicial scrutiny of rights, such as the Nordic and many former Commonwealth countries, typically adopt similarly rigorous political procedures.[11]

As with any legislation, courts play a vital role in upholding statutory bills of rights. Courts provide for their impartial application to individual cases and ensure the compatibility of other legislation with them. However, while it is desirable that judges operate independently from the democratic branches of government when deciding any given case, political constitutionalists note two key respects in which the functioning of the judicial system as a whole ought nevertheless to be democratically dependent (Ferejohn & Kramer 2002).

First, even legal constitutionalists regard a well-functioning legal system as needing to possess certain democratic qualities. They desire access to justice to be open equally to all, rather than the preserve of the wealthy or the well placed, and that the judiciary should not form a self-selecting caste or be a part of the ruling class, and hence predisposed to siding with the privileged and powerful against the unprivileged and powerless. Most will also concede that law should be in touch with the changing social circumstances or mores of those whom it affects if it is not to make arcane, arbitrary or unreasonable demands of citizens. To be followable and identified with, the law must in certain crucial respects be the 'people's law rather than merely 'lawyers' law. However, political constitutionalists argue that the legal and judicial system only comes to possess these qualities through being open to social and political pressures towards equality of access and membership. Only then are all likely to be treated as equal under the law.

[11] See Campbell et al. (2011) Part 2 for a discussion of different parliamentary systems for rights protection and Hiebert (2005) on the Commonwealth model.

It is important on their account that law operates within a democratic context, rather than being isolated entirely from democratic pressures, as legal constitutionalists sometimes propose. Though electing judges would impugn their independence and impartiality, as well as undermine the division of labour between the legislative and judicial branches, political constitutionalists believe the system for selecting judges should be open and politically criticisable should it fail to recruit in ways that are broadly representative of the political community, while judicial decisions must likewise not be isolated from public discussion and critique. Such pressures tend to exist even in legal constitutionalist regimes. For example, in the United States they have led Supreme Court decisions broadly to follow sustained, national, majority opinion (Dahl 1957).

Second, political constitutionalists contend that recognising democratic processes as the source of law plays an important role in upholding the rule of law (Waldron 2008). They regard a democratic process as necessary to ensure laws are framed in ways that treat all equitably by judging like cases alike and unalike cases in ways that are relevantly different. As we saw, they maintain this process encourages elected law-makers to take into account the various views and interests of citizens in ways that accord them equal respect and concern. Therefore, it is important that court judgments defer to the legislature rather than engaging in constructive interpretations of the legislative implications of constitutional principles. Too much judicial discretion in the application of the law risks appearing arbitrary as to both the source of law, which may then seem to be individual whim rather than a recognised public process, and its content, which may fail to give equal consideration to all relevant factors through being limited to those persons and arguments that have legal standing in the case at hand.

That said, no political process is perfect. Though political constitutionalism proves inconsistent with 'strong' judicial review, it is compatible with 'weak' judicial review. Weak review, as is found in the UK under the HRA, allows for courts to declare a measure or law as being incompatible with a democratically legitimated bill of rights, at least as it applies to a given case, but not to disapply the law or strike it down, as can occur under strong review. That remains the prerogative of the democratically elected legislature (Tushnet 2003).

The rationale for weak review follows from the two elements underlying the political constitutionalist case itself: the possibility for reasonable disagreement about rights and the fallibility of any decision about them, and the need for the equal consideration of the views and interests of citizens. Weak review provides for contestatory 'editorial' democracy rather than 'authorial' democracy.[12] It invites legislatures to think again. That can be justified if a legal challenge reveals inconsistencies between legislative acts, unearths unfortunate consequences not anticipated when framing the legislation, or when certain minorities prove so 'discreet and isolated' that their concerns fail to gain a hearing through democratic politics.

The capacity of courts to uncover such problems derives from their focus on individual cases. As a result, they can draw attention to those circumstances when legislation and policies might produce adverse effects for certain categories of persons that legislatures, which cannot explore or anticipate every possibility and are chiefly concerned with general rather than particular considerations, may have overlooked or underestimated. However, this same feature of courts makes them poorly suited for considering rights in the round and the ways the gains for rights protection overall might need to be balanced against such individual cases (Tomkins 2005). Government action may sometimes curb given rights of certain groups to promote the more equal or fuller enjoyment of the full range of rights by other groups. For example, governments may wish to regulate tobacco advertising, thereby limiting freedom of speech, for reasons of public health, or to constrain freedom of contract and exchange to protect minimum employment standards or secure certain public goods. The legal and individual focus may unduly narrow the range of moral and other considerations that need to be taken into account, and over-emphasise the danger of government power to rights (Tushnet 2007). Courts may be jurisdictionally constrained from considering, and in any case have less access to, the multifarious concerns of millions of individuals that legislatures need to respond to. Consequently, it remains important for the democratic legitimacy of such judicial opinions that the final word lies with the legislature. The purpose of such review is to enhance the democratic consideration of rights, not to substitute for it.

Therefore, from a political constitutionalist perspective, a democratically legitimate system of international human rights protection will need to be subject to ongoing democratic political control through the ordinary legislative process. Such control must apply to the content of the IHRC, the running of the legal system charged with its interpretation and – in the ultimate instance – to the decisions of the IHRCt. Before turning to the issue of whether such criteria could be met, I will briefly consider how this approach differs from a number of standard arguments for such international bodies.

[12] These terms are taken from Pettit (2000).

3. Judge in one's own cause

The standard argument for rights-based judicial review of domestic legislation by international courts is that they provide a more independent and 'impartial' view that can correct for local prejudices, self-interest or myopia (Buchanan 2004: 297–298). These arguments can be roughly grouped together under the legal norm of 'nemo iudex in sua causa'. However, from the political constitutionalist perspective, there are problems as to the applicability, effectiveness and coherence of this argument.

First, it is questionable how far it is applicable to regard a democratic state as being a 'judge in its own cause'. This position treats a state as a unitary actor, deciding an issue of rights in its own self-interest. However, given that the decisions in question tend not to be about inter-state relations, it seems inappropriate to regard these judgments as challenging the self-interest of states. The exceptions might be policies concerning access to citizenship or entry to and continued residence in a state for asylum seekers or immigrants. These cases are additionally strong given that neither group can influence the relevant domestic legal and political system via the democratic process, while most of the first and many of the second will either be citizens of regimes that are not democratic or only minimally so or stateless persons. As we shall see in the next section, democratic states have incentives to create collective arrangements to deal with such issues that can balance the rights of their citizens against those of aspirant and non-citizens, and ultimately aim to promote democracy among all states. However, it will be argued that such arrangements only require weak review. Here, though, it suffices to note that the most compelling case for strong rights-judicial review also proves the least developed in practice.

In the standard cases, which concern purely domestic measures that only affect citizens, the notion of the state being 'judge in its own cause' proves harder to sustain (Hessler 2005: 41–42). The democratic decision-making process that leads to the disputed law involves a large number of different and often opposed actors. Elected executives will have had to gain the assent of representatives in Parliament and indirectly a majority of citizens, while domestic courts will have also held the measure to be acceptable. Moreover, as we have seen, these domestic processes may well have been scrupulous in their attention to rights considerations. There will have been no single actor 'judging in its own cause' in this situation. Within most democratic systems, an electoral majority is built on a coalition of diverse groups of voters, with the executive and legislative majority often made up of a shifting coalition of different parties. In many systems, measures have to be approved by two chambers and are subject to review by domestic courts.

It will be objected that nonetheless certain 'discrete and insular' or widely dispersed minorities, with little or no bargaining power, might still be consistently ignored by these democratic and legal mechanisms. Those social groups who are likely to form part of the electoral majority and the domestic legal and political elite may suppress these minorities' individual rights – be it through self-interest, prejudice, myopia, ignorance, carelessness or plain error. Indeed, one or more of these factors could lead a majority to pay insufficient attention to their own rights in the face of an over-zealous, inept, misguided or corrupt executive, as some commentators have alleged has been the case with excessively restrictive anti-terrorist legislation. In such instances, an IHRCt offers even a well-run domestic legal and political system the benefit of an 'outsider's' perspective. For example, other legal systems may provide instances of policies that challenge the local prejudices and assumptions of the state in question. Through being more disengaged from the circumstances that give rise to a given policy, such bodies can also help guard against precipitate over reactions to a shocking incident, such as a terrorist bomb or the abduction of a child, and point to the longer term adverse consequences of over-hasty legislation.

However, the second issue of effectiveness arises here. Though such reasoning may prove valid in certain circumstances, it is doubtful that it offers a general case for anything beyond 'weak review'. Indeed, the drawbacks political constitutionalists note with relying on courts for the defence of rights may be amplified in the case of judicial review by IHRCts, in part for the very reasons that their proponents advance in their defence. For a start, the 'outsider's' view may overlook how the specification of a particular right within a given legal system forms part of a more general approach to rights, that balances different rights considerations and which taken overall is reasonable and reflects local circumstances and concerns (Hessler 2005: 43–44). Ruling on a single case does not allow for all these various factors to be taken into account and IHRCts are likely to be even less aware of the impact on other rights and moral concerns of citizens than a domestic court. An IHRCt may also be moved to assume 'one size fits all' and seek to apply a minimal standard that overlooks substantive differences between different cases and systems. For example, the ECtHR judgment in *Scoppola* could be criticised on these grounds for applying to all signatory states a somewhat arbitrary categorisation of prisoners based on length of sentence that fails to take into account any other differences in sentencing and penal policy. As a result, the Court did not differentiate between the Italian case, where prisoners may be permanently disenfranchised, and the British case, where they are only disenfranchised for the period of their incarceration.

Distance also exacerbates the potential for the underprotection of rights that can arise when IHRCts are perceived as the key agents of rights protection. Whereas political constitutionalism stresses *ex ante* rights scrutiny, courts operate *ex post*. If a higher court comes to be regarded as the prime instrument of rights protection, there is a danger that the subordinate bodies – particularly executives and legislatures – will be less scrupulous themselves and only take rights into consideration to the extent that they believe they may be legally challenged to do so. A IHRCt may exacerbate this tendency by adding to the already high costs in time and money of mounting a legal challenge. Meanwhile, though IHRCts can help dilute the influence of local factions, weakening the effects of their rent-seeking and prejudices, they may also give undue weight in their turn to those groups able to organise transnationally. As we noted, states can unjustifiably exclude underprivileged groups, such as refugees or poor migrants. However, certain exclusionary state policies – such as those regulating wages or health and safety – may serve to provide social protection for the more vulnerable within their borders. Yet, those seeking to dismantle exclusions of the latter kind, such as corporations, are likely to have more resources and be better able to mobilise to mount legal challenges, than those seeking to remove exclusions of the former kind, such as the global poor (Nicol 2011b).

There has been a move recently to enshrine some of these social protections in IHRC. However, many of these issues are matters of reasonable disagreement within most democracies and closely related to the left-right divide that forms the dominant political cleavage within them. Moreover, as we noted, courts have limitations when deciding general issues of public policy and often feel they lack the expertise as well as the legitimacy to do so. All rights are costly and how far any state may be able to meet its rights commitments is likely to be a matter of degree, involving various trade-offs that courts invariably feel reluctant to make. Again, distance can add to the court's timidity in areas that may entail more rather than less state action. Unsurprisingly, the empirical record suggests the constitutionalisation of social rights has little impact per se. The key factors are the degree of development of the country concerned and the ability of the underprivileged to organise themselves through unions and parties capable of promoting their interests (Hirschl & Rosevear 2011).

It might be thought that when courts fail to correct an injustice their influence is neutral – they have simply failed to right a wrong. That is not the case. Under strong review they add legitimacy to that wrong and render its righting harder. Meanwhile, courts may also make mistakes and in doing so commit a double wrong. Not only have the rights of those individuals directly affected by the particular decision been infringed but so has the right of all citizens to have an equal say in defining their rights. Weak review may commit the first wrong but in escaping the second also makes the rectification of the first easier to effect. Of course, strong review may still overcome an egregious wrong committed – wittingly or unwittingly – by a legislature. Yet, as the Hirst decision partly conceded, even these judgments only tend to be accepted and acted upon to the extent these rulings are perceived as correcting for flaws in the democratic process rather than as striking down a decision that has been made in a democratically legitimate way but with which the court happens to disagree. Indeed, as we noted, democratising countries are more inclined to regard such institutions as legitimate than more established democracies.

Given the legitimacy of democratic processes to decide rights issues depends on their providing an adequate means for giving equal consideration to the views and interests of those concerned, it has been argued that even if courts ought not to offer substantive rulings on the nature of rights they do have a role in deeming whether democratic procedures meet the appropriate standards for their decisions to have authority (Ely 1980). Moreover, the argument for not being judge in one's own cause appears particularly strong in this case. Those in power will always have an incentive to alter the rules of the game in their favour. The difficulty is that process issues can be as subject to reasonable disagreement as substantive questions. Citizens may agree that procedures should show those involved equal respect and concern, yet disagree as to how best to interpret these requirements. Moreover, these procedural disagreements will in all likelihood reflect their substantive disagreements. Even when agreement exists on a given understanding of political equality, the institutions most likely to bring it about can be difficult to specify and are likely to depend on the social circumstances in which they are located. As a result, it can be hard for courts to offer an impartial or satisfactory decision in such cases, with IHRCts once again hampered by distance and a lack of local knowledge.

Although a human right to democracy is controversial (Cohen 2006), such a right might be thought central for political constitutionalists – even the 'right of rights' (Waldron 1999: 232) – and, therefore, on this issue at least, strong judicial review is legitimate (Dahl 1989: 191, 359 n 9). In this area, courts could be said not just to restore the rights of those individuals who have been unjustly excluded from the process but also the rights of all those involved in it, because by ensuring their inclusion a court reinstates the authority of the process as a whole (Christiano 2008: 275–277). Yet, the principled and pragmatic objections to strong review remain given that courts may fail to uphold the democratic rights of citizens or even hamper attempts by the legislature to do so. For example, compare *Buckley v Valeo*, where the US Supreme Court prevented the legislature limiting campaign finance, to the British Parliament's considered preparedness to override potential judicial objections to its regulation of political advertising in the Communications Act 2003. At issue in both cases was freedom of speech and the appropriate way to secure its promotion.[13] The difference between the Supreme Court's perspective and that of the UK (and US) legislatures was not between a rights-based view and a non-rights-based view, but over which measures best secured this right within a democratic society. Again, the argument points at best to weak review because while it is important to draw attention to potential individual rights infringements, a court may not provide the most suitable forum for ensuring rights protection remains consistent with equal concern and respect for all citizens. In this case, it could be argued it was precisely because the politicians had an interest in the decision that they appreciated the need for regulation to ensure a roughly level playing field for fair and equal elections.

Finally, the argument against being judge in one's cause is in some respects deployed selectively and ultimately lacks coherence. For it is inescapable that some person or institution will be. After all, superior courts generally claim the competence to decide their own competences. Political constitutionalists argue that to the extent this is true of domestic democratic legislatures it can at least be justified by the countervailing principle that 'what touches all should be decided by all'. This doctrine embodies the important epistemic principle that decisions are best made by those with sufficient stake in the matter to decide responsibly. IHRCts by their very nature as outsiders lack that incentive. This issue was at the heart of the

[13] The UK Parliament (Communications Act 2003 (UK), 2003, c. 21.ss 319–321) sought to ensure political equality at election time by regulating political broadcasts – a move that had cross-party support but which it anticipated, in part because of decisions such as *Buckley v Valeo* 424 US 1 (1976), might be ruled as contrary to Article 10 ECHR, leading to a declaration of incompatibility as allowed under Article 19 HRA. In fact, the British courts subsequently upheld the measure, though arguably the reasoning of Parliament influenced their decision (*R. (Animal Defenders International) v Secretary for Culture, Media and Sport* [2008] UKHL 15, especially Lord Bingham at paras 7–21).

parliamentary debate concerning *Hirst*, where the majority of MPs voiced the fear that the ECtHR was unilaterally extending its own competence in ways that exceeded its democratically authorised competences (Nicol 2011a). It is to the question of what those competences might be and how they could be legitimised from the political constitutionalist perspective that we now turn.

4. International courts and an association of democratic states

It might be assumed that the easiest way to realise political constitutionalism at the global level would be to establish global or regional democratic legislatures in parallel with the creation of IHRCts. However, not only are such bodies some way from being practically realised, with the partial exception of the European Parliament, but also it can be doubted that they could possess the requisite constitutional qualities. The political constitutionalist case rests on the democratic process being able to promote the collective interests of those involved in a public and equal way. Unless there is a shared public sphere and reasonably clear lines of authorisation and accountability, on the one hand, and a roughly equal stake in the decisions being made and sufficient shared values and cross-cutting cleavages to overcome the problem of persistent minorities, on the other, neither of these qualities is likely to obtain (Christiano 2010).

Considerable difficulties confront attempts to represent adequately a vast and socially and culturally highly differentiated population (Miller 2009). Collective policies may only be relevant to a very restricted number of issues, and addressing these in ways that are open and give equal consideration to all the various interests involved may be extremely difficult, greatly increasing the risks of tyranny by a majority or various minorities, who abuse their bargaining power to obtain more than an equal say (see Bellamy and Castiglione 2013 for an analysis of these problems with regard to the European Union). Even if such problems could be overcome, this solution begs the question at the heart of this piece as to why democratic states would agree to IHRC in the first place. So, for present purposes, I shall assume that a political constitutionalist position must be achieved by way of an agreement between democratic states rather than by creating a global democratic state.

Three issues may motivate democratic states to establish IHRC and the judicial and other bodies necessary to monitor and enforce them. These issues can be linked in turn to three criteria for the governance of these mechanisms that follow from political constitutionalist assumptions. First, states may support such mechanisms as ways of promoting democratisation. The move to judicialisation generally occurs when hegemonic elites fear their political opponents may overturn their policies (Hirschl 2004). New democracies can rationally see such international commitments as helping to lock in the domestic status quo against their non-democratic opponents. Mature democracies may doubt the utility or legitimacy of such arrangements for themselves but regard them as helpful for less established democracies. Support for this function can be regarded as a corollary of the political constitutionalist belief that rights are best protected through democracy and because of the threat that non- or unstable democratic regimes may pose to democracies (Moravcsik 2000: 243–246).

Second, even if all states are democratic, democratic states have an incentive to ensure that their ability to operate in a democratic manner is not undermined by the decisions of other states, democratic or otherwise. Therefore, they have reason to create institutions to guarantee democracies treat each other with equal concern and respect (Pettit 2010). Examples include trade negotiations, particularly concerning the exploitation of another country's natural resources, and the promotion of global public goods such as combating climate change and protecting the environment more generally. These arguments also extend to establishing mechanisms to ensure trans- and multinational corporations and organisations respect democratic standards and decision-making.

Both the first and second issues can also be related to protecting the stateless and those seeking entry to democratic states. On the one hand, such persons lack access to the democratic process and, since democratic states are committed to spreading democracy, the reasoning underlying the first issue also extends to them. On the other hand, democratic states might fear that unless the burden of admitting them is shared equitably the democratic quality of certain states could suffer, thereby invoking the second issue. As a result, states have an interest in securing common, democracy-friendly, policies in this area.

Finally, even mature democracies can acknowledge that no democratic process is perfect. So long as the imperfections of any judicial process can also be corrected for, providing a contestatory channel at the international level may allow lessons to be learned from other democracies and certain unfounded parochial biases and prejudices to be challenged.

However, though democratic states may have an interest in using IHRCts to help tackle these three issues, they will only prove consistent with political constitutionalism to the extent they satisfy the following three criteria (Christiano 2010: 122–224, 126–129). First, these courts and the international arrangements of which they form a part must promote and be compatible with the possibility for all individuals to live in legitimate states that possess democratic systems where collective decisions are made in ways that show them equal respect and concern through being under their shared and equal control. Second, these international mechanisms should be under the equal control of such states. If the legitimacy of democratic states stems from them offering reasonably effective mechanisms for the identification and equal advancement of the interests of their citizens, then the legitimacy of international systems stems from them doing likewise through being in their turn under the shared and equal control of the signatory states. Third, membership of such international systems should be voluntary. Not all states will have an equal stake in collective arrangements on a given issue, and many will not have equal bargaining power. Voluntary arrangements allow states to tailor their international commitments to the interests of their populations and ideally to negotiate the terms of their adherence accordingly.

The basic institutional model of the international order stemming from these issues and criteria is that of a voluntary and fair association among democratic states.

A number of recommendations as to the competences and organisation of IHRC follow from this account. First, as Thomas Christiano has noted (Christiano 2010: 123), this model grounds certain international *jus cogens* norms concerning the performance of agreements duly made and against slavery, genocide and aggressive war, since these norms are prerequisites of, or internal to, such an arrangement and the importance it places on the value of consent. Therefore, there can be no problem with IHRCts seeking to uphold such norms unconditionally. Second, this model is also compatible with granting IHRCts a degree of independence from the states that bring them into being so long as they have the right of exit and the participating states can determine their competences. In other words, the functionaries of the IHRC, such as the judges, may act independently but the system itself must be democratically dependent on the contracting states. Third, the democratic legitimacy of such dependence rests on the agents of the states involved adequately reflecting the views and concerns of the populations they represent. Consequently, signatories to IHRC should be limited to states that are at least credibly democratising. The evidence suggests that non-democratic states do not respect the decisions of such bodies in any case – their formal adherence merely serves to give a spurious legitimacy to such regimes (Simmons 2009). Meanwhile, given the discretion executives of even democratic states have been accustomed to enjoy in foreign affairs, it is important to ensure the state officials involved remain accountable for their decisions to the legislature and ultimately the electorate. Fourth, if the system as a whole is to offer equal consideration to the interests of the democratic peoples that it serves, then the signatory states ought to exercise equal control over the IHRC. For example, all states should have an equal vote in decisions regarding changes to the Convention, the selection of judges and instructions as to their working methods, the implementation of the Court's judgments, the budget and so on. Fifth, a prime focus of such Conventions should be the interactions between states and those who either lack democratic representation or operate outside adequate democratic control, such as refugees and multinational corporations respectively. Finally, if IHRCts are to respect the integrity of the democratic process, particularly in their judgments on domestic legislation and policies, they must be restricted to weak review. Moreover, contestation ought to be limited to cases where domestic political and judicial avenues have been exhausted and that only involve those rights that might be considered basic to each citizen within a given polity being able to publicly advance their interests on equal terms to others, though controversy exists as to whether these involve only core civil and political rights or also certain minimum social and economic rights too (Christiano 2008: 273–274). Allowance also has to be made for the variety of ways different legal systems may choose to specify a given right and the numerous circumstances that may lead legislatures to limit the scope of one right in order to secure other rights.

Given courts may be as mistaken as legislators, the possibility for a democratic override of an IHRCt judgment must also exist, with such decisions resting with a consensus among the representatives of the democratic governments who should be ultimately charged with monitoring state compliance with the Court's rulings. From the perspective of the democratic state challenging the judgment, this would be a decision of peers (Scharpf 2009: 199–200). On the one hand, they would appreciate the need to attune rights to domestic situations and the adverse reaction an IHRCt decision perceived as insensitive to such considerations and in error might arouse. On the other hand, they would also be fully alive to the dangers of allowing states to renege on their solidaristic obligations and of undermining the Court's authority through frivolous or self-serving challenges – particularly with regard to democratising states.

Clearly, many problems stand in the way of realising such a scheme and in practice the proposed institutional arrangements may not necessarily always meet the criteria or answer all relevant issues. In particular, there is the problem of asymmetric bargaining between richer and more powerful states and poorer and weaker states, though coalitions among the latter can to some degree counteract the influence of the former (Christiano 2010: 125–126; Pettit 2010). However, as with all domestic democratic systems, the international democratic system is necessarily a work in progress, with various groups employing the existing processes to further, and occasionally to hinder, its development. The key is to establish the normative and institutional preconditions for such a system to arise.

A measure of the plausibility of this approach can be gauged by the significant degree to which the ECHR can be assimilated to it. All signatories must meet certain minimal democratic standards. The Court and Convention are overseen by the Council of Europe, the governance structure of which consists of the Committee of Ministers, comprising the Foreign Ministers or their permanent representatives of all 47 member states, along with the Parliamentary Assembly of the Council of Europe (PACE). The Committee decides the Council's budget, negotiates the treaties and conventions governing its competences and monitors the implementation of Court decisions. PACE, which includes 2–18 members, depending on population size, from the national parliaments of each of the signatory states, selects the judges – one from each member state – and the Secretary General of the Council from lists supplied by the Committee of Ministers. As a result, there is a degree of legislative oversight of executive action in this area, with PACE also receiving regular reports from, and making recommendations to, the Committee of Ministers. The danger of overlooking domestic or transnational minorities is also lessened through the involvement of a Congress of Local and Regional Authorities of the Council of Europe, composed of elected members from these bodies within the member states, charged with exploring the enhancement of local democracy and, in an advisory role, the International Non-governmental Organisations (INGOs) Conference of the Council of Europe. Meanwhile, the Court applies a margin of appreciation in making its judgments, especially where no common standard exists across the Council of Europe and it may be necessary to balance rights and other interests,[14] thereby taking account of the diverse ways a right may be specified within different legal systems. Moreover, as was noted in *Hirst*,[15] the Court has generally applied a wider margin when the case involves a

[14] See *Rasmussen v Denmark* (1984) 7 EHRR 371, paras 40–41 for the lack of a common approach, and *Dickson v United Kingdom* (2008) 46 EHRR 41, GC, paras 77–79 for the issue of balance.

[15] *Hirst v United Kingdom (No 2)* (2006) 42 EHRR 41.

choice that has been publicly debated by a democratic legislature and where opinions reasonably differ, and narrowed it where a legislature has enacted or re-enacted a measure without due consideration.[16] Its judgments also only apply to the given jurisdiction and do not necessarily serve as precedents for rulings in similar cases in another state, thereby minimising the 'one size fits all' problem. The recent Brighton declaration has proposed formally incorporating both the margin of appreciation and the principle of subsidiarity into the Preamble of the Convention,[17] thereby underlining that the primary duty for the implementation of Convention rights rests with domestic legal and especially political organs. Indeed, it proposes that all parliaments should adopt the enhanced pre-legislative scrutiny procedures currently found in the UK and Nordic countries. In fact, the record suggests that the ECtHR already operates at the margins so far as mature democracies are concerned. For example, since 1966 97 per cent of the cases brought against the UK have been deemed inadmissible, while only 271 out of the 443 cases that were heard were held to involve an infraction – 61 per cent or an average of 6.15 cases per year, less than 2 per cent of all cases brought. Five countries – Russia, Ukraine, Romania, Turkey and Italy – currently account for just over half of the cases brought before the Court, with Russia alone responsible for 27 per cent of them.

That said, the ECHR system falls down in two key respects. Notwithstanding the margin of appreciation, strictly speaking the ECtHR does not adopt weak review. Under Article 46 of the Convention its judgments have binding force on the High Contracting Parties and once a final ruling has been given by a Grand Chamber there are no further grounds of appeal. Still, it does not disapply national laws – they remain in force until the relevant domestic legislature changes them and can only offer a remedy in international not domestic law. As I noted, the Committee of Ministers is responsible for implementation of these judgments and can sanction a member for failing to comply, as in the Hirst case, and even expel them. However, it would be perfectly possible to allow the Committee to become the final court of appeal as proposed above. Hitherto, the focus of the ECtHR has been on the issue of domestic compliance with the ECHR. Although the Council of Europe has explored common issues affecting the relations between states, these have been at the margins. That will change

[16] *Hatton v United Kingdom* (2003) 37 EHRR 28 GC para 97; *Draon v France* (2006) 42 EHRR 40, GC, paras 106–108, and – for the converse argument – *Sukhovetsky v Ukraine (2007)* 44 EHRR 57, paras 65–67, and the analysis in A. Legg (2012), especially ch. 4.

[17] High Level Conference on the future of the ECtHR Brighton Declaration 19/20 April 2012, http://hub.coe.int/en/20120419-brighton-declaration/.

with the proposed accession of the EU to the ECHR, which will introduce monitoring of inter-state economic agreements for compliance with human rights. Already, an important difference between the ECtHR and the Court of Justice of the European Union (CJEU) with regard to labour rights suggests ways in which this move might lead to greater equal respect and concern between the states involved for their internal democratic processes (Fudge 2011). Yet, how far that happens is likely to depend on the degree to which both the Council of Europe and the EU are regarded as being bound by a political rather than a legal constitution.

5. Back to *Hirst*: concluding remarks

The foregoing analysis has argued that IHRC can be regarded as extensions of the domestic political constitutions of the signatory democratic states. Three elements were crucial to this possibility: first, that the IHRC result from a voluntary agreement among these states; second, that its competences and organisation remain under their equal and effective control; and third, that IHRCts should respect a principle of subsidiarity in their judgments, be as concerned with the consequences for rights of inter-state as with intra-state activities and be limited to weak, contestatory review. As we also noted, the ECHR has many of these features and could easily be adapted to adopt them all.

Does that mean the Hirst decision was legitimate? To a degree. The process can be regarded as one that the UK has voluntarily embraced and could still choose to exit from, albeit at the possible cost of a lessening of international standing. Yet, doubts can be raised as to the legitimacy of the decision itself. True, for a political constitutionalist at least, the removal of voting rights from any group of citizens represents a serious matter.[18] However, the temporary forfeiture of some rights for crimes meriting imprisonment has a long pedigree, and no consensus exists on the matter within the contracting parties.[19] Nor could it be said that MPs had self-interested motives for removing their vote, and so were acting as 'judges in their own cause' in this instance. The measure was supported by MPs from both sides of the House, with the 82,000 affected prisoners being unlikely to decide an election. Indeed, the existence of a right to vote in

[18] Jeremy Waldron, JCHR, Oral Evidence, Minutes of Evidence Taken, 15 March 2011, response to Q53.

[19] Among European states, 16 impose no formal ban on prisoners voting – although in practice it proves impossible for them to do so in many cases – 13 ban certain categories of prisoners and 13 exclude all prisoners from the franchise.

the Convention remains contentious, as does its status as a human right (Cohen 2006). As the Court has ultimately conceded, this is an issue where both a wide margin of appreciation and subsidiarity ought to apply. As things stand, the UK's best reason for complying is not because the decision is correct but so as not to weaken the authority of the Court vis-à-vis democratising states. From a political constitutionalist perspective, it would have been more legitimate to have resolved this issue not through a judicial reading in of the right, but by inviting PACE to prepare a report and then building a consensus on the measure among the Committee of Ministers, as was the case with the abolition of the death penalty across the Council of Europe. Because the ECtHR operates a soft version of strong review rather than weak review, its attempts to find a compromise in response to political pressure has arguably produced a decision, *Scoppola v Italy (no. 3)*, that is unsatisfactory from all points of view – both those who favour granting prisoners voting rights, who must now accept that certain crimes could bring permanent disenfranchisement, and those opposed, for whom an arbitrary distinction has been drawn based on the length of criminal sentence. The resolution of such dilemmas rests not in strengthening the Court as an arm of legal constitutionalism, however, but of realising its potential as part of the political constitution of an association of democratic states.

Cases

Buckley v Valeo 424 US 1 (1976)
Rasmussen v Denmark (8777/79) Chamber Judgment 28/11/1984
Hatton v United Kingdom (36022/97) Grand Chamber Judgment 08/07/2003
Hirst v United Kingdom (No. 2) (74025/01) Fourth Section Judgment 30/03/2004
Hirst v United Kingdom (No. 2) (74025/01) Grand Chamber Judgment 06/10/2005
Draon v France (1513/03) Grand Chamber Judgment 21/06/2006
Sukhovetsky v Ukraine (13716/02) Second Section Judgment 28/03/2006
Dickson v United Kingdom (44362/04) Grand Chamber Judgment 04/12/2007
R. (Animal Defenders International) v Secretary for Culture, Media and Sport [2008] UKHL 15

Bibliography

Bellamy, R., 2007. *Political Constitutionalism*, Cambridge University Press.
2011. Political Constitutionalism and the Human Rights Act. *International Journal of Constitutional Law (I-Con)*, 9, 86–111.

Bellamy, R. & Castiglione, D., 2013. Three Models of Democracy, Political Community and Representation in the EU. *Journal of European Public Policy*, 20.2, 206–223.

Bogdanor, V., 2009. *The New British Constitution*, Oxford: Hart Publishing.

Buchanan, A., 2004. *Justice, Legitimacy and Self-determination: Moral Foundations for International Law*, Oxford University Press.

Buchanan, A. & Powell, R., 2008. Survey Article: Constitutional Democracy and the Rule of International Law: Are they Compatible? *Journal of Political Philosophy*, 16 (3), 326–349.

Campbell, T., Ewing, K. D. and Tomkins, A., eds., 2011. *The Legal Protection of Rights: Sceptical Essays*, Oxford University Press.

Christiano, T., 2008. *The Constitution of Equality: Democratic Authority and its Limits*, Oxford University Press.

2010. Democratic Legitimacy and International Institutions. In S. Besson & J. Tasioulas, eds. *The Philosophy of International Law*, Oxford University Press.

2011. An Instrumental Argument for a Human Right to Democracy. *Philosophy and Public Affairs*, 39 (2), 142–176.

Cohen, J., 2006. Is There a Human Right to Democracy? In C. Sypnowich, ed. *The Egalitarian Conscience: Essays in Honour of G. A. Cohen*, Oxford University Press.

Dahl, R. A., 1957. Decision-making in a Democracy: The Supreme Court as National Policymaker. *Journal of Public Law*, 6, 279–295.

1989. *Democracy and its Critics*, New Haven: Yale University Press.

2003. *How Democratic is the American Constitution?*, New Haven: Yale University Press.

Devins, N. & Fisher, L., 2004. *The Democratic Constitution*, Oxford University Press.

Dworkin, R., 1996. *Freedom's Law: The Moral Reading of the American Constitution*, Cambridge, MA: Harvard University Press.

Ely, J. H., 1980. *Democracy and Distrust: A Theory of Judicial Review*, Cambridge, MA: Harvard University Press.

Ferejohn, J. & Kramer, L. D., 2002. Independent Judges, Dependent Judiciary: Institutionalizing Judicial Restraint, *New York University Law Review*, 77, 962–1039.

Føllesdal, A. & Wind, M., 2009. Nordic Reluctance towards Judicial Review under Siege. *Nordic Journal of Human Rights*, 27 (2), Special Issue, 131–159.

Fudge, J., 2011. Constitutionalizing Labour Rights in Europe. In Campbell et al., eds.

Gee, G. & Webber, G., 2010. What is a Political Constitution? *Oxford Journal of Legal Studies*, 30 (2), 273–299.

Griffith, J. A. G., 1979. The Political Constitution. *Modern Law Review*, 42 (1), 1–21.

Habermas, J., 1996. *Between Facts and Norms*, Cambridge, MA: MIT Press.

Hessler, K., 2005. Resolving Interpretive Conflicts in International Human Rights Law. *Journal of Political Philosophy*, 13 (1), 29–52.

Hiebert, J. L., 2005. Interpreting a Bill of Rights: The Importance of Legislative Rights Review. *British Journal of Political Science*, 35 (2), 235–255.

Hirschl, R., 2004. *Towards Juristocracy: The Origins and Consequences of the New Constitutionalism*, Cambridge, MA: Harvard University Press.

Hirschl, R. & Rosevear, E., 2011. Constitutional Law Meets Comparative Politics: Socio-economic Rights and Political Realities. In Campbell et al., eds.

Kramer, L., 2004. *The People Themselves: Popular Constitutionalism and Judicial Review*, Oxford University Press.

Legg, A., 2012. *The Margin of Appreciation in International Human Rights Law*, Oxford University Press.

Miller, D., 2009. Democracy's Domain. *Philosophy and Public Affairs*, 37 (3), 201–228.

Moravcsik, A., 2000. The Origins of Human Rights Regimes: Democratic Delegation in Postwar Europe. *International Organisation*, 54 (2), 217–252.

Nicol, D., 2011a. Legitimacy of the Commons Debate on Prisoner Voting. *Public Law*, 681–691.

2011b. Business Rights as Human Rights. In Campbell et al., eds.

Pettit, P., 2000. Democracy: Electoral and Contestatory. In I. Shapiro & S. Macedo, eds. *Designing Democratic Institutions*, New York University Press.

2010. Legitimate International Institutions: A Neo-Republican Perspective. In S. Besson & J. Tasioulas, eds. *The Philosophy of International Law*, Oxford University Press.

Scharpf, F. W., 2009. Legitimacy in the Multilevel European Polity. *European Political Science Review*, 1 (2), 173–204.

Simmons, B., 2009. *Mobilizing for Human Rights: International Law in Domestic Politics*, Cambridge, New York: Cambridge University Press.

Tomkins, A., 2005. *Our Republican Constitution*, Oxford: Hart Publishing.

Tushnet, M., 1999. *Taking the Constitution Away from the Courts*, Princeton University Press.

2003. Alternative Forms of Judicial Review. *Michigan Law Review*, 101 (8), 2781–2802.

2007. *Weak Courts, Strong Rights: Judicial Review and Social Welfare Rights in Comparative Constitutional Law*, Princeton University Press.

Waldron, J., 1999. *Law and Disagreement*, Oxford: Clarendon Press.

2006. The Core Case against Judicial Review. *The Yale Law Journal*, 115, 1346–1406.

2008. Can There Be a Democratic Jurisprudence? *Emory Law Journal*, 58 (4), 675–712.

Other sources

Decision of the Committee of Ministers 4–6 December 2012
UK Parliament (Communications Act 2003 (UK), 2003, c. 21.ss 319–321)
High Level Conference on the future of the ECtHR Brighton Declaration 19/20 April 2012, http://hub.coe.int/en/20120419-brighton-declaration/
Jeremy Waldron, JCHR, Oral Evidence, Minutes of Evidence Taken, 15 March 2011, response to Q53. HC Deb 20 December 2010 c151WS HC Deb 10 February 2011 c 493–584.

10

Much ado about nothing? International judicial review of human rights in well-functioning democracies

ANDREAS FØLLESDAL

1. Introduction

Worries about international judicial review of human rights have increased in recent years. The European Convention on Human Rights (ECHR) and the court it establishes, the European Court on Human Rights (ECtHR), have sustained particularly much criticism, not least in the Nordic countries and the UK (Campbell et al., 2001; NOU, 2003: 19; SOU, 2007: 85; Føllesdal & Wind, 2009). In these countries vocal critics have included government commissions and politicians. Such misgivings culminated in some of the proposals entertained at the Brighton conference on reforms of the ECtHR on 18–20 April 2012. Several solutions would essentially return sovereignty to the states, pruning the powers of the ECtHR not only over the UK, but across the board. Some protests against international judicial review arise from general misgivings about juridification and internationalization wrought by other influential European courts and international treaty bodies, such as the Court of Justice of the European Union. In addition, judicial review by the human

This chapter stems from two research projects: 'Should States Ratify Human Rights Conventions?', at the Centre for Advanced Study, Oslo; and MultiRights, a European Research Council Advanced Grant. It is based on some previous papers noted where appropriate, and on a draft presented at the conference 'Towards Nordic Juristocracy?' at the Faculty of Law, University of Turku, Finland, 8 December 2009, and at the University of Stirling, Scotland, 6 July 2010; as well as on a presentation of related concerns at the University of Minho, Portugal, 2 November 2009. I am grateful for all comments received at those occasions, and for comments by Geir Ulfstein, Johan K. Schaffer and Stian Øby Johansen. The Edmond J. Safra Center for Ethics, the Mossavar-Rahmani Center for Business & Government at the Kennedy School and Currier House, all at Harvard University, provided excellent working conditions for some of this research.

rights judiciary also raises particular puzzles of legitimacy, especially when performed on democratically enacted legislation. The changes to the ECHR ventured by the British government illustrate some central challenges facing the human rights judiciary as a whole. These proposals seek to enhance the legitimacy of the ECtHR by reducing its authority over national legislatures and judiciaries. The present chapter addresses some of these tensions between sovereignty, international human rights review and legitimacy, and seeks to bring these findings to bear on proposals for reform of the human rights judiciary. The objectives of such review are not obvious, the causes of non-compliance are contested, as is the legality of dynamic treaty interpretation; all of which hamper efforts to assess proposed improvements.

These concerns merit attention for several reasons. They stem from states whose 'democratic spirit' can hardly be doubted, whose citizens enjoy comparatively high scores on most standards of good governance, democracy and political trust in government, and with low levels of relative poverty.[1] On the one hand, their scepticism fits with Moravcsik's claim that resistance to the ECHR was higher in precisely such states, rather than where governments are afraid that the opposition will backslide on human rights commitments if they got to power (Moravcsik, 1995). On the other hand we would suspect that such states have little to complain about, since they can be expected to seldom violate the human rights conventions they have signed. Statistics bear this out: in 2011 the Nordic states and the UK were responsible for 1.5 per cent of the violations found by the ECtHR. This is much less than the per capita would suggest, since these states include 10.7 per cent of the population of the Council of Europe member states.[2]

Their general respect for human rights coupled with the relatively small burden of such international criticisms should give us particular ground for concern when public debates in these states concern the alleged democratic deficit of international law in general, and of human rights law and the ECtHR in particular. If widespread, such protests may hamper future

[1] Democracy Index (2008); United Nations Development Programme (2009).

[2] In 2011 the ECtHR made a total of 1157 judgments finding violations in 987 of them. Of these, the ECtHR made 37 judgments about Denmark, Finland, Iceland, Norway, Sweden and the United Kingdom, and found violations in only 15 of these cases [Denmark 6/1, Finland 7/5, Iceland 0/0, Norway 1/1, Sweden 4/0 and the UK 19/8] (European Court of Human Rights, 2012a: 12–13). In 2011 these states had [5561 + 5375 + 318 + 4920 + 9416 + 62436 =] 88 million persons, of almost 819 million living in the Council of Europe states (European Court of Human Rights, 2012c).

compliance and treaty ratification, possibly with good reason. So why are significant actors in these 'well-behaved' states worried about international human rights review, even though they have comparatively little to worry about?

Indeed, similar unease about unaccountable international judicialisation may partly explain why the path to the Lisbon Treaty was paved with negative referendums.[3] We may expect more tensions when the EU ratifies the European Convention on Human Rights, and thus becomes subject to judicial review by the ECtHR. This raises intriguing questions, inter alia about the sort of political entity the EU is and is becoming, and the relationship between the Court of Justice of the European Union and the ECtHR. EU ratification of the ECHR adds urgency to the worries of the latter's legitimacy deficit, not least if the Lisbon treaty alleviates the democratic deficit of the EU. Insofar as the EU's rules become more legitimate in the eyes of citizens and authorities, judicial review over human rights issues in the EU may be more suspect. The upshot is that concerns about the normative legitimacy of judicial review of human rights by international courts merit scrutiny.

To address these issues, this article proceeds in six parts. Section 1 presents some relevant aspects of the ECtHR. Section 2 reviews some of the recent criticism against the ECtHR practice of judicial review to protect human rights in 'well-functioning' democracies, in terms of various forms of legitimacy deficits. It also presents some of the recent proposals for reform of the ECtHR. Section 3 lays out some reasons why such judicial review of majoritarian democratic decision-making may be defensible, also for well-functioning democracies. I suggest two ways the unit of analysis needs to be clearer than often stated: we need to assess the practice as a whole, applied to both democracies and other states, and we must consider the need not only that states comply with human rights, but also that citizens are assured that such is the case. Section 4 responds to some of the criticisms, and presents a partial defence. Some standard objections are not well targeted against the practices of the ECtHR, partly due to the division of responsibility between it and national public bodies, and the different roles of legislators and of judiciaries. Section 5 returns to the proposals presented in section 2. Section 6 concludes by considering some of the important remaining normative challenges, this partial defence notwithstanding.

[3] www.voteno.ie; http://no2lisbon.wordpress.com; Marthaler (2005: 6); Siedentop (2008).

2. The European Court of Human Rights

The European Court of Human Rights is an institution of the Council of Europe, set up in 1959 on the basis of the 1950 European Convention on Human Rights. The Preamble states that the convention is a first step toward collective European enforcement of certain rights of the UN Declaration. This early warning system should help prevent lapses into totalitarianism by means of a court that holds states to account for human rights violations (Woolf, 2005). These are mainly civil and political rights, but also rights concerning such issues as education and anti-discrimination. The objective of the Convention slowly changed to fine-tune 'well-functioning democracies'. With the new crop of member states of the Council of Europe the ECtHR has again had to focus on less stable democracies.

The ECtHR monitors the ECHR, and is among the most powerful treaty-based courts. Still, the ECtHR respects states' discretion in several ways: (1) it accords states a 'margin of appreciation' with regard to assessing whether they are in compliance with the obligations of the ECHR (Bernhardt, 1994); (2) the ECtHR exercises what is sometimes referred to as 'weak' review. When the ECtHR finds a law or its application to be incompatible with the ECHR, this does not directly affect the validity of that law in the domestic legal system (Bernhardt, 1994); (3) when the ECtHR finds a state to be in violation of the ECHR, the state is still left with much leeway with regard to how to change its laws or procedures to secure compliance – in accordance with the principle of subsidiarity.

With regard to procedure, a Chamber of seven members hears most cases, while a Grand Chamber of seventeen judges hears cases found to be of great importance (ECHR article 30). A judge from the accused member state is always an *ex officio* member of the Court, to ensure relevant background information about national specifics (ECHR article 26(4)).

The judgments against a member state may include to give reparations to the particular individuals, as well as more 'general measures' necessary to avoid recurrence of violations. States have some freedom with regard to which of such measures to take, though subject to monitoring by the Committee of Ministers composed of the foreign ministers of all member states.[4] The state may amend or add to its constitution, laws, regulations or its administrative or judicial practices. The Committee of Ministers can employ a range of sanctions, ranging from the new infringement procedure under ECHR article 46(4), to different modes of bringing pressure on

[4] ECHR, *Scozzari and Giunta* [GC], no. 39221/98 and 41963/98 (2000) para 249.

the non-compliant state, suspension of voting rights in the Committee of Ministers or even expulsion from the Council of Europe (Article 8 of the Statute of the Council of Europe).

3. Backdrop: the legitimacy deficits of the human rights judiciary, especially of the ECtHR, and some proposals

Legitimacy is a complex concept with several interrelated aspects which may best be illustrated by their absence. A body such as the ECtHR may be deemed illegitimate in the eyes of ordinary citizens because of its poor *performance*: it is *ineffective* in securing or promoting certain objectives (cf. Beetham and Lord, 1998: 31). Indeed, the objectives of such review are not obvious – we turn to that in section 3. Regardless of objectives, the ECtHR currently has a backlog of approximately 140,000 applications (European Court of Human Rights, 2012c), which is taken as a further sign of ineffective protection of human rights. For citizens complaining to the Court, this backlog may weaken their support for the Court – while the states may to the contrary be more accepting of the Court due to this lack of effectiveness. But states' social acceptance seems weak when we address the next concern.

Second, the ECtHR can be regarded as illegitimate because the signatory states *fail to comply* with the rulings of the Court. Indeed, 34,000 of the cases are classified as 'repetitive' by the registry of the Court, meaning that the relevant government has failed to install suitable general measures to prevent violations identified in earlier cases.

A third form of illegitimacy concerns the lack of *legality*. For the ECtHR this occurs insofar as state governments or administration hold that judges of the ECtHR interpret a treaty unduly creatively, too far beyond the intentions of the signatories and hence *unlawful*. Some hold that this is the case when the ECtHR openly undertakes 'dynamic' interpretation of the convention. However, complaining citizens and NGOs may either downplay such 'illegality', or hold that such interpretations are necessary for many treaties to further their objectives under new societal circumstances.

Fourth, the human rights judiciary may be accused of failing to be *normatively justifiable*. Thus all judicial review, also by domestic constitutional courts, is often presented as undemocratic and generally unaccountable, and therefore normatively illegitimate in this sense (Waldron, 2006). International courts or treaty bodies raise additional fears:

(1) The treaties are even less subject to citizens' control than domestic constitutions, since they are more entrenched against popular and parliamentary preferences and more difficult to change.
(2) One consequence of such entrenchment is that the courts and treaty organs often resort to more dynamic modes of interpretation of the treaties. This raises further fears of domination by an unaccountable 'juristocracy'.
(3) By design, the treaty organs will be largely staffed by officials who are even less accountable than their domestic counterparts. The members will be less familiar with national culture, constitutional traditions and the legitimate expectations of the citizenry. Some, for instance domestic governments and administrations, fear that this lack of familiarity raises the likelihood of misjudgments about impacts and alternatives (Østerud and Selle, 2006).
(4) In addition, as a body the international court will be less accountable to the professional norms of their respective peers than are the judges of domestic courts.
(5) Adding to these risks, the increased number of international human rights treaties without a clear hierarchy may in the longer run bring familiar, possibly overstated fears wrought by the 'fragmentation of international law'. Forum shopping, divergent interpretation of the same norms and other factors may further reduce the power of legislatures and increase the ability of judges and courts to decide without much in the way of checks (Conforti, 2007).
(6) Courts and other treaty bodies must also undertake complex and often controversial balancing among norms – including among human rights (Tamanaha, 2010). Such weighing or balancing of norms and rights is something a legislature might be expected to do at least as well and responsibly as a treaty organ whose members may know little if anything about public management, local mores, preferences and opportunities. Thus human rights treaties with adjudicating bodies that perform judicial review raise understandable fears among democratically accountable executives of 'Quis custodiet ipsos custodes'?

Much of the recent criticism levelled against the ECtHR expresses such misgivings about the legitimacy of the court, in these various senses of 'legitimacy'.

No wonder that there were several proposals to reduce ECtHR's alleged legitimacy challenges, voiced during the spring of 2012 in preparation for discussions at Brighton, 18–20 April, under the British chairmanship of the Committee of Ministers of the Council of Europe. Prime Minister David Cameron pointed to the vast backlog of the Court as a main challenge to effective performance, and a further delay of justice to wronged parties (Cameron, 2012). Some critics may also take the backlog as a sign that the Court is too ambitious in its rulings, meddling in issues beyond its proper mandate.

Prime Minister Cameron maintained that part of the solution is to reduce the ECtHR's authority relative to domestic bodies of governance. The solution is in short to give more priority to sovereignty over international human rights review. Thus the British government circulated several reform proposals to ensure that the Court will heed democratic decisions by national parliaments more (UK Government, 2012). Three proposed amendments merit particular scrutiny as a matter of normative political theory.

First, some hold that the ECHR should be amended to include a clear reference to the 'Principle of Subsidiarity' (UK Government, 2012: para 19b). A 'principle of subsidiarity' regulates how to allocate or use authority within a political or legal order, typically in those orders that disperse authority between a centre and various member units (Føllesdal, 1998b). The principle holds that the burden of argument lies with attempts to centralize authority. Thus the conception of subsidiarity as laid out by the Lisbon Treaty holds that in those issue areas where the states and the EU share authority, the member states should decide – *unless* central action will ensure higher comparative efficiency or effectiveness in achieving the specified objectives (Treaty of Lisbon, 2007). According to the principle of subsidiarity, the ECtHR should only act to *supplement* the domestic legal system, and the burden of argument rests with proposals that give more authority to the international level.

A second proposal is to amend the ECHR to instruct the Court to respect states' 'margin of appreciation'. This would be a codification of the Court's long-standing practice to grant states some leeway in some cases, so that the state has the final authority to determine whether certain policies are in compliance with the ECHR.

A third proposal applies these principles to specify which cases the ECtHR should take on. The Court should not consider an application 'if it is the same in substance as a matter that has been examined by a national court taking into account the rights guaranteed by the Convention' (UK Government, 2012: para 23b). There are only two exceptions: if 'the Court considers that: i) The national court clearly erred in its interpretation or application of the Convention rights; or ii) The application raises a serious question affecting the interpretation or application of the Convention'.

The ECtHR and its President Sir Nicolas Bratza responded. In addition to the existing changes to reduce the backlog, the ECtHR urged several informal means, such as dialogue between Strasbourg and national courts, in the form of regular working meetings and 'judicial dialogue through judgments' and possibly a system of advisory opinion jurisdiction (European Court of Human Rights, 2012b: para 27–28). Judge Bratza has counselled that neither subsidiarity nor the margin of appreciation should be put in the ECHR. Such changes would would not help reduce the case load of the court significantly, thus would not enhance the effectiveness of the Court (Bratza, 2012). In response, one might argue that such changes could still increase its normative legitimacy by giving greater weight to democratic sovereignty.

The general tendency of these UK proposals is to grant more authority regarding human rights review to domestic rather than to regional bodies, and formalize this as amendments to the treaty. Assuming that they are made in good faith, what are we to think of such attempts to enhance the legitimacy of the ECtHR? Several aspects require attention. One central issue is the objectives of such human rights review. Clarity about these objectives is required in order to determine how to assess these proposals, and how the principle of subsidiarity and the margin of appreciation should be justified, specified and institutionalized.

4. In defence of international judicial review to protect human rights

There are at least three reasons in principle for international judicial review, even for well-functioning democracies which largely comply with these legal human rights obligations anyway. They concern international peer pressure, domestic safeguard of minorities and assurance of compliance. The first two may hold more obviously for citizens, and more indirectly for their governments, while the latter may also be supported by the executive branch that seeks to promote compliance with its decisions. This is not to say that these arguments support the present institutions and practices of the human rights judiciary in general, and the ECtHR in particular, but they indicate the kinds of arguments that may guide reforms.

The following brief sketch takes as a normative starting point that the 'global basic structure' – the global set of social institutions which includes domestic, regional and international bodies – should be arranged so as to be trusted to respect, protect and further the best interests of individuals globally (Føllesdal, 2013). I argue below that the citizenry should have good reasons to trust the institutions and their authorities to carry out these tasks. So institutions should not only be just, but also promote public trustworthiness that this is in fact the case. I submit that democratic rule is supported by such reasons, and go on to indicate reasons to favour democratic institutions that are constrained by a human rights judiciary over majoritarian systems of governance without such constraints.

This normative starting point rests on several normative premises. First, there is an assumption that citizens generally should be inculcated to, and be able to assume that almost all others share, a 'sense of justice'. The justification of the global set of institutions should be addressed to such individuals, motivated by what John Rawls called a 'duty of justice': 'to support and comply with just institutions that exist and apply to us. It also constrains us to further just arrangements not yet established, at least when this can be done without too much cost to ourselves … predicated on the belief that others will do their part' (Rawls, 1971: 115, 336). I interpret this to mean that citizens are 'contingent compliers' in a game theoretical sense. They can only be expected to comply if they are assured that the institutions are just, *and* that others do their share. So citizens must not only have a normally effective sense of justice, but must also be sure that most others are similarly motivated. Note that for our purposes we can bracket much disagreement about the substantive requirements of justice for the global basic structure, beyond maintaining that citizens have some obligation to promote human rights compliance even in other states than their own.

The global set of institutions must satisfy two conditions if general compliance among such contingent compliers is to occur and be predictably stable. First, the institutions must be normatively legitimate, by whatever defensible set of principles of legitimacy the normative theory defends. Second, citizens must also have reason to trust in the future compliance of other citizens and authorities with such fair institutions. In the absence of such trust even a group of persons known to be contingent compliers will have little reason to comply. Indeed, they may prefer to not comply unless institutions provide such assurance.

I venture that democratic rule combined with constraints on legislatures in the form of judicial review of human rights may provide important forms of such assurance.

I here present a fairly standard case for democratic rule, agreed by a broad range of democratic theorists (see Føllesdal, 1998a; Føllesdal and Hix, 2006). It is not intended as a complete definition, but rather as a statement about virtually all modern political systems that we would normally call 'democratic'.

(1) Institutionally established procedures that regulate
(2) competition for control over political authority,
(3) on the basis of deliberation,
(4) where nearly all adult citizens are permitted to participate in
(5) an electoral mechanism where their expressed preferences over alternative candidates determine the outcome,
(6) in such ways that the government is responsive to the majority or to as many as possible.

Essential to the case for democracy over alternative decision procedures is competitive elections. They are important to make policies and elected officials responsive to the preferences of citizens (Powell, 2000). It must be possible for an 'opposition' to form against the current leadership elites and policy status quo (e.g. Dahl, 1971). Active opposition parties and media scrutiny are crucial for fact finding, agenda setting and assessments of the effectiveness of policies.

On this line of argument, the normative case for democratic rule is comparative: forms of democratic rule by means of competitive elections to choose policies and leaders are better than alternative constitutional arrangements for decision-making. The claim is that such democratic accountability mechanisms ensure that the decisions can be trusted to be more reliably responsive to the best interests of the citizenry than other collective decision-making arrangements.

There are at least three reasons why citizens of such democracies may have good reason to subject their state to the human rights judiciary.

One reason is based on citizens' duty of justice to promote just institutions when they do not yet exist. This duty is expressed in one way by which politicians citizens vote into office, and their policies. In particular, ratification by one state is sometimes one way to promote ratification *by other states* whose citizens stand to benefit from such review. This is because ratification by some states adds pressure on other states to also ratify – states whose ratification does make a difference to citizens. Beth Simmons notes that: 'The single strongest motive for ratification in the absence of a strong value commitment is the preference that nearly all governments have to avoid the social and political pressures of remaining aloof from a multilateral agreement to which most of their peers have already committed themselves' (Simmons, 2009: 13). One consequence of this impact of the human rights judiciary is that the assessment of reforms cannot be restrained to intra-state effects, but must also heed the impact in less democratic states that form part of the present global structure. A generally well-functioning democracy may thus have to agree to submit to judicial review in order to promote human rights elsewhere – as long as the burden is not unduly hard.

Second, international judicial review of human rights can be important to correct the (few) human rights violations that can be expected even when democracies work very well. Mistakes occur even under the best procedures, and review of such decisions serves as a valuable safety mechanism. Human rights conventions address several such risks, inter alia the prerequisites for well-functioning democratic procedures such as freedom of speech, free and fair elections, etc. Other risks are those that various groups tend to face under majority rule. The majority may exploit its powers, intentionally and knowingly or not, in ways that unduly harm those that happen to find themselves in the minority. Of course, many majority decisions may harm minorities. What counts as 'undue' harm? Some such harms occur under circumstances where the case for majority rule is weaker. Brian Barry noted that the case for majority rule is stronger when the stakes for each decision are roughly equal, and where there are rotating minorities (Barry, 1991). Undue harm may thus arise for groups who find themselves in permanent minority when it comes to decisions. Some groups may also require unusual arrangements to secure the same needs as the surrounding majority. Such arrangements may include special protections, exemptions or support to maintain aspects of their own culture – 'special needs' with regard to freedom of religion, education and language, diet or other central components of what makes their lives go well in their eyes. A minority may also have special preferences which will lose out in all majoritarian decisions, each of which may be minor but with deleterious cumulative effect. Minorities may thus fear that they will be harmed even by apparently innocuous majoritarian decisions. The majority can offer some, but not many good reasons why they can be trusted to vote according to their sense of justice, even on such 'minor' issues. Standard mechanisms in a democracy that ensure responsiveness to the electorate will not work for such groups. For instance, a small minority may never get attention from political parties that seek votes.

An international human rights judiciary can serve to monitor the limits on decisions states can make within their borders. This safeguard reduces the reasonable fear that those in power will ignore their sense of justice with untoward effects on those who do not gain the majority vote.

The third reason for judicial review is related to the second. Judicial review by bodies that are independent of the domestic government may provide citizens much needed assurance about others' compliance – including that of their government. Such a mechanism helps convince 'contingent compliers' that the government will reliably continue to pursue acceptable outcomes. Compared to other modes of governance, democratic arrangements not only have better mechanisms to ensure that authorities reliably govern fairly and effectively, but they also help provide public assurance that so is the case (Przeworski et al., 1999; Pettit, 2000; Shapiro, 2001). Party contestation and media scrutiny help align the interests of the subjects to those of their rulers, and contribute to making the institutions trustworthy (Fabre, 2000: 83). Judicial review to protect human rights may provide another trust-building measure. With such review, those who fear that they will regularly be outvoted can be somewhat more certain that the majority will not subject them to undue domination, risks of unfortunate deliberations, or incompetence. This safeguard reduces reasons to fear that those in power will ignore their sense of justice, with untoward effects on minorities. This is a reason for such judicial review that may hold both for citizens and politicians: those citizens who can expect to sometimes find themselves in the minority – and that would be most citizens – will have more reason to expect that the majority will not abuse its powers. And politicians will be able to rely on citizens' duty of justice a bit more, also those who find themselves in a more or less permanent minority, because the procedures of judicial review will make it public knowledge that abuse of power is less likely.

As an example, in 2011, of the 955 applications against the UK that the ECtHR decided, the government was found to violate the ECHR in only eight cases (Bratza, 2012). Since the very large majority of cases show the government to be in compliance with its obligations under the ECHR even when alleged victims think otherwise, the ECtHR thus serves to assure the citizens that this particular government generally merits compliance. One implication of this argument is that we must assess the human rights judiciary, and reform proposals thereof not only by whether they enhance compliance with human rights within states, but whether they also provide public assurance thereof.

To conclude, note that a central normative issue is whether the benefits of the human rights judiciary – duly modified to provide the benefits indicated above – do indeed provide benefits to some, without imposing burdens of similar weight or urgency on others. One remark on such normative assessments is in order: the stakes are contested. Even when judicial review works as it should in stopping a legislative act, some will regret what they see as a loss to the *democratic* quality of the decision, since a majority decision is overturned. Some regard these losses as high – and question the likely gains (see Bellamy, 2007). On the other hand, some such limitations on the scope of legislatures' authority, and bodies entrusted to uphold such limitations, are not necessarily *non-democratic*. Indeed, minority protections of some kind, with authority placed outside the legislature itself, may be a component of any set of workable majoritarian democratic institutions worth respecting. All institutions must have a specified scope of authority, and a legislature which is corrected when it oversteps its authority is not obviously overruled in a *non-democratic* way. Which bodies may be best placed and authorized in what ways to provide such benefits remains an open question. We now turn to some details about how the ECtHR may be modified to enhance its legitimacy.[5] Recall that the normative assessment should apply an institutional perspective, including the broader impact of the human rights judiciary beyond any single state. That is, the subject of comparison is not how things would have turned out in the absence of institutions. Instead, we should compare the current ECHR regime with the best alternative institutions for binding collective action (Shapiro, 2001; Føllesdal & Pogge, 2005). Recall that the 'institutions' to be assessed must be the practice of the human rights judiciary as a whole, as the courts and treaty bodies apply to both well-functioning democracies and other states. We must also recall the need not only that states comply with human rights, but also that citizens are assured that such is the case. In the case at hand, the comparison should be with democratic legislatures of varying human rights records, without such an international judicial review of human rights, and with an improved ECHR.

[5] I have addressed other criticisms of international judicial review and of the ECtHR elsewhere (Føllesdal, 2009): that judicial review must rest on contested 'liberal' assumptions. They may be sceptical of the focus on 'negative' social and political rights found in many human rights conventions – including the ECHR. Such a priority is thought to flow from flawed premises, and leads to skewed policies: it assumes a fundamentally adversarial relationship between the individual and her state, and conveys that the paramount tasks of the state are thus limited (Bellamy, 2001). Another range of criticisms concerns the unfortunate impact of judicial review on domestic, democratic processes and outcomes. To entrench certain rights skews both the processes of decision-making and the policy outcomes. Some believe such entrenchment aims to deflect conflicts about rights and certain policies away from the political arena. But such insulation is ill advised if not impossible (Bellamy, 1999: 166; Bellamy, 2007). A bias toward civil and political rights is aggravated further by such entrenchment, at a cost to social, economic and cultural rights.

5. A partial defence of the ECtHR

We now return to several of the criticisms presented in section 2 that the ECtHR suffers from various legitimacy deficits. I shall suggest that some objections are not well targeted against the practices of the ECtHR, partly due to the division of responsibility between it and national authorities, and the different roles of legislators and of judiciaries. Other challenges merit much scrutiny.

With regard to charges of ineffectiveness expressed in the large backlog, consider several factors that alleviate the charge against the ECtHR. Recall that analyses of the case load indicates that more than 90 per cent of all applications are deemed inadmissible (European Court of Human Rights, 2012b). That is: individuals have been mistaken in assuming that the Court has the authority to decide on the case. Some ways to reduce this number are already established, such as making it easier for potential applicants to understand whether they should petition the Court at all, and to have a quick review process by a single judge. An important consideration is to ensure that potentially well-founded cases receive careful treatment.

Another major cause of backlog are *repetitive cases*. For 34,000 of the pending cases the Court has already delivered judgments finding similar violations of the ECHR, but where the state knowingly flouts its obligations to take steps to prevent future violations. That some states fail to so *comply* with the ECtHR is certainly a lack of legitimacy of the Court, but one of compliance rather than its own effectiveness. Indeed, the Court has established a streamlined procedure for these cases, using three-judge committees.

Finally, when it comes to effectiveness, we can note that of the 47 countries subject to the ECtHR, 5 were responsible for nearly half of the violations in 2011: of the 1157 judgments determining violations in 2011, Turkey was responsible for 174, Russia 133, Ukraine 105, Greece 73, Poland 71 (European Court of Human Rights, 2011). I thus submit that the main sources of ineffectiveness of the ECtHR in processing cases are partly being addressed, and partly due to states' non-compliance.

We now turn to some of the concerns about the *legality* of the ECtHR. The concern is whether the ECtHR's practice of 'dynamic interpretation' goes too far beyond the intentions of the signatories and hence beyond its legal authority. The ECtHR openly acknowledges that it develops the standards of the ECHR, e.g. in light of new social or legal circumstances. The principle of *dynamic interpretation* tends to promote judicial activism. The ECtHR has declared that 'the Convention is a living instrument which must be interpreted in the light of present-day conditions' (*Tyrer v UK*, no. 5856/72 (1977)), 'in a manner which renders its rights practical and effective, not theoretical and illusory'" (*Goodwin v UK* [GC], no. 17488/90 (2002) paras 74–75). The Court typically justifies such new interpretations by claims that there is broad consensus across most states in Europe (European Court of Human Rights, 2010). Be that as it may, it seems clear that the signatories will sometimes be bound in ways not foreseen when they consented. This will seem at clear odds with the doctrine of 'Restrictive interpretation in favour of state sovereignty' which entailed that treaties should be interpreted so as to minimize restrictions on state sovereignty (Crema, 2010): 'If the wording of a treaty provision is not clear, in choosing between several admissible interpretations, the one which involves the minimum of obligations for the Parties should be adopted' (*Interpretation of Article 3, Paragraph 2, of the Treaty of Lausanne*, Advisory Opinion, 1925 PCIJ Series B, No. 12, cited in Crema, 2010: 685). In response, several arguments defending this practice in general seem to have merit. First, one may challenge the relevance of the old case, arguing that the ICJ no longer relies on the minimum rule (Crema, 2010). Second, such a development is not unique to the ECtHR. To the contrary, 'dynamic' or 'evolutive' interpretation of treaties is widespread.

Third, given relevant changes to the facts or other circumstances, the treaty will have to be interpreted in new ways insofar as the object and purposes of the treaty diverge from the individual treaty provisions. Something will have to give, and thus necessitate 'dynamic' interpretation. The question is rather which adjustments should be made, by what guiding principles. What is special with human rights treaties is that the doctrine of Restrictive Interpretation seems quite inappropriate. In general this doctrine is no longer adhered to, witnessed by the absence of this doctrine in the Vienna Convention. Interpretations now instead focus more on the object and purpose of the specific treaty. And in particular, it is not at all obvious that this contested principle is appropriate for human rights treaties. They differ from other conventions in being explicitly aimed to protect individuals from their own state. The convention's rights are thus intended to limit state sovereignty, in ways that do not depend on whether other states violate such rights of their own citizens. The ECtHR applies a *Principle of Effectiveness*: the choice of interpretation should not be one which limits the obligations of the parties to the greatest degree, but must rather be appropriate to the aim and object of the treaty – to secure the aims of the Universal Declaration of Human Rights (*Airey v Ireland*, no. 6289/73 (1979), *Artico v Italy*, no. 6694/74 (1980)). The fact that an interpretation of such rights will be a stronger constraint on state sovereignty can hardly be decisive against such interpretations.

Fourth, this practice seems at least in principle to be in accordance with the Vienna Convention on the Law of Treaties article 31 (1), which lists the most frequently utilized interpretative methods: good faith, literal and contextual interpretation and interpretation *in light of a treaty's object and purpose*. Leaving aside the normative significance of states' intentions when signing a treaty, it thus seems clear that since the VCLT allows dynamic interpretation guided by such factors, it is reasonable that states' intentions when signing treaties have included such dynamic interpretation since 'it is now firmly rooted in the international law on interpretation' (Schlütter, 2012).

A final concern about the legitimacy of the ECtHR is that it grants undue power to non-accountable judges. This creates a risk of states being subject to the rule not of law but of lawyers, at odds with standards of legality or the normative standard to avoid domination generally. Some such risks arise for all courts, but increase for international courts, such as the ECtHR.

There thus seems to be at least two different though related kinds of concerns concerning the judges. First, the lack of accountability of various kinds which raises risks of domination by judges, and second, the epistemic risks concerning decisions made by distant judges unfamiliar with domestic circumstances and expectations.

With regard to the risk of domination, judges who are insulated from political pressure may well enjoy greater freedom to stand up to power, but they are also politically unaccountable and hence more likely to ignore citizens' legitimate claims. These risks would seem to be compounded by several features of the ECHR and its Court:

- Judges on international courts and treaty bodies may be less subject to peer pressure and less steeped in a domestic judicial culture; and their selection is not always based on merit but sometimes seems to stem from an opaque mix of nepotism and diplomatic strategy. Thus there is an added risk that judges' discretion is exploited in the service of some states' international objectives.
- Abuse of judicial power is more likely when legislation is more indeterminate, as are many parts of treaties such as the ECHR, and with an established practice of dynamic interpretation (Letsas, 2007).

- Treaties – human rights treaties as much as others – are cumbersome to amend, since unanimity is required. Partly for this reason, the ECtHR has been forced to engage in quite drastic interpretations.

There are thus risks that unelected judges of a review court will abuse their discretionary powers, unchecked by accountable politicians. This fear looms especially large with regard to treaty organs.

In partial response, these fears are somewhat alleviated insofar as the judges are still subject to professional standards and various forms of non-electoral accountability. This even holds for members of international courts and treaty bodies. Such bodies are subject to 'supervisory accountability' and 'fiscal accountability' by the various signatory states – especially toward the more powerful states (Grant & Robert, 2005: 37). The risks of unchecked judges may seem larger for *international* courts, which might be thought problematic also by those who otherwise endorse a domestic division of power. 'They are influenced by a host of structural, political and discursive constraints that states can manipulate ex ante and ex post, as well as by the pressures of professional and personal socialization within a global judicial community' (Shany, 2012, referring to Helfer & Slaughter, 1997).

The second risk is epistemic: that judiciaries generally – and international courts and tribunals in particular – are unfamiliar with the relevant details of the case. This is one reason why several critics warn that the deliberation by courts generally is of no better quality than the legislative debates. Many fear that the solutions rendered by judges are skewed or ill-informed since they are typically drawn from a narrow segment of society. Their decisions are for this and other reasons likely to be worse than those of legislatures and bureaucracies. The latter know more about the situation on the ground (Sunstein, 1996). Some make the point by comparing cases, such as the abortion debate in the US Supreme Court and British House of Commons (Waldron, 2005). Others argue on principle: Mark Tushnet holds that 'Democratic faith in the people's judgment means that the arguments liberals deploy in court should be just as good in the political arena' (Tushnet, 2005). Some arguments are empirical generalization, or doubts, e.g. against Dworkin's assertion (Dworkin, 1986: 375) that courts secure social reform and justice more effectively than do legislatures (Tushnet, 2005: 176).

In the case of the ECtHR such risks of domination and of unfamiliarity about the facts should be reduced due to one of the principles of interpretation. That court (and perhaps other courts; see Shany, 2005) grants a margin of appreciation to the states: they are allowed some discretion in how to best secure the rights of their citizens, apparently on the basis of an assumption of subsidiarity picking up on the concerns about local knowledge. The national authorities are thought better placed than an international court to evaluate local needs and conditions (*Fretté v France* no. 36515/97 (2002)). Note that this rationale is sometimes at odds with the practice of the ECtHR to grant a *wider* margin where it discerns no common European standards or values that apply (see *Handyside v UK* [PC], no. 5493/72 (1976), cf. Bernhardt, 1994). Some observe that this margin seems to be shrinking (Arai-Takahashi, 2001: 201). Insofar as this is correct, it may be due to the harmonization of European laws, which would lead to clearer and more broadly shared European standards.

Even with the caveat of the margin of appreciation doctrine, does the ECtHR subject governments – not to mention citizens – to unjustified discretion by unaccountable judges? Indeed, this doctrine may reduce the epistemic risks, but leaves some risks concerning domination. Thus critics may suspect that the ECtHR carefully picks its fights to maintain its own legitimacy. It may grant powerful states a greater margin of discretion than other states.

While such fears of domination and ignorance should give rise to concern, the weight of worry is limited. First, with regard to the epistemic concerns: one reason why a judiciary may make better decisions – and indeed induce more compliance (Shany, 2012) – is that it may therefore be, and be regarded as, more *impartial* among the parties. Such impartiality may be enhanced by the fact that few of the international judges can be suspected of parochial ties to either party to a conflict, and that they instead must rely on facts presented on behalf of the parties. They may indeed be better placed to spot widely shared yet mistaken assumptions that particular national 'local' human rights-violating practices are 'necessary' to secure certain objectives.

Second, we should keep in mind that the gains and risks of judicial review by a court are different from those of a legislature. We are concerned only with weak judicial review, where a court observes that there is a conflict between a piece of legislation and treaty obligations, but does not find the law invalid, and does not replace it. Instead, the court warns of a conflict among norms, and returns the dilemma to the democratically accountable legislature. So it is not appropriate simply to compare the failure rates of courts and legislatures. The possible risks are different than the risks a citizen faces from a legislature.

A court that performs judicial review may suffer two types of malfunction, be they the result of epistemic lapses or abuse of discretion. (1) 'False negatives', where the court stops normatively unobjectionable legislative acts. The legislature is then asked to – unnecessarily – revise its legislation to avoid alleged normative problems mistakenly labelled such by the court. (2) 'False positives' occur when a court fails to prevent normatively unacceptable legislative acts. In these cases the vital interests of some segment of the population are violated, the existence of judicial review notwithstanding. One of the crucial normative questions arises in the former cases, when a body such as the ECtHR has made a false negative decision, and thus when a parliament is urged to change its decisions but where this has not been necessary to protect citizens' vital interests – and where these changes are detrimental to some other individual. I suggest that this burden is limited: often a legislature will be able to find constructive responses that respect citizens' vital interests to the requisite degree. After all, the ECtHR leaves it to the national authorities to decide how to adjust domestic policies, legislation or constitution to avoid future violations. It is for the Committee of Ministers – which is indirectly democratically accountable (albeit not to a unified European 'demos') to decide whether these changes suffice.

Third, the range of issues where the ECtHR may intervene is limited in several ways. An indication of such limits is that 90 per cent of all applications to the ECtHR are found to be inadmissible. Furthermore, the area of intervention into legislative acts is mainly limited in the case of the ECHR to civil and political rights and equal treatment by public authorities. The more contested topics such as weighing the priority of various social and economic rights and shaping welfare policies fall somewhat beyond the scope of the ECHR – though the court has taken on some such issues (Palmer, 2009). And the margin of appreciation limits the scope of interventions by the ECtHR, especially on issues where they perceive no broad European overlap of values.

Fourth, with regard to the discretion of judges, we must first keep in mind the comparative perspective: *if* we want international judicial review based on treaties in order to secure effective human rights on the ground, the alternatives to dynamic interpretation may be even worse: judges applying outdated norms or 'original intent' to current circumstances. It is not at all clear that such interpretive practices can provide effective protection. Moreover, the 'unaccountable' judges do not enjoy a completely unregulated liberty to interpret the ECtHR any way they want. Peer pressure and professional socialization does, and should, serve to constrain such interpretations – albeit in quite other ways than we should expect among democratically accountable representatives. The appropriate, responsible consideration of reasons may well be different for judges who should largely interpret texts. The trustworthiness of judges in these regards may well be enhanced by insulation from, rather than responsiveness to, citizens' express preferences (see Moore, 2001; Ferejohn, 2002). We thus see the ECtHR engaged in several institutionalized dialogues with other parts of the human rights judiciary such as national apex courts, and the Inter-American Court of Human Rights.

The upshot of these observations is that the 'democratic deficit' of the practice of the ECtHR is not as severe as some critics might charge, due to features of the soft review, and the interpretive principles the Court applies.

Such disclaimers notwithstanding, is the defence of democratic rule compatible with judicial review by courts such as the ECtHR, of the legislation decided by elected representatives?

Valuable contributions contest whether the best interpretations of 'democracy' and 'legitimacy' in fact *support* judicial review (Ely, 1980; Dworkin, 1986: 356; Freeman, 1990; Fabre, 2000; Tamanaha, 2004); arguments that have been challenged by sceptics of judicial review. The aim here is not primarily to advance that debate. Rather, the concern is also to check whether their concerns also apply to the ECHR.

6. Reform proposals considered

We may now return to the reform proposals offered to enhance the legitimacy of the ECtHR. The general tendency of the UK proposals was to grant domestic bodies more authority regarding human rights review rather than to leave that power with the ECtHR; and formalize some aspects of current practice as amendments to the treaty.

First, consider the suggestion to include the Principle of Subsidiarity and the margin of appreciation in the treaty. In political terms such amendments are unlikely since they require unanimity. Be that as it may, it is not clear how such a reform may improve the legitimacy of the ECtHR. One concern of the UK is clearly to reduce the likelihood of the Court finding the UK in violation of the ECHR, thus respecting domestic democratic sovereignty more. This reduces the risk of 'false positives', i.e. of the Court preventing normatively unobjectionable policies. Moreover, the formalization reduces the risk of domination by the judges of the Court, by limiting and specifying their discretion. On the other hand, the risks of such reforms are high, for at least two reasons. The normative basis of these two principles is obscure with regard to human rights. Considerations of subsidiarity do not support placing protection of human rights with the national bodies alone. To the contrary, international human rights have as their objective to protect individuals against abuse by precisely such bodies. Domestic authorities should thus not have the sole responsibility, since that would make them judges in their own case. Reliance on subsidiarity would rather support a multi-level sharing of responsibility, where the regional or international level has the limited responsibility to review the actions of the national. Similarly, a margin of appreciation based on respect for local circumstance and culture stands in clear tension with the protection of human rights; for instance when it comes to the interests of minorities and women that the 'culture' of a domestic dominant group often ignores or overrules. Furthermore, a formalization of these doctrines will most likely require the Court to apply the same margin of appreciation and similar respect for subsidiarity to all states, regardless of their general willingness to comply with the ECHR. Thus the reform might reduce the risks of domination and illegality, but at the cost of effective human rights protection furthering the three objectives discussed above. Be that as it may, the central issues seem to remain how to determine and assess the appropriate margin of appreciation,

The third proposal concerned which cases the ECtHR should take on. The Court should not consider an application 'if it is the same in substance as a matter that has been examined by a national court taking into account the rights guaranteed by the Convention' (UK Government, 2012: para 23b). There are only two exceptions: if 'the Court considers that: i) The national court clearly erred in its interpretation or application of the Convention rights; or ii) The application raises a serious question affecting the interpretation or application of the Convention'. The aim of this proposal is again to reduce the workload of the ECtHR, by reducing the authority of the Court vis-à-vis national bodies, in particular to reduce the number of false negatives. Unfortunately, the effectiveness of the Court will also suffer. One reason is that the ECtHR may hesitate to thus criticize a national court for having not only erred but *clearly* erred. Similar chilling effects may have occurred in Sweden which until 2011 allowed the judiciary to arrest legislation only if parliament has committed a 'manifest error' (Nergelius, 2009), and in Finland whose Constitution requires there to be an 'evident conflict' (Section 106) for judicial review (Ojanen, 2009). In effect, this proposal would seem to remove the right of individuals to petition the Court. For citizens in well-functioning democracies the added protection by the ECtHR may not be large, but the risks of this proposal seem clearly larger for citizens in less human rights-compliant states. These effects must also be taken into account – it is not sufficient to dismiss the ECtHR because its benefits are small for citizens of the UK. Moreover, some of the benefits this proposal aims for are already secured. The Court already seems to pay attention to how carefully national courts have sought to interpret the ECHR, so that it is more likely to grant a margin of appreciation when there is evidence of such careful balancing (*Dickson v UK*, no. 44362/04 (2007)).

7. Some remaining challenges

The partial rebuttal of criticisms of the ECtHR and judicial review of human rights more generally should not be overdrawn. I conclude by pointing to some areas where such review should continue to spur caution and critical attention.

First, human rights treaties are not exempt from criticism *de lege ferenda*, as to the substantive content of the norms. For instance, it often remains to be argued whether these specific legal human rights, applied by international treaty organs, are suitable and reliable means to protect the best interests of individuals against 'standard threats' that arise in complex modern states. Note that this may be one reason in partial defence of Ron Hirschl's criticism of granting judges powers of judicial review. He argues that such authority does not in the end promote 'progressive concepts of distributive justice' (Hirschl, 2004: 13). While this may be correct and lamentable, we must also insist that the role of international judicial review may well be more limited in aspiration: its aim is more modest, and less contested than a full-fledged standard of socio-economic egalitarianism.

Second, the quality of judicial deliberation merits further scrutiny. The patterns of actual debates and decisions in the ECtHR and other courts compared to those in legislatures are indeed a crucial empirical issue relevant for assessing their normative legitimacy. However, the relevant data must go beyond one particular case, such as the abortion debate in the USA and the UK (*pace* Waldron, 2005). There are several reasons for this. The normative theory I laid out above holds that we must compare institutions and practices, so our concern must be general tendencies rather than single results. And there are institutional factors why courts and parliaments should pursue and weigh different reasons and concerns – such as rights – differently, in light of their different social functions. Judges' discretion should be more limited than that of legislatures, to interpretation of legal texts. So different modes of reasoning are to be expected. Furthermore, we may want to study how different rules affect the deliberations of parliaments, e.g., as Steiner et al. explore (Steiner et al., 2005).

Some scholars, including Tushnet, have suggested on more principled grounds that a democrat should hold that the arguments deployed in court 'should be just as good in the political arena' (Tushnet, 2005). I beg to disagree, for at least two reasons. First, there are institutional factors – mandate, rules, culture – that legitimately lead the two kinds of bodies to pursue and weigh different reasons and considerations differently. Surely, some policy choices a legislature must make should reflect the comprehensive set of preferences of representatives – both self-interested and other-regarding – and not only the elements relevant for a court. Majority rule may then be a plausible decision rule to maximize preferences over time. Judges' discretion, on the other hand, is largely limited to interpretation of legal texts, while there is clearly leeway in such interpretation. It would seem that peer pressure and professional socialization does, and should, serve to constrain such interpretations in quite other ways than we should expect among democratically accountable representatives. Thus the appropriate, responsible consideration of reasons may well be different, and the trustworthiness of legislators and judges in these regards may well be enhanced by insulation from, versus responsiveness to, citizens' express preferences, respectively (cf. Moore, 2001; Ferejohn, 2002). This is not a rebuttal of Tushnet's concern, but rather indicates that quite other sorts of arguments seem appropriate, also among democrats, on behalf of the reasoning of judges in general, and of the ECtHR in particular.

Second, recall that judicial review is a safety mechanism, not a replacement for democratic deliberation. Waldron also grants the value of weak judicial review as a safety mechanism, since legislators might not be able to see the issues of rights embedded in the proposal and its future applications (Waldron, 2006: 1370). The risks are different for such a safety mechanism, as compared to legislation. So it is not appropriate simply to compare the failure rates of courts and legislatures. We must assess the losses imposed on those whose human rights are overruled against the interests of a majority that cannot be pursued in the ways originally thought.

A third source of worry about international judicial review is that judicial solutions will likely be worse than those of legislatures and bureaucracies, because the latter know more about the situation on the ground. In response, note there are several features of the ECtHR that render this worry less weighty – but which also create other normative challenges: (1) The doctrine of the margin of appreciation explicitly recognizes and seeks to respond to this concern. (2) A judge from the accused country is always an *ex officio* member of the ECtHR, precisely to provide some such relevant information. (3) The judges' background varies to some extent, so that the ECtHR as a whole has members with experience of government administration and human rights activism – as well as academia and service on the bench. Moreover, we may also use the distance of international judges engaged in judicial review in their favour: their unfamiliarity with local conflicts and cultural mores, and their lack of stakes in the result, reduce the risk that the judges will subject a minority to wilful domination. These responses should not lead us to conclude that this concern is completely without merit. In particular, it remains to be determined whether the 'margin of appreciation' respects the domestic democratic process appropriately, and the vital interests of individuals. I return to this below.

A fourth normative concern, and related to this, the independence and professional quality of the judges on the courts – including the ECtHR – may be challenged. For instance, regarding the ECtHR, some scholars suggest that while the judges often seem sufficiently insulated from national pressures, several judges are selected by their government on quite other bases than judicial quality. The concerns about bias and independence are clearly worth further attention.

Fifth, with regard to the interpretive practices of the ECtHR, it remains to be determined whether the dynamic 'margin of appreciation' overlaps reasonably well with the scope of discretion states arguably need to accommodate local circumstances and expectations. Does this practice of recognizing such a margin, combined with the doctrine of dynamic interpretation, reliably help secure citizens' best interests against flaws in majoritarian legislation? There is no obvious reason to believe this margin overlaps precisely with the scope of the normatively permissible. There is no obvious reason to believe a broad consensus among European legal systems will always tend to converge on the normatively legitimate. And there is a real risk that the ECtHR will seek to avoid taking controversial decisions against a powerful state, and instead grant that the issue falls within the margin of appreciation. Finally, the risk of political appointees raises the spectre that judges will be affected by foreign policy concerns, rather than the best interests of individuals.

I have addressed some of the concerns that the ECtHR suffers from a lamentable 'legitimacy deficit'. Some may see such review as central to the Rule of Law, and in turn as crucial to a domestic and international constitutionalism worth respecting. At the same time, the literature reveals a long list of misgivings of such constraints on domestic democratic decision-making. We have reviewed some of the recent criticisms against the ECtHR, and some of the recent proposals for reform of the ECtHR. To assess such criticisms and proposals I have explored some of the social functions that such judicial review of human rights may play, and laid out how such treaty organs may be defended in principle, and in practice in the case of the ECtHR. I have also argued that several issues remain unresolved, before we can conclude that the ECtHR and other such bodies are normatively defensible. The answers require both normative and empirical contributions, when we ask whether these practices, better than the alternatives, provide citizens reasons to trust their authorities: that the norms and institutions in place are just, and that others in their societies act as they ought. Not only must the judges of such treaty bodies ensure that justice is done, but the institutions as a whole must also give assurance to citizens so that they have reason to believe that justice is indeed done.

Bibliography

Arai-Takahashi, Y., 2001. *The margin of appreciation doctrine and the principle of proportionality in the jurisprudence of the ECHR*, Antwerpen: Intersentia.

Barry, B., 1991. Is democracy special? In Barry, B. ed., *Democracy and Power*, Oxford University Press.

Beetham, D. & Lord, C., 1998. *Legitimacy and the European Union*, London: Longman.

Bellamy, R., 1999. *Liberalism and pluralism*, London: Routledge.

2001. Constitutive citizenship versus constitutional rights: Republican reflections on the EU Charter and the Human Rights Act. In T. Campbell, K. D. Ewing & A. Tomkins eds., *Sceptical essays on human rights*, Oxford University Press.

2007. *Political constitutionalism: A republican defence of the constitutionality of democracy*, Cambridge University Press.

Bernhardt, R., 1994. Human rights and judicial review: The European Court of Human Rights. In D. M. Beatty ed., *Human rights and judicial review: A comparative perspective*, Dordrecht: Martinus Nijhoff.

Bratza, N., 2012. Britain should be defending European justice, not attacking it. *The Independent* [Online]. Available at: www.independent.co.uk/opinion/commentators/nicolas-bratza-britain-should-be-defending-european-justice-not-attacking-it-6293689.html [Accessed 30 May 2013].

Cameron, D., 2012. Speech to the Parliamentary Assembly of the Council of Europe, 25 January.

Campbell, T., Ewing, K. D. & Tomkins, A. eds., 2001. *The Legal Protection of Rights: Sceptical essays on human rights*, Oxford University Press.

Conforti, B., 2007. The role of the judge in international law. *European Journal of Legal Studies*, 1.

Crema, L., 2010. Disappearance and new sightings of restrictive interpretation(s). *The European Journal of International Law*, 21, 681–700.

Dahl, R. A., 1971. *Polyarchy: Participation and opposition*, New Haven: Yale University Press.

Democracy Index, 2008. http://graphics.eiu.com/PDF/Democracy%20Index%20 2008.pdf [Accessed 30 May 2013].

Dworkin, R., 1986. *Law's empire*, Cambridge, MA: Harvard University Press.

Ely, J. H., 1980. *Democracy and distrust: A theory of judicial review*, Cambridge, MA: Harvard University Press.

European Court of Human Rights, 2010. *A, B & C v Ireland.*

2011. Table of Violations by Article and by State 2011.

2012a. The European Court of Human Rights in Facts and Figures 2011.

2012b. Preliminary opinion of the Court in preparation for the Brighton Conference. Available at: http://adam1cor.files.wordpress.com/2012/02/3841140-v2-2012-court-opinion-brighton-conference.doc [Accessed 30 May 2013].

2012c. Table of violations 2011. Available at: www.echr.coe.int/NR/rdonlyres/596C7B5C-3FFB-4874-85D8-F12E8F67C136/0/TABLEAU_VIOLATIONS_EN_2011.pdf [Accessed 30 May 2013].

Fabre, C., 2000. A philosophical argument for a Bill of Rights. *British Journal of Political Science*, 30, 77–98.

Ferejohn, J., 2002. Judicializing politics, politicizing law. *Law and Contemporary Problems*, 65, 41–68.

Føllesdal, A., 1998a. Democracy, legitimacy and majority rule in the EU. In: A. Weale & M. Nentwich eds., *Political theory and the European Union: Legitimacy, constitutional choice and citizenship*, London: Routledge.

1998b. Subsidiarity. *Journal of Political Philosophy*, 6, 231–259.

2009. The legitimacy of international human rights review: The case of the European Court of Human Rights. *Journal of Social Philosophy*, 40, 595–607.

2013. The legitimacy deficits of the human rights judiciary: Elements and implications of a normative theory. *Theoretical Inquiries in Law*, 14, 339–360.

Føllesdal, A. & Hix, S., 2006. Why there is a democratic deficit in the EU: A response to Majone and Moravcsik. *Journal of Common Market Studies*, 44, 533–562.

Føllesdal, A. & Pogge, T., 2005. Introduction. In A. Føllesdal & T. Pogge eds., *Real world justice: Grounds, principles, human rights standards and institutions*, Doordrecht: Springer.

Føllesdal, A. & Wind, M., 2009. Introduction: Nordic reluctance towards judicial review under siege. *Nordic Journal of Human Rights*, 27, 131–141.

Freeman, S., 1990. Constitutional democracy and the legitimacy of judicial review. *Law and Philosophy*, 9, 327–370.

Grant, R. W. K. & Robert, O., 2005. Accountability and abuses of power in world politics. *American Political Science Review*, 99, 29–43.

Helfer, L. & Slaughter, A.-M., 1997. Toward a theory of effective supranational adjudication. *Yale Law Review*, 107.

Hirschl, R., 2004. *Towards juristocracy: The origins and consequences of the new constitutionalism*, Cambridge, MA: Harvard University Press.

Letsas, G., 2007. *A theory of interpretation of the European Convention on Human Rights*, Oxford University Press.

Marthaler, S., 2005. The French referendum on ratification of the constitutional treaty. *European Parties Elections and Referendums Network – Briefing Paper.*

Moore, M., 2001. Justifying the natural law theory of constitutional interpretation. *Fordham Law Review*, 69, 2087–2117.

Moravcsik, A., 1995. Explaining international human rights regimes. *European Journal of International Relations*, 1, 157–189.

Nergelius, J., 2009. Judicial review in Swedish law: A critical analysis. *Nordic Journal of Human Rights*, 142–159.

NOU 2003: 19: Makt- og demokratiutredningen. Available at: www.regjeringen.no/nb/dep/fad/dok/nouer/2003/nou-2003-019.html?id=118893 [Accessed 30 May 2013].

Ojanen, T., 2009. From constitutional periphery toward the center: Transformations of judicial review in Finland. *Nordic Journal of Human Rights*, 194–207.

Østerud, Ø. & Selle, P., 2006. Power and democracy in Norway: The transformation of Norwegian politics. *Scandinavian Political Studies*, 29, 25–46.

Palmer, E., 2009. Protecting socio-economic rights through the European Convention on Human Rights: Trends and developments in the European Court of Human Rights. *Erasmus Law Review*, 2, 397–425.

Pettit, P., 2000. Democracy: Electoral and contestatory. In I. Shapiro & S. Macedo eds., *Designing democratic institutions*, New York University Press.

Powell, G. B., 2000. *Elections as instruments of democracy: Majoritarian and proportional visions*, New Haven: Yale University Press.

Przeworski, A., Shapiro, I. & Hacker-Cordon, C., 1999. Minimalist conception of democracy: a defense. In I. Shapiro & C. Hacker-Cordon eds., *Democracy's value*, Cambridge University Press.

Rawls, J., 1971. *A theory of justice*, Cambridge, MA: Harvard University Press.

Schlütter, B., 2012. Aspects of human rights interpretation by the UN treaty bodies. In G. Ulfstein & H. Keller eds., *UN treaty bodies – law and legitimacy*, Cambridge University Press.

Shany, Y., 2005. Toward a general margin of appreciation doctrine in international law? *European Journal of International Law*, 16, 907–940.

2012. Assessing the effectiveness of international courts: A goal-based approach. *American Journal of International Law*, 106, 225–270.

Shapiro, I., 2001. The state of democratic theory. In I. Katznelson & H. Milner eds., *Political science: The state of the discipline*, New York: Norton.

Siedentop, L., 2008. Europe is failing to restore idealism. *Financial Times*.

Simmons, B. A., 2009. *Mobilizing for human rights: International law in domestic politics*, New York: Cambridge University Press.

SOU 2007: 85: Olika former av normkontroll. Available at: www.regeringen.se/sb/d/8586/a/92025 [Accessed 30 May 2013].

Steiner, J., Bächtiger, A., Spörndli, M. & Steenebergen, M. R., 2005. *Deliberative politics in action: Crossnational study of parliamentary debates*, Cambridge University Press.

Sunstein, C. R., 1996. *Legal reasoning and political conflict*, Oxford University Press.

Tamanaha, B. Z., 2004. *On the rule of law: History, politics, theory*, Cambridge University Press.

2010. *Beyond the formalist-realist divide*, Princeton University Press.

Treaty of Lisbon, 2007. Treaty of Lisbon amending the Treaty on European Union and the Treaty establishing the European Community (adopted 13 December 2007, in force 1 December 2009) [2007] Official Journal of the European Union C306/1. *Official Journal of the European Union C306/1*.

Tushnet, M., 2005. Democracy versus judicial review: Is it time to amend the constitution? *Dissent*.

UK Government, 2012. Draft Brighton declaration on the future of the European Court of Human Rights – second version. Available at: http://adam1cor.files.wordpress.com/2012/02/2012dd220e.pdf [Accessed 30 May 2013].

United Nations Development Programme, 2009. *Human Development Report 2009*.

Waldron, J., 2005. On judicial review. *Dissent*.

2006. The core of the case against judicial review. *The Yale Law Journal*, 115, 1346–1406.

Woolf, L., 2005. *Review of the working methods of the European Court of Human Rights*, Strasbourg: The European Court of Human Rights.

INDEX